French
today 1

French today 1

Simone Oudot

Raymond Hunt

HOUGHTON MIFFLIN COMPANY Boston

Atlanta Dallas Geneva, Illinois
Hopewell, New Jersey Palo Alto Toronto

About the authors

Simone Oudot, a native of Lyon, France, received her secondary education in Lyon and was graduated from Boston University. During many years of experience as a national foreign language consultant in the United States, she has conducted numerous demonstration classes in high schools, and has given workshops at universities throughout the country on practical techniques in teaching modern foreign languages. She has written a variety of instructional materials, including French cultural readers, material for individualized study of French, and scripts for films and recordings. Ms. Oudot is an active member of the American Council on Teaching of Foreign Languages (ACTFL) and the American Association of Teachers of French (AATF), for which she edited a booklet on French history and culture in Connecticut.

Raymond Hunt is a graduate of Montclair State College and Rutgers University, and has also studied at the University of Besançon, France and Laval University, Quebec. He has taught French at the junior high and secondary levels since 1959, and is currently teacher of French and coordinator of middle school foreign language instruction for the Princeton, New Jersey Regional Schools. He has served as supervisor of student teachers for the Office of Teacher Preparation at Princeton University. Mr. Hunt is a former president of the New Jersey Foreign Language Teachers Association (NJFLTA) as well as a former ACTFL representative. He has received the award of NJFLTA for outstanding service to foreign language education.

ANNOTATIONS

Jacqueline Benevento has taught French and served as coordinator of foreign language instruction in the Collingswood, New Jersey school system since 1961. She is active in ACTFL, AATF, NJFLTA, and other organizations, and has held several elective offices. She has also acted as a consultant and has written numerous articles on foreign language education. Ms. Benevento is a graduate of Montclair State College and holds advanced degrees from Middlebury College and Temple University.

LISTENING COMPREHENSION EXERCISES

Simone Oudot

WORKBOOK

Jacqueline Benevento and **Raymond Hunt**

CHAPTER TESTS

Alice Polatschek has taught French in independent schools in New York, Pennsylvania, and Massachusetts. She has also served as a reader for Educational Testing Service. Ms. Polatschek is active in ACTFL, AATF, and other professional organizations, and she contributed testimony to the President's Commission on Foreign Language and International Studies. She is a graduate of Connecticut College and Columbia University.

Printed in U.S.A.
Student's Edition ISBN: 0-395-29299-9
Teacher's Edition ISBN: 0-395-29514-9

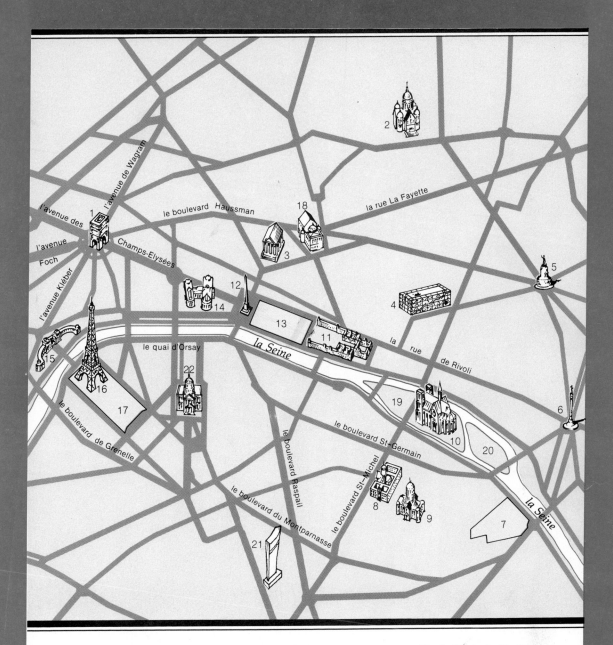

1	l'Arc de Triomphe	8	la Sorbonne	15	le Palais de Chaillot
2	le Sacré-Cœur	9	le Panthéon	16	la Tour Eiffel
3	la Madeleine	10	Notre-Dame	17	le Champ de Mars
4	le Centre Pompidou (Beaubourg)	11	le Louvre	18	l'Opéra
5	la Place de la République	12	la Place de la Concorde	19	l'Île de la Cité
6	la Place de la Bastille	13	le Jardin des Tuileries	20	l'Île St-Louis
7	le Jardin des Plantes	14	le Grand Palais	21	la Tour Montparnasse
				22	les Invalides

PARIS MONUMENTAL

1

La vie quotidienne

The French have a reputation for seriousness in academic study and for dedication to the enjoyment of life. French students find time for both. Below, university students take an exam, and a high school student works on a chemistry experiment. At right, young people enjoy free time. The background picture shows l'Île de la Cité, the oldest part of Paris.

Featured in the view of Paris on page 2 are some celebrated landmarks. Extending from **l'Arc de Triomphe,** in the foreground, toward the top left corner of the photograph is **l'Avenue des Champs-Élysées. La Seine** and **la Tour Eiffel** are visible in the distance. At ground level, the colorful bustle and detail of **la vie quotidienne** (daily life) in a large city are more evident. The street scene at left is in Dakar, Senegal. The others are in Paris.

3

5

A la maison: Apartments in Paris (left), a village in the Pyrenees mountains (above), and a farmhouse in the Loire river valley (right) are home to people in different parts of France.

7

chapitre 1
Le français dans le monde

1

There are many French-speaking areas in addition to France. It is estimated that about 100 million people either speak French as their native language or use it regularly as a second language. To get a better idea of the widespread influence of French language and culture around the world, take a few minutes to look at the map on pages xii–xiii.

In this chapter, you will meet Pierre Legrand, who lives in France, and Yvette Lebeau, who lives in Canada. In later chapters you will meet other French-speaking people from several different parts of the world.

Qui es-tu?

monologues

Pierre Legrand is a French teen-ager who lives in Paris. He introduces himself and asks who you are.

Bonjour! Je m'appelle Pierre Legrand.
Je suis français.
J'habite à Paris. Et toi?

Yvette Lebeau, a Canadian teen-ager who lives in Quebec City, introduces herself and asks who you are.

Salut! Moi, je m'appelle Yvette Lebeau.
Je suis canadienne.
J'habite à Québec. Et toi?

à vous, maintenant

It's your turn now to talk about yourself. Here are some questions and responses that will help you to do so. Practice them with a partner. Substitute your own name for the suggested names in brackets.

Comment t'appelles-tu?	[Sylvie].	Et toi?
	Je m'appelle [Bernadette].	
	Moi, je m'appelle [Charles Ledoux].	

Tu es	américain (américaine)?	Oui, je suis	américain (américaine).
	français (française)?	Non, je suis	français (française).
	canadien (canadienne)?	Moi? Non, je ne suis pas	canadien (canadienne).

Tu parles anglais?

dialogue

At a party, Pierre overhears Yvette speaking English.
He starts a conversation with her.

PIERRE	Tu parles anglais? Tu es américaine?
YVETTE	Non, canadienne. Je parle français aussi.
PIERRE	Ah, oui? Où est-ce que tu habites?
YVETTE	À Québec. Et toi, tu es français?
PIERRE	Oui. Je parle un peu anglais, mais pas très bien.

à vous,
maintenant

Now tell your partner what city or town you live in, and if you speak French or English.

Où est-ce que tu habites?	À [San Francisco]. J'habite à [Des Moines]. Moi, je suis de [Providence].
Tu parles français? espagnol anglais russe allemand italien	Oui, un peu. Pas très bien. Oui, et je parle anglais aussi. Non, je parle anglais. Non, je ne parle pas français.

Nationalités

narration

Pierre Legrand est français.
Il habite à Paris.
Il ne parle pas très bien anglais.
Yvette Lebeau est canadienne.
Elle habite à Québec.
Elle parle anglais et français.

questions

Complete the responses to the following questions based on the *monologues,* the *dialogue,* and the *narration.*

1. Où habite Pierre? Il habite _____.
2. Où habite Yvette? Elle habite _____.
3. Pierre est français. Et Yvette? Elle est _____.
4. Qui parle français et anglais? _____ parle français et anglais.

situations

Here are the names of some people and their home towns. Say where they live, what their nationalities are, and what language or languages you think they speak.

Monique: Montréal Colette: Marseille Marie: Saint-Louis
Martin: Dallas Paul: Vancouver Jacques: Paris

à vous,
maintenant

1. Ask a classmate his or her name and nationality, and where he or she lives. Then introduce yourself to your classmate, giving *your* name and nationality, and telling where *you* live.
2. Ask one classmate about another classmate's name, nationality, and home town. Then share the information with the class.

Salutations

échanges
de politesse

à vous,
maintenant

1. Say hello and good-by to several classmates.

Salut,	Marc.
Bonjour,	Simone.

Au revoir,	Annick.
À bientôt,	Pierre.

2. Now exchange greetings and farewells more formally. Pretend you and your classmates are adults who do not know each other very well.

Bonjour,	madame.
	monsieur.
	mademoiselle.

Au revoir,	madame.
À bientôt,	monsieur.
	mademoiselle.

À la française

À la française means "the French way." If you go to a French-speaking country, you will want to feel at ease with the local customs. Although people do not behave alike throughout the French-speaking world, you can learn to recognize some typical gestures and social customs.

You will find, for example, that French people usually do not use a last name when addressing someone. They say simply: **Bonjour, madame** or **Bonjour, monsieur.**

As French people greet each other, they shake hands, whether or not they know each other well. A typical handshake consists of a single strong up-and-down movement. It does not last as long as the American handshake. This is the customary gesture each time people meet, and also when they say good-by, even if they see each other many times during the day. Young people tend to shake hands less frequently than adults.

Qui est-ce?

1 une jeune fille
2 une fille
3 un garçon
4 un homme (un monsieur)
5 un bébé
6 une femme (une dame)

— Yvette est une fille?   — Oui, **c'est** une fille.
— Jean est une fille?   — Non, **ce n'est pas** une fille!
                          C'est un garçon!

A   Identify the people you see in the pictures below. Give each person an appropriate French name. (See the list in the Appendix.)

C'est un garçon. Il s'appelle Jacques.

B   Your teacher will identify several students, deliberately making some mistakes. Respond appropriately.

- ▮ɪ   [Yvette] est une fille.   *Oui, c'est une fille.*
- ▮ɪ   [Marie] est un garçon.   *Non, ce n'est pas un garçon! C'est une fille!*

Les nationalités

The following adjectives describe the nationalities of some of the characters in this book. Adjectives of nationality are not capitalized in French.

COUNTRY	NATIONALITY	
	Male	Female
France	français	française
États-Unis d'Amérique	américain	américaine
Canada	canadien	canadienne
Algérie	algérien	algérienne
Belgique	belge	belge
Haïti	haïtien	haïtienne
Maroc	marocain	marocaine
Sénégal	sénégalais	sénégalaise

M. Le Hur est **français** et Mme Le Hur est **française.**
Roger est **haïtien** et Suze est **haïtienne.**
Bruno est **belge** et Anne-Marie est **belge.**

Most French adjectives have one form to describe a male, and another form to describe a female. Some, like **belge,** have only one singular form.

C   Say that the second person mentioned is of the same nationality as the first.

- ▮ɪ   Robert est canadien. Et Claudine? *Elle est canadienne.*

1. Roger est haïtien. Et Hélène?
2. Josette est marocaine. Et M. Mustapha?
3. Pierre est français. Et Mlle Legrand?
4. Mme Diop est sénégalaise. Et M. Diop?

D   Identify a male and a female from each of the following countries by nationality. If you can, name the city where each person lives.

- ▮ɪ   France   *[Pierre] est français. Il habite à [Paris].*
      [Fanny] est française. Elle habite à [Nice].

1. Algérie	3. Sénégal	5. Haïti	7. Canada
2. Maroc	4. France	6. États-Unis	8. Belgique

Prononciation et orthographe

In the pronunciation sections of this book, special symbols in slashes are used to represent French sounds. Each symbol represents only one sound; for example, the symbol /s/ always represents the sound of **s** as in **salut.** In written French, a sound may be spelled in different ways; for example, the sound /s/ may be spelled **s, ss, c, ç.**

 /i/ **il**

/i/

There is a clear difference between French vowels and English vowels. French vowel sounds, like /i/, are short and clipped. In pronouncing /i/, smile and keep your lips, jaws, and tongue tense.

RÉPÉTEZ | Repeat after your teacher or the tape.

| il | j'habite | Paris | Sylvie |
| aussi | fille | qui | Yvette |

Note that in writing, the sound /i/ is spelled **i** or **y.**

LISEZ | Read the following sentences aloud.

1. Yvette habite à Paris.
2. Qui habite à Nice?
3. Il parle anglais aussi.

Petit à petit, l'oiseau fait son nid.

Final consonants

In writing, many French words end in a consonant that is not pronounced.

RÉPÉTEZ

comment	Paris	tu habites
salut	français	ce n'est pas
c'est	je suis	très

Liaison

The final consonant of a word, even though it is usually "silent," may be pronounced if the following word begins with a vowel sound. The consonant then links the two words together and sounds like part of the second word. This linking is called *liaison*.

Before vowel: C'est une fille. Elle est américaine. /t/ /t/
Before consonant: C'est Pierre. Il est français.

Sometimes *liaison* is required; sometimes it is optional. You will learn more about *liaison* in later chapters. For now, imitate your teacher and other French-speaking people you hear.

Grammaire

Subject pronouns: singular forms

	PRONOUNS	EXAMPLES
1st person	je (j') I	Je suis française. J'habite à Paris.
2nd person	tu you	Tu es français? Tu habites à Nice.
3rd person	il he	Il est français. Il habite à Québec.
	elle she	Elle est française. Elle habite à Montréal.

1. Subject pronouns and their verb forms must agree; for example, **je** agrees with **suis,** and **tu** agrees with **es.**
2. **Je** becomes **j'** before a verb form that begins with a vowel sound.
3. **Je** is capitalized only when it is the first word in a sentence.

A Give the subject pronoun you would use in the following situations.

■III talking about your father *il*

1. talking about a male student
2. talking about a female teacher
3. talking to a male friend
4. talking to a female friend
5. talking about yourself

B   Complete the following sentences with the correct subject pronouns.

■Ⅲ   ———— est américain.   *Il est américain.*

1. ———— suis belge.
2. ———— es de Paris?
3. ———— est canadienne.

4. ———— es américaine?
5. ———— suis de Québec.
6. ———— est français.

Negation with **ne . . . pas**

A verb form is made negative by using **ne** before the verb and **pas** after it. **Ne** becomes **n'** before a verb form beginning with a vowel sound.

Je parle français.   Je **ne** parle **pas** anglais.
Il habite à Paris.   Il **n'**habite **pas** à New York.

C   Contradict the following statements.

■Ⅲ   C'est un bébé.   *Ce n'est pas un bébé.*

1. C'est une jeune fille.
2. Elle est canadienne.
3. Elle est de Québec.

4. C'est un monsieur.
5. Il est français.
6. Il est de Paris.

D   Deny the following statements, and then correct them.

■Ⅲ   Tu parles anglais.   *Non, je ne parle pas anglais. Je parle français.*

1. Tu habites à Montréal.
2. Tu es de Paris.

3. Tu es belge.
4. Tu es à Québec.

Language and culture

A language reflects the character and the environment of the people who speak it. People use language in some way to relate to every single thing they see, hear, feel, or think about. So it's both important and interesting, when learning a language, to learn something about the people who use it — where they live, how they live, what things are important to them. As you read the cultural notes in this book, you will see that French-speaking people are both like you and different from you — just as French is both similar to and different from English.

How many French-speaking people — government officials, actors, athletes, writers, or friends — can you name? For a week, jot down the names of French-speaking people (and their countries) that you read about or hear mentioned on radio and television, and share the list with the class.

Lecture

Aux Tuileries

In the Tuileries, a public garden in Paris, Michel meets a girl pushing a baby in a stroller. Both young people are on vacation in Paris.

MICHEL	Quel joli° bébé! C'est un garçon?	What a cute
SUZANNE	Oui...	
MICHEL	Comment s'appelle-t-il?	
SUZANNE	Marc. C'est mon petit frère.°	my little brother
MICHEL	Tu habites à Paris?	
SUZANNE	Non, à Cherbourg. Je suis normande.°	from Normandy
MICHEL	Ah, oui? Moi aussi,° je suis normand. Mais j'habite à Bruxelles.	Me too
SUZANNE	Tu es belge maintenant?°	now
MICHEL	Mais non, je suis français.	
SUZANNE	Bon, maintenant, il faut que je rentre.°	I must go home
MICHEL	À bientôt, j'espère?°	I hope
SUZANNE	Oui... Demain,° ici,° aux Tuileries?	Tomorrow/here
MICHEL	D'accord!° Au revoir!	OK

questions

1. Comment s'appelle le bébé?
2. C'est une fille?
3. Qui est normand?
4. Qui habite à Bruxelles?

Résumé grammatical

The letters in parentheses following the headings indicate the related exercises in the *grammaire* section of the chapter.

Subject pronouns: singular forms (A, B)

1st person	je (j')	I
2nd person	tu	you
3rd person	il	he
	elle	she

1. Subject pronouns and their verb forms must agree.

   je suis   **j'**habite
   tu es   **tu** habites
   il est   **il** habite
   elle est   **elle** habite

2. **Je** becomes **j'** before a vowel sound, as in **j'habite.**
3. **Je** is capitalized only when it is the first word in a sentence.

Negation with ne . . . pas (C, D)

Simple negation is expressed by using **ne** before a verb form and **pas** after it. **Ne** becomes **n'** before a verb form beginning with a vowel sound.

Je **ne** suis **pas** belge.   I'm not Belgian.
Ce **n'**est **pas** un garçon.   It's not a boy.

Do you have a French name, or do you know people who do? Family names can be interesting. Many French names describe professions: Charpentier (carpenter), Maréchal (marshall), Marchand (storekeeper), Cordonnier (shoe repairman) are just a few examples. Many names have other meanings: Lebeau (the beautiful), Legrand (the tall or the great), Latour (the tower), Dumont (of the mountain).

Other family names are quite common in particular regions or countries: Le Hur in Brittany, Muller in Alsace, Calixte in Haiti, Mustapha in Morocco, and Diop in Senegal.

Many French people are immigrants or descendants of immigrants, and their names suggest the origins of their ancestors. Two famous French people of foreign origin are the scientist Marie Sklodowska Curie (Polish) and the playwright Eugène Ionesco (Rumanian).

Révision

The review exercises at the end of each chapter will help you to practice the French you have learned. Some of the review exercises require specific knowledge of vocabulary and grammar, while others ask your opinions or feelings about certain things.

A Say whether the person speaking, being spoken to, or being spoken about is a girl (*une fille*) or a boy (*un garçon*).

■⓿ Claude est canadienne.   *C'est une fille.*
■⓿ Tu es algérien?   *C'est un garçon.*

1. Tu es sénégalaise?
2. Je suis haïtien.
3. Michel est canadien.
4. Je ne suis pas française.

5. Elle parle anglais.
6. Tu es américain?
7. Il n'habite pas à Nice.
8. Je suis marocaine.

B Working with a partner, make statements about the people shown in photographs or drawings chosen from any source you like. Identify the people as completely as you can, but make some mistakes. Your partner should confirm or deny and correct what you say. For example, suppose your partner shows you a photograph of the President of the United States:

YOU — C'est un bébé.
PARTNER — Non, ce n'est pas un bébé. C'est un homme (une femme).
PARTNER — Il (elle) habite à Washington.
YOU — Oui, il (elle) habite à Washington.
PARTNER — Il (elle) parle français.
YOU — Non, il (elle) parle anglais.

C Use each of the following words or phrases in an appropriate way. Be sure you understand the meaning of each expression.

1. bonjour
2. salut
3. comment...?
4. je m'appelle...
5. où...?

6. moi
7. toi
8. ne...pas
9. au revoir
10. à bientôt

D Write a brief autobiography of about five sentences. Include information about your name, your nationality, where you live, and the languages you speak.

E Write the French names of at least ten countries, states, or provinces where French is a major language. Be sure you can locate the places on the map.

Vocabulaire

Be sure you can recognize and use actively the following words and expressions before going on to **Chapitre 2.**

NOUNS

—**un bébé**   a baby
—**une dame**   a lady, a woman
—**une femme**   a woman
—**une fille**   a girl; **une jeune fille**   a young woman (age 16–25)
—**un garçon**   a boy
—**un homme**   a man
—**un monsieur**   a man

GREETINGS AND FAREWELLS

—**bonjour**   hello
—**salut**   hi, hello
—**au revoir**   good-by
—**à bientôt**   see you soon

VERB FORMS

je suis   I am; **tu es**   you are; **il est**   he is; **elle est**   she is
je parle   I speak; **tu parles**   you speak; **il parle**   he speaks; **elle parle**   she speaks
j'habite   I live; **tu habites**   you live; **il habite**   he lives; **elle habite**   she lives

ADJECTIVES OF NATIONALITY

—**algérien(ne)**   Algerian
—**américain(e)**   American
—**belge**   Belgian
—**canadien(ne)**   Canadian
—**français(e)**   French
—**haïtien(ne)**   Haitian
—**marocain(e)**   Moroccan
—**sénégalais(e)**   Senegalese

LANGUAGES

—**anglais**   English
—**français**   French

OTHER WORDS AND EXPRESSIONS

—**à**   at, in
—**aussi**   also
—**de**   from, of
—**et**   and
mais   but
moi   me, as for me (*emphatic*)
—**non**   no
—**oui**   yes
toi   you, as for you (*emphatic*)

ah, oui?   oh, really?
c'est   it is, that is
ce n'est pas   it's not, that's not
comment t'appelles-tu?   what's your name?
je m'appelle   my name is
madame, mademoiselle, monsieur   Mrs., Miss, Mr.
où est-ce que tu habites?   where do you live?
pas très bien   not very well
qui est-ce?   who is it? who is that?
qui es-tu?   who are you?
—**un peu**   a little

chapitre 2

Au lycée

Visitors to France usually make their first stop in the capital, Paris. **La «Ville Lumière»** (City of Light) has a well-deserved reputation as a beautiful city. Its many monuments, some more than eight centuries old, give it a majestic look. Wide boulevards, large parks, and stately bridges on the Seine river provide open spaces and magnificent vistas in the heart of the city.

Paris is the home of Pierre Legrand, a high school student.

Voilà mon école

monologue

Pierre Legrand tells you a little about his high school.

Salut! C'est moi, Pierre Legrand.
Je suis lycéen.
Je vais au lycée Pasteur, à Paris.
Voilà mon école.
C'est un grand lycée, n'est-ce pas?

à vous,
maintenant

1. Your partner asks if you go to a certain high school. How would you answer?

Tu vas au lycée [Pasteur]?	Oui, je vais au lycée [Pasteur].
	Non, je ne vais pas au lycée [Pasteur].
	Non, je vais au lycée ...
	Non, je vais au collège.

2. Point out your school to your partner.

Voilà	le lycée.
	le collège.
	l'école.

3. Your partner thinks your school is big. Do you agree?

C'est un grand	lycée, collège,	n'est-ce pas?	Oui, il est très grand.
			Non, il n'est pas très grand.
			Non, il est petit.

En route pour l'école

dialogue

On his way to school, Pierre sees a classmate at the entrance to the subway.

PIERRE   Tiens! Danièle, tu vas au lycée en métro?
DANIÈLE   Oui. D'habitude, j'y vais en vélo. Mais quand il pleut...
PIERRE   En vélo? Mais tu habites loin du lycée!
DANIÈLE   Loin? Pas du tout! Quelquefois, j'y vais même à pied!
PIERRE   Ah, oui? Mais le métro, c'est bien plus pratique.

Place de la Concorde, Paris

à vous, maintenant

1. How do you get to school from your house? Here are several possible answers.

Tu vas au lycée comment?

D'habitude,	j'y vais	en métro.
Quelquefois,		en vélo.
Quand il pleut,		en autobus.
		en voiture.
		à pied.

2. Is your partner right about how far you live from the school?

Tu habites | loin | du lycée, n'est-ce-pas?
           | près |

Oui, très loin.
Oui, tout près.
Non, pas très loin.
Non, pas tout près.

Le métro

In many rural areas of France, there are school buses. Students in large cities like Paris, however, have to take public transportation, such as the **autobus** or the **métro**. **Le métro** (short for **métropolitain**) is the Paris subway system, used daily by millions of people. It serves all areas of the city and also connects with buses to the suburbs. It is fast, efficient, and economical. Many of the trains run on rubber tires, so they are quiet and comfortable.

Before boarding the train, you can plot your course from one point to another on a large map. Below the map is a list of all the stops, with a button for each one. After you push the button corresponding to your destination, your route lights up on the map.

To use the **métro,** you buy a small cardboard ticket with magnetic tape. The ticket is inserted in a machine that causes a turnstile to open automatically, allowing you to enter the boarding area.

Deux lycéens

narration

Pierre est lycéen à Paris.
L'école de Pierre s'appelle le lycée Pasteur.
Il y va en métro.
Danièle est lycéenne.
D'habitude, elle va au lycée en vélo.
Mais quand il pleut, elle y va en métro.
Le métro est très pratique, n'est-ce pas?
Mais le vélo de Danièle est pratique aussi.

questions

Complete the responses to the following questions based on the *monologue*, the *dialogue*, and the *narration*.

1. Qui est lycéen? _____ est lycéen.
2. Comment s'appelle l'école de Danièle? Elle s'appelle _____.
3. Pierre va au lycée comment? Il y va _____.
4. Et Danièle? D'habitude, elle y va _____.
5. Qui habite près du lycée? _____ habite près du lycée.

situations

The students named in the drawing below live at various distances from their *lycée.* Say whether they live close to or far from the *lycée,* and decide what means of transportation they use to get there.

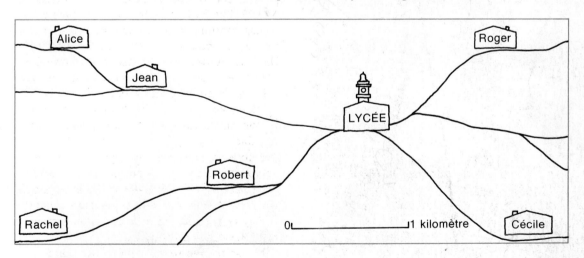

à vous, maintenant

1. You meet a girl from out of town. Introduce yourself, and ask where she lives and where and how she goes to school. Ask about the size of the school. Then give the same information about yourself.
2. Pretend that a close friend of yours lives in a different town, and give the same information about him or her.

L'éducation en France

French children generally go to nursery school or kindergarten (**l'école maternelle**) for two or three years. They start elementary school when they are five or six years old and go at least until the age of sixteen, when compulsory education ends. In France, school grades are numbered in the reverse order of American grades. Students begin in the "eleventh" grade and progress to "first" grade. The word **école** applies to school at any level, and there are three levels that correspond roughly to elementary school, junior high, and high school: **l'école primaire** (grades 11–7), **le collège d'enseignement secondaire** or **C.E.S.** (grades 6–3), and **le lycée.** The three years of the **lycée** are called **seconde** (grade 2), **première** (grade 1), and **terminale,** the final stage in the twelve-year program.

Ça va?

échanges de politesse

When Pierre arrives at school, he sees two of his classmates and joins them in the schoolyard.

PIERRE	Salut, Jean. Bonjour, Cécile. Ça va?
JEAN	Oui, ça va, merci.
CÉCILE	Pas trop mal. Et toi, Pierre?
PIERRE	Ça va mal aujourd'hui!
CÉCILE	Pourquoi?
PIERRE	Il pleut... Et j'ai un examen!

When Pierre goes to class, Mme Brochot, his biology teacher, is already there. He greets her.

PIERRE	Bonjour, madame. Comment allez-vous?
MME BROCHOT	Je vais bien, merci. Et toi, Pierre?
PIERRE	Oh! Ça ne va pas très bien, madame.
MME BROCHOT	Qu'est-ce qu'il y a? Tu es malade?
PIERRE	Non, c'est à cause de l'examen!

à vous,
maintenant

1. Ask first a classmate, then your teacher, how they are feeling. If they are not feeling well, find out what is the matter.

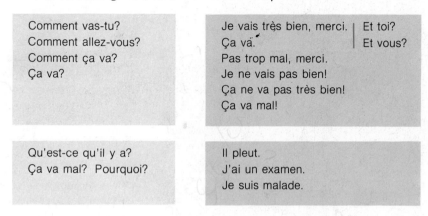

Comment vas-tu?	Je vais très bien, merci. Et toi?
Comment allez-vous?	Ça va. Et vous?
Comment ça va?	Pas trop mal, merci.
Ça va?	Je ne vais pas bien!
	Ça ne va pas très bien!
	Ça va mal!

Qu'est-ce qu'il y a?	Il pleut.
Ça va mal? Pourquoi?	J'ai un examen.
	Je suis malade.

2. Act out a scene in which you meet a teacher or another student in the hall. Exchange greetings and tell one another how things are going.

A French speaker must make a choice between the subject pronouns **tu** and **vous** when addressing an individual. In general, the use of **vous** implies a more formal relationship than **tu**. **Tu** is normally used between close friends and relatives, between students, or by an adult when speaking to a child. But **vous** is regularly used by a child in speaking to an adult, unless the adult is a relative.

In school, many teachers use **tu** with students. Students are always expected to use **vous** in addressing a teacher.

Étude de mots

Les nombres 0–10

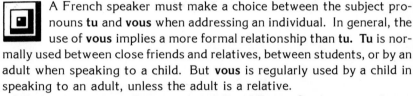

zéro	0	trois	3	six	6	neuf	9
un	1	quatre	4	sept	7	dix	10
deux	2	cinq	5	huit	8		

Note how the French write the 1 and the 7. French people sometimes interpret an American-style 7 as a 1, and Americans may read a French 1 as a 7.

A You're announcing the results at a track meet. Here's how the top three runners finished in each race. Call out the numbers.

▪▥ 5-9-3 *Cinq, neuf, trois!*

1. 2-7-5
2. 9-4-6
3. 10-1-3
4. 8-2-9
5. 7-10-1
6. 3-8-4

B You're checking your little cousin's arithmetic homework. Read the problems aloud and give the answers. (Use **et** for *plus*, **moins** for *minus*, and **font** for *equals*.)

▪▥ $1 + 1 = ?$ *Un et un font deux.*
$3 - 1 = ?$ *Trois moins un font deux.*

1. $10 - 4 = ?$
2. $2 + 7 = ?$
3. $9 + 1 = ?$
4. $6 + 4 = ?$
5. $8 - 5 = ?$
6. $3 - 3 = ?$

À la française

How do you count from 1 to 5 with your fingers? Do you touch your thumb with each finger for the numbers 1 to 4, and then open your palm to indicate 5? Or do you use your index finger for 1 and your thumb for 5?
Try it the French way:

1. Raise your thumb for **un.**
2. Raise your index finger (together with your thumb) for **deux.**
3. Then, raise your middle finger for **trois.**
4. Now fold your thumb against the palm of your hand and raise all four fingers for **quatre.**
5. Raise your thumb again with all four fingers for **cinq.**

How do you get your teacher's attention in the classroom? By raising your hand, with palm open and fingers spread? Try it the French way: just raise your index finger. Be sure not to wave your arm or hand.

La salle de classe

1 une carte
2 un élève (un lycéen)
3 une élève (une lycéenne)
4 un crayon
5 un professeur
6 un tableau
7 un livre
8 une table
9 une feuille de papier
10 un stylo
11 une cassette
12 un bureau
13 un pupitre
14 un cahier
15 une chaise

— **Qu'est-ce que c'est?**   — C'est la salle de classe de Pierre.

C   Identify each of the pictures below. Work with a partner.

— *Qu'est-ce que c'est?*
— *C'est un crayon.*

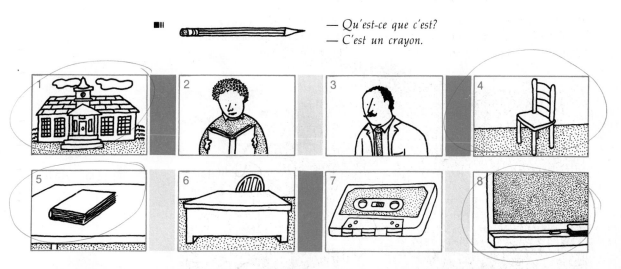

D   Point to the following things or people in your classroom, and identify them in French.

▄▥   a pencil   *Voilà un crayon.*

1. a female student
2. a student's desk
3. a piece of paper
4. a map
5. a male student
6. a notebook
7. a pen
8. a chalkboard

—————— Prononciation et orthographe ———

▋ /e/   le bébé
▋ /ɛ/   elle

/e/

When you make the sound /e/, smile and keep your lips slightly apart. The vowel does not glide, as does the vowel *a* in the English word *say*.

RÉPÉTEZ

le bébé	l'école	Roger
Québec	le lycée	et
le vélo	le métro	allez

The sound /e/ has a number of different spellings, including **é, er, et,** and **ez.**

LISEZ

1. Je vais à l'école en métro.
2. Roger va au lycée en vélo. Et Olivier?
3. Comment allez-vous, Renée?

/ɛ/

When you make the sound /ɛ/, your lips should be wider apart than when you pronounce /e/.

RÉPÉTEZ

elle	canadienne	très	la fête
je m'appelle	haïtienne	le collège	même

The sound /ɛ/ has several different spellings, including **e** (especially when followed by a double consonant), **è,** and **ê.**

LISEZ

1. C'est la fête d'Yvette.
2. Comment s'appelle l'élève canadienne?
3. Danièle va au collège.

Élision

When certain short words like **ce, de, je,** and **ne** occur before a vowel sound, the sound represented by **e** is dropped. This is called *élision*. In writing, the **e** is replaced by an apostrophe.

ce + est → **c'est**	je + habite → **j'habite**
de + Yvette → **d'Yvette**	il ne + est pas → **il n'est pas**

L'accent aigu and l'accent grave

The French spelling system includes several signs called accents. The two most common accents are *l'accent aigu* or acute accent ('), and *l'accent grave* or grave accent ('). They are used most often with the letter **e**, although *l'accent grave* also occurs with **a (voilà)**, and **u (où)**.

é always represents the sound /e/: **le bébé, le lycée**
è always represents the sound /ɛ/: **l'élève, Danièle**

Accent marks are an important part of spelling, and cannot be omitted (except on capital letters). Some words have completely different meanings when spelled with or without an accent. For example:

de   of, from
dé   thimble

ou   or
où   where

L'oisiveté est mère de tous les vices.

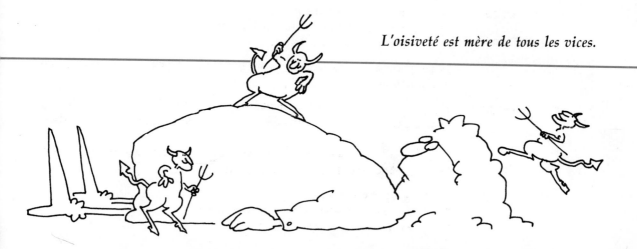

Paris presents a variety of images. Above: **la Tour Eiffel.** Top right: **Notre-Dame de Paris.** Inset: fence at **la Sorbonne,** part of the University of Paris. Bottom right: feeding the birds in Montmartre.

Grammaire

Gender of nouns

In French, all nouns have gender — that is, they are either masculine or feminine. The words for things and abstract concepts, as well as the words for people and animals, have gender. Gender determines the form of other words used with a noun. For example, **livre** is masculine and **cassette** is feminine. Notice the words in dark print in the following sentences:

Voilà **le** livre.   Voilà **la** cassette.
Voilà **un** livre.   Voilà **une** cassette.

When you learn a new noun, try to learn it together with an appropriate article (**le** or **la, un** or **une**). That way, you will know the gender, as well as the meaning, of the noun.

Singular forms of articles

The indefinite articles **un** and **une** are equivalent to *a, an*. The definite articles **le, la,** and **l'** are equivalent to *the*.

	INDEFINITE ARTICLES		DEFINITE ARTICLES	
Masculine singular	un	un garçon un examen	le, l'	le garçon l'examen
Feminine singular	une	une fille une école	la, l'	la fille l'école

1. The form of the article is determined by the gender of the noun.
2. The definite articles **le** and **la** become **l'** before a vowel.

A You're giving French lessons to a friend. Your friend points to the following objects and people, and you identify them.

◼ııı école   *C'est une école.*

1. crayon	5. professeur	9. cassette
2. fille	6. bureau	10. table
3. feuille de papier	7. garçon	11. stylo
4. cahier	8. pupitre	12. carte

B Suppose you're the artist hired to draw illustrations for a book. Show your drawings to the editor.

◼ııı un bébé   *Voilà le bébé.*

1. une table	4. une cassette	7. une jeune fille
2. un vélo	5. une chaise	8. un pupitre
3. une école	6. un professeur	9. un autobus

C A classmate notices the following things. Since you don't see them, you ask where they are.

■⫴ crayon — *Tiens! Voilà un crayon.*
— *Où est le crayon?*

1. livre	5. autobus	9. école
2. cahier	6. table	10. vélo
3. stylo	7. bureau	11. voiture
4. tableau	8. feuille de papier	12. carte

Expressing possession with **de**

One way to indicate possession or close relationship in French is to use **de** plus a person's name. Before a vowel, **de** becomes **d'**.

le livre de Pierre   Pierre's book
la chaise de Marie   Marie's chair
l'école d'Yvette   Yvette's school

D Identify the following as belonging to or as being associated with Roger.

■⫴ la table   *C'est la table de Roger.*

1. le crayon	3. le stylo	5. la cassette	7. la chaise
2. l'école	4. le professeur	6. le pupitre	8. le cahier

E Some of the following people attend a large school and some attend a small one. Describe each person's school.

■⫴ Paul va à un grand lycée.   *Le lycée de Paul est grand.*

1. Roger va à un grand lycée.	4. Bruno va à un grand lycée.
2. Annick va à un petit lycée.	5. Yvette va à un petit lycée.
3. Gilles va à un grand lycée.	6. Monette va à un petit lycée.

F A classmate points out the following things. You think they are Alain's, and you ask if that is the case.

■⫴ livre — *Voilà un livre.*
— *C'est le livre d'Alain, n'est-ce pas?*

1. carte	3. chaise	5. cassette	7. cahier
2. pupitre	4. crayon	6. vélo	8. voiture

Present tense of **aller** (to go): singular forms

The basic form of the verb is the infinitive form (the form listed in dictionaries and vocabularies). In French, the infinitive consists of one word; for example, **aller** (to go).

1st person	je vais	I go, I am going
2nd person	tu vas	you go, you are going
3rd person	il/elle va	he/she goes, he/she is going

A single present-tense form in French has several English equivalents. For example, **je vais** may mean *I go, I am going,* or in some cases *I do go.*

G Say that the following people are all walking to school today.

■III Pierre *Aujourd'hui, Pierre va au lycée à pied.*

1. tu	3. je	5. il	7. Cécile
2. elle	4. Alain	6. Sylvie	8. Jacques

H To which city is each of the following people going? You decide.

■III Roger *Roger va à [Paris].*

1. je 2. elle 3. M. Legrand 4. tu

Referring to destinations with **y**

The word **y** (*there*) is used to refer to a destination that has been previously identified. **Y** comes right before the verb.

— Tu vas au lycée comment? — J'**y** vais à pied.
— Anne va à Paris en vélo? — Non, elle **y** va en voiture.
— Paul va à Chicago? — Non, il n'**y** va pas.

I Say how the following people are going to school, using *y*.

■III Danièle: en vélo *Danièle y va en vélo.*

1. je: en vélo	3. il: en autobus	5. elle: en métro
2. Marie: à pied	4. tu: en voiture	6. Paul: à pied

J Identify somebody (a celebrity, a friend, yourself, or an imaginary person) who normally or sometimes goes to the following places.

■III à Paris — *Qui va à Paris?*
— *Pierre y va d'habitude.* / *Moi, j'y vais quelquefois.*

1. à Québec	3. à Montréal	5. à Miami
2. à Seattle	4. à Hollywood	6. à Washington

Lecture

Un rendez-vous

Serge Forey is on his way out of his apartment. His mother asks where he is going.

MME FOREY	Où est-ce que tu vas, Serge?
SERGE	Je vais à la Tour Eiffel, Maman. J'ai rendez-vous avec° Christianne.
MME FOREY	Tu n'y vas pas en vélo, j'espère.° Il pleut!
SERGE	Non, Maman. J'y vais en autobus.
MME FOREY	Qui est Christianne?
SERGE	Elle va au lycée avec moi. Elle est canadienne, mais elle habite à Paris maintenant.°
MME FOREY	Bon, alors, amuse-toi bien.°
SERGE	Merci. Au revoir, Maman. À tout à l'heure.°

avec° I have a date with
j'espère.° I hope
maintenant.° now
amuse-toi bien.° Well, then, have a good time
À tout à l'heure.° See you later

vrai ou faux?

Say whether the following statements are true (*C'est vrai*) or false (*C'est faux*). Correct the false statements.

1. Serge va à la Tour Eiffel.
2. Il y va en métro.
3. Christianne est lycéenne.
4. Elle est française.
5. Il ne pleut pas.

Résumé grammatical

Singular forms of articles (A-C)

	INDEFINITE (a, an)	DEFINITE (the)
Masculine singular	un	le (l')
Feminine singular	une	la (l')

1. The gender of the noun determines the form of the article.
2. The articles **un** (*a, an*) and **le** (*the*) are used with masculine singular nouns: **un stylo, le stylo.** The articles **une** (*a, an*) and **la** (*the*) are used with feminine singular nouns: **une chaise, la chaise.**
3. Both **le** and **la** contract to **l'** before a vowel, because of élision.

Expressing possession with **de** (D-F)

A phrase consisting of a noun with a definite article, followed by **de** plus a person's name, indicates possession or close relationship. Before a vowel, **de** contracts to **d'.**

> Voilà **le crayon de Marie.**   *There's **Marie's** pencil.*
> Où est **l'école d'Alain?**   *Where is **Alain's** school?*

Present tense of **aller** (to go): singular forms (G-H)

1st person	je vais	I go, I am going
2nd person	tu vas	you go, you are going
3rd person	il/elle va	he/she goes, he/she is going

1. The form of **aller** that is used must agree with the subject.
2. Each French form has several English equivalents: **je vais** may mean *I go, I am going,* or in some cases *I do go.* French verbs do not have separate forms to express these different meanings.

Referring to destinations with **y** (I, J)

The word **y** is used to refer to a destination that has been identified.

> —Pierre va à l'école à pied? —Non, il **y** va en vélo.
> —Tu vas à New York comment? —J'**y** vais en voiture.

1. The word **y** must be included if the destination is not named in the sentence (unlike the English equivalent *there*, which may be dropped).
2. **Y** comes right before the verb, which is often a form of **aller.**

Révision

A Identify the following persons and objects. Complete each sentence with *un* or *une*, as appropriate.

■ll   C'est ____ feuille de papier.   *C'est une feuille de papier.*

1. C'est ____ pupitre.
2. C'est ____ dame.
3. C'est ____ fille.
4. C'est ____ stylo.
5. C'est ____ lycée.
6. C'est ____ carte.
7. C'est ____ livre.
8. C'est ____ monsieur.

B Point out the following people and objects to a friend. Use the correct form of the definite article.

■ll   garçon   *Voilà le garçon.*

1. chaise
2. crayon
3. cassette
4. cahier
5. professeur
6. bureau
7. examen
8. jeune fille
9. stylo

C Choose the logical response to each of the following questions.

1. Tu es français?
    a. Non, à bicyclette.   b. Non, canadien.   c. Non, à Paris.
2. Le lycée est grand?
    a. C'est Pierre.   b. Non, petit.   c. Il va au lycée.
3. Comment vas-tu?
    a. En vélo.   b. Au lycée.   c. Bien, merci.
4. Où est-ce que tu habites?
    a. Yvette.   b. En métro.   c. À Québec.
5. Qui est-ce?
    a. C'est un cahier.   b. C'est le professeur.   c. Pas mal.

D Solve the following arithmetic problems.

■ll   1 + 1 = ?   *Un et un font deux.*
      2 − 1 = ?   *Deux moins un font un.*

1. 4 + 3 = ?
2. 7 + 3 = ?
3. 9 − 6 = ?
4. 5 − 4 = ?
5. 2 + 6 = ?
6. 8 − 3 = ?

E   State where the following people are going.

   ▪▥   je / au lycée   *Je vais au lycée.*

1. il / à Montréal   3. je / à New York
2. tu / à l'école   4. elle / à Dallas

F   Say that the following people and things are related in some way to Yvette.

   ▪▥   l'école   *C'est l'école d'Yvette.*

1. le professeur   2. la classe   3. le livre   4. le lycée

G   Respond to the following questions. Indicate your destination with *y*.

   ▪▥   Tu vas à l'école comment?   *J'y vais à pied.*

1. Et le professeur, comment va-t-il/elle à l'école?
2. Est-ce que Pierre va à l'école en vélo?
3. Est-ce que Danièle va à l'école en voiture?

H   You are in Paris. You want to visit the monuments shown on the map below. Plot your trip. Say how you will go from one monument to the next. Identify the *métro* stations, and tell when you must change lines.

1   Tour Eiffel
2   Arc de Triomphe
3   Place de la Con-
     corde
4   Centre Beaubourg
5   Jardin des Tuileries
6   Notre-Dame
7   Sacré-Cœur
8   Sorbonne

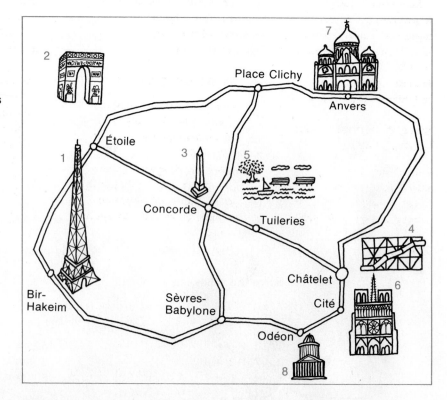

le collégian - French junior high school student

la collégienne

ARTICLES AND NOUNS

le bureau   teacher's desk
le cahier   notebook
la carte   map
la cassette   cassette
la chaise   chair
le collège   French junior high school
le crayon   pencil
l'école (f.)   school
l'élève (m./f.)   pupil
l'examen (m.)   exam
la feuille de papier   sheet of paper
le livre   book
le lycée   French high school
le lycéen, la lycéenne   French high school student
le professeur   teacher
le pupitre   pupil's desk
la salle de classe   classroom
le stylo   pen
la table   table
le tableau   chalkboard

SUBJECT PRONOUNS AND VERB FORMS

j'ai   I have
aller   to go (**je vais**   I go; **tu vas**   you go; **il va**   he goes; **elle va**   she goes)

NUMBERS 0–10

zéro = 0   **six** = 6
un = 1   **sept** = 7
deux = 2   **huit** = 8
trois = 3   **neuf** = 9
quatre = 4   **dix** = 10
cinq = 5

ADJECTIVES

grand(e)   big, large
malade   sick
petit(e)   small
pratique   practical

MEANS OF TRANSPORTATION

en autobus   by bus
en métro   by subway
en vélo   by bicycle
en voiture   by car
à pied   on foot

EXPRESSIONS OF HEALTH

comment vas-tu? (comment allez-vous?)   how are you?
(comment) ça va?   how are things?
très bien   very well, fine
pas (trop) mal   not (too) bad
ça va   OK, things are all right; **ça va mal**   things are bad

OTHER WORDS AND EXPRESSIONS

au   to the
aujourd'hui   today
aussi   also
comment   how
merci   thanks, thank you
même   even
quand   when
plus   more; **bien plus**   much more
pourquoi   why
quelquefois   sometimes
tiens!   why! well! look!
voilà   there is, there are, here is, here are
à cause de   because of
d'habitude   usually
n'est-ce pas?   isn't that so? right?
qu'est-ce que c'est?   what's that? what's this?
qu'est-ce qu'il y a?   what's the matter?
près du (loin du) lycée   near (far from) the lycée
tout près   close by
pas du tout   not at all
j'y vais   I go (there)
il pleut   it's raining

chapitre 3

Chez moi

The city of Quebec is the capital of Canada's largest province, and one of the loveliest cities in North America. Perched on top of a bluff, the Upper Town overlooks the St. Lawrence River. Near the waterfront, where many cargo and passenger ships dock in the harbor, is the Lower Town. Narrow, winding, picturesque streets link the two sections of the city.

In the Upper Town, between the Château Frontenac and a park called *Les plaines d'Abraham,* is Yvette Lebeau's home.

Bienvenue à Québec!

Yvette Lebeau invites you to come visit her in Quebec.

Bonjour! Je suis Yvette Lebeau de Québec.
J'ai presque quinze ans.
J'habite dans une jolie petite maison.
Elle n'est pas loin du Château Frontenac.
Je t'invite chez moi.

à vous,
maintenant

1. Invite first one classmate, then several classmates, to your home. They may accept or refuse, depending on their plans.

| Je t'invite | chez moi. |
| Je vous invite | |

| Très bien, j'accepte. |
| D'accord, merci. |
| Merci, mais je suis occupé(e). |
| Merci, mais je ne peux pas. |

2. A classmate asks if you live in a house or an apartment, and then asks you to describe it.

Tu habites dans une maison ou
dans un appartement?

| J'habite dans | une maison. |
| | un appartement. |

Comment est la maison?	Elle est	jolie.
		grande.
		petite.

Comment est l'appartement?	Il est	joli.
		grand.
		petit.

3. Tell one of your classmates how old you are. Then inquire about the age of another classmate.

Quel âge as-tu?

J'ai	treize	ans.
	quatorze	
	quinze	

Le Château Frontenac

Bon anniversaire!

dialogue

Today is Yvette's birthday. Two of her friends arrive at her party.

YVETTE   Salut, les amis! Bienvenue chez moi!

JOËL   Bon anniversaire! Tiens! Voilà un petit cadeau pour toi.

YVETTE   Merci beaucoup, Joël. C'est gentil!

SYLVIE   Moi aussi, j'ai quelque chose pour toi.

YVETTE   Merci bien. Tu es gentille, Sylvie. Eh bien, entrez dans le salon. Tout le monde est là.

à vous, maintenant

1. How should you respond when someone gives you a gift? Here are a few suggestions.

Voilà un petit cadeau. Voilà quelque chose pour toi.	Merci, [Joël]. Merci bien! Merci beaucoup! C'est gentil! Tu es gentil(le).

2. Your friend is carrying a present. Can you guess whom it is for?

C'est pour	moi? Yvette? Alain?	Oui, c'est pour	toi. elle. lui.

La fête

In most of the French-speaking world, children are given from two to five first names, often including names of parents, grandparents, or godparents. (However, people normally use only one or two first names, and they do not use middle initials.) In Catholic families, at least one name is that of a Catholic saint.

Many people celebrate their name day **(la fête)** as well as their birthday. A person's **fête** is the day of the saint whose name was given to that person. Practically every date on the calendar is a saint's day. The list of saints' days is revised from time to time by the Vatican. Post offices, banks, and other offices in France give their customers calendars that indicate **les fêtes.** On their name day, people are often given cards, presents, and a cake. Their families and friends wish them a **bonne fête!**

L'anniversaire d'Yvette

narration

La maison d'Yvette est près du Château Frontenac.
Yvette invite Joël et Sylvie chez elle.
Joël a un petit cadeau pour Yvette.
Sylvie aussi a quelque chose pour elle.
Pourquoi? C'est l'anniversaire d'Yvette!
Aujourd'hui, elle a quinze ans.

questions

1. Où est la maison d'Yvette? Elle est _____.
2. Comment est la maison d'Yvette? Elle est _____.
3. Quel âge a Yvette aujourd'hui? Elle a _____.
4. Qui est-ce qu'elle invite chez elle? Elle invite _____.
5. Qu'est-ce que Joël a pour Yvette? Il a _____ pour elle.
6. Et Sylvie? Elle a _____ aussi.

situations

Pretend that you have a birthday present for a friend. Offer your congratulations and present your gift. Your friend responds appropriately.

— Bon anniversaire, [Yvette].
　Voilà un cadeau pour toi.
　C'est [un stylo].

— Merci bien, [Joël].
　Tu es gentil!

à vous,
maintenant

1. You invite a new friend from out of town to your home. Your friend accepts or declines the invitation.
2. Your guest arrives with a gift for you. You welcome him or her and accept the gift politely.

Le français au Québec

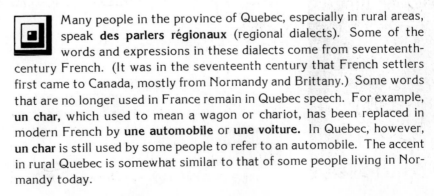

Many people in the province of Quebec, especially in rural areas, speak **des parlers régionaux** (regional dialects). Some of the words and expressions in these dialects come from seventeenth-century French. (It was in the seventeenth century that French settlers first came to Canada, mostly from Normandy and Brittany.) Some words that are no longer used in France remain in Quebec speech. For example, **un char,** which used to mean a wagon or chariot, has been replaced in modern French by **une automobile** or **une voiture.** In Quebec, however, **un char** is still used by some people to refer to an automobile. The accent in rural Quebec is somewhat similar to that of some people living in Normandy today.

échanges
de politesse

à vous,
maintenant

Invite first a classmate, then an adult, to come in, sit down, and feel at ease in your home.

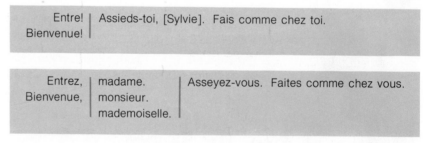

L'hospitalité

In Quebec, as in France, home and family are the center of life. People who are invited into a French-Canadian home are often greeted with a hearty **Bienvenue chez moi!** or **Vous êtes les bienvenus!** If you are invited to stay for a few days in a French home, you might be told **Faites comme chez vous!** or **Fais comme chez toi!** These expressions are meant to put guests at ease, to make them feel as comfortable as they would in their own homes.

À la française

In France, it is considered polite to repay one compliment with another instead of merely thanking someone for a compliment directly. For example, if someone compliments you on your lovely home, you might respond **Vous êtes très gentil(le)**, instead of **Merci.**

―――――――――― Étude de mots ――――――――――

Les nombres 11–20

11 = onze	16 = seize
12 = douze	17 = dix-sept
13 = treize	18 = dix-huit
14 = quatorze	19 = dix-neuf
15 = quinze	20 = vingt

Note that **vingt** ends in a /t/ sound only before a vowel:

Onze et neuf font vingt. J'ai vingt livres. *But:* J'ai vingt ans.

A   Roger is the oldest of ten children. His parents had one child each year for ten years. The children are listed below from *oldest to youngest*. Say how old each person is.

■Ⅲ   Roger a 20 ans. Et Sylvie?   *Elle a dix-neuf ans.*

1. Et Paul?
2. Et Yvette?
3. Et François?
4. Et Chantal?
5. Et Charles?
6. Et Josette?
7. Et Richard?
8. Et Béatrice?
9. Et Renée?

B   You are at an auction. Outbid the previous offer for a book by one *franc* (a unit of French currency).

■Ⅲ   Seize!   *Dix-sept!*

1. Quinze!
2. Dix-neuf!
3. Dix-huit!
4. Onze!
5. Douze!
6. Treize!

C   Solve the following addition problems.

■Ⅲ   8 + 2 = ?   *Huit et deux font dix.*

1. 7 + 6 = ?
2. 12 + 5 = ?
3. 10 + 1 = ?
4. 8 + 7 = ?
5. 5 + 9 = ?
6. 18 + 2 = ?
7. 10 + 6 = ?
8. 14 + 5 = ?

La maison d'Yvette

Il y a sept pièces dans la maison d'Yvette: un salon, une salle à manger, une cuisine, trois chambres et une salle de bains. Il y a aussi un corridor.

Il y a combien de pièces chez vous?

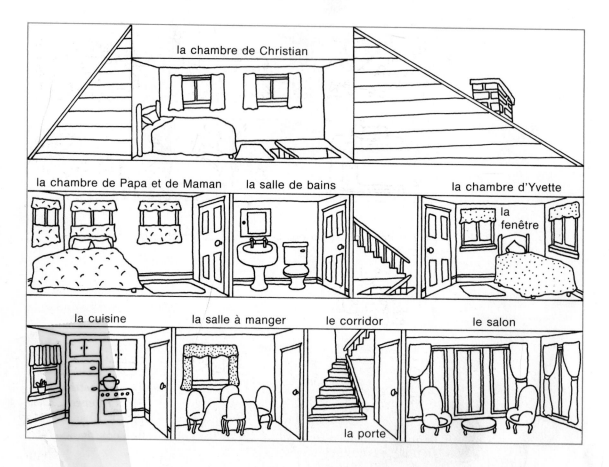

la chambre de Christian

la chambre de Papa et de Maman   la salle de bains   la chambre d'Yvette

la fenêtre

la cuisine   la salle à manger   le corridor   le salon

la porte

D   Discuss with a partner how many of the following items there are in Yvette's home.

■ⅲ   fenêtres / chambre d'Yvette   *Il y a combien de fenêtres dans la chambre d'Yvette?*
      Il y a deux fenêtres.

1. fenêtres / la cuisine   4. fenêtres / la salle à manger
2. portes / le salon   5. salles de bains / la maison
3. chambres / la maison   6. fenêtres / la maison

E You are in the same room as the objects pictured below. Say what room you are in.

Je suis dans la cuisine.

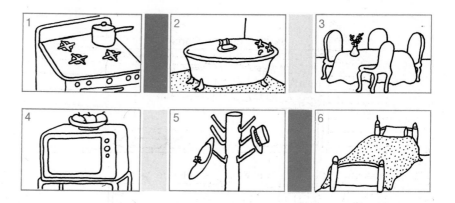

F Paul is engaged in various activities. Say which room he is in.

Il est dans la cuisine.

à vous, maintenant

Imagine you are designing your dream house. Describe it briefly. How many rooms are there? How many of each type? Look back at the plan of Yvette's home for ideas.

Prononciation et orthographe

▌ /a/   la
▌ /wa/ moi

/a/

The French vowel /a/ is close in sound to the English vowel /a/ in *aha*, but it is pronounced with lips and jaws held in a tense position.

RÉPÉTEZ

la table	canadienne	je m'appelle
l'appartement	américaine	à
la carte	j'habite	là
madame	Paris	l'âge

The sound /a/ is most often spelled **a, à,** or **â.**

LISEZ

1. Anne habite à Paris.
2. Je m'appelle Alice.
3. Quel âge as-tu?
4. Mardi, Jacques va à Strasbourg.

/wa/

The sound /a/ also occurs in words like **moi** and **toi.** The spelling **oi** represents the combination of sounds /wa/ (except when followed by **n,** as in the words **loin** and **moins**).

RÉPÉTEZ

moi	mademoiselle	quelquefois
toi	au revoir	voilà
trois	François	Leroi

LISEZ

1. Au revoir, mademoiselle.
2. Voilà un cadeau pour toi.
3. Vous êtes François Leroi?

Les chiens aboient, la caravane passe.

Pronunciation of numbers 1–10

Most numbers **un** to **dix** change in pronunciation according to whether they are followed by a pause (at the end of a phrase), a vowel or a consonant. Exceptions: **quatre** and **sept** do not change.

Before a pause	Before a vowel	Before a consonant
un	/n/ un‿an	un livre
deu$x$	/z/ deux‿ans	deu$x$ livres
troi$s$	/z/ trois‿ans	troi$s$ livres
/R/ quatre	/R/ quatre‿ans	/R/ quatre livres
/K/ cinq	/K/ cinq‿ans	cin$q$ livres
/s/ six	/z/ six‿ans	si$x$ livres
/t/ sept	/t/ sept‿ans	/t/ sept livres
/t/ huit	/t/ huit‿ans	hui$t$ livres
/f/ neuf	/v/ neuf‿ans	/f/ neuf livres
/s/ dix	/z/ dix‿ans	di$x$ livres

Note: In the number **neuf,** the /f/ sound changes to /v/ only in the phrases **neu/v/f‿ans** and **neu/v/f‿heures** (*nine o'clock*). But: **neuf /f/ écoles.**

Intonation

Intonation refers to the rise or fall of the voice in speaking. In French, as in English, you can use the same words to make a statement or ask a question, depending on your intonation. In a statement, the voice falls slightly at the end of the sentence. In a question asking for a **oui** or **non** answer, the voice rises at the end of the sentence.

RÉPÉTEZ   Tu as une jolie maison.   Tu as une jolie maison?

Elle est grande.   Elle est grande?

LISEZ   Say each of the following sentences, first as a statement, then as a question.

1. Il habite à Québec.
2. Elle est française.
3. Le livre est dans le salon.
4. Tu as seize ans.

La cédille and l'accent circonflexe

In addition to the *accent aigu* (´) and the *accent grave* (`), you have probably noticed two other marks that occur in written French: *la cédille* (cedilla) and *l'accent circonflexe* (circumflex accent).

La cédille (̧) occurs only under the letter **c** in the combinations **ça, ço,** and **çu.** The letter **ç** represents the sound /s/, as in **ça.**

RÉPÉTEZ   français   le garçon   ça va?   la leçon

L'accent circonflexe (ˆ) occurs over the vowels **a, e, i, o,** and **u.**

RÉPÉTEZ   le château   même   s'il vous plaît   à bientôt

L'accent circonflexe often indicates that the vowel used to be followed by **s** in an older form of the word. This fact may help you in reading some new words: **la bête** (beast, animal), **la croûte** (crust), **la fête** (festival).

French-speaking Canada

The French were among the first Europeans to explore Canada. Jacques Cartier sailed from St.-Malo, Brittany, in 1534, and entered the Gulf of St. Lawrence by the Strait of Belle Isle. He explored the St. Lawrence River and claimed the region of New Brunswick, the Gaspé Peninsula, and the St. Lawrence Valley in the name of the French king. He named the entire area **la Nouvelle-France** (New France).

In 1608, Samuel de Champlain built a trading post where the city of Quebec now stands. More than fifty years later, King Louis XIV established a royal government in New France. The early French inhabitants were mostly missionaries, explorers, and fur traders. They had to fight for control of the territory, first against the native Indians, and later against the rival British. After a century of struggle, the British won a decisive victory at Quebec City in 1759, on the Plains of Abraham.

Today approximately eighty percent of the population of Quebec Province are of French descent, and French is their native language. The government of the province has passed laws making French the official language. In

Jacques Cartier

the public schools, English is taught as a second language.

Although the majority of Canada's francophone population live in Quebec, there are French-speaking areas in other parts of the country, such as the city of St.-Boniface, near Winnipeg. In addition, just fifteen miles off the southern coast of Newfoundland are St.-Pierre and Miquelon, two islands that are French territories.

Grammaire

Subject pronouns: plural forms

	SUBJECT PRONOUNS		EXAMPLES
1st person	**nous**	we	Nous habitons près du lycée.
2nd person	**vous**	you	Vous habitez loin du château.
3rd person	**ils**	they (*masculine*)	Ils habitent à Québec.
	elles	they (*feminine*)	Elles habitent à Montréal.

1. **Vous** is always used in addressing two or more people. **Vous** is also used in addressing one person with whom one is on a relatively formal basis.
2. The masculine plural pronoun **ils** is used in referring to any group that includes at least one male. **Elles** is used for an all-female group.

A   Give the subject pronoun you would use in the following situations.

■III   You are talking to three people.   *vous*

1. You are talking about two boys.
2. You are talking about yourself and your friends.
3. You are talking to a group of your friends.
4. You are talking to your teacher.
5. You are talking about one boy and two girls.
6. You are talking about six girls.

Subject pronouns referring to things

1. The pronouns **il** and **elle** mean *he* and *she* when they refer to people. **Il** and **elle** can also refer to things, in which case they are both equivalent to *it*. **Il** refers to a masculine noun; **elle** refers to a feminine noun.
2. The plural forms **ils** and **elles** can likewise refer to things. **Ils** refers to a group of masculine nouns, or to a mixed group of masculine and feminine nouns; **elles** refers to a group of feminine nouns. **Ils** and **elles** mean *they*.

— **Le livre** est dans le salon?

— Non, **il** est dans la chambre.

— **La maison** est petite?

— Non, **elle** est très grande.

— Où sont **le cahier et la cassette**?

— **Ils** sont chez moi.

— Voilà **une table et une chaise.**

— **Elles** sont jolies.

B Tell your classmate where to find the following things. Pick any location you like.

▪ Où est le crayon de Jacques?   *Il est dans la cuisine.*

1. Où est la maison d'Yvette?
2. Où sont la carte et la cassette de Chantal?
3. Où sont la feuille de papier et le stylo d'Hélène?
4. Où est l'appartement de Pierre?
5. Où sont le livre et le cahier d'Alain?

Present tense of **être** (to be)

The verb **être** is the most common verb in the French language.

	SINGULAR		PLURAL	
1st person	je **suis**	I am	nous **sommes**	we are
2nd person	tu **es**	you are	vous **êtes**	you are
3rd person	il/elle **est**	he/she, it is	ils/elles **sont**	they are

C Say that the following people are in the classroom.

▪ tu   *Tu es dans la salle de classe.*

1. elle   3. je   5. nous
2. vous   4. le professeur   6. Mme Lebeau

D Ask a classmate if the following people and things are in the places indicated. Your classmate answers with *oui* or *non*.

▪ tu / dans la cuisine   — *Tu es dans la cuisine?*
                           — *Non, je ne suis pas dans la cuisine.*

1. la table / dans le salon   5. tu / à Paris
2. vous / au collège   6. nous / dans la salle à manger
3. elles / dans le corridor   7. le stylo / dans la chambre
4. il / chez Luc   8. la carte / à l'école

Present tense of **avoir** (to have)

	SINGULAR		PLURAL	
1st person	j'**ai**	I have	nous **avons**	we have
2nd person	tu **as**	you have	vous **avez**	you have
3rd person	il/elle **a**	he/she, it has	ils/elles **ont**	they have

The basic meaning of **avoir** is *to have*. **Avoir** is also used in many phrases with the meaning *to be*.

J'ai treize cassettes.	*I have* thirteen cassettes.
J'ai treize ans.	*I am* thirteen years old.

E Say that the following people have a pretty house.

◼ll M. Delacroix *M. Delacroix a une jolie maison.*

1. je
2. elles
3. ils
4. M. et Mme Renoir
5. tu
6. nous
7. Yvette
8. Robert

F Ask whether the following people have a gift for Yvette. A classmate answers affirmatively.

◼ll tu — *Tu as un cadeau pour elle?*
— *Oui, j'ai un cadeau pour elle.*

1. Pierre
2. elles
3. tu
4. nous
5. Marie
6. vous

G State the ages of the following people. Use any age from 1 to 20.

◼ll je *J'ai quatorze ans.*

1. Paulette
2. Richard
3. vous
4. tu
5. nous
6. ils

H Complete each of the following sentences with the correct form of *avoir* or *être*, depending on the sense of the sentence.

◼ll Il ____ grand. *Il est grand.*
Nous ____ un joli appartement. *Nous avons un joli appartement.*

1. Elle ____ neuf ans.
2. Ils ____ de Montréal.
3. Sylvie ____ une jolie chambre.
4. Tu ____ quinze ans?
5. Je ____ petite.
6. Nous ____ américains.

Emphatic pronouns: singular forms

moi	me, I
toi	you
lui	him, he
elle	her, she

Emphatic pronouns are used:

1. To give emphasis to the subject of a sentence.
    Moi, je m'appelle Pierre Legrand.
    Lui, il va à Montréal.

2. In compound subjects.
    Paul et moi, nous sommes américains.
    Anne et lui sont lycéens.

3. After prepositions.
    Je vous invite **chez moi.**
    Voilà un cadeau **pour toi.**

4. After **c'est** to express identity.
    — C'est Yvette?   — Oui, c'est **elle.**

5. In phrases without a verb.
    J'ai quatorze ans. Et **toi?**

I You and a friend are looking at an old class picture. Identify the following people as you recognize them.

> ▪▥ Tiens! C'est Jacqueline?   *Oui, c'est elle!*
>   *Non, ce n'est pas elle!*

1. C'est Charles?   3. C'est moi?
2. C'est toi?   4. C'est Alice?

J Say that the following people are going home.

> ▪▥ M. Lebeau   *Il va chez lui.*

1. je   4. Mme Lebeau
2. Jean   5. il
3. tu   6. elle

K Pierre is going to school. Say emphatically that the following people are going to school, too.

> ▪▥ Pierre va au lycée. Et toi?   *Moi aussi, je vais au lycée.*

1. Et Josette?   3. Et moi?
2. Et Paul?   4. Et Gilles?

L Expand the subject of each sentence below to include yourself. Remember to change the verb form.

> ▪▥ Paul a une voiture.   *Paul et moi, nous avons une voiture.*

1. Luc a un vélo.   3. Yvette a une carte de France.
2. Richard est à Montréal.   4. Josette est dans le salon.

Lecture

La fête de Christian

The Lebeau family is celebrating the name day of Yvette's older brother. One of Yvette's classmates arrives unexpectedly.

ANDRÉ	Qu'est-ce que c'est? C'est ton anniversaire?
YVETTE	Non, c'est la fête° de mon frère Christian.
ANDRÉ	Ah, oui? Il a quel âge?
YVETTE	Vingt ans.
ANDRÉ	Oh là là! C'est un vieux°!
YVETTE	Eh bien, entre et va souhaiter° une bonne fête à mon vieux frère.
ANDRÉ	Oh non! C'est une fête de famille.
YVETTE	Mais non, André, entre!
ANDRÉ	Euh ... euh ...°
YVETTE	Mais va dans le salon! Tout le monde est là.
ANDRÉ	Eh bien, d'accord! Et merci ...

name day

He's an old man!

wish

euh ... euh ... (*stalling expression*)

questions

1. Qui a vingt ans?
2. Est-ce que le frère d'Yvette est vieux?
3. Qui est André?
4. Est-ce qu'André accepte l'invitation d'Yvette?

Subject pronouns: plural forms (A)

SUBJECT	EXAMPLES
nous	Nous parlons français.
vous	Vous parlez anglais, Yvette et toi?
	Vous parlez anglais, mademoiselle?
ils	Ils parlent avec moi.
elles	Elles parlent avec Jean.

1. **Vous** is used in addressing two or more people, no matter what the relationship is. **Vous** (rather than **tu**) is also used in addressing one person with whom one has a relatively formal relationship.
2. The masculine plural **ils** is used in referring to any group that includes at least one male. The feminine plural **elles** is used when the entire group is female.

Subject pronouns referring to things (B)

The pronouns **il, elle, ils,** and **elles** can refer to things as well as to people. (**il/elle** = it; **ils/elles** = they)

Le livre est sur la table.   **Il** est sur la table.
La carte est sur la table.   **Elle** est sur la table.

Les livres sont sur la table.   **Ils** sont sur la table.
Les cartes sont sur la table.   **Elles** sont sur la table.

Present tense of **être** and **avoir** (C-H)

être to be	
je suis	nous sommes
tu es	vous êtes
il/elle est	ils/elles sont

avoir to have	
j'ai	nous avons
tu as	vous avez
il/elle a	ils/elles ont

The basic meaning of **avoir** is *to have*. **Avoir** is also used in some expressions with the meaning *to be*.

J'ai une carte.   *I have* a map.
J'ai quinze ans.   *I am* fifteen years old.

Emphatic pronouns: singular forms (I-L)

moi	me, I
toi	you (*fam.*)
lui	him, he
elle	her, she

Emphatic pronouns are used:

1. To give emphasis to a subject pronoun: **Moi, je m'appelle Pierre Legrand.**
2. In compound subjects:
   A compound subject that includes **moi** or **toi** is set off by a comma and followed by **nous** or **vous: Paul et moi, nous sommes américains.**
   After a compound subject that includes **lui** or **elle**, the subject pronoun **ils** or **elles** is usually omitted: **Anne et lui sont canadiens.**
3. After prepositions: **Je vous invite chez moi. C'est pour toi?**
4. After **c'est** to express identity: **C'est Yvette? Oui, c'est elle.**
5. In phrases without a verb: **J'ai quatorze ans. Et toi?**

Révision

A Say that the following people and things are at school. Use the appropriate subject pronouns.

■III Suzanne et Josette *Elles sont à l'école.*

1. Marc et toi
2. Paul et Pierre
3. la carte de France
4. Julie et Nicole
5. les livres d'Olivier
6. toi et moi

B Form complete sentences, using the cues provided.

■III je / avoir / une cassette *J'ai une cassette.*

1. ils / avoir / une jolie maison
2. elle / être / chez Pierre
3. vous / avoir / vingt ans
4. nous / avoir / un petit appartement
5. je / être / dans le salon
6. tu / être / français
7. elles / être / au lycée
8. il / avoir / quinze ans

C A moving van has just delivered the following things to your house. Say where each item should go.

◼▥ (a sofa) *C'est pour le salon.*

1. (a bed)
2. (a medicine cabinet)
3. (a refrigerator)
4. (a china cabinet)
5. (a television set)
6. (a wall clock)

D Choose the logical response to each of the following statements or questions.

1. Il va au lycée?
    a. Oui, il a cinq ans.
    b. Oui, il est chez lui.
    c. Oui, il a seize ans.
2. Ils ont un cadeau?
    a. Qui? Paul?
    b. Qui? Marie et Luc?
    c. Qui? Josette et Marie?
3. Elle vous invite chez elle.
    a. Elle est petite.   b. Elle est belge.   c. Elle est gentille.
4. Je vais chez elle.
    a. Chez Marc?   b. Chez Yvette?   c. Chez M. Dumont?
5. Tu habites dans une grande maison, n'est-ce pas?
    a. Non, j'habite à Québec.
    b. Non, j'habite dans un grand appartement.
    c. Oui, j'habite dans un grand appartement.
6. Entrez! Asseyez-vous.
    a. Au revoir.   b. Oui, je vais chez moi.   c. Merci.

E You receive a phone call from a new friend, who is full of questions. Respond with logical answers.

1. Tu habites dans une maison? Comment est-elle?
2. Il y a combien de pièces chez toi?
3. Tu invites qui chez toi?
4. Josette et Marc sont français?
5. Tu vas au lycée?
6. Tu as rendez-vous avec Paul?

F Look for some products made in Canada with labels printed in French and English. Bring the labels to class and discuss their geographical origin. See how many different parts of the country are represented.

G Use a road map to plot a car trip from Montpelier, Vermont to Montreal and Quebec. Tell your class what cities and towns you plan to visit or pass through.

Vocabulaire

NOUNS

l'anniversaire (*m.*)   birthday
l'appartement
(*m.*)   apartment
le cadeau   gift
la chambre   bedroom
le château   castle
le corridor   hall
la cuisine   kitchen
la fenêtre   window
la maison   house
(la) maman   mom, mother
(le) papa   dad, father
la pièce   room
la porte   door
la salle à manger   dining
  room
la salle de bains   bathroom
le salon   living room

SUBJECT PRONOUNS

elles   they (*feminine*)
ils   they (*masculine*)
nous   we
vous   you (*plural or formal*)

OTHER PRONOUNS

elle   her, she
lui   him, he
te (t')   you

VERBS

avoir   to have; **avoir 16 ans**
  to be sixteen years old (**j'ai,**
  tu as, il/elle a, nous avons,
  vous avez, ils/elles ont)
être   to be (**je suis, tu es,**
  il/elle est, nous sommes,
  vous êtes, ils/elles sont)

ADJECTIVES

gentil(le)   nice, kind
joli(e)   pretty
occupé(e)   busy

NUMBERS 11–20

onze   eleven
douze   twelve
treize   thirteen
quatorze   fourteen
quinze   fifteen
seize   sixteen
dix-sept   seventeen
dix-huit   eighteen
dix-neuf   nineteen
vingt   twenty

OTHER WORDS AND EXPRESSIONS

bienvenue   welcome
combien   how many, how
  much
dans   in
entre (entrez)   come in
là   there
pour   for
presque   almost

assieds-toi or asseyez-vous
  sit down
bon anniversaire   happy
  birthday
chez moi   at my house
d'accord   O.K., fine
fais comme chez toi or faites
  comme chez vous   make
  yourself at home
il y a   there is, there are
j'accepte   I accept
je t'invite (je vous invite)   I
  invite you
je ne peux pas   I can't
merci   thank you; merci
  beaucoup or merci bien
  thanks a lot
quel âge as-tu?   how old are
  you?
quelque chose   something
salut, les amis   hello, friends
tout le monde   everybody

61

chapitre 4
À l'étude

Strasbourg is the capital of **Alsace,** one of France's old provinces. Situated on the Rhine river, France's natural border with Germany, Strasbourg has witnessed many historic conflicts between the two countries. Now the seat of the Council of Europe, the city has both a cosmopolitan atmosphere and an Old-World flavor. Many of its houses, with their long, sloping roofs, are historical monuments dating back to the 14th and 15th centuries. Other beautiful monuments include a pink sandstone Gothic cathedral, famous for its remarkable astronomical clock, which indicates solar time and phases of the moon.

It is there, in the shadow of the cathedral, that Bernadette Muller lives and goes to a **lycée.**

Les leçons et les devoirs

monologue

Bernadette Muller, a high school student in Strasbourg, describes her study habits.

Salut de Strasbourg!
Je suis dans le séjour avec une amie.
J'étudie souvent avec elle après l'école.
On est toutes les deux en seconde.
Maintenant, on étudie une leçon d'histoire.
On a aussi des devoirs de maths.

à vous,
maintenant

1. Say whether you often, always, sometimes, or usually study with a friend.

J'étudie	souvent	avec	une amie.
	tout le temps		un ami.
	quelquefois		une copine.
	d'habitude		un copain.

2. Tell what grade you and your friend are in, using the French grade equivalents. (See the cultural note at the top of page 26 if you need to review the way grades are numbered in France.)

On est	toutes les deux	en première.
Nous sommes	tous les deux	en seconde.
		en troisième.

Bernadette est lycéenne à Strasbourg, en Alsace.

Les leçons et les devoirs

After school, students have many assignments for the following day, both **leçons** (study of facts, historical events, poems, etc.) and **devoirs** (written exercises, compositions, or essays). These homework assignments are graded on a scale of either 20 or 10. Grading is very strict. A passing grade is 10 out of 20 (or 5 out of 10). An 18 is considered excellent. A 20 is practically unheard of — the paper would have to be perfect in every way. Grading takes into consideration not only content, but also grammar, neatness, and legibility.

Mauvaises nouvelles!

dialogue

Bernadette's classmate Gérard has missed school because of illness. He calls Bernadette to ask about the assignments.

BERNADETTE	Allô, oui?
GÉRARD	Allô, c'est toi, Bernadette? Ici, Gérard.
BERNADETTE	Bonjour. Comment ça va, Gérard? Tu es malade?
GÉRARD	Non, ça va maintenant. Dis donc, qu'est-ce qu'on a comme devoirs pour demain?
BERNADETTE	On a des problèmes de maths, et ils ne sont pas faciles, tu sais.
GÉRARD	Et la leçon d'histoire?
BERNADETTE	Elle est barbante.
GÉRARD	Zut, alors! Mauvaises nouvelles!

à vous,
maintenant

1. One of your friends missed school today. Tell her or him what the homework is.

Qu'est-ce qu'on a comme devoirs?		On a	des devoirs de (maths).
			une leçon de (géographie).

2. Now tell your friend your reaction to the homework.

Comment est	le problème	de (maths)?	Il est	facile.
	la leçon	d'(histoire)?	Elle est	difficile.
				intéressant(e).
				barbant(e).

Beaucoup de devoirs

narration

Bernadette étudie souvent avec une amie, Marianne.
Aujourd'hui, elles ont des devoirs de maths.
Elles ont aussi une leçon d'histoire.
Gérard téléphone à Bernadette.
Il ne sait pas quels devoirs ils ont pour demain.
Mauvaises nouvelles! Les devoirs sont difficiles, la leçon est barbante.

questions

Complete the responses based on the *monologue, dialogue,* and *narration.*

1. Avec qui est-ce que Bernadette étudie? Elle étudie ____.
2. Quels devoirs ont Bernadette et Marianne? Elles ont ____.
3. Qui téléphone à Bernadette? ____ téléphone à Bernadette.
4. Qu'est-ce qui est difficile? ____ sont difficiles.
5. Est-ce que la leçon d'histoire est intéressante? ____, elle est ____.

situations

How would you react if you got the following homework grades (on a scale of 0 to 20)? Here are two possible reactions on which you can model your own.

Zut, alors! J'ai un cinq en maths! Mauvaise nouvelle!
Chic, alors! Un seize en français! C'est une bonne nouvelle!

1. anglais: 10
2. histoire: 0
3. biologie: 8
4. français: 16
5. algèbre: 2
6. géographie: 12

à vous, maintenant

1. Relatives have come to visit your family. One of them finds you studying with a friend and asks you about your study habits. You give a brief account of what you are doing and how you feel about your school work.
2. While you are studying with a classmate, a friend from another school calls and tells you about her or his school work. Afterward, you tell your classmate about the phone conversation.

L'amitié

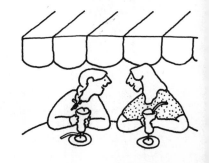

Most French people have only two or three close friends, or **ami(e)s.** More casual acquaintances may be **copains, copines,** or **camarades de classe** (*classmates*). Bernadette, of course, has many **copains** and **camarades,** but she may have only one or two close friends other than Marianne. True friendship is reserved for a few, and it usually is a relationship that lasts a lifetime.

La Maison Kammerzell, un restaurant célèbre à Strasbourg. À gauche: dans un vignoble alsacien.

L'Alsace

The province of Alsace has been the site of invasions and battles ever since Louis I, son of the Emperor Charlemagne, tried to divide his empire among his three sons. In A.D. 842, two of the brothers swore an alliance against the third in the **Serment** (Oath) **de Strasbourg,** the oldest known document written in French. The brothers fought each other for a year before the Treaty of Verdun divided the empire among them, into: 1) what is now Germany; 2) what is now the Netherlands, Belgium, and most of Italy, plus the provinces of Alsace, Lorraine, Burgundy, and Provence; 3) the rest of what is now France, minus Brittany.

These early conflicts were the first of many border wars that have occurred in the region over the centuries. During World War I, France reconquered Alsace and the neighboring province of Lorraine, which had been held by Germany since 1871. The two provinces again came under German rule from 1940 to 1945, when they were liberated by French and American troops.

Not surprisingly, there is a strong German cultural influence in Alsace. Many Alsatians speak a dialect of German origin in addition to French.

Alsatian food specialties include **pâté de foie gras** (goose liver pâté), **choucroute** (sauerkraut with pork and sausages) and light beers. The many vineyards in the pretty, hilly countryside along the Rhine yield famous Alsatian wines.

A note about French provinces: The provinces of France were divided in 1790 into smaller **départements.** Since that time, the provinces have had no official standing. However, French citizens still refer to them and think of them as clearly defined regions of the country.

Pardon, monsieur!

échanges de
politesse

Bernadette is late for class and tries to apologize.

BERNADETTE	Pardon, monsieur. Je suis en retard!
LE PROFESSEUR	Oui, mademoiselle. Vous êtes souvent en retard. Pourquoi?
BERNADETTE	Je vais chez moi pour déjeuner, et...
LE PROFESSEUR	Vous avez le devoir d'anglais pour aujourd'hui?
BERNADETTE	Non, monsieur. Excusez-moi.
LE PROFESSEUR	Alors, vous avez un zéro en anglais.
BERNADETTE	Oh non, monsieur, s'il vous plaît...!

à vous,
maintenant

1. Your teacher scolds you for being late to class. Offer a suitable apology.

Vous êtes en retard!

Oui. Excusez-moi, s'il vous plaît,	monsieur.
Oui. Pardon,	madame.
	mademoiselle.

2. You have a *rendez-vous* with a friend. When you arrive, your friend says you are late. How do you respond?

Tu es en retard!

Oui... Excuse-moi, s'il te plaît.
Mais non! Je suis à l'heure!
Pas du tout! Je suis en avance!

Étude de mots

Les nombres 21–69

21 = vingt et un	24 = vingt-quatre	27 = vingt-sept
22 = vingt-deux	25 = vingt-cinq	28 = vingt-huit
23 = vingt-trois	26 = vingt-six	29 = vingt-neuf

30, 31, 32 ... 39: **trente**, trente et un, trente-deux ... trente-neuf
40, 41 ... 49: **quarante**, quarante et un ... quarante-neuf
50, 51 ... 59: **cinquante**, cinquante et un ... cinquante-neuf
60, 61 ... 69: **soixante**, soixante et un ... soixante-neuf

— Il y a combien d'élèves dans la classe? — Trente-cinq.

The word **et** is used only in the numbers 21, 31, 41, 51, 61, and 71.

A A friend visiting your school tries to guess how many students there are in each class. Each guess is too low by ten. Correct the guesses accordingly.

  ■ⅲ 25   — *Il y a combien d'élèves dans la classe? Vingt-cinq?*
                    — *Non, trente-cinq.*

1. 30	3. 42	5. 33
2. 55	4. 29	6. 59

B Solve the following addition problems.

  ■ⅲ 41 + 24 = ?   *Quarante et un et vingt-quatre font soixante-cinq.*

1. 25 + 36 = ?	3. 13 + 21 = ?	5. 23 + 26 = ?
2. 31 + 22 = ?	4. 21 + 20 = ?	6. 43 + 24 = ?

C **Zut!** This is a game for the entire class. A number is chosen as the *unmentionable*. For example, if 7 is chosen, you may not say 7, any multiple of 7, or any number that contains a 7. Instead, you must say **Zut!** One student begins with **un,** the next says **deux,** and so on around the room — but **Zut!** must be substituted for 7, 14, 17, etc. You are *out* if you give a wrong number or fail to say **Zut!** at the appropriate time. The winner is the person who gives the last correct number (or **Zut!**) after the rest of the class has been eliminated.

Les cours au lycée

l'allemand (*m.*)	les sciences (*f. pl.*)
l'anglais (*m.*)	la biologie *ou* les sciences naturelles
l'espagnol (*m.*)	(sciences nats)
le français	la chimie
le latin	la physique
la géographie	l'histoire (*f.*) de l'art
l'histoire (*f.*)	le dessin
	la littérature
les mathématiques (les maths)	la musique
(*f. pl.*)	
l'algèbre (*m.*)	l'éducation physique (*f.*) *ou* la gym
la géométrie	

  ■ⅲ   — Tu as **un cours de maths?** — Non, j'ai **un cours de latin.**

D Discuss with your classmates which of your courses you find easy or difficult.

  ■ⅲ   — [*Le cours de français*] *est facile.*
             — *Non,* [*le français*] *est difficile!*

L'emploi du temps de Bernadette

Bernadette va à l'école le lundi, le mardi, le mercredi, le jeudi, le vendredi et le samedi. Elle n'y va pas le dimanche.

	Lundi	Mardi	Mercredi	Jeudi	Vendredi	Samedi	Dimanche
8 h 30	éducation physique (gym)	latin	latin	histoire de l'art	anglais	littérature française	
9 h 30			physique		éducation physique (gym)		
10 h 30	histoire	physique	littérature française	géographie		espagnol	
11 h 30					anglais	anglais	
12 h 30	déjeuner	déjeuner		déjeuner	déjeuner		
2 h	dessin	dessin		maths	maths		
3 h	maths				espagnol		
4 h	littérature française	espagnol					
5 h							

E Say what subjects Bernadette has on the following days.

   ■ⅲ   le mercredi   *Le mercredi, elle étudie le latin, la physique et la littérature française.*

1. le mardi   2. le jeudi   3. le samedi

F According to Bernadette's schedule, what days does she have these subjects?

   ■ⅲ   le latin   *Elle a un cours de latin le mardi et le mercredi.*

1. les maths   2. l'espagnol   3. la physique

à vous, maintenant

Talk about your own schedule and your courses. Tell your classmates what courses you are taking, what days they meet, and who the teachers are. Which of your classes are easy, difficult, interesting, or boring?

The school day in a French **lycée** begins at about 8:30 A.M., Monday through Saturday. Classes last until about 5:50 on Mondays and Tuesdays, and until about 3:50 on Thursdays and Fridays, with a 90-minute lunch recess from 12:30 to 2:00. There is no school on Wednesday and Saturday afternoons; classes on those days end at lunch time.

À la française

Here is the report card of Bernadette's cousin, Cécile. How does it compare with yours? (Some of the new vocabulary is given below.)

Lycée du Parc LYON	Nom *Cécile Muller* Classe de *Terminale D*	
Matières	**Notes**	**Evaluation des professeurs**
Maths	*10*	*Élève douée mais doit travailler plus*
Sciences physiques	*15*	*Bon travail*
Sciences naturelles	*17*	*Élève intelligente et sérieuse*
Philosophie	*8*	*Trop distraite*
Anglais	*11*	*Bonne à l'oral devoirs moins satisfaisants*
Russe	*9*	*A besoin de faire des progrès*
Moyenne	*11,67*	*Honnête moyenne peut faire mieux*

doué(e)   gifted
doit travailler plus   must work more
le travail   work
distrait(e)   absent-minded

a besoin de faire des progrès   needs to improve
la moyenne   average
honnête   satisfactory
peut faire mieux   can do better

Prononciation et orthographe

▌ /u/	**vous**	
▌ /y/	**tu**	

/u/

The sound /u/ is fairly close to the English vowel in the word *do*, but when you make the French sound, your lips should be rounded and tense.

RÉPÉTEZ

vo**us**	do**u**ze	bonj**ou**r	po**u**rquoi	**où**
no**us**	t**ou**t	aujo**u**rd'hui	beauc**ou**p	Strasbo**ur**g

The sound /u/ is spelled **ou, où,** or **oû.**

LISEZ

1. Bonjour, tout le monde!
2. Les Latour et moi, nous sommes à Strasbourg.
3. Aujourd'hui, nous avons beaucoup de devoirs.

/y/

To pronounce the sound /y/, which has no equivalent in English, first say /i/ (as in **ami**). Your lips should be in a smiling position. As you make the /i/ sound, round your lips; the sound changes to /y/. Be careful not to substitute the sound /u/ for the sound /y/. If you do, you may change the meaning of the word. For example:

Tout va bien?	All is well?
Tu vas bien?	Are you well?

RÉPÉTEZ

t**u**	Br**u**no	M**u**ller	**u**ne voit**u**re	d'habit**u**de
d**u**	S**u**zanne	la m**u**sique	le p**u**pitre	pl**u**s

The sound /y/ is spelled **u** or **û.**

LISEZ

1. D'habitude, tu étudies la musique avec lui.
2. Le pupitre de Bruno Muller est plus pratique.

Plus on est de fous, plus on rit.

Stress

In French speech, all syllables are pronounced evenly — that is, they are given equal stress — except that the last syllable in a phrase or sentence is held a little longer than the others.

Pronounce the following French and English words, and notice how the stress patterns of the two languages differ:

biologie biology   **géométrie** geometry

RÉPÉTEZ

Bonjour!	Salut!	Comment allez-vous?
Bonjour, madame!	Salut, les copains!	Asseyez-vous!
Bonjour, tout le monde!	Comment ça va?	Faites comme chez vous!

L'alphabet

In order to say abbreviations or to spell aloud, you need to know the French names for the letters of the alphabet. Your teacher will model the letters for you, and there is a pronunciation guide on page 352. Practice spelling your own name, and then try these sentences:

Je vais au C.E.S.   Voilà la carte des U.S.A.

Cognates

Cognates are words in different languages that are derived from the same "parent" word. Thousands of English words have the same Latin root as their French counterparts; therefore, the French and English words are cognates. (In fact, many English words came directly from French.)

Many French cognates are easy to recognize in writing (for example, **le latin, les sciences, la musique**), though they sound different from their English counterparts. Here are some guidelines.

1. Many English nouns ending in *-tion* or *-sion* are spelled identically in French: **l'éducation, la division.**
2. Many nouns ending in *-y* in English have French cognates ending in **-ie: la biologie, la géométrie.**
3. Many English words ending in *-ic, -ics,* or *-ical* have French cognates ending in **-ique: la musique, la physique, logique.**

Guess the French equivalents of the following words. Say the French words aloud.

nation	anthropology	political	magical
illusion	philosophy	photographic	identical
composition	symphony	optics	practical

See how many cognates you can identify in the *narration* on page 65.

The vineyard harvest, an open-air concert, and a time-honored form of transportation make up a selection of scenes of Alsace.

Grammaire

Plural nouns and articles

INDEFINITE ARTICLES		
Singular	Plural	
un livre		livres
une chaise	des	chaises
un cours		cours

DEFINITE ARTICLES		
Singular	Plural	
le livre		livres
la chaise	les	chaises
l'ami		amis

1. French nouns generally form their plural by adding **-s** to the singular form. If the singular form ends in **-s,** the noun does not change in the plural. Because the final **-s** is *silent,* the plural form of a noun sounds the same as the singular. The form of the article tells the listener that the noun is plural.
2. The gender of the noun does not affect the plural form of the article.
3. *Liaison* always occurs with **des** or **les** before a vowel.

$$\text{Voilà les}_{\overset{/z/}{\frown}}\text{amis de Jacques.}$$

A You have the following items on your shopping list. Ask the salesperson (a classmate) whether the store has the things you need.

▪▥ un livre — *Vous avez des livres?*
— *Oui, nous avons des livres.*

1. une chaise
2. un stylo
3. un cahier
4. une cassette
5. une carte
6. un crayon

B Now you ask where to find the different things on your list, and the salesperson points them out.

▪▥ le cahier — *Où sont les cahiers?*
— *Voilà les cahiers.*

1. la cassette
2. le crayon
3. le stylo
4. la carte
5. la chaise
6. le livre

C Point out one member of each of the following groups.

▪▥ des professeurs *Voilà un professeur.*
les appartements *Voilà l'appartement.*

1. les maisons
2. les lycées
3. des chambres
4. des bébés
5. des livres
6. les écoles
7. des dames
8. les copains
9. les autobus

The subject pronoun **on**

The subject pronoun **on** takes the same verb form as **il** and **elle.** It has two uses:

1. In informal conversation, **on** is often substituted for **nous.**

    On est tous les deux   *We are* both in tenth grade.
    en seconde.

2. **On** is used to refer to *people in general.*

    En France, **on va** au lycée   In France, *they go (people go,*
    le samedi.   *you go, one goes)* to school
                                    on Saturdays.

D   A relative asks about you and your friends. Answer affirmatively or negatively, using *on.*

    ■Ⅲ   Vous avez des cours de   *Oui, on a des cours de*
                littérature?   *littérature.*

1. Vous allez au lycée Pasteur?
2. Vous allez au lycée en métro?
3. Vous êtes en seconde?
4. Vous avez des devoirs de maths?
5. Vous avez un cours de sciences naturelles?

à vous, maintenant

Use the pronoun *on* to tell a little about your school.

1. What days do students go to school?
2. What are some of the ways people get to school?
3. What subjects do people take?

Present tense of **aller** (to go)

	SINGULAR	PLURAL
1st person	je **vais**	nous **allons**
2nd person	tu **vas**	vous **allez**
3rd person	on/il/elle **va**	ils/elles **vont**

The basic meaning of **aller** is *to go.* **Aller** is also used to refer to health or state of mind.

Nous allons au lycée.   We're going to school.
Je ne vais pas bien.   I'm not feeling well.

E   Say that the following people are going to the *lycée.*

■ııı   les élèves   *Les élèves vont au lycée.*

1. nous
2. Robert
3. les jeunes filles
4. Yolande
5. les garçons
6. Paul et toi

F   A classmate asks about the health of several people. Say that they are not feeling well.

■ııı   Irène   — *Irène va bien?*
                    — *Non, elle ne va pas très bien.*

1. Elizabeth
2. Yvette et toi
3. les garçons
4. toi
5. François
6. Lise et Anne

Agreement of adjectives

MASCULINE		FEMININE	
Singular	Plural	Singular	Plural
Le garçon est grand.	Les garçons sont grands.	La fille est grande.	Les filles sont grandes.
Le livre est joli.	Les livres sont jolis.	La carte est jolie.	Les cartes sont jolies.
Jacques est malade.	Paul et Luc sont malades.	Michèle est malade.	Michèle et Anne sont malades.

The form of a French adjective agrees in gender and number (singular or plural) with the noun it describes.

1. In most cases, the plural form of an adjective is the singular form plus **-s.** However, because the **-s** represents no sound, the singular and plural forms sound the same. If the singular form already ends in **-s** **(français),** nothing is added in the plural.
2. In writing, the feminine form for most adjectives is the masculine form plus **-e.** No letter is added if the masculine ends in **-e (pratique).**
3. In speech, the masculine and feminine forms of many adjectives sound different **(grand-grande);** however, many adjectives sound the same in the masculine and feminine **(joli-jolie, facile-facile).**

G   One of you says that the following school subjects are boring. A classmate disagrees and says that they are interesting.

■ııı   l'histoire   — *L'histoire est barbante.*
                        — *Non, l'histoire est intéressante.*

1. le français
2. les maths
3. la musique
4. le dessin
5. la géographie
6. le latin

H   Say that the same description applies to both things or people mentioned.

> ■‖   Le salon est petit. Et   *Elle est petite aussi.*
> la salle à manger?

1. Le garçon est petit. Et la fille?
2. Le salon est joli. Et les chambres?
3. La dame est américaine. Et le monsieur?
4. Le latin est intéressant. Et la géographie?
5. L'élève est canadienne. Et le professeur?
6. La maison est grande. Et l'appartement?

Descriptive **de**-phrases

In French, a phrase consisting of **de** + a noun is often used to describe another noun.

> C'est **un livre d'histoire.**   It's *a history book.*
> J'ai **des devoirs de français.**   I have *some French homework.*

I   Say that the following people have homework in the subjects indicated.

> ■‖   moi/français   *J'ai des devoirs de français.*

1. elle/maths   3. vous/sciences   5. moi/latin
2. toi/anglais   4. Bernard/histoire   6. elles/géographie

J   Michèle has decorated her *emploi du temps* with small drawings that illustrate her different subjects. Using the drawings as cues, say what courses she is taking.

> ■‖ $(b+c)+(-c)=b.$ *Elle a un cours d'algèbre.*

Lecture

Quel bac?

Bernadette's cousin Cécile is visiting her in Strasbourg. They have not seen each other for a long time. They talk about their studies.

BERNADETTE	Alors, tu es en terminale? Et quel bac° est-ce que tu prépares?	baccalauréat degree
CÉCILE	Le bac D, mathématiques et sciences naturelles.	
BERNADETTE	Quels cours est-ce que tu as?	
CÉCILE	J'ai des maths, bien sûr,° des sciences phy-siques, des sciences nats et de la philosophie. J'ai aussi des cours d'anglais, comme tout le monde, et des cours de russe.°	naturally Russian
BERNADETTE	C'est un bac difficile!	
CÉCILE	Oui, mais ton° bac A-7 est difficile aussi. Les sciences physiques et les sciences nats, pour moi, c'est intéressant! Mais l'art, alors là,° c'est barbant!	your as for that
BERNADETTE	Mais non, c'est très intéressant, le dessin et les arts plastiques... Et tes profs, ils sont comment?	
CÉCILE	Oh, comme° d'habitude, tu sais, il y a des profs barbants et des profs intéressants...	as

questions

1. Qu'est-ce qu'on étudie pour le bac A-7?
2. Quel bac est scientifique?
3. Quel bac prépare Bernadette?
4. Qu'est-ce qui est intéressant pour Cécile?
5. D'après (*according to*) Cécile, comment sont les professeurs?

Le bac

French students who hope to go to college must pass a national exam called **le baccalauréat,** known as **le bac.** This exam is given in two parts. The first, which covers French language and litera-ture, takes place at the end of **première.** The second part comes at the end of **terminale.** Its content depends on the student's course of study.

By the time students enter **troisième,** the equivalent of 9th grade, they must choose which **baccalauréat** degree they will study for. There are eight categories, identified by letter (**Bac A, B, C,** etc.); **Bac A,** a liberal arts program, has seven numbered sub-sections. All of the programs in-clude at least one foreign language.

Students dread **le bac** because, traditionally, one third of them fail; but those who do fail can try again the following year, and it is now possible in some rare cases to enter certain universities without the **bac** degree. There is plenty of competition among the schools, since they are under great pressure to produce students capable of passing the exam. For stu-dents, parents, administrators, and teachers, the percentage of students who pass **le bac** each year is all-important.

—————— Résumé grammatical ——————

Plural nouns and articles (A-C)

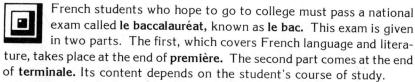

INDEFINITE ARTICLES			DEFINITE ARTICLES		
Singular		Plural	Singular		Plural
un livre		livres	le livre		livres
une chaise	des	chaises	la chaise	les	chaises
un cours		cours	l'ami		amis

1. Nouns generally form the plural by adding **-s** to the singular form. If the singular form ends in **-s,** the noun does not change in the plural.
2. The plural form of the indefinite articles **un** and **une** is **des.** The plural form of the definite articles **le, la,** and **l'** is **les.**

The subject pronoun **on** (D)

The subject pronoun **on** always takes a third-person singular verb form. It is used:

1. as a conversational equivalent for **nous** (we).

    — Vous allez chez Jean?
    — Non, **on va** au lycée.

2. to refer to a group of people in general.

    En France, **on va** à l'école le samedi.

Present tense of **aller** (to go) (E-F)

	SINGULAR	PLURAL
1st person	je **vais**	nous **allons**
2nd person	tu **vas**	vous **allez**
3rd person	on/il/elle **va**	ils/elles **vont**

The basic meaning of **aller** is *to go*; however, **aller** is also used in expressions of health: **Je vais bien.** *I'm feeling fine.*

Agreement of adjectives (G-H)

Adjectives agree in gender with the nouns they describe. There are three types of adjectives:

1. Some have masculine and feminine forms that sound different and are spelled differently, such as **grand-grande, petit-petite.**
2. Some have forms that sound alike but are spelled differently, such as **joli-jolie, bienvenu-bienvenue.**
3. Some have forms that are pronounced and spelled alike, such as **malade-malade, facile-facile.**

Adjectives also agree in number (singular or plural). In most cases, the plural form is the singular form plus **-s: petit-petits, grande-grandes.**

Descriptive **de**-phrases (I-J)

A noun preceded by **de** may be used to modify or describe another noun. The entire phrase follows the noun being described.

un livre de latin   a Latin book

Révision

A You are helping take inventory in a small college bookstore. Say how many there are of each type of book indicated.

▪▮▮ latin: 38   *Il y a trente-huit livres de latin.*

1. anglais: 41   3. géographie: 56   5. littérature: 27
2. dessin: 60   4. sciences nats: 34   6. histoire: 63

B Choose the most logical response to each of the following statements or questions.

1. Il va au lycée?
   a. Oui, il est belge.   b. Oui, elle est grande.
   c. Oui, il est en seconde.
2. J'ai un cours de sciences nats.
   a. Dans la cuisine?   b. En métro?   c. Au lycée?
3. Vous allez tous les deux chez Paul?
   a. Oui, on va chez lui.   b. Oui, il va chez Paul.
   c. Oui, je vais chez Paul.
4. Tu étudies d'habitude avec Roger?
   a. Oui, j'étudie souvent avec lui.
   b. Oui, j'étudie quelquefois avec toi.
   c. Des devoirs d'histoire.
5. Je suis en retard le jeudi.
   a. Excusez-moi, s'il vous plaît.   b. Tout le temps?
   c. Maintenant?

C Prepare a French *emploi du temps* for yourself.

D Give the plural of each of the following noun phrases.

▪▮▮ un élève   *des élèves*

1. une chaise   3. un ami   5. le cours   7. la chambre
2. la table   4. l'autobus   6. un bébé   8. un livre

E Restate each sentence, substituting the words in parentheses for the words in italics. Make any necessary changes.

▪▮▮ *Le latin* est barbant. (l'histoire)   *L'histoire est barbante.*

1. *Le français* est intéressant. (les sciences)
2. *Le dessin* est facile. (la musique)
3. *La chambre* est jolie. (le salon)
4. *Les maisons* sont grandes. (le salon)
5. *Marc* est petit. (Marie et Danièle)

F Use an atlas to learn the distances and directions from Strasbourg to the following European cities: Paris, Berlin, Brussels, and Geneva.

G Learn the names of five French provinces. Locate them on the map on page xiv.

Vocabulaire

NOUNS

l'algèbre (*m.*)   algebra
l'allemand (*m.*)   German
l'ami (*m.*), **l'amie** (*f.*)   friend
l'art (*m.*)   art
le baccalauréat (le bac)
French secondary school diploma
la biologie   biology
la chimie   chemistry
la classe   class
le copain, la copine   friend
le cours   school subject, course
le déjeuner   lunch
le dessin   drawing
les devoirs (*m. pl.*)   homework
l'éducation physique (*f.*)
(la gym)   gym
l'espagnol (*m.*)   Spanish
la géographie   geography
la géométrie   geometry
l'histoire (*f.*)   history
le latin   Latin
la leçon   lesson
la littérature   literature
les mathématiques (les maths)
(*f. pl.*)   math
la musique   music
la physique   physics
le problème   problem
les sciences naturelles (*f. pl.*)
natural science, biology
le séjour (la salle de séjour)
living-dining room

VERBS

aller   to go **(je vais, tu vas, on/il/elle va, nous allons, vous allez, ils/elles vont)**
étudier   to study **(j'étudie, tu étudies)**

CLASSES IN FRANCE

la troisième   9th school year (last year of *C.E.S.*)
la seconde   10th school year (first year of *lycée*)
la première   11th school year (second year of *lycée*)
la terminale   12th school year (last year of *lycée*)

DAYS OF THE WEEK

le lundi   Monday
le mardi   Tuesday
le mercredi   Wednesday
le jeudi   Thursday
le vendredi   Friday
le samedi   Saturday
le dimanche   Sunday

NUMBERS

vingt   twenty; **vingt et un** twenty-one; **vingt-deux** twenty-two
trente   thirty
quarante   forty
cinquante   fifty
soixante   sixty

ADJECTIVES

barbant(e)   boring
difficile   difficult
facile   easy
intéressant(e)   interesting

OTHER WORDS AND EXPRESSIONS

allô   hello (on telephone)
après   after
avec   with
demain   tomorrow
ici   here
maintenant   now
on   we; one, they, people, you
quel(le)   what, which
souvent   often

à l'heure   on time
chic, alors!   great!
dis donc!   say!
en avance   early
en retard   late
excusez-moi   excuse me
pardon   pardon me
qu'est-ce qu'on a comme devoirs?   what do we have for homework?
s'il vous plaît   please
tous les deux (*m.*), **toutes les deux** (*f.*)   both
tout le temps   all the time, always
tu sais   you know
zut, alors!   darn it!

chapitre 5
En famille

The Republic of **Haïti,** in the West Indies, is
sometimes called **la perle des Antilles** (Pearl of
the Antilles). Beautiful, lush vegetation thrives
in the tropical climate of Haiti. Pink and purple
bougainvilleas, red flamboyants, and other
flowers dot the countryside.

Port-au-Prince, the capital of the country and
the home of Raymond Calixte, lies on a beautiful bay in the Caribbean Sea. The weather is
hot in Port-au-Prince, but as one goes up into
the hills that overlook the city, the air gradually
gets cooler. About ten miles south of the capital, one comes to the town of Kenscoff, on top of
a tree-covered mountain. From time to time,
Raymond makes this trip by bus to visit his
grandmother in Kenscoff.

Une famille nombreuse

monologue

Raymond Calixte, a teen-ager in Port-au-Prince, introduces his family to you.

Bonjour de Port-au-Prince!
J'habite ici avec ma famille.
C'est une famille nombreuse!
Nous sommes cinq enfants, et je suis l'aîné.
J'ai trois sœurs et un frère.
J'aime bien ma petite sœur Suze. Elle est adorable.
Mon frère, lui, est insupportable.

à vous,
maintenant

1. You are interested in the size of a classmate's family. Ask whether he/she has any brothers and sisters.

Tu as	des frères? des sœurs?

Oui, j'ai une grande famille.
Oui, j'ai [trois frères] et [une sœur.]
Non, je n'ai pas | de frères. | de sœurs.
Non, je suis fille/fils unique.

2. Now ask your classmate to describe a sister or brother.

Comment est	ta sœur? ton frère?

Elle est	formidable.
Il est	sympathique.
	égoïste.
	insupportable.

Une bonne nouvelle!

dialogue

Raymond unexpectedly meets Berthe, a former neighbor. She seems very happy.

RAYMOND	Berthe! Qu'est-ce qu'il y a?
BERTHE	Il y a un nouveau bébé chez moi... C'est un garçon.
RAYMOND	C'est formidable! Tu es contente?
BERTHE	Je suis ravie... On est deux maintenant!
RAYMOND	Eh oui! Vous n'êtes pas trop nombreux, comme chez moi!
BERTHE	Mais non. Tu as de la chance, toi! Tu joues tout le temps avec tes sœurs. C'est bien d'avoir une grande famille.

Have a short conversation with a classmate on the subject of your families. Use some of the words and expressions from the *monologue* and the *dialogue*, making changes to fit your own situation.

Le français et le créole

 Standard French is taught in Haitian schools and is the official language of government and business. About ten percent of Haitians speak French, and thirty percent understand it. Most Haitians speak **créole,** which is derived from French and from African and Indian languages. There is a **créole** saying, **Bel français pas lesprit pou' ça** ("speaking good French doesn't make you smart"). That is, there is more to wisdom than the ability to speak standard French.

Frères et sœurs

narration

Raymond Calixte est haïtien.
Sa famille est une famille nombreuse: ils sont cinq enfants.
Raymond aime bien sa petite sœur, mais il n'aime pas du tout son frère.
Sa copine, Berthe Rigaud, a un petit frère.
Elle est ravie, parce qu'ils sont deux maintenant.
Elle aime les grandes familles.

questions

Answer these questions based on the *monologue, dialogue,* and *narration.*

1. Comment est la famille de Raymond? C'est une famille ____.
2. Combien sont-ils? Ils sont ____.
3. Est-ce que Berthe est contente? ____, elle est ____.
4. Pourquoi est-elle ravie? Parce qu'____.
5. Qui est l'aîné chez Berthe? ____ est l'aînée.

situations

Describe the families pictured below, as well as each of the family members. Give ages and use appropriate descriptive adjectives.

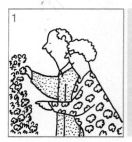  

Une visite chez grand-mère

Raymond has gone by tap-tap (a Haitian bus) to take a cake to his grandmother Calixte in Kenscoff.

GRAND-MÈRE — Ah! Raymond, c'est toi! Comment ça va, mon petit?

RAYMOND — Ça va, grand-mère. Et toi?

GRAND-MÈRE — Oh! tu sais, comme ci, comme ça. Et ton papa? Et ta maman?

RAYMOND — Tout va bien à la maison, grand-mère. Tiens, voilà quelque chose pour toi.

GRAND-MÈRE — Merci, mon garçon. Alors, entre un moment.

RAYMOND — Oui, d'accord.

(When it begins to get dark, Raymond leaves.)

RAYMOND — Bonsoir, grand-mère. Porte-toi bien.

GRAND-MÈRE — Bonne nuit, Raymond. À bientôt.

à vous, maintenant

You have gone to visit your grandparents. Now it's time to take leave of them. Act out the scene with several other classmates, using appropriate farewells.

Bonsoir,	[grand-mère].
Bonne nuit,	[grand-père].

Au revoir,	mon petit.	Porte-toi bien.
	ma petite.	
	mes enfants.	Portez-vous bien.

Le café est un produit important d'Haïti.

Des femmes haïtiennes en route pour le marché

_____ Étude de mots _____

Les nombres 70–100

70 = soixante-dix (60 + 10)	80 = quatre-vingts (4 × 20)
71 = soixante et onze (60 + 11)	81 = quatre-vingt-un (4 × 20 + 1)
72 = soixante-douze (60 + 12)	82 = quatre-vingt-deux (4 × 20 + 2)
73 = soixante-treize (60 + 13)	
74 = soixante-quatorze (60 + 14)	90 = quatre-vingt-dix (4 × 20 + 10)
75 = soixante-quinze (60 + 15)	91 = quatre-vingt-onze (4 × 20 + 11)
76 = soixante-seize (60 + 16)	92 = quatre-vingt-douze (4 × 20 + 12)
77 = soixante-dix-sept (60 + 17)	
78 = soixante-dix-huit (60 + 18)	100 = cent
79 = soixante-dix-neuf (60 + 19)	

A Raymond's cousin sells Haitian woodcrafts in Paris. His business is hit by inflation. Note how the price (in *francs*) of a sculpture went up each month from March to October. Say the prices aloud.

1. 70F		3. 77F		5. 90F		7. 99F
2. 74F		4. 80F		6. 95F		8. 100F

B *Un jeu* (Game): The class is divided into two teams, and every student draws the name of a student from the opposite team. Each person makes up an arithmetic problem and reads it aloud to the opponent who drew her or his name. That student repeats the problem and gives an answer, which must be confirmed or corrected by the person who made up the problem. Score one point for correctly stating a problem and checking the answer; score two points for a correct answer.

La famille de Raymond Calixte

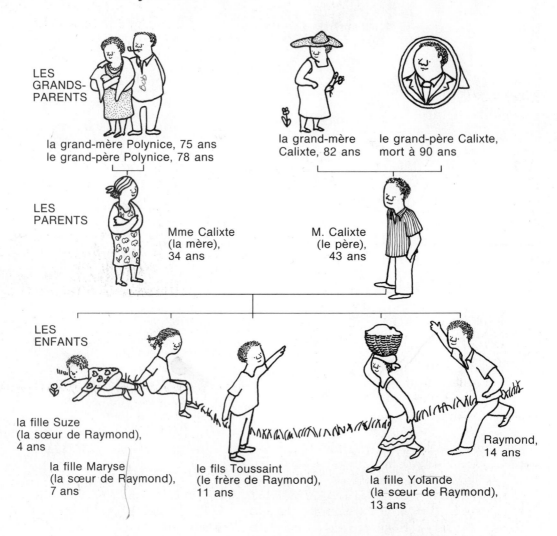

LES GRANDS-PARENTS

la grand-mère Polynice, 75 ans
le grand-père Polynice, 78 ans

la grand-mère Calixte, 82 ans

le grand-père Calixte, mort à 90 ans

LES PARENTS

Mme Calixte (la mère), 34 ans

M. Calixte (le père), 43 ans

LES ENFANTS

la fille Suze (la sœur de Raymond), 4 ans

la fille Maryse (la sœur de Raymond), 7 ans

le fils Toussaint (le frère de Raymond), 11 ans

la fille Yolande (la sœur de Raymond), 13 ans

Raymond, 14 ans

C Identify some of Raymond's family members, using their ages as clues.

▪▥ 78 ans *Le grand-père de Raymond a 78 ans.*

1. 34 ans
2. 7 ans
3. 4 ans
4. 11 ans
5. 82 ans
6. 13 ans

D State the relationships between the following members of Raymond's family.

▪▥ Maryse / Raymond *Maryse est la sœur de Raymond.*

1. Raymond / Toussaint
2. M. Calixte / Yolande
3. M. Polynice / Toussaint
4. la grand-mère Polynice / Mme Calixte
5. Toussaint / Mme Calixte
6. Suze / Maryse
7. Mme Polynice / Maryse
8. Suze / Mme Calixte

La personnalité

timide

bavard, bavarde

intelligent, intelligente

bête

généreux, généreuse

égoïste

sympathique

snob

beau, belle

moche

gentil, gentille

méchant, méchante

à vous, maintenant

1. Use each adjective listed above to describe a celebrity or a character in a book, movie, play, or TV show. For example: *Tom Sawyer est intelligent.*
2. Make your own family tree. Then describe one member of your family as completely as you can.
3. Describe your ideal friend, using at least five adjectives. Use *ne...pas* with some adjectives to say what traits your friend *does not* possess.

L'histoire d'Haïti

The Republic of Haiti occupies the western third of the island of Hispaniola, located in the Caribbean Sea west of Puerto Rico. The Dominican Republic occupies the eastern two thirds of the island. Christopher Columbus landed on the island in 1492 and named it **Española.** It was later referred to as **Saint-Domingue** or **Haïti** (a term that means "the land of the mountains" in the language of the early Indian inhabitants).

During the centuries following the arrival of Columbus, the French and Spanish established settlements in various parts of the island. In 1697, Spain recognized France's claim to the western part of Saint-Domingue. Large plantations of sugar, cotton, coffee, and indigo were established, and slaves were brought from Africa to work on the plantations. Gradually a ruling class was formed of European-born plantation owners and **Créoles,** people of European descent born on the island. The white ruling class was greatly outnumbered by black slaves, freed blacks, and mulattos (people of mixed black and white ancestry).

In the late eighteenth century, there was a general slave revolt, and the blacks rallied behind their remarkable leader Toussaint Louverture. Skilled as a soldier and administrator, Toussaint became the most powerful person on the island. Napoleon was forced to send in troops in an attempt to restore French control. Even after Toussaint was captured and sent to prison in France, where he died in 1803, the blacks were not subdued and the French had to withdraw.

Haiti finally gained its independence from France in 1804. Its current boundaries were set forty years later when the Dominican Republic was created.

Statue d'un Haïtien devant le Palais National à Port-au-Prince

90

Prononciation et orthographe

▌ /R/ père
▌ /ɑ̃/ dans

/R/

The French /R/ is different from the English /R/. The French /R/ is formed far back in the mouth and throat, without moving the lips and jaws.

The /R/ sound is relatively soft at the end of a word. It is more distinct in the middle of a word, and most distinct at the beginning of a word or after a consonant.

RÉPÉTEZ

le père	la carte	Raymond
la sœur	merci	ravi
le cours	barbant	grand

LISEZ

1. Roger a trois sœurs et un frère.
2. Merci pour la carte de Strasbourg.
3. Mon grand-père et ma grand-mère sont généreux.

/ɑ̃/

The sound /ɑ̃/ is called a nasal vowel, in contrast to an oral vowel like /a/. A nasal vowel is formed by passing air through the nose and the mouth at the same time. The sound /a/ changes to /ɑ̃/ when air is allowed to pass through the nasal passage.

RÉPÉTEZ

| dans | comment | la chambre |
| méchant | gentil | ensemble |

The sound /ɑ̃/ is spelled **an, en am,** or **em.**

LISEZ

1. Maman va souvent en France.
2. Les enfants jouent tout le temps dans la chambre.
3. Ma grand-mère française est intelligente et gentille.

Rira bien qui rira le dernier.

Le tréma

Le tréma (¨) is a spelling symbol that is used in certain words with the letters **e, i,** and **u** when they follow another written vowel. *Le tréma* indicates that the letter represents a second vowel sound, separate from the vowel that precedes it.

RÉPÉTEZ Joël   égoïste   Saül
           Noël   Haïti

Rhythm and pitch in sentences

The pitch of the voice falls slightly at the end of a French sentence (except for a *oui-non* question). However, if the sentence contains several phrases, or "thought groups," the pitch rises slightly at the end of each phrase except the last one.

RÉPÉTEZ J'ai un livre,   j'ai un cahier   et j'ai des crayons.

Practice saying the following groups of phrases. First say them separately, as if each one were a complete sentence. Then run all three together as one sentence: raise the pitch of your voice at the end of each of the first two phrases, and lower it at the end of the third phrase (the end of the sentence).

LISEZ
1. Voilà mon frère,   voilà mon ami,   et voilà ma grand-mère.
2. Moi et mes frères,   Roger, Paul, et Jean,   nous allons au collège.
3. J'aime bien ma sœur   et mes trois grands frères,   mais je n'aime pas mon petit frère.

Grammaire

Formation of **oui-non** questions

The following are three ways to form questions that may be answered by **oui** or **non:**

1. Use rising intonation.
2. Add **est-ce que** before a statement.
3. Add **n'est-ce pas?** at the end of a statement. (**N'est-ce pas?** normally indicates that the speaker expects an affirmative answer: **oui.**)

STATEMENT	QUESTION
Tu as une grande famille.	Tu as une grande famille? ↗ **Est-ce que** tu as une grande famille? Tu as une grande famille, **n'est-ce pas?**

A Change the following statements to questions in three different ways.

> ▰⫶ Il s'appelle Jacques.

Il s'appelle Jacques?
Il s'appelle Jacques, n'est-ce pas?
Est-ce qu'il s'appelle Jacques?

1. C'est un ami de Marie.
2. Vous êtes dans le salon.
3. La maison est grande.
4. Tu es en retard.

5. Il aime sa sœur.
6. Elles vont au lycée.
7. Raymond est haïtien.
8. On va à la maison.

B Make up three questions that require *oui-non* answers, one with rising intonation, one with *est-ce que,* and one with *n'est-ce pas?* Be prepared to ask the questions in class.

À la française

If you observe French-speaking people carefully, you will see that many of them express their feelings through active body movements. For example:

1. A person may point the right thumb upward to show approval.
2. Someone who thinks another person is stupid may raise the right shoulder in disgust, while saying **Elle/Il est bête!**
3. To show boredom, a person rubs one side of the face or chin with the knuckles, as if to feel whether the face is well shaved. This gesture is usually accompanied by a phrase such as **C'est barbant!** or **Quelle barbe!** (**La barbe** means *beard;* the idea suggested is: "This is old enough to wear a beard.")
4. Someone who is very enthusiastic about something may exclaim **C'est formidable!** with the arm raised high, fist shaking joyously.

93

Regular -er verbs: present tense

1. Every verb has a basic form called the infinitive. A great many French infinitives end in the sound /e/, spelled **-er.** **Jouer** (to play) is an infinitive form.
2. All regular **-er** verbs take the present-tense endings **-e, -es, -e, -ons, -ez, -ent,** as shown in the chart on the left below.
3. The present tense of regular **-er** verbs is formed by adding the endings to the infinitive stem. The stem is the infinitive minus **-er,** as shown in the chart on the right below.

JOUER (to play)			OTHER -ER VERBS	
			Infinitive	Stem
je	jou	e	aimer	aim-
tu	jou	es	étudier	étudi-
on/il/elle	jou	e	habiter	habit-
nous	jou	ons	inviter	invit-
vous	jou	ez	parler	parl-
ils/elles	jou	ent	téléphoner	téléphon-

C The schedule has just been announced for a city-wide tennis tournament. Ask where the following people are playing.

▮▮▮ lui   *Où est-ce qu'il joue?*

1. toi
2. Paul et Jean
3. vous
4. on
5. Véronique
6. nous

D Say whether or not the following people like school.

▮▮▮ moi   *J'aime l'école. / Je n'aime pas l'école.*

1. lui
2. nous
3. elles
4. on
5. toi
6. Roger
7. les amis
8. vous
9. moi

E These people are departing from de Gaulle airport in Paris for many different destinations. Say that they live in the cities they are going to.

▮▮▮ Roger va à Lyon.   *Roger habite à Lyon.*

1. Nous allons à Dakar.
2. Elles vont à Bruxelles.
3. Les Calixte vont à Port-au-Prince.
4. Tu vas à Montréal.
5. Vous allez à Boston.
6. Je vais à Nice.
7. Il va à Rome.
8. On va à Madrid.
9. Elle va à Amsterdam.

F Different people, when asked how they felt about Sylvie, gave the following responses. Say whether or not they invite Sylvie to their homes, based on their stated opinions of her.

> ▣▥ Paul: «Pas très intelligente.» *Il n'invite pas Sylvie.*

1. Alain: «Très gentille!»
2. toi: «Elle est bête!»
3. moi: «Très sympathique!»
4. nous: «Un peu snob.»
5. les Dupont: «Généreuse.»
6. vous: «Insupportable!»

Possessive adjectives

SINGULAR NOUNS				PLURAL NOUNS				ENGLISH EQUIVALENT
Masculine		Feminine		Masculine		Feminine		
mon	frère	ma	sœur	mes	frères	mes	sœurs	my
ton		ta		tes		tes		your
son		sa		ses		ses		her/his/its

1. A French possessive adjective agrees in number and gender with the noun it modifies, *not* with the possessor.

> Pierre est avec **sa sœur.**   Pierre is with *his sister.*
> Yvette est avec **son père.**   Yvette is with *her father.*

2. Before a feminine singular noun beginning with a vowel, **mon, ton,** and **son** are used rather than **ma, ta,** and **sa.**

> Je suis avec ma sœur et **mon amie** Hélène.

G Point out the following members of your family or friends.

> ▣▥ frère   *Voilà mon frère.*

1. père
2. mère
3. grand-père
4. grand-mère
5. amis
6. parents
7. copain
8. amie
9. copine

H Your young cousin, who is visiting for the weekend, asks where various things are. You point them out. Act out the exchanges with a classmate.

> ▣▥ vélo   — *Où est ton vélo?*
>   — *Voilà mon vélo.*

1. crayons
2. stylo
3. chambre
4. cahier
5. voiture
6. livres
7. chaise
8. école

I   Say whether or not you like the people asked about in the following questions.

     ◼▥   Tu aimes le grand-père   *Oui, j'aime bien son grand-père. / Non,*
            de Marie?   *je n'aime pas son grand-père.*

1.   Tu aimes le père de Suzanne?
2.   Tu aimes les copains d'Éric?
3.   Tu aimes la mère de Roger?
4.   Tu aimes l'amie de Yolande?
5.   Tu aimes les frères de Maryse?
6.   Tu aimes le fils de M. Calixte?
7.   Tu aimes les parents de Pierre?
8.   Tu aimes la fille de Mme Calixte?

Negative sentences: **pas de**

After a verb in the negative, the articles **un, une,** and **des** are replaced by **de.**

     — Tu as **un** frère?   — Non, je n'ai pas **de** frère.
     — Tu as **une** sœur?   — Non, je n'ai pas **de** sœur.
     — Tu as **des** amis?   — Non, je n'ai pas **d'**amis.

Exception: the above rule does not apply with the verb **être.**

     Ce n'**est** pas **un** garçon, c'est un monsieur.

J   Mme Victor is the sole surviving member of her family. Answer the following questions about her in the negative.

     ◼▥   Est-ce qu'elle a un frère?   *Non, elle n'a pas de frère.*

1.   Est-ce qu'elle a des sœurs?
2.   Elle a un fils?
3.   Elle a des frères, n'est-ce pas?
4.   Est-ce qu'elle a une fille?
5.   Elle a une mère?
6.   Est-ce qu'elle a un père?

K   Jean-Pierre is looking for a cheap apartment, but the one he's visiting now may be too cheap. He asks where various things are; the landlord replies that there are none. Act out the conversation with a classmate.

     ◼▥   la salle à manger   — *Où est la salle à manger?*
                              — *Il n'y a pas de salle à manger.*

1.   la chambre   3.   les fenêtres
2.   le salon   4.   la salle de bains

Lecture

Because there are so many French-English cognates, it is often relatively easy to read an unfamiliar French passage. Read the following *lecture* and try to understand its general meaning. Then read it again and make a list of the cognates you recognize. For words that are not exactly alike in French and in English, write the English equivalent also. (You will notice that not all of the words have exactly the same meaning as their English counterparts — one example is **la circulation.**)

Le retour à Port-au-Prince

Avant de reprendre° le tap-tap pour retourner à Port-au-Prince, Raymond décide d'aller rendre° visite à des copains. Il fait° un détour sur la route du village. Il fait bon° dans les montagnes et l'air est pur. L'atmosphère y est calme; ce n'est pas comme dans la grande ville de Port-au-Prince où il y a beaucoup de circulation.

 C'est une surprise pour les garçons qui sont réunis° dans un garage. Ils parlent d'automobiles, de bicyclettes et de motocyclettes. Raymond, qui travaille° quelquefois dans le studio d'un fameux artiste haïtien, leur° parle des clients. Il y a beaucoup de touristes qui achètent° les sculptures et les masques de l'artiste.

 Mais c'est l'heure de° partir. Raymond rentre° chez lui, ravi de son petit voyage.

Before taking again
pay a/makes
The weather is nice

gathered

works/to them
buy

time to/goes home

questions

1. Où est Kenscoff?
2. Où est-ce qu'il y a beaucoup de circulation?
3. De quoi parlent les garçons?
4. Qui travaille dans le studio d'un artiste?
5. Est-ce que Raymond est content de son voyage?

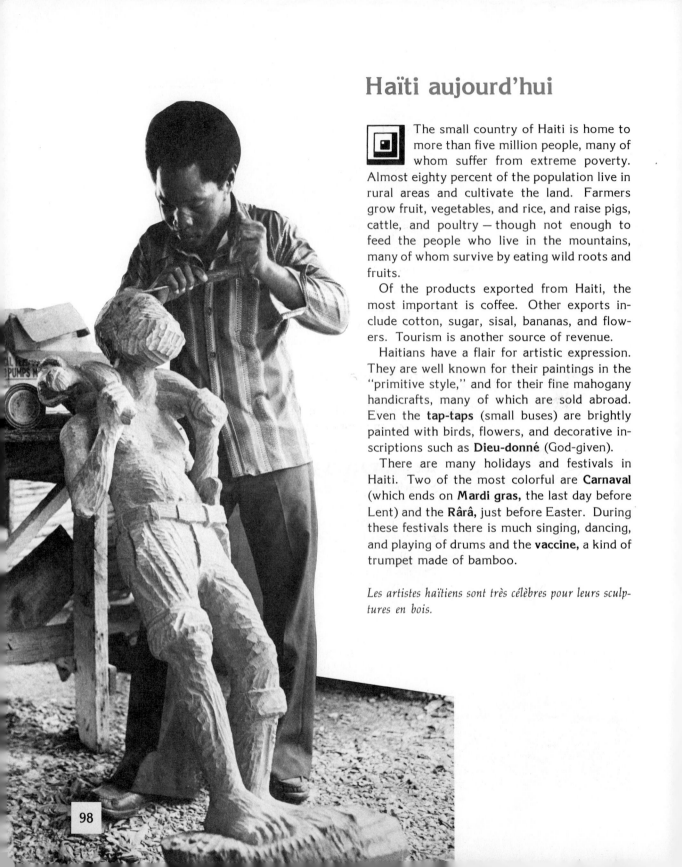

Haïti aujourd'hui

The small country of Haiti is home to more than five million people, many of whom suffer from extreme poverty. Almost eighty percent of the population live in rural areas and cultivate the land. Farmers grow fruit, vegetables, and rice, and raise pigs, cattle, and poultry — though not enough to feed the people who live in the mountains, many of whom survive by eating wild roots and fruits.

Of the products exported from Haiti, the most important is coffee. Other exports include cotton, sugar, sisal, bananas, and flowers. Tourism is another source of revenue.

Haitians have a flair for artistic expression. They are well known for their paintings in the "primitive style," and for their fine mahogany handicrafts, many of which are sold abroad. Even the **tap-taps** (small buses) are brightly painted with birds, flowers, and decorative inscriptions such as **Dieu-donné** (God-given).

There are many holidays and festivals in Haiti. Two of the most colorful are **Carnaval** (which ends on **Mardi gras,** the last day before Lent) and the **Rârâ,** just before Easter. During these festivals there is much singing, dancing, and playing of drums and the **vaccine,** a kind of trumpet made of bamboo.

Les artistes haïtiens sont très célèbres pour leurs sculptures en bois.

Résumé grammatical

Formation of **oui-non** questions (A-B)

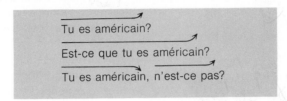

Questions that may be answered by **oui** or **non** may be formed:

1. by using rising intonation at the end of a statement;
2. by using **est-ce que (est-ce qu')** before a statement;
3. by adding a tag expression like **n'est-ce pas** to the end of a statement.

Regular **-er** verbs: present tense (C-F)

The present tense of regular **-er** verbs is formed by adding the endings **-e, -es, -e, -ons, -ez,** and **-ent** to the infinitive stem (the infinitive minus the **-er** ending).

AIMER Stem: **aim-**	
j'	aime
tu	aimes
on/il/elle	aime
nous	aim**ons**
vous	aim**ez**
ils/elles	aim**ent**

JOUER Stem: **jou-**	
je	joue
tu	joues
on/il/elle	joue
nous	jouons
vous	jouez
ils/elles	jouent

Possessive adjectives (G-I)

SINGULAR				PLURAL				ENGLISH
Masculine		Feminine		Masculine		Feminine		EQUIVALENT
mon	copain	ma	copine	mes	copains	mes	copines	my
ton	amie	ta		tes		tes		your
son		sa		ses		ses		her/his/its

1. Possessive adjectives agree with the noun that follows, not with the possessor.

> — C'est **la sœur** de Paul?   — Oui, c'est **sa** sœur.
> — C'est **le père** d'Yvette?   — Oui, c'est **son** père.

2. **Mon, ton,** and **son** are used in place of **ma, ta,** and **sa** before a feminine noun that begins with a vowel sound.

> Mon amie Gisèle est haïtienne.

Negative sentences: **pas de** (J-K)

After a negative verb (other than **être**), the markers **un, une,** and **des** are replaced by **de.**

> J'ai un frère. Toi, tu n'as pas **de** frère.
> J'ai une sœur. Toi, tu n'as pas **de** sœur.
> J'ai des amis. Toi, tu n'as pas **d'**amis.

_____ Révision _____

A   Make clear the relationship between various members of the Calixte family by completing the following sentences.

> ▪◽   Suze est ____ de Raymond   _la sœur_

1. Mme Calixte est ____ de Raymond.
2. Raymond est ____ de M. Calixte.
3. ____ de Raymond est mort.
4. Toussaint est ____ de Raymond.
5. Yolande est ____ de Raymond.
6. Mme Calixte est ____ de la grand-mère Polynice.

B   Say what the following people are doing after school. Use the correct form of _étudier, inviter, jouer,_ or _parler,_ as appropriate.

> ▪◽   On ____ une leçon de chimie.   _étudie_

1. Vous ____ au tennis.
2. Tu ____ la leçon de biologie.
3. Marc et moi, nous ____ au football.
4. Je ____ anglais avec mon copain américain.
5. Richard ____ des copains chez lui.
6. Elles ____ une leçon de maths.

C   You are the basketball team manager. One of the lockers won't open. You have the following list of combinations to try. Read them aloud to your assistant.

1. 73-26-90
2. 84-35-59
3. 61-42-76
4. 89-57-60
5. 96-16-78
6. 75-91-80

D   Ask questions that logically lead to the following answers.

▪▥   Oui, j'aime bien mon petit frère.   *Tu aimes ton petit frère?*
Est-ce que tu aimes ton petit frère?
Tu aimes ton petit frère, n'est-ce pas?

1. Oui, j'habite à Port-au-Prince.
2. Non, Martine n'a pas de frères.
3. Non, Raymond et Pierre ne parlent pas anglais.
4. Non, je suis fille unique.
5. Oui, c'est le bureau de Mme Ledoux.
6. Non, je n'ai pas de fils.

E   Complete each of the following sentences with the correct form of the possessive adjective that matches the subject.

▪▥   Je n'ai pas _____ vélo.   *mon*

1. Tu as _____ livres aujourd'hui?
2. J'aime bien _____ cours de français.
3. Richard joue avec _____ frères.
4. Tu parles de _____ école.
5. Yvette et _____ sœur vont au lycée.
6. J'habite avec _____ parents.
7. Voilà Marianne et _____ copain Jules.

F   A classmate asks whether you have the following. Answer in the negative.

▪▥   une maison   — *Tu as une maison?*
— *Non, je n'ai pas de maison.*

1. un cadeau pour Anne
2. un vélo
3. une voiture
4. une carte de France
5. des amis sénégalais
6. des livres de géographie

G   In English, identify or define briefly each of the following:

1. Port-au-Prince
2. un tap-tap
3. Toussaint Louverture
4. le créole
5. Carnaval
6. Hispaniola

Vocabulaire

NOUNS

la famille family
le moment moment

THE FAMILY

l'aîné(e) the oldest
l'enfant (*m./f.*) child
la fille daughter; **fille unique** only child (female)
le fils son; **fils unique** only child (male)
le frère brother
la grand-mère grandmother
les grands-parents (*m. pl.*) grandparents
le grand-père grandfather
les parents (*m. pl.*) parents
la sœur sister

VERBS

aimer to like, love
entrer to enter, go in
habiter to live
inviter to invite
jouer to play
parler to speak
téléphoner to telephone

ADJECTIVES

adorable adorable
bavard(e) talkative *TIM*
beau, belle beautiful *MOCH*
bête stupid, dull
bon(ne) good
content(e) happy
égoïste selfish *Gener.*
formidable terrific
généreux, généreuse generous
insupportable unbearable, insufferable
intelligent(e) intelligent *Bet*
méchant(e) mean
moche ugly
mort(e) dead
nombreux, nombreuse numerous
nouveau, nouvelle new
ravi(e) delighted
snob snobbish
sympathique nice, likeable *MECH.*
timide shy

MAIG / GROS

POSSESSIVE ADJECTIVES

mon, ma, mes my
ton, ta, tes your (*fam.*)
son, sa, ses his, her, its

NUMBERS 70–100

soixante-dix seventy
quatre-vingts eighty
quatre-vingt-dix ninety
cent one hundred

OTHER WORDS AND EXPRESSIONS

bien well, good
bonne nuit good night
comme as, like
parce que because
trop too, too much
à la maison at home
comme ci, comme ça so-so
mon petit, ma petite (my) dear (*affectionate*)
porte-toi (portez-vous) bien take care of yourself
tu as de la chance you're lucky
c'est formidable! it's fantastic!

102

première étape

A **Le jeu des portraits.** This is a game **(un jeu)** that can be played by two teams. The first team chooses a person known to most of the class, and invites the other team to guess who the individual is. Each member of the opposing team asks or answers one **oui-non** question, until the person is identified.

B **Une autobiographie.** The characters in the first stage of your text have described themselves and their daily lives to you. Prepare a short autobiography in French to send to a pen pal in a French-speaking area of the world. You may wish to include a photograph of yourself, and perhaps record a few words of greeting on a cassette.

C **Une visite.** Convert your classroom into an imaginary home by preparing large signs that will serve to label the rooms. One student should be the invited guest. The other students are members of the family who will welcome the guest, introduce her or him to the parents, show the various rooms of the house, and ask various questions about the guest's own home and family.

D **Un peu de culture.** Make believe that you are going to Paris, Strasbourg, Québec, or Port-au-Prince. Tell *in English* what you know about the country, what you would like to see, what you think the people are like, and what you expect to do there. Look at the color photo essay on pages 1–8 and the black and white photos in chapters 1–5 to get ideas of places you might want to visit.

E **Le français dans le monde.** Collect photographs from magazines that pertain to French-speaking people around the world. Bring in items that friends, relatives, or you yourself might have brought back from travels to French-speaking areas. Go on a walking tour of your city or town and see how many signs are in French. Look in the telephone directory to see if you can spot names of people who might be French or who might have come to this country from French-speaking areas. You'll be surprised at the amount of French around you!

Les petits
événements

Qu'est-ce qu'on achète?
Displays of food and clothing entice French shoppers (left), while a Senegalese merchant (right) offers both. The women in the inset are content with the most basic of purchases: **une baguette** for each.

107

Qu'est-ce qu'on mange? In France, there is ample evidence that enjoyment of food is a national passion. The scenes here are in Paris, but most of them could be almost anywhere in the country.

The everyday work of people like those pictured on these pages makes possible many of the **petits événements** that add pleasure to life. Page 110: Moroccan workers dye wool in Marrakech; a woman works in a watch factory in Besançon; a man hangs a movie poster in Paris. Page 111: This scene in central France is typical of the lovely farmland that characterizes much of the country.

110

chapitre 6
Les cousins à la mode de Bretagne

In the province of **Bretagne** (Brittany), in north-western France, the lives of many people revolve around the sea. Brittany's rocky coast is home to the thousands of Bretons whose living depends on fishing.

In Brittany, the family is a close-knit unit. It is traditional to keep in touch with relatives, including distant relatives, or **cousins à la mode de Bretagne.** Annick Le Hur, whose father is a lobster fisherman, lives on the coast in Douarnenez. The Le Hurs have come by train to the inland city of Rennes for a family reunion at the home of relatives who have recently moved there.

Quel est le chemin?

scène 1

The Le Hurs have lost their way while walking from the train station to their relatives' home. M. Le Hur is worried that his sister will be angry if they are late.

M. LE HUR	On est en retard. La tante Soizic va être furieuse.
MME LE HUR	Mais non, ne t'en fais pas! On apporte des langoustes! Elle va être ravie!
M. LE HUR	Bon! Ils habitent vingt-deux, rue de la Monnaie... C'est en face de la cathédrale... C'est par ici, mais où?
5 ANNICK	Je demande le chemin? (*à un passant*) Monsieur, s'il vous plaît! Où est la cathédrale?
LE PASSANT	Ce n'est pas loin d'ici, mademoiselle. Vous allez tout droit jusqu'à la place Foch. D'abord, vous passez devant le cinéma Gaumont.
ANNICK	La place Foch, c'est la petite place au coin, là-bas?
10 LE PASSANT	Oui. Quand vous y arrivez, vous tournez à droite. Vous suivez la rue jusqu'à la cathédrale.
ANNICK	Merci bien, monsieur.
LE PASSANT	Je vous en prie.
ANNICK	Alors, maintenant, dépêchons-nous!

questions

1. Qui est en retard, les Le Hur ou la tante Soizic?
2. Où habite la tante Soizic?
3. Est-ce que la tante Soizic habite loin de la place Foch?
4. Qu'est-ce que les Le Hur apportent?
5. Est-ce que la tante Soizic va être furieuse?

**parlons de
la scène**

The items illustrated below are all mentioned in *scène 1*. Make a statement, ask a question, or have a short conversation with a classmate about each item as it relates to *scène 1*.

— *Vous allez tout droit jusqu'à la place Foch.*
— *C'est la petite place au coin?*

**à vous,
maintenant**

Can you answer these questions about yourself? Model your answers on lines from the *scène*.

1. Où est-ce que vous habitez?
2. Est-ce que vous avez une tante? Où est-ce qu'elle habite? Est-ce que vous habitez loin de chez elle?
3. Dans la salle de classe, qui est à votre droite? Qui est à votre gauche? Qui est en face du professeur?

**petites
scènes**

1. You are on your way to a new school for the first time. Your father hurries you to get ready. Act out this dialogue with a classmate.

PAPA	Tu es en retard! *même*
VOUS	Ne t'en fais pas, Papa!
PAPA	Voilà tes livres.
VOUS	Oui, merci, Papa. *même*
PAPA	Dépêche-toi! Ton professeur va être furieux!

2. Create a dialogue modeled on *scène 1* in which one student asks another for directions to a place in your town.

Étude de mots

Jouons avec les mots

In the *Jouons avec les mots* sections, you will see how certain words are related to one another, in meaning or in form. In general, you will find that it is easier to learn words in logical groups than to learn a number of unrelated words. Also, by seeing how words are related, you will increase your understanding of how language works.

1. *Prépositions.* You already know some of the words below. Study their antonyms (or opposites) in the right column, so that you can give the opposite of each one without looking.

à droite de (à ma droite)	à gauche de (à ma gauche)
devant	derrière
près de	loin de

A Say where several students are in the class, in relation to you and to others. For example:

■III *Jean est devant moi. Jeanne est derrière moi. Suzanne est à ma droite et à gauche de Marc. Pierre est loin de Béatrice.*

2. *La famille.* The following words are paired with logical opposites in gender. Take a few minutes to learn the new words.

la tante	l'oncle (*m.*)
la cousine	le cousin
la nièce	le neveu

B Identify each relative in terms of her or his relationship to other family members.

■III la tante *La tante est la sœur de la mère ou du père.*

1. le neveu
2. la cousine
3. l'oncle
4. la nièce
5. le cousin
6. la tante

C Try an "add-on" game with family terms. Each student repeats the relatives that have been named, and adds to the list.

FIRST STUDENT: J'ai une tante.
SECOND STUDENT: J'ai une tante et deux frères.
THIRD STUDENT: J'ai une tante, deux frères et...

Le plan de la ville

1 le stade
2 la piscine
3 l'hôpital
4 la gare
5 la banque
6 les magasins
7 la poste
8 le cinéma
9 le théâtre
10 le restaurant
11 l'hôtel de ville
12 l'église (f.)

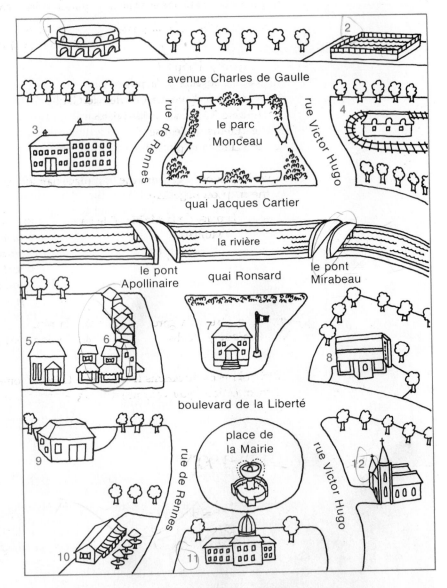

D Answer the following questions based on the map above.

1. Dans quelle rue est le théâtre?
2. Les magasins sont au coin de quelles rues?
3. Qu'est-ce qu'il y a dans le boulevard de la Liberté?
4. Est-ce que l'hôpital est sur le quai Ronsard?
5. Qu'est-ce qu'il y a sur la place de la Mairie?

E Locate the following landmarks in relation to one another, according to the map. More than one response is possible in each case.

▪▥ le cinéma / la poste   *Le cinéma est tout près de la poste.*
                                       Le cinéma est à droite de la poste.

1. la gare / l'hôpital
2. l'hôtel de ville / la poste
3. le stade / l'avenue Charles de Gaulle
4. le parc Monceau / la rivière
5. le cinéma / l'église
6. le stade / la piscine

F Give directions to go from the first place named to the second place. Refer to the map on page 116.

▪▥ la place de la Mairie / le parc Monceau   *Vous suivez la rue de Rennes. Vous allez tout droit jusqu'à la rivière. Vous passez sur le pont Apollinaire et vous tournez à droite. Le parc est à gauche.*

1. le théâtre / la gare
2. le stade / l'église

3. la piscine / l'hôtel de ville
4. le pont Mirabeau / les magasins

à vous,
maintenant

A friend needs directions from school to your home. Give the most complete directions you can, mentioning a number of landmarks along the route.

Les nombres: 100–1.000.000

100 = cent	200 = deux cents	1.000 = mille
101 = cent un	201 = deux cent un	2.000 = deux mille
102 = cent deux	202 = deux cent deux	1.000.000 = un million

1. In numbers representing even hundreds 200 and up (**deux cents, trois cents,** etc.), the word **cents** ends in **-s.** In numbers other than even hundreds (**deux cent un, trois cent dix,** etc.), the **-s** is dropped.
2. Note that in French, a period is used rather than a comma in figures 1.000 and above.

G Give in French the approximate population of your class, your school, your town, and your state, province, or territory.

La Bretagne et ses ressources

Brittany is a peninsula roughly the size of Connecticut and Massachusetts, jutting out into the Atlantic Ocean between the English Channel and the Bay of Biscay. Natural harbors and small, rocky coves are typical of its rugged, beautiful coast. Inland are farmlands, heath-covered moors, and low hills. The climate is generally temperate, with cool summers and mild winters, but rain and fog often make the landscape look like a place fit for witches and goblins.

Brittany has several important ports. The biggest are Brest, Nantes, and Saint-Nazaire, all major shipbuilding centers. In smaller harbors there are numerous fishing ports like Douarnenez. Some of the boats from these towns stay close to the Brittany coast, harvesting tuna, sardines, and shellfish. Others venture much farther out into the Atlantic.

Many towns are known for particular types of fishing. In Douarnenez, for example, the specialty is lobster fishing. Fishing boats go all the way from Douarnenez to Mauritania and the tip of South Africa, staying out from September to May. At sea, the catch is kept alive in sea water in the hulls of the boats. When the boats return home, some of the lobsters are frozen or canned in Douarnenez, and others are sold alive to wholesalers.

Breton farmers raise cattle and grow wheat, apples, and vegetables. The first crops of vegetables grown in the spring, called **les primeurs,** are highly regarded throughout France.

Brittany was settled around A.D. 500 by the Britons, a Celtic tribe that was driven out of what is now Great Britain by Anglo-Saxon invaders. Bretons have maintained their own traditions. Many older people speak a language that is very close to Welsh, because of the common Celtic origin of Wales and Brittany. In fact, the Welsh and the Bretons carry on an active trade in vegetables, with little or no language problem.

À la française

In France, when relatives or close friends of either sex greet or say good-by to one another, they usually exchange kisses on both cheeks. Within the immediate family, this may take place several times each day: on saying good morning, on leaving for and returning from school or work, and on saying good night. Many people give two kisses, but in various parts of the country a third or fourth kiss is given.

Prononciation et orthographe

The sound /ə/

The sound /ə/ (spelled **e**) is often dropped.

RÉPÉTEZ
je	Jé m'appelle Suze.	petit	Le pétit garçon est beau.
ne	Je né vais pas bien.	demande	Je démande le chémin?
de	C'est la maison dé Paul.	le monde	Tout lé monde est là?

LISEZ
1. Jé n'ai pas dé frères.
2. Au révoir, madémoiselle.
3. Est-cé que tu vas bien?

Intonation in questions

When you ask a **oui-non** question, your voice normally rises in pitch.

Tu vas à Rennes?   Est-ce que c'est loin d'ici?

In questions asking for specific information, the intonation is like that of a statement. The voice goes down in pitch.

Où est la cathédrale?   Quel est le chemin?

REPÉTEZ

Tu aimes le cinéma?
Est-ce que nous sommes en retard?
Ils sont de Douarnenez?
Vous avez des langoustes?

Comment allez-vous?
Qui est-ce?
Où est la banque?
Qu'est-ce que c'est?

The letter h

The letter **h** never represents a sound in French.

REPÉTEZ

Haïti
Hélène
l'hôtel
l'hôpital

Marthe
Théodore
j'habite
l'homme

Liaison and *élision* occur with most words beginning with the letter **h**, since **h** is silent.

$$/t/$$
un grand homme
l'homme

$$/t/$$
un petit hôtel
l'hôtel

Some words beginning with **h** are treated as if they began with a consonant. *Liaison* and *élision* do not occur.

Le Hur
le héros

le hockey
les hors-d'œuvre

LISEZ

1. Marthe Le Hur est à l'hôpital.
2. Hélène et Henri habitent près de l'hôtel de ville.

Les jours se suivent et ne se ressemblent pas.

Chez les Kervendal

Annick's aunt and uncle, M. and Mme Kervendal, and her second cousin Patrick Le Floch greet the Le Hurs at the door. Mme Kervendal is not upset that they are late, but concerned that they must be tired after their long walk.

MME KERVENDAL	Vous arrivez de la gare à pied! Mes pauvres enfants!
M. LE HUR	Tiens, Soizic, voilà les langoustes.
MME KERVENDAL	Merci beaucoup, Jacques-Yves. Tu es vraiment gentil.
M. LE HUR	Pas de quoi, pas de quoi...
PATRICK	Des langoustes! Chic, alors!
MME LE HUR	Tout le monde est là?
M. KERVENDAL	Oui, tout le monde est dans le salon.

In the living room, the Le Hurs exchange kisses on the cheeks with other relatives who are there for the family reunion. When M. Kervendal asks Annick about her first impressions of Rennes, she shows mixed feelings.

M. KERVENDAL	Eh bien, Annick, comment trouves-tu notre ville?
ANNICK	Oh, elle n'est pas mal... mais il n'y a pas la mer.
PATRICK	Tu es bien une fille de marin. Tu vas faire du bateau pendant l'été?
ANNICK	Peut-être. J'aimerais bien faire de la voile.
PATRICK	Moi, je vais aller chez mon copain Jean-Marie à Concarneau. Il a un bateau à voiles, tu sais.
ANNICK	Ah, formidable! Tu as de la chance!

questions

1. Comment est-ce que les Le Hur arrivent chez les Kervendal?
2. Est-ce qu'Annick aime bien Rennes? Pourquoi?
3. Qui aime la mer?
4. Pourquoi est-ce que Patrick a de la chance?

parlons de la scène

Use each pair of cues listed below to form a logical statement based on *scène 2.*

▬Ⅲ   Annick / Patrick   *Annick est la cousine de Patrick.*

1. M. Le Hur / Mme Kervendal
2. Annick / M. Kervendal
3. Patrick / Concarneau
4. Annick / marin
5. copain / bateau à voiles
6. Rennes / la mer

à vous, maintenant

1. Discuss with a classmate what you plan to do, might do, or would like to do during the summer.

Qu'est-ce que	tu vas faire tu aimerais faire	pendant l'été?

Je vais Je vais peut-être J'aimerais bien	faire	du bateau. du camping. de la voile. du sport.

2. Express your opinions of some places and people.

Comment trouves-tu	notre ville? notre école? ton cousin?

Formidable! Je l'aime bien. Pas mal. Je ne l'aime pas beaucoup.

situations

Use the following expressions of appreciation, acknowledgment of appreciation, enthusiasm, and sympathy to help create a suitable dialogue for the series of events shown in the drawings below.

Merci bien! Merci beaucoup! Merci, c'est gentil!	Je t'en prie. Pas de quoi. De rien.	Tu as de la chance! Formidable! Chic, alors!	Ma/Mon pauvre! Zut, alors! Tu n'as pas de chance!

Grammaire

Contraction of **à** + definite article

Je vais **au** cinéma. Je vais **à la** banque.
Je vais **aux** grands magasins. Je vais **à l'**école.

À contracts with **le** and **les** to form **au** and **aux**. It does not contract with **la** or **l'**.

A Say that Robert is going to the following places.

> ◼⫶ lycée *Il va au lycée.*

1. stade
2. parc
3. mairie
4. magasin
5. poste
6. hôtel

B Ask a friend if he or she is going to the first place mentioned. Your friend isn't going there; he/she is on the way to the second place mentioned instead.

> ◼⫶ l'hôpital / la cathédrale
>
> — *Tu vas à l'hôpital?*
> — *Non, je n'y vais pas. Je vais à la cathédrale.*

1. le restaurant / le théâtre
2. l'église / la maison
3. la banque / l'école
4. la gare / les magasins
5. le cinéma / le parc
6. l'hôtel de ville / la cathédrale

Contraction of **de** + definite article

J'habite près **du** parc. J'habite près **de la** poste.
J'habite près **des** magasins. J'habite près **de l'**église.

De contracts with **le** and **les** to form **du** and **des**. It does not contract with **la** or **l'**.

C Identify the owner of each boat in the harbor at Douarnenez, using the cues indicated.

> ◼⫶ le professeur *C'est le bateau du professeur.*

1. la nièce de Paul
2. le marin
3. l'élève
4. la sœur de Guy
5. les parents d'Annick
6. le cousin Kervendal
7. le copain d'Annick
8. les Le Floch

D   Locate Paul's house in relation to the places indicated.

▰▰   (près de) la poste   *Sa maison est près de la poste.*

1. (en face de) le métro
2. (loin de) les quais
3. (près de) l'hôtel
4. (près de) les magasins
5. (à droite de) la banque
6. (à gauche de) le cinéma

à vous,
maintenant

Say where you and your friends are going on Saturday. Use place names you have learned.

Moi, je vais au cinéma. Paul et Roger vont au théâtre. Alice va...

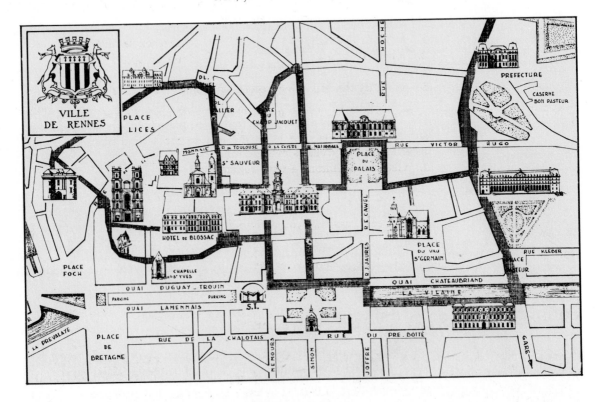

Future plans and events: **aller** + infinitive

Je vais faire du camping.   I'm going to go camping.
Il va être en retard.   He's going to be late.
On ne va pas habiter à Paris.   We aren't going to live in Paris.

A present-tense form of **aller** plus an infinitive is used to refer to future plans and events.

E Say where the following people plan to live when they finish school.

■▌▌▌▌ moi: Port-au-Prince   *Moi, je vais habiter à Port-au-Prince.*

1. nous: Paris
2. lui: Montréal
3. vous: Québec
4. toi: Nice

5. elles: Dakar
6. moi: Rennes
7. on: Douarnenez
8. elle: Bruxelles

F Say that Jacques-Yves isn't going to do the following things on Saturday. He's going to do them on Sunday.

■▌▌▌▌ aller au parc   *Il ne va pas aller au parc samedi. Il va aller au parc dimanche.*

1. faire du bateau
2. aller au cinéma

3. aller chez sa tante
4. faire du sport

G Answer that the following people are going to do the things tomorrow.

■▌▌▌▌ Monique étudie aujourd'hui?   *Non, elle va étudier demain.*

1. Gilles joue avec Paul aujourd'hui?
2. Anne invite Charles aujourd'hui?
3. Georges téléphone à Guy aujourd'hui?
4. Marie arrive de Lyon aujourd'hui?

à vous, maintenant

State three things that you plan to do today, and three things that you do not plan to do. Then ask some of your friends about their plans.

Moi, je vais... Je ne vais pas... Et toi, qu'est-ce que tu vas faire?

Possessive adjectives: **notre, votre, leur**

SINGULAR NOUNS				PLURAL NOUNS				ENGLISH
Masculine		Feminine		Masculine		Feminine		EQUIVALENT
notre		notre		nos		nos		our
votre	cousin	votre	cousine	vos	cousins	vos	cousines	your
leur		leur		leurs		leurs		their

1. **Notre, votre,** and **leur** modify either a masculine singular or a feminine singular noun. **Nos, vos,** and **leurs** modify either a masculine plural or a feminine plural noun.
2. *Liaison* occurs when **nos, vos,** and **leurs** are used with a noun beginning with a vowel sound: **nos /z/ amis, vos /z/ oncles, leurs /z/ enfants.**

H   You and your brother are planning a trip to Paris. A classmate asks whether you are traveling with other members of your family. Give a logical answer, using *notre* or *nos*.

      ▪▮   parents   — *Vous y allez avec vos parents?*
                               — *Non, nous y allons avec notre tante.*

1. soeur
2. grands-parents
3. cousins
4. oncle
5. cousine
6. tante

I   The Dupont twins are hosting a family reunion. Say where their relatives are arriving from, according to the cues.

      ▪▮   grand-père (Marseille)   *Leur grand-père arrive de Marseille.*

1. nièce (Port-au-Prince)
2. cousins (Montréal)
3. neveu (Dakar)
4. parents (Grenoble)
5. soeur (Saint-Louis)
6. oncles (Bruxelles)

à vous, maintenant   Comment on or ask about various possessions or relationships of your family and friends. Try to use all of the possessive adjectives.

> *Notre bateau est très joli. Vos cousins ont un bateau, n'est-ce pas? Comment est leur bateau?*

Information questions

où (where)	Où est-ce que tu habites?
quand (when)	Quand est-ce que Jean arrive?
que (what)	Qu'est-ce que vous allez faire?
pourquoi (why)	Pourquoi est-ce que vous êtes en retard?
comment (how)	Comment est-ce que vous allez au lycée?
qui (whom)	Qui est-ce que tu invites?
qui (who)	Qui va au cinéma?

1. Many questions asking for information have the word order:

     interrogative word + **est-ce que** + subject and verb

2. **Qui** followed by **est-ce que** means *whom*. **Qui** (meaning *who*) may also be the subject of a third-person singular verb, in which case **est-ce que** is not used.

    Qui est-ce que tu invites?   Whom are you inviting?
    Qui habite ici?   Who lives here?

J   Ask for specific information based on the following statements. Use the question words in parentheses.

> ▬◖◗   Il va au cinéma. (quand)   *Quand est-ce qu'il va au cinéma?*

1. Tu joues. (où)
2. Elle arrive à la gare. (qui)
3. Vous étudiez. (que)
4. Ils vont à Québec. (quand)
5. Elle est furieuse. (pourquoi)
6. Tu vas au parc. (comment)

K   Form information questions that would produce the following answers. More than one question may be possible.

> ▬◖◗   Paul aime les langoustes.   *Qui aime les langoustes?*
> *Qu'est-ce que Paul aime?*

1. Nous étudions la leçon d'histoire.
2. J'invite mes copains.
3. Il habite à Paris.
4. On accepte le cadeau.
5. Elle arrive maintenant.
6. Nous y allons à pied.

L   Make up six original information questions about the photograph below.

On arrive à la gare.

127

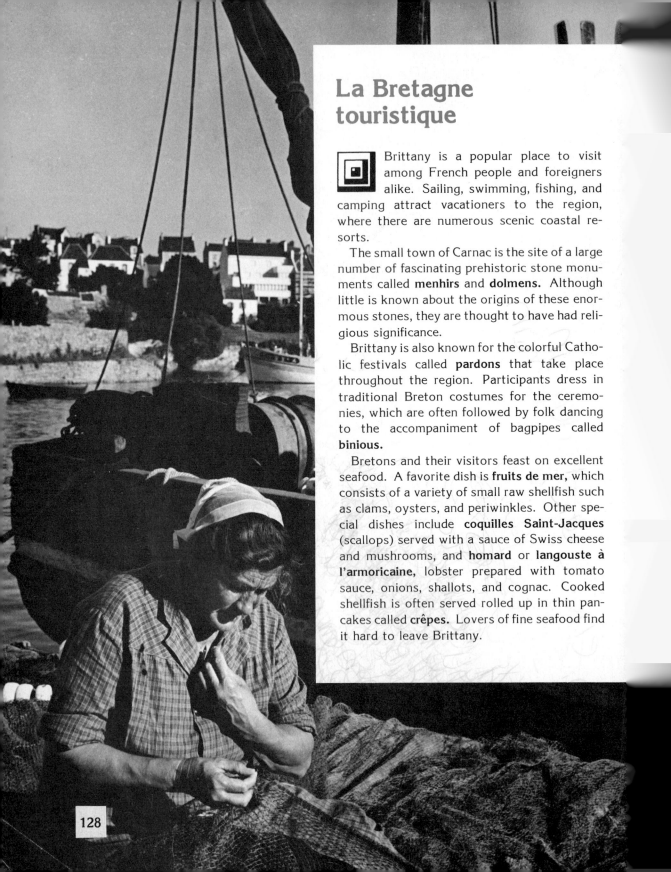

La Bretagne touristique

Brittany is a popular place to visit among French people and foreigners alike. Sailing, swimming, fishing, and camping attract vacationers to the region, where there are numerous scenic coastal resorts.

The small town of Carnac is the site of a large number of fascinating prehistoric stone monuments called **menhirs** and **dolmens**. Although little is known about the origins of these enormous stones, they are thought to have had religious significance.

Brittany is also known for the colorful Catholic festivals called **pardons** that take place throughout the region. Participants dress in traditional Breton costumes for the ceremonies, which are often followed by folk dancing to the accompaniment of bagpipes called **binious.**

Bretons and their visitors feast on excellent seafood. A favorite dish is **fruits de mer,** which consists of a variety of small raw shellfish such as clams, oysters, and periwinkles. Other special dishes include **coquilles Saint-Jacques** (scallops) served with a sauce of Swiss cheese and mushrooms, and **homard** or **langouste à l'armoricaine,** lobster prepared with tomato sauce, onions, shallots, and cognac. Cooked shellfish is often served rolled up in thin pancakes called **crêpes.** Lovers of fine seafood find it hard to leave Brittany.

Page 128: fishing nets need constant mending. Left: workers at a sardine cannery in Douarnenez wear traditional costumes. Below: **menhirs** stand like sentries near Carnac; a young couple enjoys one of Brittany's many festivals.

Une réunion de famille

La famille Le Hur habite à Douarnenez, une petite ville de pêcheurs° en   fishermen
Bretagne. À Douarnenez, on est pêcheur de père en fils. M. Le Hur, qui est
pêcheur de langoustes, part° pendant neuf mois de l'année.° Il va pêcher   leaves/months of the
jusque sur les côtes° de la Mauritanie en Afrique. Annick est bien con-   year
5 tente quand son père retourne chez lui en été.   shores

    Aujourd'hui ils vont tous à Rennes pour rendre visite aux Kervendal.
Toute la famille est là, quand ils arrivent un peu en retard de la gare: les
Kervendal, des cousins germains° d'Annick; les Le Floch, des cousins   first cousins
éloignés;° les grands-parents d'Annick; et tout un assortiment d'oncles et   distant
10 de tantes.

    L'aîné des Le Floch, Patrick, est le cousin préféré d'Annick. Comme°   Like
elle, il aime la mer et les bateaux à voiles. Au salon, ils admirent
ensemble° des photos du dernier° bateau d'Éric Tabarly, un champion de   together/latest
voile et un héros national en France. Annick et Patrick rêvent° de faire des   dream
15 courses° transatlantiques comme lui. Mais d'abord, ils vont apprendre° à   races/learn
faire de la voile.

    Maintenant, le déjeuner est prêt.° Tout le monde va bien se régaler de°   ready/feast on
langoustes à l'armoricaine. C'est bien agréable, les réunions de famille!

questions
1. Quelle est la profession principale à Douarnenez?
2. Où est-ce que M. Le Hur va pêcher la langouste?
3. Qui est présent à la réunion de famille chez les Kervendal?
4. Qui est Éric Tabarly?
5. Qu'est-ce qu'Annick et Patrick rêvent de faire?

à vous, maintenant	1. Comment s'appellent vos cousins? vos cousines?
	2. Est-ce que vous avez quelquefois des réunions de famille chez vous? chez vos oncles et vos tantes?
	3. Est-ce que vous allez pêcher quelquefois avec des amis? Où est-ce que vous allez pêcher?
	4. Est-ce que vous aimez la langouste?

résumés oraux

Give some information in two or three sentences on the topics suggested below.

1. la ville de Douarnenez
2. les Le Hur
3. Patrick Kervendal ~~Le Floch~~
4. Rennes

résumé écrit

Retell the story of the Le Hurs' trip to Rennes by answering the following questions in complete sentences.

1. Qui habite à Douarnenez?
2. Pourquoi est-ce que les Le Hur vont à Rennes?
3. Qui est là quand les Le Hur arrivent?
4. Qu'est-ce qu'Annick et Patrick admirent dans le salon?
5. Comment est la réunion?

_____ Résumé grammatical _____

Contractions: à and de + definite articles (A-D)

à + le = au	de + le = du
à + les = aux	de + les = des
à + la = à la	de + la = de la
à + l' = à l'	de + l' = de l'

1. The preposition **à** contracts with **le** and **les** to form **au** and **aux.** The preposition **de** contracts with **le** and **les** to form **du** and **des.** No contraction occurs with **la** or **l'**.

   Je vais **au** théâtre.   Tu habites près **du** lycée.
   Ils vont **aux** grands magasins.   Il habite en face **des** quais.

2. _Liaison_ occurs when **aux** or **des** precedes a word beginning with a vowel sound.

   /z/
   aux écoles

   /z/
   des écoles

Future plans and events: **aller** + infinitive (E-G)

The present-tense form of **aller** plus an infinitive is often used to indicate a future action.

Je vais aller à une fête samedi.

I'm going to go to a party on Saturday.

Possessive adjectives: all forms (H-I)

mon, ma, mes	my	notre, nos	our
ton, ta, tes	your	votre, vos	your
son, sa, ses	her/his/its	leur, leurs	their

Mon, ton, and **son** are used with a feminine singular noun that begins with a vowel sound: **mon amie, ton école, son église.**

Specific information questions (J-L)

Specific information questions begin with a question word like **où** or **comment.** The interrogative phrase **est-ce que** is often used directly after the question word.

Où est-ce que tu vas?
Quand est-ce que tu arrives?
Pourquoi est-ce que tu es en retard?
Comment est-ce que tu vas au lycée?

When **qui** is used as the subject of a verb, it is followed by a verb form. When **qui** is used as the object of a verb, it may be followed by **est-ce que.**

Qui va au cinéma? (**qui** = subject)
Qui est-ce que tu invites? (**qui** = object)

The legend of King Arthur may have originated in Brittany. According to the stories of the Knights of the Round Table, the sorcerer Merlin roamed the huge forest of Brocéliande, in north central Brittany. There are no written texts to prove that the Round Table stories originally came from Brittany, but many literary historians believe that the legend was created in the oral tradition of the region and passed along from generation to generation.

Révision

A Reverse the order of the two landmarks mentioned in the statements below.

▪‖ Le théâtre est à gauche de *La banque est à droite du théâtre.*
la banque.

1. La cathédrale n'est pas loin du musée.
2. L'église est à gauche de l'hôpital.
3. Le cinéma est en face du théâtre.
4. La poste est à droite de la gare.
5. La piscine est près du parc.
6. L'hôtel de ville est devant le quai.
7. Les magasins sont loin du stade.
8. Le théâtre est derrière l'hôtel de ville.

B Tell the class who lives at the following addresses. Use names of your choice.

▪‖ 201, rue Malar *[Michèle] habite 201, rue Malar.*

1. 108, quai de Brest
2. 147, place de la Mairie
3. 206, avenue Foch
4. 259, boulevard de la Madeleine
5. 312, rue de la Poste
6. 244, avenue Pasteur
7. 589, rue de la Gare
8. 96, place Charles de Gaulle

C You and a friend disagree about which relatives are described below. Correct each statement by changing the relative mentioned to one of the opposite sex.

▪‖ Le neveu de Mme Le Hur *La nièce de Mme Le Hur est*
est gentil. *gentille.*

1. Le cousin de Paul est mort.
2. La tante de Lucienne est bavarde.
3. Le grand-père de Luc est sympathique.
4. La fille de Mme Leclerc est insupportable.
5. La nièce de M. Leblanc est timide.
6. Le père de Guillaume est formidable.
7. Le neveu de Roger est beau.
8. L'oncle de Véronique est snob.

D   Say that the people identified in parentheses are going to do the things that you would like to do.

> ▣‖   Je voudrais habiter à   *Elles vont habiter à Paris.*
>   Paris. (elles)

1. Je voudrais acheter un bateau. (elle)
2. Je voudrais aller à la mer. (toi)
3. Je voudrais faire du camping. (les Kervendal)
4. Je voudrais manger des langoustes. (on)
5. Je voudrais faire de la voile. (vous)
6. Je voudrais aller en France. (lui)

E   Describe the people and things mentioned, using the appropriate possessive adjectives.

> ▣‖   Ils ont des amis.   *Leurs amis sont américains.*

1. Nous avons des copains. _____ copains sont grands.
2. Vous avez un bateau à voiles. _____ bateau à voiles est beau.
3. Vous avez des livres. _____ livres sont intéressants.
4. Nous avons une sœur. _____ sœur est petite.
5. Ils ont un appartement. _____ appartement est joli.
6. Les Le Hur ont une fille. _____ fille est française.

F   Ask questions that would elicit the specific information given in parentheses. Use *est-ce que* (*est-ce qu'*) in each question.

> ▣‖   Il va au lycée. (en voiture)   *Comment est-ce qu'il va au lycée?*

1. Elle étudie. (dans sa chambre)
2. Le professeur est furieux. (parce que les élèves sont en retard)
3. Les enfants vont au parc. (l'après-midi)
4. On accepte. (une invitation)
5. Elle va demander. (le chemin)
6. Il va aller au cinéma. (en vélo)

G   Say that you are going on foot to the following places.

> ▣‖   parc   *Je vais au parc à pied.*

1. les magasins	3. la piscine	5. la banque
2. le stade	4. l'hôpital	6. le théâtre

H   Pretend you are going to visit Brittany. What would you want to see and do? Are there similarities between Brittany and the part of the country where you live, or do you feel that Brittany is quite different from your region?

Vocabulaire

NOUNS

l'avenue (f.)   avenue
la banque   bank
le bateau   boat
le boulevard   boulevard
le camping   camping
la cathédrale   cathedral
le chemin   way
le cinéma   movie theater
le cousin   male cousin
la cousine   female cousin
l'église (f.)   church
l'été (m.)   summer
la gare   railroad station
l'hôpital (m.)   hospital
l'hôtel de ville (m.)   city hall
la langouste   spiny lobster
le magasin   store
la mairie   town hall
le marin   sailor
la mer   sea
le neveu   nephew
la nièce   niece
l'oncle (m.)   uncle
le parc   park
le passant   passer-by
la piscine   swimming pool
la place   square

NOUNS (cont.)

le pont   bridge
la poste   post office
le quai   pier; street bordering
   a body of water
le restaurant   restaurant
la rivière   river
la rue   street
le sport   sport
le stade   stadium
la tante   aunt
le théâtre   theater, playhouse
la ville   city

29

VERBS

apporter   to bring
arriver   to arrive
demander   to ask
passer   to pass
tourner   to turn

ADJECTIVES

furieux, furieuse   furious
pauvre   poor

PREPOSITIONS

au coin de   at the corner of
à droite de   to (on) the right of
à gauche de   to (on) the left of
derrière   behind
devant   in front of
en face de   opposite; facing
sur   on
tout droit   straight ahead

OTHER WORDS AND EXPRESSIONS

alors   well, then
beaucoup   very much
comment trouvez-vous...?
   what do you think of...?
d'abord   first
dépêchons-nous!   let's hurry!
de rien   you're welcome
faire   to do; faire du bateau
   to go boating; faire du camping   to go camping; faire
   du sport   to play sports;
   faire de la voile   to go
   sailing
jusqu'à   up to, as far as
il n'y a pas de quoi   don't
   mention it; you're welcome
j'aimerais   I would like
je vous en prie (je t'en prie)
   don't mention it, you're welcome
leur   their
mille   one thousand
un million   one million
ne t'en fais pas!   don't worry!
notre   our
par ici   around here
pendant   during
peut-être   perhaps
vous suivez   you follow
votre   your

tout le monde — everybody

chapitre 7

Dans un magasin algérien

Constantine, in Algeria, is a city built on both sides of a deep ravine created by the Rhumel River. The bridges that span the gorges high above the river are a spectacular sight.

An important center for grain trade and for the manufacture of textiles and leather goods, Constantine bustles with life. People come from faraway villages and towns to shop there. On his days off from school, Si Farid works in his father's clothing store in Constantine.

Ici, on marchande

scène 1

Si Farid is helping his father in the family store in Constantine, Algeria. A woman dressed in European clothes appears at the entrance to the shop.

M. FARID	Entrez, madame. Vous désirez?
LA CLIENTE	Je cherche un foulard pour aller avec ma robe verte.
M. FARID	Par ici, madame. Si, montre les foulards à madame.
SI	Voilà un joli foulard vert et rouge.
5 LA CLIENTE	Non, je n'aime pas le rouge.
SI	Vous préférez le bleu? Voilà un beau foulard en soie bleue.
LA CLIENTE	Oui, il est superbe. Il coûte combien?
SI	Cent cinquante dinars, madame.
LA CLIENTE	C'est trop cher, jeune homme!
10 SI	Mais non, madame. C'est vraiment bon marché pour de la soie. Et il va très bien avec vos yeux bleus.
LA CLIENTE	Oh, le flatteur! Je l'achète à cent dinars.
SI	Cent vingt-cinq!
LA CLIENTE	Bon, d'accord. Je le prends.

questions

1. Qu'est-ce que la cliente cherche? Pourquoi?
2. Qui montre les foulards à la cliente?
3. Quelles couleurs est-ce que la cliente aime?
4. Quel foulard est-ce que la cliente achète?
5. Le foulard en soie coûte combien?

Comment marchander

 It is a tradition in Arabic countries to bargain **(marchander)**, especially when buying valuable objects. The philosophy is that you should pay what the item is worth to you, emotionally as well as monetarily. For example, the seller may ask you what you are prepared to pay, and you give as low a bid as you can in good conscience. The merchant will indicate that he can't afford to sell you the item for that figure, and then mention a price much higher than yours. You compromise and the merchant compromises until you reach a happy medium and are both satisfied — although both of you may try not to show it.

In department stores, however, prices are generally fixed, and one is not expected to bargain.

Si Farid habite à Constantine, en Algérie.

parlons de la scène	Make a statement or ask a question about each of the drawings below as it relates to the *scène*.

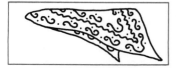

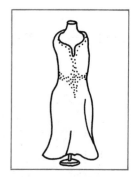

à vous, maintenant	Pay a compliment to a classmate. Your classmate should choose an appropriate response.

Ta robe [verte] va très bien avec tes yeux.
Ton pull-over [rouge] est très beau.
Tes yeux [bruns] sont très jolis.

Vraiment?
Tu trouves?
Tu es gentil(le).
Oh, le flatteur! / la flatteuse!

petite scène	Act out the following scene, which takes place in a clothing store. Then vary the scene, making as many logical changes as you can.

CLIENT(E)	Je cherche un tee-shirt.
EMPLOYÉ(E)	C'est pour vous?
CLIENT(E)	Non, c'est pour mon frère.
EMPLOYÉ(E)	De quelle couleur?
CLIENT(E)	Rouge, s'il vous plaît.
EMPLOYÉ(E)	Voilà un joli tee-shirt rouge.
CLIENT(E)	Il coûte combien?
EMPLOYÉ(E)	Huit dollars. C'est bon marché!
CLIENT(E)	Oui, c'est bon marché. Je le prends.

À la française

French people do not pay compliments very easily. One has to feel strongly about something to compliment another person. In response to a compliment, one may ask: **Vraiment? Tu trouves?** (Do you really think so?) Sometimes, the person complimented endorses the other person's judgment: **Oui, je l'aime bien.** Or he/she may return another compliment: **[Ta robe] aussi est jolie.**

Étude de mots

Les vêtements

1 la jupe
2 le chemisier
3 le pull-over
4 les bottes (f. pl.)
5 le jean
6 la chemise
7 le blouson
8 les tennis (m. pl.)

1 la robe
2 le manteau
3 le collant
4 les chaussures (f. pl.)
5 le foulard
6 le parapluie
7 le pantalon
8 la ceinture
9 les chaussettes (f. pl.)
10 l'imperméable (m.)

1 les lunettes de soleil (f. pl.)
2 le chapeau
3 le tee-shirt
4 le maillot de bain
5 les sandales (f. pl.)

A Ask somebody to tell you who in the class is wearing each of the following items. (**porter** = to wear)

  ▣ⅲ un pull-over   — *Qui porte un pull-over?*
                          — *[Marie] porte un pull-over.*

  1. une jupe   4. un foulard   7. des chaussures
  2. un tee-shirt   5. une chemise   8. un jean
  3. des tennis   6. des bottes   9. un pantalon

B Comment on the price of each item. Use *c'est cher* or *c'est bon marché*.

  ▣ⅲ une robe: $20   *Une robe à vingt dollars! C'est bon marché.*

  1. un chapeau: $50   4. un imperméable: $35
  2. des bottes: $12   5. un collant: $5
  3. un pull-over: $100   6. un blouson: $70

C   Say what articles of clothing you consider appropriate under the following circumstances.

> ■III   quand vous allez au cinéma

Quand je vais au cinéma, je porte un jean...,

1. quand il pleut
2. à l'école
3. à la mer
4. à une réunion de famille

à vous, maintenant

1. What articles of clothing are you wearing today?

   Je porte une chemise, un pantalon...

2. What clothes are you going to buy before next summer?

   Je vais acheter un maillot de bain, des sandales...

Les couleurs

blanc, blanche white	**jaune** yellow	**rose** pink
bleu(e) blue	**marron** red-brown	**rouge** red
brun(e) brown	**noir(e)** black	**vert(e)** green
gris(e) gray	**orange** orange	**violet(te)** purple

Most adjectives of color, like other descriptive adjectives, agree in gender and in number with the noun they modify. The adjectives **marron** and **orange** are exceptions; they do not change form, whether they describe a masculine, feminine, singular, or plural noun.

> un pull-over **marron**   une jupe **orange**
> une robe **marron**   des chaussettes **orange**

D   Describe the color or colors of the following things.

> ■III   une orange   *Elle est orange.*

1. la mer
2. le tableau de la salle de classe
3. votre livre de français
4. une langouste
5. une banane
6. une feuille de papier
7. une rose
8. vos yeux

E   The class is divided into two teams. A name card for each student is prepared in advance. A member of the first team stands at the front of the room, facing away from the class. A name card is chosen at random. Without turning around, the student at the front of the room must describe an item of clothing worn by the person whose name is on the card. (For example, *Georges porte des chaussures jaunes.*) A correct response earns a point for the team.

à vous,
maintenant

1. Où est-ce que vous achetez vos vêtements?
2. Quelle couleur est-ce que vous préférez pour vos vêtements? pour une maison? pour une voiture?
3. Où est-ce que vous portez un maillot de bain?
4. De quelle couleur est votre chemise ou votre chemisier?
5. Est-ce que vous avez des chaussures marron?
6. Quand il pleut, est-ce que vous portez un chapeau? un imperméable?
7. Est-ce que vous avez un parapluie? Il est de quelle couleur?

Échanges de mots

The French names for many articles of clothing, such as **le tee-shirt** and **le jean,** are taken directly from English. French people facetiously describe these "borrowed" words as **franglais.** Other clothing-related examples of **franglais** are **le short, le smoking** (tuxedo), **le pull-over,** and **le cardigan.**

The linguistic exchange works both ways, as English has borrowed many words from French — including such clothing words as **négligé** and **lingerie.** And the word for the material used to make jeans, denim, comes from the name of the French city of Nîmes, where it was first made. The French called the fabric **serge de Nîmes.**

Prononciation et orthographe

/o/	jaune
/ɔ/	la robe
/ɔ̃/	bon

/o/

When you say /o/, your lips should be rounded and close together.

RÉPÉTEZ

jaune	beau	nos	trop
les chaussettes	le chapeau	le métro	l'hôtel

The sound /o/ has many different spellings, including **au, eau, o,** and **ô.**

LISEZ

1. Le chapeau jaune est beau.
2. L'hôtel est à gauche du métro.

/ɔ/

When you say /ɔ/, your lips should be wider apart than for /o/.

RÉPÉTEZ

la robe	joli	notre	la porte
la botte	orange	Simone	l'hôpital

The sound /ɔ/ is spelled **o** or **ô.**

LISEZ

1. Votre robe est jolie.
2. Simone porte des bottes à l'école.

/ɔ̃/

The sound /ɔ̃/ is a nasal vowel. No /n/ is heard.

RÉPÉTEZ

bon	le pantalon	la maison	l'oncle
mon	marron	le pont	je compte

The sound /ɔ̃/ is spelled **on** or **om.**

LISEZ

1. Allons bon! Où est mon pantalon marron?
2. La maison de notre oncle est près du pont.

Les bons comptes font les bons amis.

Les voiles et les voilettes

It's almost one o'clock. Before closing the store for lunch, Si's father has ordered hot mint tea at a café nearby. A waiter brings the tea to the store. Si and his father drink their tea as they get an order ready.

LE GARÇON	Voilà deux thés, Monsieur Farid. Je les pose sur la table?
M. FARID	Oui, merci, Ahmed. C'est combien?
LE GARÇON	Cinq dinars.
M. FARID	Voilà! Au revoir, Ahmed. Alors, Si, à ta santé!
SI	Merci, Papa. Je ferme le magasin maintenant?
M. FARID	Oui, d'accord. Mais avant d'aller déjeuner, je voudrais préparer la commande des Ben Kim.
SI	Les robes de mariage, c'est pour eux?
M. FARID	Oui, six robes blanches et des voiles et des voilettes assortis.
SI	Bon. Je range les six robes dans le carton. Où sont les voiles?
M. FARID	Tiens, les voilà. Maintenant, compte six voilettes. Elles sont là sur le rayon.
SI	Il y a cinq voilettes seulement.
M. FARID	Allons bon! Regarde dans le tiroir de la table.
SI	Oui, voilà une voilette blanche comme les autres.
M. FARID	Range-la avec le reste et rentrons à la maison. Tu as faim?
SI	Oui, Papa, j'ai toujours faim pour le couscous.

questions

1. Qu'est-ce que le garçon de café pose sur la table?
2. Pourquoi est-ce que Si et son père ferment le magasin?
3. Qu'est-ce qu'il y a dans la commande des Ben Kim?
4. Où sont les voilettes? Est-ce qu'elles sont assorties?
5. Où est-ce que Si range la commande?
6. Qu'est-ce qu'il y a pour le déjeuner chez les Farid?
7. Est-ce que Si aime le couscous?

parlons de la scène

In the *scène*, a few questions are asked and a few commands are given. See if you can recall the question or command that leads to each of the following replies.

1. Oui, merci, Ahmed.
2. Oui, d'accord. Mais avant d'aller déjeuner, je voudrais préparer la commande des Ben Kim.
3. Oui, six robes blanches, et des voiles et des voilettes assortis.
4. Il y a cinq voilettes seulement.
5. Voilà une voilette blanche comme les autres.
6. Oui, Papa, j'ai toujours faim pour le couscous.

à vous,
maintenant

1. Order one or more of your classmates to do something.

> Regarde le tableau!
> Ferme la porte!
> Rangez vos livres!
> Cherchez vos devoirs!

2. Suggest something for you and a classmate to do.

> Achetons un bateau!
> Rentrons chez nous!
> Allons au cinéma!

Le couscous et le thé à la menthe

Couscous is a favorite dish in Algeria. It is served at lunch time as the main meal of the day. It is often served on Friday, a Moslem holy day. **Couscous** is made of semolina, or coarse wheat, which is steamed in a fine sieve over boiling vegetables like carrots, onions, red pimentos, and chick peas. Served with boiled chicken and lamb, it makes a hearty and healthy dish.

Thé à la menthe is tea brewed in a teapot and served steaming hot over mint leaves in a glass. It is very refreshing, especially in temperatures that reach thirty-five degrees Celsius. Algerian men often sip it at cafés, where Moslem tradition forbids the serving of alcoholic beverages.

La préparation du couscous

Grammaire

Position of adjectives

1. In noun phrases, many French adjectives (including adjectives of color and of nationality) follow the noun.

    un foulard **bleu**   des vêtements **algériens**
    des yeux **verts**   un chapeau **français**

2. Certain other adjectives, including the ones in the following phrases, usually precede the noun.

    un **grand** hôtel   une **petite** famille   un **joli** bateau

A   Respond in the affirmative or negative, as indicated.

▪ⅲ   L'appartement est petit? (oui)   *Oui, c'est un petit apparte-*
                                         ment.

1. Le vélo est jaune? (oui)
2. Le magasin est grand? (non)
3. La maison est jolie? (oui)
4. Le carton est marron? (non)
5. Le bateau est blanc? (oui)
6. La ville est petite? (non)
7. Le parc est joli? (oui)
8. L'église est grande? (non)

B   Combine each of the following pairs of sentences into one descriptive sentence.

▪ⅲ   C'est un garçon. Il est   *C'est un garçon intelligent.*
     intelligent.

1. J'ai des devoirs. Ils sont barbants.
2. On a des cousines. Elles sont égoïstes.
3. Nous avons une voiture. Elle est petite.
4. Il a une maison. Elle est jolie.
5. Marie a une robe. Elle est rouge.
6. Voilà des hommes. Ils sont généreux.
7. Elles invitent des amis. Ils sont algériens.
8. C'est un magasin. Il est grand.

à vous,
maintenant

Look around your classroom and describe as many people and things as you can, using a variety of adjectives.

Il y a un professeur formidable...

Commands

	FAMILIAR (tu-form)	FORMAL/PLURAL (vous-form)	SUGGESTION (nous-form)
compter	Compte les robes.	Comptez les robes.	Comptons les robes.
entrer	Entre!	Entrez!	Entrons!
aller	Va au café.	Allez au café.	Allons au café.

1. Subject pronouns are not used with the command forms.
2. Commands are derived from the **tu-, vous-,** and **nous-**forms of the present tense. However, the final **-s** is dropped from the **tu-**form of all **-er** verbs and **aller.**
3. A command, or suggestion, derived from the **nous-**form of the present tense is equivalent to the English *Let's....*

    Allons au cinéma.   Let's go to the movies.
    Jouons au tennis.   Let's play tennis.

4. Negative commands are formed according to the pattern: **ne +** verb **+ pas.**

    N'achète pas de sandales.   Don't buy (any) sandals.
    Ne fermez pas la porte.   Don't close the door.

C You are in charge of straightening up your classroom. Order a classmate and then your teacher to do the following things.

 ◼⫼ regarder dans le tiroir   *Regarde dans le tiroir!*
                                     Regardez dans le tiroir!

1. poser les cahiers là-bas
2. compter les stylos
3. ranger les livres sur le rayon
4. fermer les fenêtres

D Tell the following people *not* to perform the actions indicated.

 ◼⫼ Paul: jouer en classe   *Ne joue pas en classe.*

1. M. Farid: fermer le magasin
2. votre cousin: demander le chemin
3. Mme Farid: arriver en retard
4. votre copain: aller à la piscine
5. votre ami: commander deux thés
6. la cliente: acheter la ceinture noire
7. votre mère: entrer dans votre chambre

E Suggest the following activities to a friend. Your friend disagrees with all of your suggestions.

> ▪▥ aller au parc — *Allons au parc.*
> — *Oh non! N'allons pas au parc.*

1. inviter Marie au cinéma
2. acheter un cadeau pour le professeur
3. parler anglais
4. demander le chemin à un passant
5. entrer dans le magasin
6. aller au restaurant

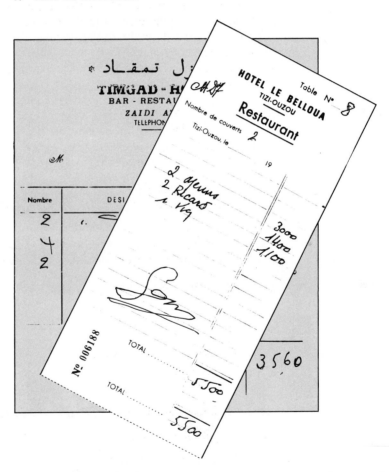

à vous, maintenant

Tell a friend to do or not to do three different activities. Choose verbs from the following list.

aller	fermer	poser
compter	montrer	ranger
entrer	parler	regarder

Les vêtements
à la mode algérienne

L'Algérie, like many Arabic countries, is changing to adapt to modern times. Clothing, for example, is a visible sign of change, especially in the cities. People are likely to wear European-style clothes in cosmopolitan **Alger,** the capital; but in Constantine, which is more conservative, most people dress in the Arabic fashion.

The traditional outfit for an Arab woman is an ankle-length dress with long sleeves, a veil **(le voile),** and a kind of handkerchief **(la voilette)** over the nose and mouth. While Arab women in Algiers generally wear white, in Constantine they usually wear black dresses and veils with white lace handkerchiefs. Women are distinguished in wealth or rank by the number of silver bracelets and rings that they wear.

The tradition of women wearing veils came from an ancient Mediterranean custom that was adopted and reinforced by the Islamic religion. According to custom, a father may decide that his daughter should be veiled at the traditional age of sixteen. Later, her husband may insist that she continue to wear the veil, or — if he has modern ideas — he may allow her to wear European-style clothes.

Men generally wear a lightweight, simply cut garment, like a **djellaba** (a knee-length loose garment with long sleeves). Many men wear a turban or skullcap, and slippers called **babouches.** In colder weather, they put on a **burnous** (a sleeveless coat with a hood). Boys are more likely to wear short pants, a shirt, and sandals.

Femmes algériennes, en voiles et voilettes blancs, en train de voter

Plural emphatic pronouns

nous	we, us	Pierre et **nous**, nous allons à Alger.
vous	you	Votre grand-mère habite chez **vous**?
eux	they, them (*m.*)	**Eux**, ils aiment marchander.
elles	they, them (*f.*)	Ils parlent anglais. Et **elles**?

The uses of the plural emphatic pronouns are the same as for the singular emphatic pronouns:

1. To give emphasis to the subject of a sentence.
   Eux, ils sont canadiens.
   Lui, il va à Montréal.

2. In compound subjects.
   Paul et nous, nous sommes américains.
   Anne et lui sont lycéens.

3. After prepositions.
   Elles vous invitent chez **elles.**
   Voilà un cadeau pour **vous.**

4. After **c'est** to express identity.
   — C'est **vous?** — Oui, c'est **nous.**

5. In phrases without a verb.
   Nous allons au cinéma. Et **eux?**

F   Say that the following people like *couscous.*

   ■||| Jacques   *Lui, il aime le couscous.*

1. nous   3. vous
2. Marc et Hélène   4. Anne et Marie

G   Complete each of the following sentences with the emphatic pronoun that corresponds to the subject.

   ■||| Les filles sont chez ____.   *Les filles sont chez elles.*

1. Nous allons chez ____ maintenant.
2. Les Farid vont chez ____ plus tard.
3. Martine et Jeanne ne sont pas chez ____.
4. Les copains vont chez ____ après le cinéma.
5. Vous étudiez toujours chez ____?
6. Marie et Paul arrivent chez ____.

Stem-changing verbs

acheter to buy	
j'achète	nous achetons
tu achètes	vous achetez
on/il/elle achète	ils/elles achètent

préférer to prefer	
je préfère	nous préférons
tu préfères	vous préférez
on/il/elle préfère	ils/elles préfèrent

Acheter, préférer, and certain other **-er** verbs undergo a stem change in present-tense forms that have silent endings: the vowels **e** and **é** in the last syllable of the stem both change to **è**. This change occurs in the **je-, tu-,** and **il(s)/elle(s)-**forms. The endings, however, are regular.

H   Say that the following people are buying clothes.

■▥   lui   *Il achète des vêtements.*

1. nous 3. on   5. elle   7. eux
2. toi   4. moi 6. vous 8. le client

I   The following people have a choice between European clothing and Algerian clothing. State which type of clothing they are likely to prefer.

■▥   Si   *Il préfère des vêtements algériens.*

1. les cousins de Si   3. Mme Farid   5. Pierre Legrand
2. nous   4. vous   6. toi

à vous, maintenant

1. List some of the things that you and members of your family buy every year.

   Mon père achète... Ma sœur et moi, nous achetons...

2. State your preferences regarding colors. Guess at the preferences of some of your friends also, based on what you know or are able to observe about them.

   Moi, je préfère... Dominique et Sylvie, vous préférez...

À l'algérienne

In Algeria and other Arab countries, the following greeting is exchanged when two friends meet: first, both people lightly touch the fingertips of their right hands together. Then each person touches her/his chest, lips, and forehead with the right hand, while saying in Arabic: "May your thoughts be in my heart, on my lips, and in my mind."

Direct-object pronouns le, la, les

Je prends **le foulard**.	Je **le** prends.
Je cherche **ma sœur**.	Je **la** cherche.
Julie n'aime pas **son oncle**.	Julie ne **l'**aime pas.
Vous n'achetez pas **la robe**?	Vous ne **l'**achetez pas?
Il va ranger **les vêtements**.	Il va **les** ranger.
Range **les vêtements**.	Range-**les**.
Ne ferme pas **la fenêtre**.	Ne **la** ferme pas.

1. The direct-object pronouns **le, la, les** refer to both things and people.
2. **Le** and **la** become **l'** before a vowel sound.
3. Object pronouns precede the verb in affirmative and negative sentences. In constructions with **aller** + infinitive, the object pronouns precede the infinitive.
4. In affirmative commands, object pronouns follow the verb. In writing, a hyphen joins the verb and the object pronoun.
5. In negative commands, object pronouns precede the verb. No hyphen is used.

J   Restate each sentence below, replacing the phrase in italics with a direct-object pronoun.

     ■॥॥   Elle achète *les bottes canadiennes*.   *Elle les achète.*

1. Tu aimes *les jeans?*
2. Ils préfèrent *les chaussettes noires.*
3. Achetez *les sandales blanches!*
4. Ne montrez pas *le foulard* à la cliente.
5. Elle prend *la robe rouge.*
6. Nous allons acheter *les chaussures marron.*
7. Je n'aime pas *la ceinture noire.*
8. Ne regarde pas *le maillot de bain.*

K   Answer each of the following questions first in the affirmative, then in the negative. Use direct-object pronouns in your responses.

     ■॥॥   Il achète l'imperméable?   *Oui, il l'achète.*
                                              Non, il ne l'achète pas.

1. Tu aimes les sandales?
2. Brigitte et toi, vous cherchez le carton de chaussettes?
3. Nicole porte la jupe verte?
4. Ils vont regarder les chemises?
5. Vous achetez le parapluie, monsieur?
6. Tu préfères le pantalon bleu?
7. Il achète la robe pour sa fille?

Expressing purpose with **pour**

The preposition **pour,** when followed by a noun or pronoun, means *for.*

C'est vraiment bon marché **pour** de la soie.	It's really a good price for silk.

To express the purpose of a thing or an action, **pour** may be used with a verb infinitive.

Je cherche un foulard **pour aller** avec ma robe verte.	I'm looking for a scarf to go with my green dress.
Sylvie va au magasin **pour acheter** un pull-over.	Sylvie is going to the store to buy a sweater.

L   You are downtown with a friend. Suggest to your friend that the two of you go home to do the following things.

◼▥ préparer le dîner   *Rentrons pour préparer le dîner.*

1. téléphoner à Bernadette
2. regarder la télévision
3. faire les devoirs d'anglais
4. écouter la radio
5. déjeuner
6. étudier la leçon d'histoire

M   Explain what the following people are shopping for.

◼▥ Lise a une robe verte.   *Elle cherche un foulard pour*
Elle cherche un foulard.   *aller avec sa robe verte.*

1. Alain a des chaussures marron. Il cherche des chaussettes.
2. Michèle a une jupe noire et blanche. Elle cherche un chemisier.
3. M. Couret a un pantalon bleu. Il cherche une ceinture.
4. Mme Ménard a un imperméable gris. Elle cherche un parapluie.
5. Roger a une chemise rouge. Il cherche un pull-over.

N   You are jealous of friends who are traveling. Express your wish that you could go and do the things they are doing.

◼▥ Jean-Paul visite des   *Moi aussi, je voudrais aller*
musées à Rennes.   *à Rennes pour visiter*
des musées.

1. Chantal étudie la littérature allemande à Bonn.
2. Jacques fait de la voile à Concarneau.
3. Isabelle achète des vêtements à Londres (London).
4. Marianne joue au base-ball aux États-Unis.
5. André visite des monuments à Paris.

à vous, maintenant

State the purpose of a trip you intend to take somewhere, whether to a place in your home town or to any place in the world.

L'Algérie

The first known inhabitants of North Africa were the Berbers, who still form the principal ethnic group in Algeria. During the first five centuries A.D., the coast of North Africa was part of the Roman Empire. (The city of Constantine owes its name to the emperor Constantine.) Arabs invaded the country in the seventh century and introduced the Moslem religion, which was adopted by the Berbers. Today, Arabs and Berbers make up the majority of Algeria's population. Many Arabs are merchants or nomadic shepherds, while many Berbers are farmers.

France conquered Algeria in the nineteenth century, and French became the language of business and education. But Algerians were discontented with their colonial status. A bloody eight-year war with France ended in 1962, when the French government under President Charles de Gaulle granted independence to Algeria. This action triggered angry and sometimes violent protests by some French citizens who felt that de Gaulle had betrayed **l'Algérie française.** Algeria, as an independent republic, still maintains close ties with France.

Lecture

Si Farid et son père

Si est un jeune Algérien de quinze ans. Il habite avec ses parents à Constantine. Son père a un petit magasin de vêtements. Quand Si ne va pas à l'école, il aide son père au magasin.

Aujourd'hui, Si montre des foulards à une cliente algérienne. La cliente
5 n'aime pas le rouge, mais elle aime beaucoup un foulard en soie bleue.
Comme° elle le trouve cher, elle marchande avec Si. Finalement,° elle
l'achète pour cent vingt-cinq dinars.

M. Farid et son fils ferment le magasin vers une heure° pour préparer
une commande. Pour se rafraîchir,° ils boivent° du thé à la menthe.
10 Ensuite,° ils rangent des robes, des voiles et des voilettes dans un carton
pour des clients de Djemila. Ce° petit village près de ruines romaines
importantes n'est pas très loin de Constantine.

Après ça, Si et son père ont faim. C'est vendredi, et le couscous tra-
ditionnel les attend° à la maison. Les deux hommes rentrent chez eux pour
15 déjeuner. Plus tard,° ils vont faire la sieste avant de retourner au magasin
à cinq heures.°

As/Finally

around one o'clock
For refreshment/drink
Then
This

waits for
Later
five o'clock

1. Dans quel magasin sont les Farid?
2. Qui marchande au magasin?
3. Qu'est-ce que Si compte?
4. C'est pour qui, les vêtements dans le carton?

à vous,
maintenant

1. Est-ce que vous avez faim maintenant? Est-ce que vous avez toujours faim?
2. Est-ce que vous aimez le thé? la menthe? le couscous?
3. Est-ce que vous rentrez à la maison pour déjeuner?
4. Est-ce que vous aidez souvent votre mère? votre père?

résumés
oraux

1. Prepare a brief biography of Si Farid. Include information about how old he is, where he goes to school, and what he does to help his father.
2. Tell which types of European and Arabic clothing there are at M. Farid's store.

résumé
écrit

Write a summary of Si's story by answering the following questions based on the *scènes* and the *lecture*.

1. Qui montre des foulards? À qui?
2. Qu'est-ce que la cliente achète?
3. Qu'est-ce que le père et le fils préparent?
4. Quand est-ce qu'ils préparent la commande?
5. Où est-ce qu'ils vont rentrer?
6. Pourquoi est-ce que Si est content de rentrer?

chanson

The following song has to do with one of the themes of Chapter 7. (**Les souliers** is another word for **les chaussures. Ça use les souliers** means "It wears out your shoes.") The song is meant to be sung while walking, and can be carried on for as long as the hikers like, just by adding one verse for each kilometer traveled.

> Un kilomètre à pied,
> Ça use, ça use,
> Un kilomètre à pied,
> Ça use les souliers!

> Un, deux kilomètres à pied,
> Ça use, ça use,
> Deux kilomètres à pied,
> Ça use les souliers!

> Un, deux, trois kilomètres à pied,
> Ça use, ça use,
> Trois kilomètres à pied,
> Ça use les souliers!

Résumé grammatical

Position of adjectives (A-B)

Many descriptive adjectives in French follow the noun. Some descriptive adjectives, including **grand, petit,** and **joli,** usually precede the noun.

un homme **sympathique**	un **grand** salon
une femme **intelligente**	une **petite** chambre
des garçons **sociables**	deux **jolies** pièces

Commands (C-E)

The command forms of most verbs are derived from the present tense. (For **-er** verbs and **aller,** the **-s** is dropped from the **tu-**form.) Subject pronouns are not used with commands.

Parle français!	*Speak* French!
Entrez, s'il vous plaît.	*Come in,* please.
N'allons pas à l'école.	*Let's not go* to school.

Emphatic pronouns: all forms (F-G)

SINGULAR	PLURAL
moi	nous
toi	vous
lui	eux
elle	elles

Four of the emphatic pronouns are identical to the corresponding subject pronouns: **elle, elles, nous,** and **vous.** Four are different: **moi, toi, lui,** and **eux.**

Emphatic pronouns are used:

1. To give emphasis to the subject of a sentence.
   Nous, nous allons à la piscine.

2. In compound subjects.
   Josette et **eux** sont lycéens.

3. After prepositions.
   Voilà des cadeaux pour **elles.**

4. After **c'est** or **ce sont** to express identity.

   Ce sont les élèves? Non, ce ne sont pas **eux.**

5. In phrases without a verb.

   Ils vont ranger leurs vêtements. Et **elles?**

Stem-changing **-er** verbs (H-I)

The following charts show the present-tense forms of **acheter** and **préférer.**
Note the stem vowel changes in the singular and in the third-person plural.

acheter to buy	
j'achète	nous achetons
tu achètes	vous achetez
on/il/elle achète	ils/elles achètent

préférer to prefer	
je préfère	nous préférons
tu préfères	vous préférez
on/il/elle préfère	ils/elles préfèrent

Direct-object pronouns **le, la, les** (J-K)

The direct-object pronouns **le, la, les** refer to either people or things.
Object pronouns immediately precede the verb in all constructions except
for affirmative commands. Before a vowel, **le** and **la** become **l'.**

Je regarde **le tableau.**	Je **le** regarde.
Elle n'aime pas **la robe.**	Elle ne **l'**aime pas.
Tu as **les voilettes?**	Tu **les** as?
On va chercher **la voiture.**	On va **la** chercher.

Note the word order of an affirmative command: a hyphen links the verb
and the object pronoun.

Fermez **vos livres.**   Fermez-**les.**

In a negative command, the object pronoun precedes the verb. No hyphen
is used.

Ne fermons pas **la fenêtre.**   Ne **la** fermons pas.

Expressing purpose with **pour** (L-N)

The purpose of an action or a thing may be expressed by using **pour** (in
order to) followed by an infinitive.

Je vais à Boston **pour** **étudier** l'anglais.	I'm going to Boston in order to study English.

Révision

A Express surprise to a friend who is buying the items mentioned. Then express your own preference.

> ▄▍▍ le pantalon jaune/rose   *Tu achètes le pantalon jaune?*
> *Moi, je préfère le rose.*

1. le pull-over rouge/noir
2. les chaussures blanches/marron
3. le manteau bleu/gris
4. la chemise verte/bleue
5. la jupe orange/blanche
6. le chapeau vert/violet

B Call a friend's attention to the following items on display in a shop window.

> ▄▍▍ *Regarde les chaussures!*
> ▄▍▍ *Regarde la robe!*

C Suggest that the following people do the things indicated.

> ▄▍▍ vous et vos cousins: aller   *Allons au cinéma.*
> au cinéma

1. un copain: acheter un vélo
2. vous et vos amis: aller au parc
3. les élèves: arriver à l'heure
4. Étienne et Guy: étudier l'histoire algérienne
5. vous et votre frère: tourner à gauche
6. Geneviève: inviter le professeur

D   Express your opinion of the following things, using object pronouns.

    ■III   votre école   *Je la trouve formidable.*

1. votre maison ou appartement
2. votre salle de classe
3. les vêtements de vos parents

4. votre ville
5. votre livre de français
6. vos devoirs

E   Describe the cars at an automobile show. Place the adjective before or after the noun, as required.

    ■III   beau   *Voilà une belle voiture.*
    ■III   américain   *Voilà une voiture américaine.*

1. petit
2. bleu
3. blanc

4. français
5. vert
6. joli

F   Say with whom you are going to have lunch. Use emphatic pronouns in your responses.

    ■III   les amis   *Je vais déjeuner avec eux.*

1. Monique et Marie
2. Philippe et Janine
3. Charles

4. Henri
5. Michèle
6. François et Jacques

G   Discuss some of the ways in which Algerian culture differs from your own culture and that of France. You may wish to talk about food, clothing, religion, and the status of women.

H   Locate the places mentioned in this chapter on the map below. Figure approximate distances from place to place, using the scale.

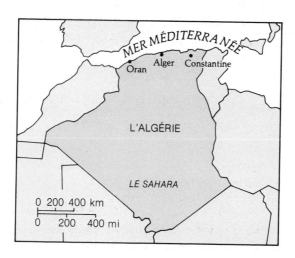

Vocabulaire

NOUNS

le blouson windbreaker
les bottes (*f. pl.*) boots
le carton box
la ceinture belt
le chapeau hat
les chaussettes (*f. pl.*) socks
les chaussures (*f. pl.*) shoes
la chemise shirt
le chemisier woman's shirt
le collant pantyhose
la commande order
la couleur color
le flatteur, la flatteuse flatterer
le foulard scarf
le jean jeans
l'imperméable (*m.*) raincoat
les lunettes de soleil (*f. pl.*) sunglasses
le maillot de bain swimming suit
le manteau coat
le mariage marriage
le pantalon pants
le parapluie umbrella
le pull-over sweater
le rayon shelf
le reste rest
la robe dress
les sandales (*f. pl.*) sandals
la soie silk
le thé tea
le tee-shirt T-shirt
les tennis (*m. pl.*) sneakers
le tiroir drawer
les vêtements (*m. pl.*) clothes
le voile veil
la voilette veil that covers face
les yeux (*m. pl.*) eyes

ADJECTIVES

assorti(e) matching
autre other
blanc, blanche white
bleu(e) blue
bon marché cheap, inexpensive
brun(e) brown
cher, chère expensive
gris(e) gray
jaune yellow
marron reddish brown
noir(e) black
orange orange
rose pink
rouge red
superbe superb
vert(e) green
violet(te) purple

PRONOUNS

la, le her, him, it; **les** them (*direct object*)
nous, vous, eux, elles us, you, them (*emphatic*)

PREPOSITIONS

avant de (+ *inf.*) before (*...ing*)
comme like

ADVERBS

seulement only
toujours always
vraiment really

VERBS

acheter to buy
chercher to look (for)
compter to count
coûter to cost
désirer to want
fermer to close
montrer to show
porter to wear
poser to put
préférer to prefer
préparer to prepare
ranger to put away; to straighten
regarder to look (at)
rentrer to go back, go home

OTHER WORDS AND EXPRESSIONS

je voudrais I would like
allons bon! oh no!
je le/la prends I'll take it
tu trouves? do you think so?
à ta santé! to your health!
avoir faim to be hungry
par ici this way

chapitre 8

La vie de château

The gently rolling countryside of the Loire River Valley is the site of some of the world's most magnificent castles. Although many are now government-owned, some are privately owned and are still inhabited. The château de Beauregard is the home of the family of Ivana du Pavillon. The du Pavillons keep part of their castle open to the public as a museum, where Ivana conducts tours during the summer.

CHATEAU
DE
CHENONCEAU
Propriété Privée

Entrée pour
1 personne
Prix : 8 F
510177

161

Une visite de musée

Château de Beauregard — *Cellettes (Loire-et-Cher)*
Château Renaissance construit aux 16ème et 17ème siècles. Monument historique: propriété privée; musée ouvert tous les jours de 9 h 30 à midi et de 2 h à 5 h. *Entrée: 8 francs.* Toit en ardoise grise et hautes cheminées typiques de la région; murs en belles pierres. Dans la galerie des portraits, trois siècles d'histoire: rois et reines de France, princes et princesses, et hommes célèbres de chaque époque.

---

scène 1

As the museum opens, Ivana du Pavillon greets a group of visitors who are waiting to begin their tour.

IVANA Mesdames et messieurs, il est neuf heures et demie. La visite va commencer. Au rez-de-chaussée, nous avons deux pièces, la salle d'entrée et la cuisine. Mais nous allons commencer par le premier étage. Entrez et tournez à gauche vers l'escalier. Au passage, admirez la belle horloge hollandaise...

5

UNE VISITEUSE L'horloge est de quelle époque, mademoiselle?

IVANA Du dix-huitième siècle, madame. Montez par ici... Faites attention à la marche!

(Quelques minutes plus tard, au premier étage)

IVANA Nous sommes maintenant dans la galerie des portraits. Il y a ici trois cent soixante trois portraits. Regardez aussi le beau plafond en bois peint. Le sol en carreaux bleus est unique en France. Il représente une armée en marche.

10

LA VISITEUSE Sur les murs, est-ce qu'il y a des portraits de vos ancêtres, mademoiselle?

IVANA Oui, madame, mais ce sont des ancêtres éloignés. Dans le salon bleu chez nous, nous avons un portrait du chevalier du Pavillon. Il est mort pendant la guerre d'indépendance des États-Unis. Ça, c'est plus récent!

15

vrai ou faux?

Decide whether the following statements are true or false. If a statement is true, say *C'est vrai.* If a statement is false, say *C'est faux,* and correct it.

1. Il y a une cuisine au rez-de-chaussée du musée.
2. La visite du musée commence à neuf heures.
3. L'horloge est du dix-septième siècle.
4. La galerie des portraits est au premier.
5. Le plafond de la galerie des portraits est en bois.
6. Le sol représente des rois et des reines de France.
7. Un des ancêtres d'Ivana est mort aux États-Unis.

<table>
<tr><td>parlons de
la scène</td><td>Use the pairs of words given below to form sentences that relate to scène 1.</td></tr>
</table>

parlons de la scène

Use the pairs of words given below to form sentences that relate to *scène 1*.

1. pièces / rez-de-chaussée
2. horloge / siècle
3. attention / marche
4. portraits / murs
5. sol / armée
6. tourner / escalier

à vous, maintenant

1. Combien d'étages a votre école? votre maison?
2. En quoi est votre maison? En bois? En briques? En pierres?
3. À quel étage est votre chambre?
4. De quelle(s) couleur(s) sont les murs de votre chambre? de votre salle de séjour?
5. Préférez-vous habiter dans un château Renaissance ou dans une maison moderne?

petite scène

Act out the following scene, in which a new classmate has come to your house to do homework. You suggest going upstairs to your room.

VOUS	Montons dans ma chambre.
ELLE/LUI	Tu as une chambre à toi? Tu as de la chance!
VOUS	Oui, mais elle est au deuxième. L'escalier est par ici. Fais attention!
ELLE/LUI	Pourquoi?
VOUS	C'est un petit escalier et le plafond n'est pas très haut.

After studying the *étude de mots* section on pages 166–169, see how many variations you can think of for the *petite scène*.

...laissez-vous séduire par le charme de cette demeure encore habitée.

Beauregard

Les châteaux de la Loire

Between the cities of Angers and Orléans, in the lovely region of **la Vallée de la Loire,** French monarchs, aristocrats, and a few financiers built many castles as country retreats. Although the era of fabulously wealthy French royalty and nobility has long since passed, the castles remain, many designated as national historical monuments.

The castles naturally attract many visitors. Some of the privately-owned chateaux may be leased for weddings or other special occasions. A number of private owners open some rooms of their castles as public museums; in return, the French government subsidizes the maintenance of the property.

The **château de Chambord,** originally used as a rendez-vous for hunting parties, was transformed in the 16th century by the king François Premier into the biggest castle of the time: 440 rooms, each one with a fireplace; 13 stairways; and 800 cornices. It is famous for its **grand escalier,** a double spiral staircase that two people can use at the same time without seeing one another.

The **château de Chenonceau** was built in 1513 by a French financier who was then forced to surrender it to François Premier in order to pay debts. Chenonceau, built in the middle of the Cher River, was originally a square castle connected to only one shore by a small drawbridge. Later, a beautiful arched bridge supporting a three-story gallery connected the castle to the other shore.

The **château d'Azay-le-Rideau** was built by another 16th-century financier. This small castle has a grace and elegance attributed to the good taste of the financier's wife. A small pond with water lilies, swans, and goldfish reflects the perfect proportions of the castle and gives a romantic atmosphere to the setting.

Quelques événements historiques

Many key historical events have taken place in the Loire Valley. The château de Langeais, for example, was a medieval castle with a huge dungeon when the English king Richard Cœur de Lion (Richard the Lion-hearted) seized it at the end of the 12th century. By the 15th century the castle, which was remodeled over the years, had acquired the majestic appearance that is preserved today. The marriage of Charles VIII, king of France, and the Duchesse Anne de Bretagne, heir to the Duchy of Brittany, took place at Langeais in 1491. This forced union ended the long-standing independence of Brittany, as it became part of the kingdom of France.

During the Hundred Years' War between France and England (1337–1453), the château de Chinon witnessed the first encounter between Jeanne d'Arc (Joan of Arc) and the dauphin of France, later King Charles VII. According to historical tradition, Jeanne d'Arc heard the voices of saints urging her to come to the aid of the dauphin. Dressed as a man, she made the journey to Chinon and convinced the dauphin to let her go into battle against the English. She led French troops to victory, ending the siege of Orléans in 1429. Jeanne d'Arc was recognized as a saint by the Catholic church in 1920.

Page 164: un escalier du château de Blois. Page 165: le château de Beauregard, et l'armure d'un noble chevalier.

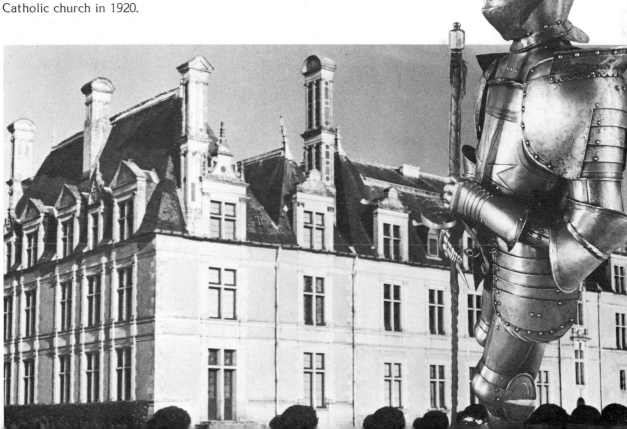

Jouons avec les mots

1. *Position et direction:* You should recognize the words in the left column below from *scène 1*. They are paired with their opposites in the right column. Take a few minutes to learn the meaning of all the words.

haut, haute	bas, basse
en haut	en bas
sur	sous
monter	descendre

A   Look at the following drawings and complete each of the accompanying sentences with an appropriate word or phrase.

1. La chaise de Simone est _____. La chaise de Pierre est _____.

2. Jacques est _____. Michèle est _____.

3. Le garçon est _____ la table. La fille est _____ la table.

4. Hélène va _____ les marches. Robert va _____ les marches.

2. *Les nombres ordinaux:* Ordinal numbers (first, tenth, etc.) in French are formed by adding the ending **-ième** to a cardinal number. The word **premier** is an exception to the pattern.

1	premier, première	6	sixième
2	deuxième	7	septième
3	troisième	8	huitième
4	quatrième	9	neuvième
5	cinquième	10	dixième

Note certain minor spelling changes:

Quatre drops the **e** to form **quatrième.**
Cinq adds **u** to form **cinquième.**
Neuf changes **f** to **v** to form **neuvième.**

B Say where each entrant in the race is probably going to finish, based on the drawing.

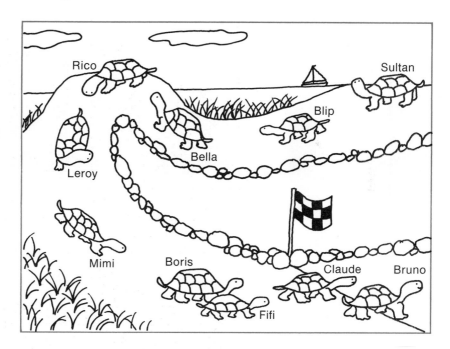

■III   Bruno   *Bruno va arriver premier.*

1. Claude
2. Fifi
3. Boris
4. Mimi
5. Leroy

6. Rico
7. Bella
8. Blip
9. Sultan
10. Bruno

Quelle heure est-il?

Il est une heure.

Il est une heure et demie.

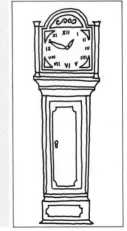
Il est une heure
moins dix.

Il est deux heures.

Il est deux heures
et quart.

Il est quatre heures
moins le quart.

Il est six heures
moins cinq.

Il est midi.

Il est minuit.

— Quelle heure est-il?
— Paul arrive à quelle heure?

— Deux heures et demie du
  matin?

— Il est midi.
— Il arrive à deux heures et
  demie.
— Ah non! De l'après-midi!

C   The times listed below are for New York. Say what time it is in New York
and Paris, remembering that it is six hours later in Paris. Use the expressions *du matin*, *de l'après-midi*, and *du soir*, as appropriate.

▤▥   10:00 A.M.   *Il est dix heures du matin à New York.*
                      À Paris, il est quatre heures de l'après-midi.

1. 7:00 P.M.   3. 4:00 P.M.   5. 2:00 P.M.
2. 1:00 A.M.   4. 11:00 A.M.   6. 8:00 P.M.

D Your watch is running fifteen minutes faster than your friend's. Disagree about the time.

    ■╫   Il est deux heures.   *Non, il est deux heures et quart.*

1. Il est cinq heures vingt.
2. Il est dix heures et quart.
3. Il est six heures moins le quart.
4. Il est midi.
5. Il est trois heures et demie.
6. Il est quatre heures seize.

Le building

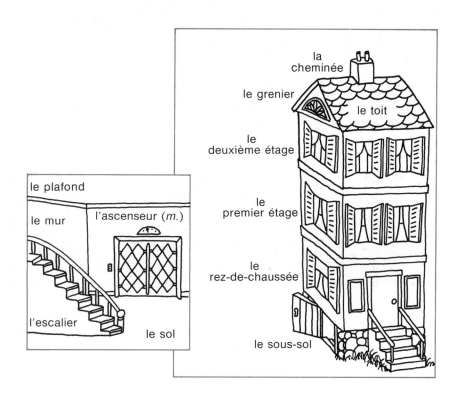

E Make an observation about each of the following parts of your home or school. You may talk about color, construction, contents, appearance — or anything you like.

    ■╫   le sol   *Le sol [est moche].*
    ■╫   l'ascenseur   *[Il n'y a pas d'ascenseur ici!]*

1. les murs	4. l'escalier	7. le plafond
2. le sous-sol	5. le grenier	8. l'ascenseur
3. le toit	6. le rez-de-chaussée	9. le sol

Prononciation et orthographe

/ʃ/	le **ch**âteau
/ʒ/	l'horlo**g**e
/ɛ̃/	le ma**t**in

/ʃ/

The sound /ʃ/ is spelled **ch** in French. Do not include a /t/ sound, as in the English word *chew;* /ʃ/ is similar to the English sound spelled *sh*, as in *shoe.*

RÉPÉTEZ

le **ch**âteau	la **ch**eminée	la mar**ch**e
le **ch**eval	la **ch**ambre	le **ch**evalier
chercher	**Ch**arles	le rez-de-**ch**aussée

LISEZ

1. Je vais acheter une chemise et des chaussettes.
2. Chantal cherche des chaussures blanches.
3. Charles achète un chapeau bon marché.

/ʒ/

The sound /ʒ/ is spelled **j** or **g.** Do not include a /d/ sound, as in the English words *jump* and *gem;* /ʒ/ is similar to the consonant sound in the middle of the English word *measure.*

RÉPÉTEZ

l'horlo**g**e	l'â**g**e	la **j**ournée
l'éta**g**e	au passa**g**e	**j**eudi
gentil	au**j**ourd'hui	le dé**j**euner
généreux	**j**ouer	bon**j**our

LISEZ

1. L'horloge est au premier étage.
2. La jupe jaune de Janine est jolie.
3. Jeudi, je vais chercher Serge à la gare.

La fin justifie les moyens.

/ɛ̃/   The sound /ɛ̃/ is a nasal vowel.

RÉPÉTEZ

le matin	le copain	bien	j'ai faim
le chemin	maintenant	de rien	peint
le magasin	demain	algérien	sympathique

The sound /ɛ̃/ has many spellings, including **-in, -ain, -en, -aim, -ein, -ym.**

LISEZ

1. Demain, j'invite mon copain le marin.
2. Martin est sympathique et sociable.
3. J'ai bien faim le matin.

Ivana a un invité

scène 2

Ivana is having lunch at the chateau with a guest, Philippe Delacroix. She met him in Paris, and he is visiting relatives in Blois.

PHILIPPE   Qu'est-ce que vous faites de beau toute la journée?

IVANA   Eh bien, le matin, je me lève à sept heures. Je fais du cheval jusqu'à huit heures. Ensuite, je m'habille pour la journée. Après le petit déjeuner, je fais le guide jusqu'à midi.

5   PHILIPPE   Et vous continuez les visites l'après-midi?

IVANA   Non, l'après-midi, j'étudie dans la bibliothèque... Quelquefois, je me promène dans le parc avec mes chiens.

PHILIPPE   Qu'est-ce que vous étudiez?

IVANA   Je me prépare à l'examen d'entrée de Sciences-Po. C'est assez dure comme

10   école!

PHILIPPE   Oui, c'est vrai. Vous êtes donc très occupée...

IVANA   Oui, mais pas tout le temps. Je m'amuse bien aussi. Et vous, Philippe, quand est-ce que vous rentrez à Paris?

PHILIPPE   Dans une semaine. Mais j'aimerais bien vous revoir avant mon départ.

15   Est-ce que vous êtes libre mardi soir?

IVANA   Je pense que oui.

PHILIPPE   Alors, je vous emmène dîner à Amboise, d'accord?

IVANA   Avec plaisir!

questions

1. À quelle heure est-ce qu'Ivana fait du cheval?
2. Qu'est-ce qu'elle fait après le petit déjeuner?
3. Quand est-ce qu'elle se promène avec ses chiens?
4. Où est-ce qu'elle étudie l'après-midi?
5. Trouvez-vous l'emploi du temps d'Ivana très occupé? Pourquoi?
6. Qu'est-ce que Philippe et Ivana vont faire mardi soir?

parlons de
la scène

Make statements or ask questions related to *scène 2*, using the drawings below as cues.

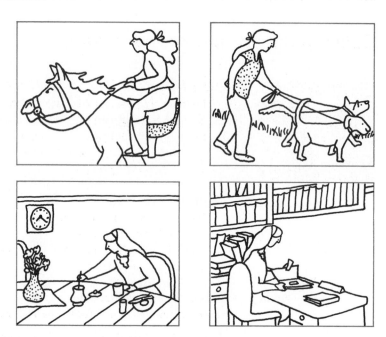

à vous,
maintenant

Give a brief summary of your daily routine, modeling your statements on sentences from *scène 2.* Then answer the following questions about yourself.

1. Est-ce que vous faites du cheval?
2. Est-ce que vous avez un chien?
3. Combien d'heures est-ce que vous étudiez par jour?
4. Quels jours est-ce que vous êtes très occupé(e)? Qu'est-ce que vous faites?
5. Est-ce que vous êtes libre l'après-midi? le soir? Qu'est-ce que vous aimez faire?
6. Quand est-ce que vous vous amusez?

petite scène

Make a date with a friend to go to the movies, as in the following scene.

VOUS	Qu'est-ce que tu vas faire de beau samedi?
VOTRE AMI(E)	Je ne sais pas...
VOUS	Alors, tu es libre? Est-ce que tu aimerais aller au cinéma?
VOTRE AMI(E)	Oui, d'accord. À quelle heure?
VOUS	À huit heures. Ça va?
VOTRE AMI(E)	Oui, ça va. À samedi!

Grammaire

Object pronouns **me, te, nous, vous**

OBJECT PRONOUNS		EXAMPLES	
		Direct object	Indirect object
me (m')	me	Il **me** trouve bête.	Il ne **me** parle pas.
te (t')	you	Elle **te** regarde en classe.	Elle **te** téléphone souvent.
nous	us	Grand-père **nous** aime bien.	Il **nous** achète un cadeau.
vous	you	Je **vous** invite chez moi.	Je voudrais **vous** montrer ma maison.

1. The pronouns **me, te, nous,** and **vous** are used both as direct objects and as indirect objects.
2. The object pronoun precedes the verb in affirmative or negative statements and questions.

A Isabelle has strong opinions of people. Use direct-object pronouns in describing how she feels about the following people.

■▥ (toi) intelligent *Elle te trouve intelligent.*

1. (vous) insupportable
2. (moi) bête
3. (toi) sympathique
4. (nous) égoïstes
5. (moi) formidable
6. (nous) adorables
7. (toi) méchant
8. (vous) timides

B Say that Georges reciprocates the following actions. Use the appropriate indirect-object pronouns.

■▥ Je parle à Georges. *Il me parle aussi.*

1. Nous montrons notre maison à Georges.
2. Tu téléphones souvent à Georges.
3. Vous apportez un cadeau à Georges.
4. Je montre mes devoirs à Georges.

C Try to cheer up Danièle, who is fond of Robert but is convinced that he doesn't care about her. A classmate takes the part of Danièle.

■▥ trouver sympathique — *Il te trouve sympathique!*
— *Non, il ne me trouve pas sympathique.*

1. regarder tout le temps
2. parler beaucoup
3. inviter chez lui
4. montrer ses dessins
5. téléphoner souvent
6. emmener au restaurant

D   Make up a logical answer to each question.

> ▪▥   Qu'est-ce que tu vas   *Je vais te montrer [un beau*
>   me montrer?   *château].*

1. Pourquoi est-ce que Jacques va te téléphoner?
2. Où est-ce que tu emmènes tes copains français ce soir?
3. Pour quand est-ce que les Lebeau vous invitent?
4. Qui va nous montrer les appartements du château?
5. Comment trouves-tu le guide?
6. Qu'est-ce que tu vas m'apporter pour mon anniversaire?

Reflexive constructions

A reflexive construction is one in which the subject and the object of the verb represent the same person. All verbs used reflexively take the object pronouns shown in the following chart of the present-tense forms of **se préparer** (to prepare oneself, to get ready).

SINGULAR	PLURAL
je **me** prépare	nous **nous** préparons
tu **te** prépares	vous **vous** préparez
on/il/elle **se** prépare	ils/elles **se** préparent

1. A reflexive construction in English includes a pronoun ending in *-self* or *-selves.* Some verbs can be used both reflexively and non-reflexively:

   amuser   to amuse   **s'amuser**   to enjoy oneself, to have a good time

   demander   to ask   **se demander**   to ask oneself, to wonder

   excuser   to excuse   **s'excuser**   to excuse oneself

2. Reflexive constructions are very common in French. They are used in many situations where a non-reflexive construction is used in English.

   Je me lève à huit heures.   I get up at eight.
   Janine s'habille.   Janine is getting dressed.
   Ils se promènent.   They are taking a walk.

3. Other reflexive verbs you have seen in this book:

   s'appeler   to be called, to be named
   s'asseoir   to sit down
   se dépêcher   to hurry
   se porter (bien)   to be (well)

E Use the verb *se préparer* to say that the following people are getting ready to carry out their plans.

▪▥ On va visiter les États-Unis. *On se prépare à visiter les États-Unis.*

1. Tu vas faire du camping.
2. Je vais entrer à Sciences-Po.
3. Annick va faire de la voile.
4. Elles vont aller au cinéma.
5. Vous allez jouer.
6. Nous allons faire du sport.

F Use the following cues to form complete sentences.

▪▥ Elle / s'appeler / Maryse   *Elle s'appelle Maryse.*

1. Nous / se dépêcher / pour arriver à l'heure
2. Vous / se lever / à 7 h 30
3. On / s'amuser bien / au musée
4. Les garçons / s'excuser / pour aller regarder les portraits
5. Je / se demander / si c'est une horloge hollandaise

à vous, maintenant

Use each of the following reflexive constructions, first in a statement about yourself, then in a question to a classmate: **s'appeler, se lever, s'habiller, s'amuser, se promener.**

Je m'appelle [Anne]. Et toi, tu t'appelles [Alain], n'est-ce pas?

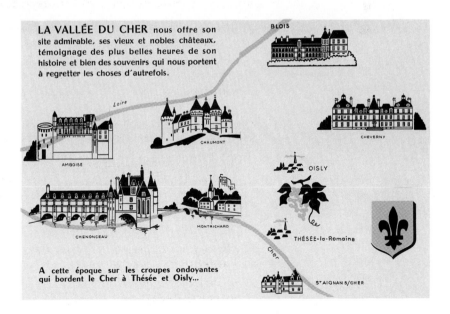

LA VALLÉE DU CHER nous offre son site admirable, ses vieux et nobles châteaux, témoignage des plus belles heures de son histoire et bien des souvenirs qui nous portent à regretter les choses d'autrefois.

BLOIS

Loire

CHAUMONT

CHEVERNY

AMBOISE

OISLY

CHENONCEAU

MONTRICHARD

THÉSÉE-la-Romaine

Cher

A cette époque sur les croupes ondoyantes qui bordent le Cher à Thésée et Oisly...

ST AIGNAN S/CHER

Les grandes écoles

Sciences-Po is a popular name for l'Institut d'Études Politiques, a school for advanced study in government and political science. Graduates of Sciences-Po are often leading candidates for prominent positions in government and public office. Sciences-Po is one of the institutions the French call **les grandes écoles,** universities offering rigorous training for specialized careers. Students applying to these schools must pass difficult entrance exams in competition for very limited numbers of openings.

Other **grandes écoles** include Polytechnique, which offers degrees in engineering, and Saint-Cyr, where future military officers are trained. While l'Institut d'Études Politiques has produced many successful and prominent female graduates over the years, many of the **grandes écoles** were not open to women until the 1970's.

Object pronouns in commands

The form of a command containing an object pronoun depends on whether the command is negative or affirmative.

1. In a negative command, the word order is the same as that of a statement or question. The object pronoun precedes the verb.

   Ne me parle pas.   Don't talk to me.

2. In an affirmative command, the object pronoun follows the verb. A hyphen links the verb and the pronoun.

   Regardez-nous.   Look at us.
   Levez-vous.   Get up.

3. In affirmative commands *only*, the pronouns **me** and **te** become **moi** and **toi**.

   Téléphone-moi.   Call me on the phone.
   Assieds-toi.   Sit down.

G You're taking care of a young child in your home. The child expresses the following wishes. Respond with an affirmative or negative command, as you think best.

   ▣▥ Je voudrais me lever   *Eh bien, lève-toi. / Non, ne te*
        maintenant.   *lève pas.*

   1. Je voudrais m'habiller.
   2. Je voudrais te demander quelque chose.
   3. Je voudrais te montrer mon tee-shirt.
   4. Je voudrais t'acheter un cadeau.
   5. Je voudrais me promener avec le chien.
   6. Je voudrais me préparer à rentrer.

H Everyone is getting on your nerves. Order the people mentioned below either to stop what they are doing, or to get busy and do what they are supposed to do.

   ▣▥ Tu achètes le tee-shirt bleu?   *Ne l'achète pas!*
   ▣▥ Vous ne vous préparez pas?   *Préparez-vous!*

   1. Tu ne te lèves pas?
   2. Vous ne cherchez pas le chien?
   3. Tu ne me regardes pas?
   4. Vous ne faites pas vos devoirs?
   5. Vous vous promenez?
   6. Tu me demandes pourquoi?

I Respond to each question with a command. Use object pronouns.

■Ⅲ On invite Dominique?   *Oui, invitons-la.*

1. Quand est-ce que je te téléphone?
2. Où est-ce que je range les livres?
3. Je m'habille maintenant?
4. On se lève à sept heures?

The interrogative adjective **quel**

	SINGULAR	PLURAL
Masculine	**quel** château?	**quels** étages?
Feminine	**quelle** époque?	**quelles** cheminées?

1. The interrogative adjective **quel** (*what, which*) agrees in number and gender with the noun it modifies.
2. *Liaison* occurs when **quels** and **quelles** are followed by a noun that begins with a vowel sound: **quels‿ancêtres? quelles‿horloges?**

J You're with a tour group at a chateau. You aren't sure which objects the tour guide is talking about. Apologize, and ask him to be more specific.

■Ⅲ Les carreaux représentent   *Pardon, monsieur, vous parlez de*
une armée en marche.   *quels carreaux?*

1. Les horloges sont de l'époque de François Premier.
2. La chaise est du dix-huitième siècle.
3. Les murs sont en pierres.
4. C'est un portrait du Marquis de la Fayette.
5. Les escaliers ont cent marches.

K You are interviewing a potential roommate. Ask for the following information.

■Ⅲ le numéro de téléphone   *Quel est ton numéro de téléphone?*

1. l'adresse   3. la nationalité
2. le nom   4. l'âge

L Your friend is shopping for the following items. Ask her which of the ones she has considered she intends to buy.

■Ⅲ un pantalon   *Tu achètes quel pantalon?*

1. un parapluie   3. des foulards   5. des chaussures
2. une ceinture   4. deux imperméables 6. une robe

The verb **faire:** present tense

SINGULAR	PLURAL
je fais	nous faisons
tu fais	vous faites
on/il/elle fait	ils/elles font

The basic meaning of **faire** is *to do* or *to make*. **Faire** is also used in a variety of expressions with different English equivalents.

Elle aime faire du camping.	She likes to go camping.
Je fais du cheval.	I go horseback riding.
Faites attention!	Pay attention! Watch out!

M Say that the people mentioned below are doing homework for the courses they are taking.

■III Nous avons un cours de   *Nous faisons nos devoirs de bio-*
      biologie.   *logie.*

1. Tu as un cours de maths.
2. Lise a un cours de physique.
3. On a un cours d'histoire.
4. J'ai un cours d'anglais.
5. Vous avez un cours d'algèbre.
6. Mes frères ont un cours de géographie.

N Ask a classmate what the following people are doing Saturday. Your classmate should give a logical answer.

■III Philippe   *— Qu'est-ce que Philippe fait samedi?*
                   — Il fait [du bateau].

1.	on	3.	nous	5.	vous
2.	Marie	4.	toi	6.	Paul et Michel

O Below are the plans that various people made for the summer. Confirm that the people are doing as they planned.

■III Ivana va faire le guide   *Ivana fait le guide dans*
      dans un château.   *un château.*

1. Nous allons faire de la voile à Douarnenez.
2. Elles vont faire du sport.
3. Gilles va faire du camping en Bretagne.
4. Je vais faire du bateau à Nice.
5. Vous allez faire du cheval à Blois.

La journée d'Ivana

Le Comte et la Comtesse du Pavillon habitent un merveilleux° petit   marvelous
château dans la vallée de la Loire. Une partie du château est ouverte au
public, et leur fille, Ivana, est guide du musée pendant l'été.

  La journée d'Ivana est très occupée. Le matin, elle se lève à sept heures
5 pour faire du cheval. Après le petit déjeuner, elle fait le guide de neuf
heures et demie à midi. De toutes les pièces du musée, elle préfère la
galerie des portraits, où il y a des tableaux° de rois de France et de leurs   paintings
célèbres contemporains.° L'après-midi, elle étudie pour se préparer à   contemporaries
entrer à Sciences-Po.

10 Aujourd'hui, Ivana a un invité pour le déjeuner. Philippe Delacroix est
un jeune homme parisien qui est en visite chez ses cousins à Blois. Il
questionne Ivana sur son emploi du temps au château, car° il aimerait bien   because
la revoir avant de rentrer à Paris.

  Pendant le déjeuner, Philippe, qui étudie l'architecture aux Beaux-Arts à
15 Paris, demande à Ivana pourquoi elle veut° entrer à Sciences-Po. La jeune   wants
fille explique que° la politique l'intéresse, et que Sciences-Po est une   explains that
excellente école pour entrer dans l'Administration. Les deux jeunes gens°   people
pensent que c'est une bonne chose qu'il y ait° des femmes dans l'Adminis-   that there are
tration. Ils concluent que plus° il y a de femmes au gouvernement,   the more
20 moins° il y a de chances de guerre.   the less

  Quand ils se séparent, Philippe et Ivana prennent rendez-vous° pour   make a date
dîner à Amboise mardi soir. Ils pensent aussi qu'ils vont se revoir à Paris.

1. Où est-ce que Philippe habite?
2. Qu'est-ce que Philippe étudie?
3. Qu'est-ce qu'Ivana étudie? Pourquoi?
4. Quand est-ce qu'il y a moins de chances de guerre?

une situation
embrouillée

Unscramble the following account of Ivana's day.

1. Ivana se lève à sept heures.
2. Ivana montre la galerie des portraits aux visiteurs.
3. Philippe déjeune chez Ivana.
4. Ivana fait du cheval jusqu'à huit heures.
5. Ivana étudie dans la bibliothèque.
6. Ivana se promène dans le parc avec ses chiens.

à vous,
maintenant

Share with the class some of the things you would like to do. Use the expression **je voudrais** with appropriate infinitives.

poème

Jacques Prévert, one of France's best-loved poets, died in 1977. In the following poem, he poked fun at some illustrious monarchs.

Les belles familles

Louis I
Louis II
Louis III
Louis IV
Louis V
Louis VI
Louis VII
Louis VIII
Louis IX
Louis X (dit le Hutin°)   called the Headstrong
Louis XI
Louis XII
Louis XIII
Louis XIV
Louis XV
Louis XVI
Louis XVIII
et plus personne plus rien...°   nobody else, nothing
Qu'est-ce que c'est que ces gens-là   more
qui ne sont pas foutus
de° compter jusqu'à vingt?   aren't capable of

Jacques Prévert

Paroles, © 1949 Editions Gallimard

L'aristocratie française

Until the end of the eighteenth century, France was governed by monarchy. French society was dominated by the aristocracy, noble families who owned land by birthright or by royal gift. The majority of French people were peasants with little money or political power.

The social hierarchy was changed radically by the French Revolution of 1789, a bloody uprising in which the middle class united to overthrow the monarchy and the aristocracy. From the Revolution came the democratic principles on which the current French republic is based. Members of the aristocracy now living in France trace their ancestry back to pre-Revolutionary times, but their noble heritage is no longer a significant factor in today's society.

La reine Marie-Antoinette, femme du roi Louis XVI

Résumé grammatical

Object pronouns **me, te, nous, vous** (A-D)

The pronouns **me, te, nous,** and **vous** are used as both direct and indirect objects. Object pronouns precede the verb in affirmative or negative statements and questions.

Il **me** parle souvent.	He speaks *to me* often.
Je **t'**aime bien.	I like *you*.
Est-ce qu'il **nous** cherche?	Is he looking for *us?*
Je ne **vous** trouve pas bête.	I don't find *you* stupid.

Reflexive constructions (E-F)

A phrase in which the subject and the object of the verb represent the same person is called a reflexive construction. A reflexive construction includes a reflexive pronoun. (Reflexive pronouns in English end in *-self* or *-selves*.)

French uses a great many reflexive constructions, many of which have non-reflexive English equivalents.

Je **me lève**.	I'm getting up.
Tu **t'habilles?**	Are you getting dressed?
Elle **se promène**.	She's taking a walk.
Nous **nous préparons**.	We're preparing ourselves.
Vous **vous amusez** bien?	Are you enjoying yourselves?
Ils **se dépêchent**.	They're hurrying.

Object pronouns in commands (G-I)

The form of a command containing an object pronoun depends on whether the command is affirmative or negative.

1. In negative commands, the object pronoun precedes the verb.

   Ne l'achète pas!   Don't buy it!

2. In affirmative commands, the object pronoun follows the verb. It is linked to the verb with a hyphen.

   Cherchez-les!   Look for them!
   Habillez-vous!   Get dressed!

3. In affirmative commands only, the pronouns **me** and **te** become **moi** and **toi**.

   Écoute-moi!   Listen to me!
   Assieds-toi!   Sit down!

The interrogative adjective **quel** (J-L)

The interrogative adjective **quel** (what, which) agrees in gender and number with the noun it modifies.

quel livre?	what book?
quelle fille?	which girl?
quels châteaux?	which chateaux?
quelles maisons?	what houses?

The verb **faire:** present tense (M-O)

SINGULAR	PLURAL
je fais	nous faisons
tu fais	vous faites
on/il/elle fait	ils/elles font

1. The basic meaning of **faire** is *to do* or *to make.*
2. **Faire** is often used in idiomatic expressions with a variety of English equivalents:

Ils font de la voile.	They are sailing.
Je fais du cheval.	I go horseback riding.
Faites attention!	Pay attention! Watch out!

À la française

Members of aristocratic families can be distinguished by certain characteristics. One is the use of *de* before the last name. In recent years, two aristocrats have been President of the French Republic: Charles de Gaulle and Valéry Giscard d'Estaing. Some aristocrats use titles of nobility, including *chevalier, baron(ne), comte/comtesse,* and *duc/duchesse.* (The titles *prince* and *princesse* are reserved for the immediate family of *le Comte de Paris,* who theoretically is the heir to the throne, although a return of the monarchy in France is unlikely.)

Young people in aristocratic circles tend to use *vous,* rather than *tu,* with one another, unless they are close friends; some use *vous* in speaking to their own parents. Another upper-class tradition is *le baise-main,* or hand-kiss, in which a gentleman meeting a married woman bows and brings the back of her hand to his lips.

M. et Mme Valéry Giscard d'Estaing

A   Arrange the following activities in the order in which they would normally occur on a school day.

1. J'arrive à l'école.
2. Je prépare le petit déjeuner.
3. Je m'habille.
4. Je joue avec mes amis.
5. Je dîne.
6. Je me lève.
7. Je fais mes devoirs.
8. Je déjeune.

B   Say that it is five minutes later than the time indicated.

    ◼ⅠⅠⅠ   10:00   *Il est dix heures cinq.*

1. 10:55
2. 1:55
3. 11:15
4. 1:25
5. 3:05
6. 7:10
7. 8:20
8. 4:50

C   Argue with a classmate over whether the two of you should do the following things now.

    ◼ⅠⅠⅠ   faire les devoirs   — *Faisons-les maintenant!*
                                          — *Non, ne les faisons pas maintenant!*

1. se promener
2. préparer la leçon
3. inviter les copains
4. se lever
5. visiter la cathédrale
6. s'habiller pour le dîner

D   Confirm the following invitations by answering the questions in the affirmative. Use appropriate object pronouns.

    ◼ⅠⅠⅠ   Elle t'invite chez elle?   *Oui, elle m'invite chez elle.*

1. Geneviève invite Jacques et toi au cinéma?
2. Philippe invite Marie et moi au café?
3. Elle t'invite à dîner?
4. Tu m'invites à jouer au tennis?

E   Ask what the following people are doing tomorrow.

    ◼ⅠⅠⅠ   vos cousins   *Qu'est-ce que vous faites demain?*

1. toi
2. on
3. Jacques et Paul
4. vous
5. Anne et Henri
6. le monsieur
7. nous
8. votre sœur
9. vos cousines
10. eux

F The following people are doing various things. Say what they are doing and whether or not they are enjoying themselves.

> ▪Ⅲ   Hélène (faire du cheval)

Hélène fait du cheval. Elle s'amuse bien.

> Henri (faire ses devoirs)

Henri fait ses devoirs. Il ne s'amuse pas.

1. Alfred (faire du bateau)
2. Béatrice (préparer le dîner)
3. les amis (aller au cinéma)
4. Anne et Lise (faire du sport)
5. Marie et Jean (aller à l'hôpital)
6. nous (se promener)

G Identify the parts of buildings that you can see in the photograph below, and point them out to your classmates. (The photograph shows the town of Amboise as seen from the chateau.)

H Summarize in English a few important facts about each of the following topics.

1. the French Revolution
2. the Loire River Valley
3. French royalty and aristocracy

Vocabulaire

NOUNS

l'ancêtre (m./f.)   ancestor
l'après-midi (m./f.)   after-noon
l'armée (f.)   army
B l'ascenseur (m.)   elevator
la bibliothèque   library
le bois   wood
le carreau   tile
A la cheminée   fireplace
le chien   dog
le départ   departure
l'entrée (f.)   entrance
l'époque (f.)   period, epoch
B l'escalier (m.)   ~~stairway~~
A l'étage (m.)   floor _premier_
A le grenier   attic
la guerre   war
l'horloge (f.)   clock
l'indépendance (f.)   inde-pendence
le jour   day
la journée   day
B la marche   step
le matin   morning
B le mur   wall
le petit déjeuner   breakfast
B le plafond   ceiling
le portrait   portrait
A le rez-de-chaussée   first (ground) floor
la semaine   week
le siècle   century
le soir   evening
le sol   floor
A le sous-sol   basement
A le toit   roof

ADJECTIVES

bas(se)   low
dur(e)   hard
éloigné(e)   distant
haut(e)   high
hollandais(e)   Dutch
libre   free
peint(e)   painted
récent(e)   recent
unique   unique

VERBS

admirer   to admire
s'amuser   to enjoy oneself; to play
commencer   to start
continuer   to continue
descendre   to go down
dîner   to have dinner
emmener   to take out
s'habiller   to get dressed
se lever   to get up
monter   to go up
penser   to think
se préparer   to get ready
se promener   to take a walk
représenter   to represent

ORDINAL NUMBERS

premier/première, deuxième...
seizième, dix-septième,   etc.

TELLING TIME

il est une heure   it's one o'clock
il est une heure et quart (et demie)   it's quarter past (half past) one
il est une heure moins le quart   it's quarter to one
il est midi   it's noon
il est minuit   it's midnight
quelle heure est-il?   what time is it?

OTHER WORDS AND EXPRESSIONS

assez   rather, quite
ensuite   then
vers   toward

au passage   on the way
avec plaisir   with pleasure
c'est vrai   it's true
en bas   down below
en haut   up above
en marche   on the march
faire: faire attention   to be careful, to pay attention; faire du cheval   to go horseback riding; faire le guide   to act as a guide; faire quelque chose de beau   to do something in-teresting

chapitre 9
La saison des pluies

The Republic of Senegal, in West Africa, has a rainy season during the summer months. Even during the rainy season, however, the much-needed rain is sometimes scarce in the area around the modern and elegant capital of Dakar. The Senegalese count on rainstorms to water the peanuts and other crops on which the country depends. The weather is important for other reasons as well to Karim Diop's father, an air traffic controller in Dakar.

À l'aéroport de Dakar

scène 1

A rainstorm would be welcome in Dakar, but it might cause problems for incoming flights. In the tower at Yoff Airport, M. Diop discusses the weather with M. Camara, who has come to relieve him.

M. DIOP — Quel temps fait-il dehors? Il fait chaud?

M. CAMARA — Oui, très chaud. J'espère qu'il va faire de l'orage. Nous voilà au mois de juillet, et il ne pleut toujours pas!

M. DIOP — C'est vrai, on a bien besoin de pluie. Mais si l'avion d'Air Afrique ne peut pas atterrir à cause de l'orage...

M. CAMARA — C'est le vol de Casablanca?

M. DIOP — Oui, avec escale à Nouakchott. Il est en retard.

M. CAMARA — Qu'est-ce qu'on annonce à la météo?

M. DIOP — Il fait beau à Casa. Mais ils ont une tempête de sable à Nouakchott. Le vent souffle du désert à soixante-quinze kilomètres à l'heure. Et il fait trente-cinq degrés à l'ombre!

M. CAMARA — Ouf! Quelle chaleur!

M. DIOP — Alors, au revoir, et bonne journée! Il va faire bon ici, avec l'air climatisé. Pas chez moi, malheureusement! Mais j'ai sommeil et je vais bien dormir.

questions

1. Quel temps fait-il à Dakar?
2. Est-ce que le vol d'Air Afrique est à l'heure?
3. Où est-ce qu'il y a une tempête de sable?
4. Quelle température fait-il à Nouakchott?
5. Pourquoi est-ce que M. Diop va bien dormir?

parlons de la scène

Use the visual cues below to form sentences that relate to what happens in *scène 1*.

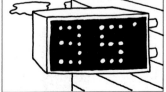

à vous,
maintenant

1. Est-ce qu'il y a une saison des pluies chez vous? Quand? Est-ce que vous aimez la pluie?

2. Au mois de juillet chez vous, est-ce qu'il fait chaud? Est-ce qu'il fait souvent de l'orage?

3. Est-ce que vous aimez la chaleur? Est-ce que vous trouvez que c'est difficile de dormir quand il fait très chaud?

petite scène

With a classmate, act out the following scene: one person proposes an activity, but the other hesitates and makes excuses. Then see how many variations you can come up with.

VOUS	On joue au tennis?
ELLE/LUI	Je ne sais pas... Je me demande s'il ne va pas pleuvoir.
VOUS	Mais non, il fait beau.
ELLE/LUI	Il fait trop chaud et il fait du vent!
VOUS	Mais qu'est ce qu'il y a? Tu ne veux pas jouer?
ELLE/LUI	J'ai sommeil!
VOUS	Eh bien, va dormir! Moi, je vais m'amuser!

_____ Étude de mots _____

Les saisons et les mois de l'année

le printemps	**l'automne** (*m.*)
mars	septembre
avril	octobre
mai	novembre
l'été (*m.*)	**l'hiver** (*m.*)
juin	décembre
juillet	janvier
août	février

1. In dates, cardinal numbers are used except for the *first* day of the month.

   Aujourd'hui, c'est **le trente avril.** Demain, c'est **le premier mai.**

2. In specifying the season during which something takes place, **au** is used before **printemps; en** is used before **été, automne,** or **hiver.**

   Je vais à l'école **en automne, en hiver** et **au printemps** — mais pas **en été.**

A   Identify the following months by name.

> ▪ⅲ   Quel est le cinquième mois?   *C'est mai.*

1. Quel est le premier mois?
2. Quel est le troisième mois?
3. Quel est le septième mois?

4. Quel est le neuvième mois?
5. Quel est le onzième mois?
6. Quel est le huitième mois?

B   Specify the seasons in which the following holidays occur, and give the exact dates.

> ▪ⅲ   New Year's Day   *C'est en hiver, le premier janvier.*

1. American Independence Day
2. Halloween
3. Christmas
4. Martin Luther King Day

5. May Day
6. April Fool's Day
7. Veterans' Day
8. Valentine's Day

à vous, maintenant

1. Quelle est la date aujourd'hui?
2. Quelle est la date de votre anniversaire?
3. Quel mois est-ce que vous préférez? Quelle saison?

Quel temps fait-il?

Il fait beau et il fait chaud.

Il fait frais et il fait du vent.

Il neige et il fait froid.

Il fait mauvais: il pleut.

C   Guess what kind of weather prompts each of the following comments.

▪ꞮꞮꞮ   Brrrrr! Il fait zéro!   *Il fait froid.*

1. Formidable! C'est une belle journée pour faire de la voile.
2. Quelle tempête! On ne va pas à l'école aujourd'hui.
3. Oh, zut! Où est mon parapluie?
4. Ouf! Trente-deux degrés! Allons à la piscine!
5. Allô! Apporte ton pull-over au stade.

D   See how many different weather conditions you can identify in photographs in this book. Describe the weather as completely as you can.

à vous,
maintenant

1. Pretend that you are a weatherperson for a local TV or radio station. Report today's weather. Then give a report for a very different kind of weather.
2. Describe the typical weather for your region in January, May, August, and November.

Jouons avec les mots

Many personal feelings, sensations, or conditions are expressed in French by **avoir** followed by a noun without an article. (The feelings are expressed in English by *to be* + adjective.)

Some of the most common of these expressions are listed below. The noun, given with its English equivalent, should enable you to figure out the meaning of each expression.

avoir besoin (de)	**le besoin** = need
avoir chaud	**le chaud** = heat
avoir envie (de)	**l'envie** (*f.*) = desire
avoir faim	**la faim** = hunger
avoir froid	**le froid** = cold
avoir peur (de)	**la peur** = fear
avoir raison	**la raison** = rightness, reason
avoir soif	**la soif** = thirst
avoir sommeil	**le sommeil** = sleep
avoir tort	**le tort** = wrong

E   Use an appropriate expression with *avoir* to complete each of the following sentences.

1. ＿＿＿ d'un stylo pour faire mes devoirs.
2. Je voudrais déjeuner maintenant. ＿＿＿!
3. Je voudrais un coca, s'il te plaît! ＿＿＿!
4. Deux et deux font quatre, n'est-ce pas, Papa? Oui, ＿＿＿.

5. Je vais aller dormir parce que _____.
6. Tu n'as pas ton manteau? Tu vas _____!
7. Quand Josette achète une nouvelle robe, sa petite sœur _____ d'une robe aussi.
8. Je vais descendre par l'escalier parce que _____ des ascenseurs.
9. Non, Jacqueline, _____. Dakar n'est pas en France.
10. Il n'y a pas l'air climatisé au restaurant. On va _____!

À la française

The French, like people everywhere, like to talk about the weather. Here are some of their favorite expressions.

Il fait lourd.	It's muggy.
Ça tape aujourd'hui!	It's really hot today!
On gèle!	It's freezing!
Il tombe des cordes! / **Il pleut à seaux!**	It's pouring rain!
Quel sale temps! / Quel **temps de chien!**	What horrible weather!
Le temps est détraqué.	The weather is crazy.

There are also a number of figurative expressions based on the weather. **Une personne qui fait la pluie et le beau temps** is someone of power and influence, a person who has the means to control a situation. **Il y a de l'orage dans l'air** describes a tense situation where something explosive is about to happen. **Parler de la pluie et du beau temps** means to discuss matters of no great importance, or to make small talk. Finally, the proverb **Après la pluie, le beau temps** is supposed to reassure those who are experiencing difficulties that better days are ahead.

Le climat en Afrique Occidentale

The republic of **Sénégal** is about 1400–1800 kilometers north of the equator, in the region known in colonial times as French West Africa. Because countries of the region have predominantly agricultural economies, many people depend upon the rain for survival.

In northern Senegal, there is an average of only thirty-three days of rain per year; in Dakar, the average is forty-six days, mostly in June and July. In the southern part of the country, called the **Casamance,** the rainy season brings storms from June to November. The Senegalese consider the Casamance, with its abundant rainfall, fertile soil, and lush vegetation, to be a sort of paradise.

The **Fleuve Sénégal** (Senegal River), the boundary between Senegal and Mauritania, is a source of water for agriculture. When rain comes, the river floods and enriches the surrounding land. The river, which then becomes navigable over much of its length, swarms with life as boats transport products from the interior to the coast.

The eastern part of Senegal, Mali, and southern Mauritania (where Nouakchott is located) belong to the subregion of the Sahara Desert called the **Sahel.** The rainy season in the Sahel is very short; in some years, it is practically nonexistent. Severe droughts in recent decades have caused a southward expansion of the Sahara.

Le Fleuve Sénégal

194

Prononciation et orthographe

/ø/	un p**eu**	
/œ/	la chal**eur**	
/œ̃/	**un**	

/ø/

The sound /ø/ is like the sound /ə/ in *je*, except that the lips are slightly rounded. Also, unlike /ə/, the sound /ø/ may not be dropped.

RÉPÉTEZ

un p**eu**	les y**eu**x	le déj**eu**ner
il pl**eu**t	furi**eu**x	malh**eu**r**eu**sement
bl**eu**	je p**eu**x	monsi**eu**r

The sound /ø/ is spelled **eu**.

LISEZ

1. Malheureusement, il pleut!
2. Ses yeux bleus sont furieux.
3. Tu peux te promener un peu après le déjeuner.

/œ/

The sound /œ/ is pronounced with the lips unrounded and slightly wider apart than for /ø/.

RÉPÉTEZ

la chal**eur**	la coul**eur**	s**eu**l
l'h**eu**re	j'ai p**eur**	la s**œur**

The sound /œ/ is spelled **eu** or **oeu**.

LISEZ

1. J'ai peur d'être seul dans l'ascenseur.
2. Le professeur est toujours à l'heure.
3. Leur sœur porte une robe d'une jolie couleur.

Qui vole un œuf vole un bœuf.

/œ̃/	The sound /œ̃/ is a nasal vowel.		

RÉPÉTEZ **un** brun lundi

The sound /œ̃/ is spelled **un.**

LISEZ
1. Lundi, je vais chez un ami qui a vingt et un ans.
2. M. Lebrun est un brun aux yeux bruns.

Le griot

Modern technology and lifestyles have come to Senegal, but the nation has maintained its African culture and traditions. Many of the traditions have been transmitted for generations by **griots.** A historian, poet, and musician, the **griot** fills a complex social role in Black Africa. He can be compared to the medieval minstrels of Europe as he keeps alive oral traditions in languages that have no written form. Alex Haley, the author of Roots, used the services of **griots** to trace his ancestry in Gambia.

Senegalese people invite the **griot** to help celebrate such family events as weddings and births. At the celebration, the **griot** recalls the history of his client's ancestors and sings the praises of the person being honored. He may also retell legends of the region, sometimes including his own poems in the narrative. As he sings, he may accompany himself on the **kora** (a stringed instrument), the **balafon** (a type of xylophone), or the **tam-tam** (drum).

«**Écoutons battre le pouls profond de l'Afrique dans la brume des villages perdus.**» (Let us listen to the beat of the deep pulse of Africa in the mist of lost villages.) These words, written by the Senegalese poet-President Léopold Sédar Senghor, may one day lead you to the foot of a baobab tree, where, when nature is quiet, the **griot** speaks.

On va écouter le griot

scène 2

At the Diops' home that evening, Karim and his four-year-old sister, Yacine, have been cooped up all day in the house because of the rainstorm. Karim is eager to get out of the house.

KARIM	Maman, j'ai chaud! J'ai envie de sortir!
MME DIOP	Mais il pleut, Karim.
KARIM	Mais non, Maman, il ne pleut plus.
MME DIOP	Tu as raison. Bon, tu peux sortir avec ta sœur.
YACINE	Non! Je ne veux pas m'amuser dehors! J'ai peur du tonnerre!
KARIM	Mais ça ne fait pas mal, le tonnerre! Et tu as ton gri-gri, n'est-ce pas?
YACINE	Oui, mais j'ai peur quand même!
KARIM	Alors, je vais aller tout seul écouter le griot. Il est en train de chanter chez les voisins.
YACINE	Ah! Pourquoi il est là?
KARIM	Pour la naissance du fils des Sambène. Toute la famille est là. Le griot va raconter l'histoire de leurs ancêtres.
YACINE	Alors, je veux y aller, moi aussi.
KARIM	Eh bien, allons-y, petite sœur... (*dehors*) Tiens! Voilà l'avion d'Air Afrique! Papa va être content...

questions

1. Est-ce qu'il pleut?
2. Pourquoi est-ce que Yacine ne veut pas sortir?
3. Qu'est-ce que Karim veut faire?
4. Où est le griot? Qu'est-ce qu'il fait?
5. Pourquoi est-ce que le père de Karim va être content?

petite scène

Try to persuade a classmate to accompany you somewhere, as in the following *petite scène* or one similar to it. See how many variations you and your partner can come up with.

ELLE/LUI	Ouf! Quelle chaleur!
VOUS	Je vais sortir! Tu viens avec moi?
ELLE/LUI	Qu'est-ce que tu vas faire?
VOUS	J'ai besoin de livres. Je voudrais aller à la bibliothèque.
ELLE/LUI	Moi, je n'ai pas envie de sortir!
VOUS	Pourquoi pas?
ELLE/LUI	Je pense qu'il va faire de l'orage.
VOUS	Alors, si tu as peur...
ELLE/LUI	Non, je n'ai pas peur, mais je n'ai pas de parapluie.
VOUS	Ne t'en fais pas! Tiens! Voilà l'imperméable de mon frère.
ELLE/LUI	Eh bien, d'accord. Allons-y!

Indicate why each of the following remarks is made by recalling its context in *scène 2.*

1. Ça ne fait pas mal, le tonnerre.
2. J'ai peur quand même.
3. Tu as raison. Bon, tu peux sortir avec ta sœur.
4. Il est en train de chanter.
5. Papa va être content.

à vous,
maintenant

1. Mention to a classmate (who plays the role of your parent) your desire to do something. Your classmate either gives or refuses permission.

J'ai envie de (d')	aller au théâtre.
Je veux	me promener.
	sortir.

| D'accord, tu peux... |
| Non, tu ne peux pas... |

2. Express your hope that something will take place.

J'espère que (qu')	il va faire beau.
	l'avion va arriver à l'heure.
	tu peux jouer avec nous.

L'histoire du Sénégal

Until the 11th century, West Africa was made up of many kingdoms and empires. Then came Islam. The Moslem dynasty of the Almoravides, the converted Berbers who had moved southward from southern Morocco to Ghana, ruled the region for several centuries. In 1444, the Portuguese, seeking a safe route to India, began exploring the coast and trading in the commodities for which Africa became famous: spices, ivory, gold, diamonds — and slaves. Some territories changed hands many times during the next few centuries, belonging at various times to the Dutch, the English, or the French.

Senegal was the first part of Africa to be settled by the French, who established Fort Saint-Louis on the mouth of the Senegal River in the 1650s. From there, they went on to conquer and colonize other areas. By the 19th century, Senegal had become the leading French colony in West Africa. It was a center for the slave trade, especially on the small island of Gorée off the coast near Dakar.

In 1822, Catholic missionaries started arriving in Fort Saint-Louis. One of them, Mère Anne-Marie Javouhey, devoted her life to the liberation of the slaves. It was not until 1848, however, that slavery was abolished.

In 1958, the French government headed by President de Gaulle offered all French territories except for Algeria a choice of remaining colonies, becoming part of France, or becoming independent. Senegal, like most colonies, chose independence.

Three glimpses of a vibrant nation: a computer center in Dakar, the port city of Saint-Louis, and a Senegalese woman with her child.

Grammaire

Negative expressions

The word **ne** is used in combination with several different negative words in addition to **pas.** The negative phrases shown in the following chart are more specific in meaning than the simple negation expressed by **ne...pas.**

NEGATIVE PHRASE	EXAMPLES
ne...plus (no longer)	Il ne pleut plus.
ne...jamais (never)	Elle n'écoute jamais ses parents.
ne...rien (nothing)	Je ne vais rien acheter aujourd'hui.
ne...personne (nobody)	Il n'y a personne à la maison.

As in the case of **ne...pas, ne** precedes the verb, and the word that completes the negation follows the verb.

A You choose not to reveal any information to your inquisitive friend. Answer each of the following questions with *personne* or *rien*, depending on the meaning.

■││ Qu'est-ce que tu cherches? *Je ne cherche rien.*
■││ Qui est-ce que tu regardes? *Je ne regarde personne.*

1. Qui est-ce que tu invites chez toi?
2. Qui est-ce que tu aimes?
3. Qu'est-ce que tu vas faire samedi?
4. Qu'est-ce que tu achètes?
5. Qu'est-ce que tu écoutes?
6. Qui est-ce que tu cherches?
7. Qu'est-ce que tu regardes?

B A former classmate who has not seen you for a long time asks if you still do the following things. Answer that you no longer do them.

■││ aller au collège — *Tu vas toujours au collège?*
— *Non, je ne vais plus au collège.*

1. habiter à Paris
2. étudier la musique
3. rentrer très tard le soir
4. faire du bateau
5. se lever à 7 h
6. acheter des vêtements chers

C   A classmate claims that he or she does not do the following things, but you aren't convinced. Express your doubt by asking if your classmate really never does them.

■Ⅲ   téléphoner à Yvette   — *Je ne téléphone pas à Yvette.*
                                      — *Vraiment? Tu ne téléphones jamais à Yvette?*

1. aller au cinéma
2. étudier les leçons
3. faire les devoirs
4. parler anglais

5. jouer au tennis
6. demander la voiture
7. s'amuser
8. chanter

à vous, maintenant   Tell the class something that you *never* do, and something that you *no longer* do.

More on forms of adjectives

There are many French adjectives whose written forms do not follow the regular pattern (feminine = masculine + **e**). Two groups of exceptions to the regular pattern are illustrated by the following charts.

MASCULINE	FEMININE
gentil	gentille
bon	bonne
canadien	canadienne
bas	basse

MASCULINE	FEMININE
heureux	heureuse
malheureux	malheureuse
furieux	furieuse
généreux	généreuse

1. Many adjectives with masculine singular forms ending in **-l, -n,** or **-s** double the final consonant and add **-e** in the feminine singular.
2. The ending **-eux** changes to **-euse** in the feminine singular. (Note: Masculine singular adjectives ending in **-x** do not add **-s** in the plural.)

D   Complete each of the following descriptions. Use the adjective that is used in the first part of the sentence.

■Ⅲ   Les langoustes sont bonnes,   *...et le couscous est bon aussi.*
         et le couscous...

1. Maman est furieuse, et Papa...
2. Voilà un monsieur haïtien, et voilà une dame...
3. Mon frère est très gentil, et ma sœur...
4. Le plafond est bas, et la table...
5. Le bébé est heureux, et sa mère...

Exclamations with **quel**

A form of **quel** may introduce an exclamation as well as a question. **Quel** agrees with the noun about which the speaker exclaims. The exclamation may or may not include an adjective.

Quel beau temps!	What beautiful weather!
Quelle chance!	What good luck!
Quels grands avions!	What big planes!
Quelles tempêtes!	What storms!

E Respond to each of the following remarks with a suitable exclamation. (There may be several appropriate responses.)

■⫿ Il va pleuvoir toute la journée. *Quelle pluie! / Quel mauvais temps! / Quelle journée!*

1. Le vent souffle à soixante kilomètres à l'heure.
2. Le château de Chambord a 440 pièces.
3. Les robes là-bas coûtent 2.000 francs.
4. Au déjeuner, il y a des langoustes pour tout le monde.
5. Mon lycée a seulement cent élèves.
6. Il fait trente-trois degrés à l'ombre.
7. Les enfants n'ont pas de chaussures.

à vous,
maintenant

1. Comment on each of the following things, using **quel** and an adjective: **le temps; votre ville; vos voisins; les vêtements de vos copains; vos livres; vos cours.**
2. Exclaim about the people and things you see in the photograph below.

Present tense of **vouloir** and **pouvoir**

vouloir (to want)	
je **veux**	nous **voulons**
tu **veux**	vous **voulez**
on/il/elle **veut**	ils/elles **veulent**

pouvoir (to be able; can, may)	
je **peux**	nous **pouvons**
tu **peux**	vous **pouvez**
on/il/elle **peut**	ils/elles **peuvent**

1. **Je voudrais** is a special polite form of **vouloir.**

   Je voudrais vous parler, s'il vous plaît.

2. **Vouloir** may be followed by either a noun phrase or an infinitive.

   Je veux une robe bleue.
   Je veux m'acheter une robe bleue.

3. **Pouvoir** is usually followed by an infinitive.

   D'accord, tu peux t'acheter une robe.

F   A friend invites you to do the following things. Respond politely that you would like to, but can't.

■▥   faire du bateau   — *Tu veux faire du bateau?*
                           — *Je voudrais bien faire du bateau, mais je ne peux pas.*

1. aller au cinéma
2. jouer au tennis
3. faire du cheval

G   Say that the following people want to visit the cities indicated.

■▥   elles: New York   *Elles veulent visiter New York.*

1. elle: Marrakech
2. Marie et Héléne: Québec
3. toi: Bruxelles
4. vous: Boston
5. nos amis: Rome
6. on: Dakar
7. moi: Madrid
8. nous: Berlin

H   Somebody asks whether the following people may go out Friday evening. Grant or refuse permission, as you think best.

■▥   Marc   — *Est-ce que Marc peut sortir vendredi soir?*
                — *Oui, il peut sortir. /Non, il ne peut pas sortir.*

1. Robert
2. moi
3. nous
4. on
5. Jacqueline et Marie
6. Jean-Paul et Serge

I   Say that the people listed below can visit the chateau if they wish.

    ▪▥   elle   *Elle peut visiter le château si elle veut.*

    ▪▥   les hommes   *Ils peuvent visiter le château s'ils veulent.*

1. nous
2. toi
3. eux
4. on

5. vous
6. moi
7. le prof
8. les élèves

J   While looking through magazines, you and your friends all see pictures of things that you would like to have. Imagine that you are fabulously rich. Express your willingness to make everybody's dreams come true, as in the model.

    ▪▥   Tu as envie du vélo rouge?   *Si tu veux le vélo rouge,*
                                                           tu peux l'avoir.

1. Tu as envie de la robe en soie bleue?
2. Christine a envie de la voiture de sport?
3. Maurice a envie de la maison en Californie?
4. Moi, j'ai envie de la piscine.
5. Nous avons envie du château de la Loire.
6. Vous avez envie du beau cheval blanc?
7. Bernadette et Georges ont envie du petit avion?
8. Annick et Patrick ont envie du bateau à voiles?

K   **Vouloir, c'est pouvoir** is a French proverb. Can you give an equivalent proverb in English?

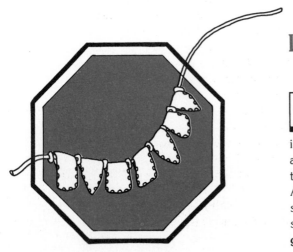

Le gri-gri

A **gri-gri** is a charm or amulet worn by people of animist beliefs for protection against danger and disease. Animism is a religion whose followers believe that, in addition to a supreme God, there are lesser deities embodied in natural forces and objects. Although most Senegalese are Moslems and some are Catholics, many continue to practice some forms of animism, including wearing the **gri-gri.**

Lecture

Un jour d'orage au Sénégal

M. Diop est contrôleur aérien à l'aéroport de Dakar-Yoff. Quand son collègue, M. Camara, arrive pour le remplacer,° ils parlent des prévisions de la météo. Tous les deux espèrent bien qu'il va pleuvoir. Mais s'il fait de l'orage, l'avion de Casablanca ne va peut-être pas pouvoir atterrir.

₅   M. Diop rentre chez lui pour dormir. Comme il pleut à seaux dehors, ses enfants jouent à la maison tout l'après-midi. Quand la pluie s'arrête,° Karim voudrait sortir. Sa petite sœur Yacine ne veut pas, parce qu'elle a peur du tonnerre, même avec son gri-gri. Pourtant,° quand Karim annonce qu'il va aller écouter le griot chez les voisins, elle décide d'aller avec lui.

₁₀   Chez les Sambène, le griot est en train de chanter les louanges° du grand-père et de tous les ancêtres du bébé. Karim écoute attentivement le récit° du griot. Il pense à la vie° de ces hommes qu'il admire. Sa vie à lui° va être bien différente. D'abord, il parle français et il va à l'école. Plus tard, il voudrait être pilote d'avion et visiter le monde: la France, l'Europe ₁₅ et d'autres pays° d'Afrique. Mais il sait qu'il reviendra° toujours chez lui, car il fait partie de° la grande famille des Ouolofs et son pays est le Sénégal.

Tout le monde admire le bébé et la soirée se termine° dans la joie et le plaisir d'être ensemble.° M. Diop est content aussi, parce que l'avion d'Air ₂₀ Afrique atterrit sans° incident à l'aéroport.

replace

stops

However

praises

narration/life/his own life

countries/will return

for he is part of

ends

together

without

1. Qu'est-ce que M. Diop fait à l'aéroport?
2. Qu'est-ce que M. Diop va faire à la maison?
3. Où vont Karim et Yacine? Pourquoi?
4. Qu'est-ce que le griot chante?
5. À quoi pense Karim?
6. Qu'est-ce que Karim voudrait faire plus tard?
7. Pourquoi est-ce que M. Diop est content?

une situation embrouillée

Unscramble the following account of the day by giving the sentences in the proper sequence.

1. Pendant l'orage, les enfants s'amusent.
2. Yacine décide d'aller l'écouter avec son frère.
3. Karim pense à sa future vie de pilote.
4. Quand il rentre à la maison, M. Diop va dormir.
5. Ils vont chez les voisins.
6. Le vol d'Air Afrique arrive à Dakar.
7. M. Diop et son collègue espèrent la pluie pour aujourd'hui.
8. Le griot chante chez les Sambène.

à vous, maintenant

Discuss with your classmates some of the things you like to do, don't like to do, and hope to do. Use expressions like the ones given below, and try to think of your own activities.

J'aime bien	me promener dehors
J'aime beaucoup	sortir sous la pluie
J'adore	m'amuser tout(e) seul(e)
...et j'espère	jouer avec mes copains
...mais je préfère	voyager en avion
...mais je n'aime pas	visiter l'Afrique
	aller à la mer
	marcher sur le sable

composition orale ou écrite

Assume the identity of one of the characters in this chapter. Tell what you are doing and what you are going to do on this particular day, the first day of the rainy season in Dakar. For example:

Je m'appelle Yacine. Aujourd'hui, il fait de l'orage. Alors, je m'amuse à la maison. Maintenant, mon frère veut sortir, mais moi, j'ai peur du tonnerre. Mais Karim parle du griot, qui chante chez les voisins. Les Sambène ont un nouveau bébé. Alors moi, je décide d'y aller aussi. Karim et moi, nous allons écouter le griot chanter.

poème

Jacques Prévert's poetry provides countless examples of clever wordplay, such as the following verses asking why the masculine pronoun is favored over the feminine in impersonal expressions.

Extrait de «Refrains enfantins»

Il pleut Il pleut
Il fait beau
Il fait du soleil°   sunshine
Il est tôt°   early
Il se fait° tard   is getting
Il
Il
Il
Toujours Il
Toujours Il qui pleut et qui neige
Toujours Il qui fait du soleil
Toujours Il
Pourquoi pas Elle
Jamais Elle
Pourtant° Elle aussi   And yet
Souvent se fait° belle!   makes herself

— Jacques Prévert

Spectacle, © *Editions Gallimard*

Résumé grammatical

Negative expressions (A-C)

ne...pas	not
ne...plus	no longer, no more
ne...jamais	never, not ever
ne...personne	nobody, no one
ne...rien	nothing

Je **ne** chante **jamais**.	I never (don't ever) sing.
Je **ne** veux **plus** jouer.	I don't want to play any longer.

Negative expressions follow the basic word order pattern:

ne (n′) + verb form + negative word

More on forms of adjectives (D)

Many adjectives whose masculine singular form ends in **-l, -n,** or **-s** double the final consonant and add **-e** in the feminine singular.

gentil, genti**lle**   bon, bo**nne**   bas, ba**sse**

The masculine singular ending **-eux** becomes **-euse** in the feminine singular.

heureux, heur**euse**   furieux, furi**euse**

Exclamations with **quel** (E)

A form of **quel** may introduce an exclamation as well as a question. **Quel** agrees with the noun it modifies.

Quel méchant garçon!   **Quels** beaux cadeaux!
Quelle bonne nouvelle!   **Quelles** belles avenues!

Present tense of **vouloir** and **pouvoir** (F-K)

vouloir (to want)	
je veux	nous voulons
tu veux	vous voulez
on/il/elle veut	ils/elles veulent

pouvoir (to be able; can, may)	
je peux	nous pouvons
tu peux	vous pouvez
on/il/elle peut	ils/elles peuvent

1. **Je veux** (I want, I wish) expresses a strong desire or wish. **Je voudrais** (I would like) is often used instead of **je veux** in making a polite request.

   Je veux vous parler.   I want to talk to you.
   Je voudrais vous parler.   I would like to talk to you.

2. **Vouloir** may be followed by either a noun phrase or an infinitive.

   Je veux une robe blanche.   I want a white dress.
   Je veux m'acheter une robe   I want to buy myself a white
   blanche.   dress.

3. **Pouvoir** may be followed by an infinitive, never by a noun phrase. Sometimes the infinitive is understood.

   Tu **peux jouer** avec nous demain?
   Joue avec nous demain, si tu **peux (jouer).**

A   Give a negative answer to each of the following questions, using *ne* with the negative words *rien, jamais, plus,* and *personne.*

■⫿   Tu écoutes le griot?   *Non, je n'écoute personne.*

1. Tu as quelque chose pour moi?
2. Tu vas souvent au théâtre?
3. Est-ce qu'ils vont quelquefois à Dakar?
4. Tu habites toujours à Saint-Louis?
5. Il regarde les enfants, n'est-ce pas?
6. Pierre achète un cadeau pour sa sœur?
7. Il y a des élèves dans la salle de classe?

B   Make up a sentence, paragraph, or conversational exchange to illustrate the meaning of each of the following expressions.

avoir peur	avoir chaud	avoir besoin de
avoir raison	avoir sommeil	avoir envie de

C   Say that the people would like to do the things indicated, but can't.

■⫿   nous: visiter le Sénégal   *Nous voulons visiter le Sénégal, mais nous ne pouvons pas.*

1. Henri: acheter une voiture
2. moi: faire du camping
3. toi: aller à Paris
4. on: se promener
5. vous: jouer au tennis
6. nous: dormir

D   M. Laroche has a very disagreeable personality, but Mme Laroche is easy-going and is well liked by everyone. Use each of the following adjectives in describing both people.

■⫿   méchant   *M. Laroche est toujours méchant. Mme Laroche n'est jamais méchante.*

1. sympathique
2. heureux
3. généreux
4. gentil
5. furieux
6. content

E   You're shopping for clothes with a friend. Your friend points out the following items. Respond with a suitable exclamation about each of them.

■⫿   une jupe   — *Voilà une jupe.*
                   — *Quelle jolie jupe!*

1. des chaussures
2. un imperméable
3. une chemise
4. un pantalon
5. des foulards
6. une robe

F   Give answers in French to the following questions about the weather and about your feelings on the subject.

1. Quel temps fait-il chez vous au mois de septembre? au mois de février? au mois de juin?
2. Pendant quels mois est-ce qu'il neige souvent chez vous? Pendant quels mois est-ce qu'il pleut souvent?
3. Pendant quelle saison est-ce que vous aimez aller à la mer? faire du camping? vous promener?
4. Préférez-vous avoir chaud ou avoir froid? Qu'est-ce que vous faites quand il fait chaud et quand il fait froid?

G   Choose one of the following topics and write a brief report on it in English.

1. Look at a map to learn more about the geography of West Africa. With what countries does Senegal share borders? How far is Dakar from Nouakchott and Casablanca?
2. Do some research on the first president of Senegal, Léopold Senghor. What themes are important in Senghor's literary works?
3. Find out more about the climate of Senegal. What are the average temperatures at different times of year? If you could visit Senegal, at what time of year would you like to go? What would you like to see and do?

H   With a little extra research, you should be able to identify all of the places on the map below. What is Niokolo Koba? Use an atlas and an encyclopedia to get more information about the region.

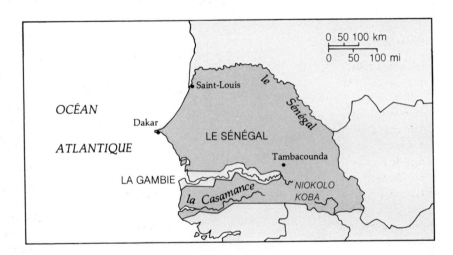

Vocabulaire

NOUNS

l'aéroport (m.) airport
l'air climatisé (m.) air conditioning
l'avion (m.) airplane
la chaleur heat
le degré degree
le désert desert
l'escale (f.) flight stop
le kilomètre kilometer
la météo weather report
le mois month
la naissance birth
l'ombre (f.) shade
l'orage (m.) thunderstorm
la pluie rain
le sable sand
la saison season
la tempête storm
le tonnerre thunder
le vent wind
le voisin/la voisine neighbor
le vol flight

WEATHER EXPRESSIONS

quel temps fait-il? what's the weather like?
il fait beau it's beautiful
il fait bon it's nice
il fait chaud it's warm, it's hot
il fait de l'orage it's stormy
il fait du vent it's windy
il fait frais it's cool
il fait froid it's cold
il fait mauvais it's bad weather
il neige it's snowing
il pleut it's raining

VERBS

adorer to love
annoncer to announce
atterrir to land
chanter to sing
dormir to sleep
écouter to listen (to)
espérer to hope
marcher to walk
pouvoir to be able; can; may
raconter to tell
sortir to go out, to leave
souffler to blow
vouloir to want, to wish

ADVERBS

alors then, so
dehors outside
malheureusement unfortunately
quand même just the same
toujours still, always

SEASONS

le printemps spring
l'été (m.) summer
l'automne (m.) autumn, fall
l'hiver (m.) winter

MONTHS

janvier	juillet
février	août
mars	septembre
avril	octobre
mai	novembre
juin	décembre

NEGATIVE EXPRESSIONS

ne...jamais never, not ever
ne...plus no longer, not any longer
ne...rien nothing, not anything
ne...personne no one, nobody

EXPRESSIONS WITH AVOIR

avoir besoin (de) to need
avoir chaud to be warm, to be hot
avoir envie (de) to want
avoir faim to be hungry
avoir froid to be cold
avoir peur (de) to be afraid (of)
avoir raison to be right
avoir soif to be thirsty
avoir sommeil to be sleepy
avoir tort to be wrong

OTHER EXPRESSIONS

ouf! exclamation indicating amazement or relief
seul(e) alone; tout(e) seul(e) all alone
si if
à (65) kilomètres à l'heure at (65) kilometers per hour
allons-y let's go
bonne journée have a good day
être en train de + inf. to be in the process of ...-ing
faire mal to hurt
nous voilà here we are

chapitre 10
Un repas bourguignon

Beaune, a medieval town in the heart of the wine region of **Bourgogne** (Burgundy), is surrounded by vineyards that climb the nearby hills. Small villages with picturesque red-tiled roofs and church steeples nestle in the midst of Burgundy's vineyards, from which come some of the world's most celebrated wines.

The Cordier family (thirteen-year-old Jacques, his older sister Alice, and his parents) live on a farm a few kilometers east of Beaune. There the land is relatively flat, and the fertile fields are planted with grains, potatoes, and sugar beets. During the week the Cordiers work long hours, but on Sundays they enjoy a day of rest and a big midday meal. Nobody takes the matter of eating more seriously than do the French, and Sunday dinner is an occasion that is eagerly anticipated by the whole family.

Le gourmand

scène 1

*Everyone in the family is helping Mme Cordier prepare Sunday dinner. Jacques, who has gone by motorbike to a **charcuterie** in town to get pâté, ham, and sausage, returns from his errand.*

MME CORDIER	Tu as la charcuterie, Jacques?
JACQUES	Oui, Maman. Voilà le pâté en croûte, le jambon et le saucisson.
MME CORDIER	Tiens, il manque un morceau du pâté! Comment ça se fait? Mon charcutier est pourtant honnête d'habitude!
5 JACQUES	Euh... Euh... Tu sais bien que j'adore le pâté, Maman.
MME CORDIER	Oh! Ce que tu es gourmand, Jacques! Enfin, ça ne fait rien! On va bien déjeuner.
JACQUES	Qu'est-ce qu'on va manger?
MME CORDIER	Eh bien, après la charcuterie, on a des escargots et du civet de lapin. Comme légumes, il y a des pommes de terre et des petits pois frais.
10 M. CORDIER	(*à la porte de la cuisine*) Je vais chercher le vin à la cave, Suzanne?
MME CORDIER	Oui, si tu veux.
M. CORDIER	Quand est-ce qu'on mange?
MME CORDIER	Dans une heure. Je viens de mettre le lapin à cuire. Demande à Alice de m'apporter de la salade du jardin, s'il te plaît.
15 M. CORDIER	Bon, d'accord.
JACQUES	Est-ce qu'il y a du fromage et du dessert, Maman?
MME CORDIER	Bien sûr! Du fromage blanc à la crème, et une tarte aux fraises, spécialement pour toi.
20 JACQUES	Chic, alors! Merci, Maman.
MME CORDIER	Et maintenant, laisse-moi faire la cuisine!

1. Qu'est-ce que Jacques apporte à la maison?
   a. du civet de lapin
   b. des légumes
   c. de la charcuterie
2. Qu'est-ce qui manque?
   a. un morceau du pâté
   b. des pommes de terre
   c. des petits pois
3. Où est-ce qu'Alice va chercher la salade?
   a. à la cave
   b. à la charcuterie
   c. au jardin
4. Pourquoi est-ce que M. Cordier va à la cave?
   a. pour chercher du fromage
   b. pour chercher du vin
   c. pour tuer le lapin

parlons
de la scène

Try to recall what is said in *scène 1* about each of the foods shown in the drawings below.

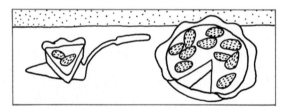

pourquoi?

Explain briefly in French why Mme Cordier makes the following remarks to her husband (*son mari*) or her son, Jacques.

■ⅲ *à son fils:* Une tarte aux fraises, spécialement pour toi.   *Parce qu'il demande ce qu'il y a comme dessert.*

1. *à son fils:* On va bien déjeuner.
2. *à son mari:* Oui, si tu veux.
3. *à son fils:* Ce que tu es gourmand!
4. *à son mari:* Dans une heure.

| à vous,
maintenant | You and a friend are having a picnic. Reassure your friend, who is concerned because you are out of a particular food. |

Comment ça se fait? Il n'y a plus de [pâté].

| Ça ne fait rien!
Ne t'en fais pas! | Il y a | du jambon.
de la salade.
du saucisson. |

| petite scène | Create a four-line dialogue that might take place at the market. Model your dialogue on the following samples. |

AMI(E)   Je vais acheter des escargots.
VOUS   Des escargots? Pourquoi?
AMI(E)   Pour le petit déjeuner.
VOUS   Ce que tu es bête! On ne mange jamais d'escargots au petit déjeuner!

AMI(E)   On achète du pâté en croûte?
VOUS   Pourquoi?
AMI(E)   Parce qu'il n'y a pas de pâté pour le déjeuner.
VOUS   Ça ne fait rien! Je viens d'acheter du jambon et du saucisson.

Chez le marchand de primeurs

Étude de mots

Les magasins alimentaires

On achète du pain à la boulangerie.

On achète du porc à la charcuterie.

On achète du lait à la crémerie.

On achète des gâteaux à la pâtisserie.

On achète du poisson à la poissonnerie.

On achète des fruits et des légumes frais chez le marchand de primeurs.

On achète de la viande à la boucherie.

On achète des conserves à l'épicerie.

On achète de tout au supermarché.

A Tell which store Jacques is going to in order to buy the following groceries.

■ⅲ des pommes de terre   *Il va chez le marchand de primeurs ou au supermarché.*

1. de la crème
2. du jambon
3. du pain
4. des langoustes

5. des tartes aux fraises
6. de la viande
7. des oranges
8. des petits pois en conserves

B Ask a classmate the following questions.

1. *Où est-ce que tu vas pour acheter des gâteaux?*
2. *Où est-ce que tu vas pour acheter de la viande?*
3. *Est-ce que tu vas à l'épicerie pour acheter des conserves?*
4. *Est-ce que tu vas à la poissonnerie pour acheter des légumes?*

La nourriture

Learn the French names for the following common foods. Some cognates are given without English equivalents. You should be able to guess their meaning.

la viande meat
le jambon ham
le poulet chicken
le poisson fish
le bœuf
le porc

les légumes (*m. pl.*)
  vegetables
les haricots verts
  (*m. pl.*) green
  beans
les petits pois
  (*m. pl.*) peas
les pommes de terre
  (*f. pl.*) potatoes
les carottes (*f. pl.*)
les oignons (*m. pl.*)
la salade
les tomates (*f. pl.*)

le beurre butter
les conserves (*f. pl.*)
  canned goods
le fromage cheese
les œufs (*m. pl.*)
  eggs
le pain bread
le poivre pepper
le sel salt
le sucre sugar
la crème
la soupe

l'eau (*f.*) water;
  l'eau minérale
  mineral water
  (bottled)
le lait milk
le vin wine
le café
le chocolat
le thé

les fraises (*f. pl.*)
  strawberries
les pommes (*f. pl.*)
  apples
les fruits (*m. pl.*)
les bananes (*f. pl.*)
les oranges (*f. pl.*)

le gâteau cake,
  pastry
la glace ice cream
le dessert
la tarte

C   Your friends waiting with you in the cafeteria line ask what you are going to have for lunch. Answer their questions.

> ▪▥   de la soupe   — *Tu vas manger de la soupe?*
> — *Oui, j'aime la soupe./Non, je n'aime pas la soupe.*

1. du poisson
2. du fromage
3. des haricots verts
4. des pommes de terre
5. des tomates
6. de la glace

D   Compare the prices of the following items in a neighborhood store and in the supermarket, and share the information with the class.

> ▪▥   six oranges   *Dans un petit magasin, six oranges coûtent...*
> *Dans un supermarché, elles coûtent...*

1. une tarte aux pommes
2. douze œufs
3. un poulet
4. un kilo (*2.2 lbs.*) de beurre
5. dix bananes
6. un gâteau au chocolat

à vous, maintenant

What foods do you like or dislike? Comment on some of your personal tastes.

J'adore	les légumes.
J'aime beaucoup	la viande.
Je n'aime pas	le poisson.
Je déteste	
Je préfère	

Les repas français

In France, **le petit déjeuner** (breakfast) is always simple. It generally consists of rolls or bread, butter, jelly or jam, and **café au lait** (coffee with milk) or hot chocolate. For most families, **le déjeuner** (noon meal) is the main meal of the day. Many people go home for lunch between noon and two o'clock. In the afternoon, around four o'clock, it is customary to serve bread and chocolate to small children for **le goûter** (afternoon snack). Some adults have tea and a pastry in a **pâtisserie** or a **salon de thé. Le dîner** (equivalent to supper) is served at home around eight o'clock. It is usually a light meal and often includes soup.

Meals, especially the noon and evening meals, are an important part of the day for French people: good food, good conversation and relaxation make a nice combination.

Le couvert

En France, on met la fourchette et la serviette à gauche de l'assiette. On met le couteau et la cuillère à soupe à droite de l'assiette. On met la petite cuillère devant le verre. Comment est-ce qu'on met le couvert chez vous?

Jouons avec les mots

Adverbes en -ment   A great many French adverbs have the ending **-ment**. In most cases, the adverb is formed by adding **-ment** to the feminine singular form of an adjective. Some adverbs are exceptions, with the ending **-ment** added to a stem that is related to an adjective but is *not* the feminine singular form. Note: an adverb has only one form; it does not agree with any noun.

REGULAR FORMATION		EXCEPTIONS	
Adjective (f. sing.)	Adverb	Adjective (f. sing.)	Adverb
spéciale	spécialement	vraie	vraiment
furieuse	furieusement	gentille	gentiment
timide	timidement	méchante	méchamment

E   Complete the following sentences with appropriate adverbs.

■Ⅲ   Alain est *sérieux*. Il raconte   *sérieusement*
       ＿＿ l'histoire à sa copine.

1. Jean est un garçon *timide*. Il demande ＿＿ un morceau de pâté.
2. Les devoirs sont *faciles*. Alice les fait ＿＿.
3. Monique est *méchante*. Elle parle ＿＿ à son frère.
4. Mon oncle est toujours *généreux*. Il nous invite ＿＿ chez lui.
5. C'est *vrai*. Les voitures sont ＿＿ chères.
6. Le charcutier est *honnête*. Il prépare ＿＿ la commande du monsieur.
7. Mme Cordier est très *gentille*. Elle aide ＿＿ ses voisins.

À la française

Most French shoppers are very particular about the stores where they buy food. Even though there are many supermarkets in France (**le supermarché, l'hypermarché, la superette**), many people prefer to do their food shopping in small, specialized stores, like the **boulangerie, boucherie,** or **charcuterie.** They are fussy about quality and insist that prepared foods, such as the **pâté,** sausage, and cold cuts sold at the **charcuterie,** be freshly made. They also like to establish personal relationships with the storekeepers so that they will receive personal attention.

Here is a typical scene at a **boucherie:**

LE BOUCHER	Bonjour, Mme Cordier. Comment ça va aujourd'hui? Et la petite famille?
MME CORDIER	Ça va bien, merci. Et chez vous?
LE BOUCHER	Ça va, ça va. Alors, qu'est-ce que vous désirez? Un petit rôti de veau (*veal*)? Il est bien aujourd'hui.
5 MME CORDIER	Eh bien, d'accord. Donnez-moi un kilo de veau.
LE BOUCHER	Un kilo seulement? Les enfants ne sont pas à la maison?
MME CORDIER	Non, ils sont en camp. Ils vont rentrer dans deux semaines.
LE BOUCHER	Ah oui? Ils ont le beau temps, alors. Voilà, chère madame, un bon petit rôti. (*He wraps the roast and turns to his wife at the cash register.*) Jeanne, ça fait vingt-huit francs pour Mme Cordier.
10 MME CORDIER	Voilà trente francs.
LA BOUCHÈRE	Et voilà deux francs, madame. Merci beaucoup.
MME CORDIER	Au revoir, madame.
LA BOUCHÈRE	Au revoir, Mme Cordier. À demain.

Prononciation et orthographe

/g/	le **g**arçon
/ɲ/	la Bour**g**o**gn**e

/g/

The French /g/ is similar to the English sound /g/ as in *go*.

RÉPÉTEZ

le **g**arçon	le lé**g**ume	la **g**uerre
le **g**âteau	**G**ustave	le **g**uide
le **g**ourmand	la **g**lace	**G**uy

The sound /g/ is spelled **g** before the letters **a, o, u,** and before a consonant. It is spelled **gu** before the letters **e, i,** and **y.**

LISEZ

1. Les Anglais adorent la glace et les gâteaux.
2. Guy et Gustave sont des garçons gourmands.
3. J'aime la langouste, mais pas les escargots.

/ɲ/

The French sound /ɲ/ is similar to the sound spelled *ny* in the English word *canyon*.

RÉPÉTEZ

la Bour**gogn**e	l'oi**gn**on	la monta**gn**e
la Breta**gn**e	la Champa**gn**e	ma**gn**ifique
bour**gu**i**gn**on	l'Espa**gn**e	i**gn**orer

The sound /ɲ/ is spelled **gn.**

LISEZ

1. On visite la Bourgogne, la Bretagne et la Champagne.
2. Les montagnes en Espagne sont magnifiques.
3. Les Bourguignons adorent les oignons.

Au royaume des aveugles, les borgnes sont rois.

Les animaux de la ferme

Animals make the same sounds everywhere, although the sounds are expressed in different ways by speakers of different languages. Here is how the French represent the sounds made by some common farm animals. Review and practice some French sounds by imitating the animals.

Jacques meurt de faim

scène 2

An hour later, dinner is still not quite ready. In the kitchen, Jacques is getting restless, Alice is teasing her brother, and both are getting on Mme Cordier's nerves.

JACQUES   Ça sent bon! Il ne va pas être mauvais, ce petit civet! Oh là là! Je meurs de faim!

MME CORDIER   Eh bien, fais quelque chose pour m'aider... Va mettre le couvert dans la salle à manger.

5   ALICE   Maman, quand Jacques met le couvert, il manque toujours quelque chose... les petites cuillères pour le dessert... les serviettes...

JACQUES   Oh! Tu m'embêtes! Tu peux le faire, si tu veux.

MME CORDIER Soyez gentils tous les deux! Ne vous disputez pas! Et ne restez pas ici pendant que je fais la cuisine. Alice, va mettre le pain sur la table.

ALICE Oh, zut alors! Il n'y a plus de pain... Je vais vite en vélo à la boulangerie.

MME CORDIER Bon, voilà cinq francs. Achète deux baguettes.

ALICE D'accord, je reviens dans une minute. Jacques, ne mange pas tout le pâté pendant que je ne suis pas là!

JACQUES Oh, laisse-moi tranquille!

vrai ou faux?

Confirm or correct the following statements, saying either *C'est vrai* or *C'est faux,* as appropriate.

1. Le civet sent mauvais.
2. Jacques met toujours bien le couvert.
3. Alice est très gentille avec son frère.
4. Mme Cordier fait la cuisine.
5. Il manque du pain pour le déjeuner.
6. Alice va à la charcuterie.

à vous, maintenant

1. Someone offers you something to eat. Accept or decline the offer, adding a comment like one of the ones suggested below.

Tu veux | du pain?
de la charcuterie?

Oui, je l'aime bien.
Oui, j'ai faim.
Oh, oui, je meurs de faim!
Oui, ce n'est pas mauvais.
Merci, je n'ai pas faim.

2. Show your irritation to somebody who pesters you about something.

Tu ne peux pas ranger la cuisine?
Je meurs de faim. Quand est-ce qu'on mange?
Tu vas mettre le couvert, oui ou non?

Zut, alors! | Tu m'embêtes!
Tu ne peux pas m'aider?
Laisse-moi tranquille!

French people often use **petit** to express fondness for something. When Jacques says «**ce petit civet,**» he does not really mean "little;" he implies "good." Another characteristic way of showing approval is to use **mauvais** (bad) in a negative statement. When Jacques says, «**Il ne va pas être mauvais!**» he really means, «**Il va être très bon!**»

Grammaire

The partitive article

Certain nouns, because of their physical nature, are usually used only in the singular. Partitive articles are used in referring to unspecified quantities of such nouns.

AFFIRMATIVE	NEGATIVE
On a **du** fromage.	On n'a pas **de** fromage.
On a **de la** viande.	On n'a pas **de** viande.
On a **de l'**eau.	On n'a pas **d'**eau.

1. A masculine noun beginning with a consonant takes the partitive form **du;** a feminine noun beginning with a consonant takes **de la.** A noun beginning with a vowel takes **de l'.**
2. Partitive articles, like the indefinite articles **un, une, des,** become **de** following a negative verb.
3. In French, partitive articles must be expressed, even in cases where their English equivalents (*some, any*) may be omitted.

> Je voudrais **du** poisson.   I'd like (some) fish.
> Nous n'avons pas **de** poisson.   We don't have (any) fish.

A   You are at a buffet supper. Predict whether or not the following people are going to eat any of the foods indicated, according to their tastes.

> ▪▥   Serge déteste la salade.   *Il ne va pas manger de salade.*

1. Marie adore le poisson.
2. Alain n'aime pas le fromage.
3. Robert aime beaucoup la soupe.
4. Danièle aime le jambon.
5. Jean-Marc déteste la charcuterie.
6. Lise adore le pâté.
7. Tout le monde aime la glace.

B   Tell a friend who is helping you shop to look for the following items from your grocery list.

> ▪▥   charcuterie   *Va chercher de la charcuterie.*

1. lait	4. fromage blanc	7. viande
2. eau minérale	5. pain	8. crème
3. oignons	6. œufs	9. carottes

à vous,
maintenant

You are having dinner in a French restaurant. Order a main course, a vegetable, and a beverage. You might also have salad, cheese, fruit, and dessert. Refer to the list of foods on page 217.

Je voudrais du poisson, des tomates,...

Le pain et le fromage français

Bread is an important staple of the French diet and is served at every meal. As the French say, «**Repas sans pain, repas de rien.**» The government regulates the price of wheat to ensure that everyone can afford bread. French bread comes in various sizes and shapes and is bought fresh every day. The best-known type of French bread may be the long, skinny loaf called **la baguette,** but many other kinds are available as well in every **boulangerie.**

Nothing goes better with fresh bread than cheese, which the French generally serve at the end of the noon and evening meals. Over 350 kinds of cheese are made in France from the milk of cows, goats, and ewes. Many individual types of cheese are produced only in specifically defined parts of the country. Some of the most famous are **brie, camembert, roquefort,** and **gruyère.** Each of these names is an **appellation d'origine** (title of origin). No cheese may be sold under an **appellation d'origine** unless it is actually made within the district to which that name applies.

The verb **venir** (to come): present tense

SINGULAR	PLURAL
je **viens**	nous **venons**
tu **viens**	vous **venez**
on/il/elle **vient**	ils/elles **viennent**

1. Note the three stems of **venir** in the present tense: **vien-, ven-, vienn-.**
2. **Revenir** (to return, come back) is conjugated like **venir: je reviens, nous revenons,** etc.

C Confirm or deny that the following people are coming at two o'clock.

■꣼ Paul (oui) *Oui, Paul vient à deux heures.*

1. nous (non)
2. on (oui)
3. toi et moi (non)
4. eux (oui)
5. toi (non)
6. les cousins (oui)

D What stores are you and your friends returning from?

■꣼ Jacques: la charcuterie *Jacques revient de la charcuterie.*

1. Alice: la boulangerie
2. vous: la boucherie
3. moi: l'épicerie
4. les voisins: la poissonnerie
5. toi: la crémerie
6. nous: la pâtisserie

à vous, maintenant

Interview your teacher and some of your classmates about their usual routine with regard to coming to school. Compare your own habits with those of the people you interview. The following guidelines may be helpful.

> *Demandez à votre professeur et à vos copains: comment ils viennent à l'école (à pied, en voiture, etc.); à quelle heure ils viennent à l'école; s'ils viennent quelquefois à l'école le samedi ou le dimanche; s'ils aiment venir à l'école.*

The recent past: **venir de**

A present-tense form of **venir** followed by **de** plus an infinitive is used to tell about something that has just happened.

Je viens de tuer le lapin.	I have just killed the rabbit.
Ils viennent de déjeuner.	They have just had lunch.

E   Your friend suggests the following things to do. You aren't interested, because you've just done them.

   ▪▥   visiter le musée   — *Tu veux visiter le musée?*
                            — *Non, je viens de visiter le musée.*

   1.   jouer au tennis
   2.   aller au supermarché
   3.   étudier la leçon de maths
   4.   téléphoner à Jacques
   5.   écouter des cassettes
   6.   faire du cheval

F   The chef checks with you to be sure the necessary dinner preparations are being made. Reply that you and the other assistants have just completed the tasks indicated.

   ▪▥   Nicole achète la charcuterie?   *Elle vient d'acheter la charcuterie.*

   1.   Tu mets le couvert?
   2.   Pierre va aller à la boulangerie?
   3.   Est-ce que Maryse et Paul préparent la salade?
   4.   Hélène et toi, vous achetez du fromage?
   5.   Tu apportes des pommes de terre du jardin?

à vous,   Give an account of what the various members of your household have
maintenant   been doing at a particular time on a particular day.

   C'est samedi. Il est six heures du soir. Moi, je viens de [me promener].
   Mon père vient de [préparer le dîner]. Ma sœur...

The verb **mettre:** present tense

SINGULAR	PLURAL
je **mets**	nous **mettons**
tu **mets**	vous **mettez**
on/il/elle **met**	ils/elles **mettent**

1.   The basic meaning of **mettre** is *to put* or *to place.*
2.   In a clothing context, **mettre** means *to put on* or *to wear.*

   Elle met une robe.   She's putting on a dress.
   Qu'est-ce que tu vas mettre?   What are you going to wear?

3.   Note also the expression **mettre le couvert** (to set the table).

G Flowers can brighten any room. Say where the following people put the flowers that their guests bring with them when they come to dinner.

> ▪▥ Jacques (la cuisine)   *Jacques les met dans la cuisine.*

1. nous (le salon)
2. toi (ta chambre)
3. Sarah (la salle à manger)
4. moi (le corridor)
5. vous (le séjour)
6. M. et Mme Cordier (la cuisine)

H Say what everyone is wearing to the soccer game, according to the cues.

> ▪▥ Pierre (un tee-shirt)   *Pierre met un tee-shirt.*

1. moi (un pull-over)
2. vous (un imperméable)
3. Michel (un blouson)
4. toi (un manteau)
5. eux (des tennis)
6. nous (des bottes)

La Bourgogne

The province of **Bourgogne** was once a separate kingdom, later a duchy. At one point it covered territories all the way from Belgium to Provence, in southern France. The Dukes of Burgundy were powerful rivals of the kings of France. Most of them were well loved within their own domain, for they were just rulers who cared for the poor among their subjects. A hospital built for the poor, **les Hospices de Beaune,** is a monument to the humanitarian rule of the dukes. The hospital is also one of the architectural showcases of Burgundy. Each year, some of the finest wines of the region are sold by the hospital. The profits help to support the hospital services.

Wine is the leading product of modern Burgundy. Other agricultural products include wheat, corn, and sugar beets. Burgundy also produces cattle; in fact years ago some cattle of the famous **charolaise** breed were exported to Texas, where they are now extensively raised.

Les vendanges en Bourgogne

Question formation with inversion

A question may be formed by inverting (reversing the order of) a subject-verb phrase so that the verb precedes the subject. Inversion most often occurs in questions asking for specific information other than *oui* or *non*.

> Pourquoi **viens-tu** à Beaune?
> Où **mettez-vous** le pain?
> Quand **va-t-il** mettre le couvert?

1. In written French, a hyphen links an inverted verb with its subject pronoun.
2. When a third-person subject-verb phrase is inverted, a /t/ sound is heard between the verb and the subject pronoun. In writing, **-t-** is inserted, *unless* the verb form itself ends in **-t** or **-d.**

> /t/
> Mange-**t**-elle ses carottes?
>
> /t/
> Fait-il bien la cuisine?
>
> /t/
> Où va-**t**-on maintenant?
>
> /t/
> Comment s'appellent-ils?

3. Inversion rarely occurs with the subject pronoun **je;** rising intonation or **est-ce que** is generally used instead.
4. Noun subjects (as opposed to pronoun subjects) may not themselves be inverted to form *oui-non* questions. However, a noun subject may be followed by an inverted verb-pronoun phrase to form a *oui-non* question.

> Alice **va-t-elle** à la boulangerie?
> Les verres **sont-ils** sur la table?

5. Noun subjects are sometimes inverted in specific information questions; however, no hyphen is used in this case.

> Où sont **les assiettes?**
> Comment va **votre père?**

I   Restate the following questions, using inversion.

▪▥   Pourquoi est-ce qu'il achète des oignons?   *Pourquoi achète-t-il des oignons?*

1. Comment est-ce qu'elle fait la tarte?
2. Quand est-ce que tu prépares les escargots?
3. Où est-ce que vous achetez le beurre?
4. Combien d'œufs est-ce que tu veux?
5. Quels verres est-ce qu'ils cherchent?
6. Pourquoi est-ce qu'elle met le couvert?
7. Est-ce que tu manges du poisson?

J   Hugo is dying to tell his news: he's going to visit the United States. Humor him by asking him what he wants you to ask, using questions formed by inversion.

     ▥   Demande-moi où je vais.   *Où vas-tu?*

1. Demande-moi quand je vais à New York.
2. Demande-moi quelles villes je vais visiter.
3. Demande-moi combien de jours je vais rester aux États-Unis.
4. Demande-moi pourquoi j'y vais.
5. Demande-moi quand je reviens en France.
6. Demande-moi si je suis heureux.

à vous,
maintenant

Interview one of your classmates or your teacher. Using inversion questions, ask where the person buys different foods, or whether he or she grows them in a garden. Ask what foods he or she likes and likes to prepare. Use your imagination to think of as many appropriate questions as you can.

     Où allez-vous pour acheter des légumes? Quels légumes aimez-vous?
     Mangez-vous souvent du poisson? . . .

À table!

Quand Alice revient de la boulangerie, son père est en train de servir le vin dans les verres. Il remarque:

— Alors, le pain est bien frais, ma fille? Il est encore tout chaud, je parie.°   I'll bet

— Tu plaisantes,° Papa! dit° Alice.   You're joking/says

5   Mme Cordier, le visage° rouge de chaleur, arrive de la cuisine.   face

— Ouf! dit-elle, en soupirant de soulagement.°   Maintenant, à table, les   sighing with relief
enfants! Le déjeuner est prêt.°   ready

    Tout est frais dans ce bon repas bourguignon: le lapin, les petits pois, les
pommes de terre, la salade, les fraises, le pain. Et il ne manque plus rien
10 sur la table. Tout le monde s'assied avec anticipation.

— Bon appétit! dit Mme Cordier, en passant° le plat de charcuterie à son   passing
mari.

— Tiens, il n'y a pas beaucoup de pâté! remarque M. Cordier.

    Jacques devient° tout rouge et baisse la tête.°   becomes/bows his head

15 — C'est encore Jacques! s'exclame Alice, furieuse. Ce garçon est vraiment
insupportable...

— Ça alors, c'est le comble!° Jacques, tu es privé° de dessert, dit sa mère   that's the last straw/deprived
fermement.

    Mais le pauvre Jacques a l'air tellement déçu° que ses parents finissent   seems so disappointed
20 par° le laisser manger un morceau de tarte.   end up by

questions

1. Qu'est-ce qu'il y a sur la table de la salle à manger?
2. Pourquoi Alice est-elle furieuse?
3. Est-ce qu'il manque quelque chose sur la table?
4. Qu'est-ce qui est frais?
5. Est-ce que finalement Jacques mange du dessert?

à vous,
maintenant

1. Est-ce que vous aimez faire la cuisine? Qui fait la cuisine chez vous?
2. Est-ce que vous préférez dîner à la maison ou au restaurant?
3. Voilà le menu d'un restaurant. Qu'est-ce que vous allez manger comme déjeuner?

Au Relais Bourguignon

HORS D'ŒUVRE	Jambon, saucisson, pâté en croûte, pâté de foie gras
	Olives vertes, olives noires
	Salade de tomates
ENTRÉES	Escargots de Bourgogne
	Fruits de mer
PLATS DU JOUR	Bifteck frites ou rosbif
	Civet de lapin
	Filet de sole au beurre noir
	Langouste à l'armoricaine ou à la mayonnaise
	Couscous
	Côtelettes de mouton
	Poulet à la crème
LÉGUMES	Petits pois, carottes, haricots verts
SALADES	Laitue, cresson
FROMAGES	Camembert, roquefort, gruyère
DESSERTS	Tarte aux pommes, glace à la vanille, gâteau au chocolat
BOISSONS	Vin rouge, vin blanc, eau minérale, café, thé

résumé oral
ou écrit

Summarize the contributions of each member of the Cordier family to the Sunday dinner.

The partitive article (A-B)

A form of the partitive article is used to express an indefinite quantity (*some, any*) of a singular noun. The partitive article may not be omitted in French.

Je voudrais **du** lait.	I'd like (some) milk.
Je voudrais **de la** tarte.	I'd like (some) pie.
Je voudrais **de l'**eau.	I'd like (some) water.

All forms of the partitive article, as well as the indefinite articles (**un, une, des**), change to **de** after a negative verb.

Present tense of **venir**; the expression **venir de** (C-F)

The verb **venir** means *to come*. A present-tense form of **venir** followed by **de** plus an infinitive refers to something that has just happened. The verb **revenir** (to return, to come back) is conjugated like **venir**.

SINGULAR	PLURAL
je viens	nous venons
tu viens	vous venez
on/il/elle vient	ils/elles viennent

Nous venons de déjeuner.	We've just had lunch.
Il revient mardi.	He's coming back Tuesday.

Present tense of **mettre** (G-H)

The basic meaning of **mettre** is *to put*. **Mettre** also means *to put on* or *to wear* in talking about clothing. The expression **mettre le couvert** means *to set the table.*

SINGULAR	PLURAL
je mets	nous mettons
tu mets	vous mettez
on/il/elle met	ils/elles mettent

Question formation with inversion   (I-J)

A question may be formed by reversing the order of the subject pronoun and the verb. A hyphen is placed between the verb and the pronoun.

> Où sommes-nous?
> Allez-vous au restaurant?

In all inversion questions with the subjects **on, il(s),** and **elle(s),** the sound /t/ occurs between the verb and the subject pronoun. If the verb form does not end in a written **-t** or **-d, -t-** is inserted.

> À qui parle-t-elle?
> Comment trouvent-ils la maison?

Inversion rarely occurs with **je.** Noun subjects may be inverted *only* when preceded by a question word (such as **où, comment,** etc.). No hyphen is used with a noun subject. A noun may be followed by a verb-pronoun phrase to form a **oui-non** question.

> Où sont Dominique et Richard?
> La dame parle-t-elle français?

_____ Révision _____

A   You are going grocery shopping. Name at least one item that you intend to buy at each of the following stores.

   ■ⅲ   la boulangerie   *À la boulangerie, je vais acheter du pain.*

1. la boucherie
2. l'épicerie
3. la crémerie

4. la pâtisserie
5. chez le marchand de primeurs
6. la charcuterie

B   Tell the class how you feel about each of the following foods, and whether you often, sometimes, or never eat them.

   ■ⅲ   le pain   *[J'aime bien] le pain. [Je mange souvent] du pain.*

1. les escargots
2. le fromage
3. la glace
4. la salade
5. le poisson

6. les tomates
7. les pommes
8. le jambon
9. la charcuterie
10. le civet

C   M. Moreau has planned the following schedule for the day that relatives are coming for dinner. Take his role and report that fifteen minutes after each time mentioned, the various chores have just been done.

> ▪ıı   À huit heures, je vais acheter   *Il est huit heures et quart. Je viens*
> du pain frais.   *d'acheter du pain frais.*

1. À neuf heures, je vais téléphoner à Pierre.
2. À dix heures, Martin va arriver de Rennes.
3. À dix heures et demie, nous allons ranger la cuisine.
4. À onze heures moins le quart, les enfants vont aller à l'épicerie.
5. À onze heures dix, tu vas préparer le dessert.
6. À midi, vous allez apporter des légumes du jardin.

D   Say whose job it is to set the table on each of the following days, according to the cues.

> ▪ıı   lundi: Jacques   *Jacques met le couvert le lundi.*

1. mardi: nous
2. mercredi: toi
3. jeudi: Guillaume et Marcel

4. vendredi: Sylvie
5. samedi: moi
6. dimanche: vous

E   Ask the person who makes the following statements to clarify them, as you aren't sure you hear them correctly. Use logical questions formed by inversion.

> ▪ıı   Nous allons à Constantine.   *Où allez-vous?*

1. Jean-Paul arrive le 5 juin.
2. Les Cordier habitent en Bourgogne.
3. Toi et ton copain, vous pouvez venir demain.
4. Je trouve la ville très jolie.
5. Nous revenons parce qu'il fait mauvais.
6. On va aller au supermarché.

F   With your class, compile a list of French foods and food expressions that you see or hear mentioned near where you live. Cookbooks, restaurant menus, TV cooking shows, and magazine advertisements are good sources for such phrases. Try to learn the meaning of as many words and phrases as you can.

G   French people take food and everything associated with eating very seriously. Think about what you have learned in this chapter and compare French customs with your own and your family's eating and shopping habits. Explain in English some of the similarities and differences that you have noticed.

Vocabulaire

NOUNS

l'**assiette** (*f.*)   plate
la **baguette**   a kind of bread
la **banane**   banana
le **beurre**   butter
le **bœuf**   beef
la **boucherie**   butcher shop
la **boulangerie**   bakery
le **café**   coffee
la **carotte**   carrot
la **cave**   cellar
la **charcuterie**   pork-butcher
   shop, delicatessen; products
   sold in such a store
le **charcutier**   delicatessen
   owner
le **chocolat**   (hot) chocolate
le **civet**   stew
le **couteau**   knife
le **couvert**   table setting
la **crème**   cream
la **crémerie**   dairy store
la **cuillère**   spoon
le **dessert**   dessert
l'**eau** (*f.*)   water; l'**eau**
   minérale   mineral water
l'**épicerie** (*f.*)   grocery store
l'**escargot** (*m.*)   snail
la **fourchette**   fork
la **fraise**   strawberry
le **fromage**   cheese
le **fruit**   fruit
le **gâteau**   cake
la **glace**   ice cream
les **haricots verts** (*m.pl.*)   string
   beans
le **jambon**   ham
le **jardin**   garden
le **lait**   milk
le **lapin**   rabbit
le **légume**   vegetable

NOUNS (cont.)

le **marchand**, la **marchande**
   merchant
le **morceau**   piece
l'**œuf** (*m.*)   egg
l'**oignon** (*m.*)   onion
l'**orange** (*f.*)   orange
le **pain**   bread
le **pâté**   finely chopped meat;
   le **pâté en croûte**   a kind of
   pâté with a pastry crust
la **pâtisserie**   pastry shop
les **petits pois** (*m.pl.*)   peas
le **poisson**   fish
la **poissonnerie**   fish store
le **poivre**   pepper
la **pomme**   apple
la **pomme de terre**   potato
le **porc**   pork
le **poulet**   chicken
les **primeurs** (*m.pl.*)   fresh
   fruits and vegetables
le **repas**   meal
la **salade**   salad
le **saucisson**   salami
le **sel**   salt
la **serviette**   napkin
la **soupe**   soup
le **sucre**   sugar
la **tarte**   pie; tart
la **tomate**   tomato
le **verre**   glass
la **viande**   meat
le **vin**   wine

ADJECTIVES

frais, fraîche   fresh
gourmand(e)   fond of eating
honnête   honest
mauvais(e)   bad
tranquille   quiet, peaceful

VERBS

aider   to help
détester   to dislike, to hate
se disputer   to have an argument, to quarrel
embêter   to annoy
laisser   to let; to leave
manger   to eat
prendre   to take
préparer   to prepare
rester   to stay
revenir   to come back
tuer   to kill
venir   to come

ADVERBS

furieusement   furiously
gentiment   nicely
méchamment   nastily
pourtant   however
sérieusement   seriously
spécialement   especially
tranquillement   quietly

OTHER EXPRESSIONS

ça ne fait rien   it doesn't
   matter
ça sent (bon)   it smells
   (good)
comment ça se fait?   how can
   that be?
faire la cuisine   to cook
il manque (quelque chose)
   (something) is missing
je meurs de faim   I'm starving
mettre à cuire   to start cooking
mettre le couvert   to set the
   table
soyez gentil   be nice

deuxième étape

A **Une autobiographie.** One of the suggested activities in the **première étape** section of Stage 1 was to write a short letter about yourself to a French-speaking pen pal. Now is a good time to send another letter, in which you will be able to tell your friend a great deal more about your life. Describe your home, your town and its climate, your daily routine, and some of your interests and tastes (in food and clothing, for example).

If you would like to have a pen pal but have not yet found one, ask your teacher to help you. There are a number of organizations that provide names of people who would like to correspond with pen pals in foreign countries. It might also be possible for your class as a group to correspond with an English class in a French-speaking school.

B **Quelques personnages.** Describe as many as possible of the characters you have met in the **scènes** of Stage 2. Tell in French where they live, their ages, and what some of their interests and activities are. You may have formed some opinions of your own about these people and the way they live. Include your own impressions, and the reasons for them, in the descriptions you give.

C **Au restaurant.** Enact a scene in a restaurant. Assign the roles of diners, maître d'hôtel, waiter or waitress, chef, and cashier to various students. The skit should include ordering, serving, eating, and paying for the meal. For reference, you may wish to use the menu on page 232 or actual menus from French restaurants. The diners can exchange comments on the food and service, while the restaurant personnel may wish to gossip about the patrons.

D **Votre famille.** Give a brief summary in French of your family tree. Give the names of at least some of your relatives, such as grandparents, parents, aunts, uncles, cousins, nieces, and nephews. Tell where they live and give brief descriptions or identifying information about some of them. You may wish to show photographs or portraits of some family members.

E **Une ville imaginaire.** Set up your classroom as an imaginary city or town, with different areas designated as various streets, shops, and landmarks. Have some students act as local residents and others as out-of-town visitors. The visitors may ask the natives for directions and advice on where to go for particular needs. Use your imagination and create as much lively dialogue as you can. For example, the local residents may ask the visitors questions about where they come from, where they are staying, and what their interests are.

F **La haute couture.** Conduct a fashion show in your class. Several students should volunteer to be contestants, and others should be chosen as commentators whose role is to describe the outfits in French. There should also be a panel of judges, and perhaps one or more students serving as reporters to write brief summaries in French for the fashion columns of local newspapers. Afterwards, you and your classmates can exchange remarks and opinions about the spectacle. Try to make the show lively and entertaining by encouraging unusual or outrageous costumes, perceptive judging, and spirited commentary.

G **Les courses.** Divide the class into groups of three to five students. Each group prepares and presents a skit related to shopping. Some possible settings include a department store, a supermarket or various small food shops, a clothing store, an automobile showroom, a gift shop, or a souvenir shop. Factors such as complaints, hard-to-fill requirements, inefficient or overenthusiastic salespersons, and family disputes among shoppers can contribute to lively scenes.

H **La grande cuisine.** Find several recipes for French dishes. Some popular dishes that are not difficult or expensive to make are **soupe à l'oignon, crêpes, quiche,** and **ratatouille.** (French cookbooks are easy to find, and many general cookbooks contain several French recipes.) Interested students may volunteer to prepare one recipe each and bring the dish to share with the class. It may be possible to arrange to do the cooking at school in the home economics room.

I   **Une vente aux enchères.** Conduct an auction in French. Use play money and pictures clipped from magazines or catalogues to represent sale items. Each participant is given a fixed sum of money to spend, perhaps fifty thousand francs. Bidding is held on each item, with the teacher or a student acting as auctioneer. The item goes to the highest bidder in exchange for the sale price. Students may sell items they have already purchased to classmates in separate deals if they need more money in order to bid on other things. When all of the goods have been sold, you and your classmates can compare your purchases and expenditures.

J   **Le temps qu'il fait.** Keep a weather journal for one week, and then present a summary in French. Give as many details as possible about the weather for each day of the week. For a varied and comprehensive weather picture, keep a journal for locations in several different parts of the country or even of the world. (Information on national weather patterns is given on local television news programs; weather data for major foreign cities can be found in most newspapers.) Every student may be assigned a single location to monitor, or a smaller number of students may each report on several different locations.

K   **Actualités.** Watch the news for current events related to the themes and locales of Stage 2. When you come across interesting information about Brittany, the Loire Valley, Burgundy, Algeria, or Senegal, report it to the class in English. Reserve space on your classroom bulletin board for articles from newspapers and magazines.

L   **Voyages et rencontres.** Look at the color photographs on pages 105 to 112. Which of the places shown would you most like to visit? Which person or people shown would you most like to meet? Discuss in French your choices and the reasons for them. Then pretend that you are in the situation depicted in one of the photographs, and make up a short dialogue that might take place in that situation. Work with classmates as necessary.

Les joies
et les peines

241

A festival atmosphere prevails on these pages, in
street scenes of Paris (above), Nice at **Mardi gras**
(top right), and Concarneau (bottom right). One man
who seems to prefer to get away from it all floats
peacefully on the Seine near Paris.

Four of the most popular sports in France are represented here. Professional teams from Nantes and Bordeaux meet in a big soccer game; a skier meets the challenge of the giant slalom; racers in the **Tour de France** climb through the Alps; sailors rig their boats for an outing near Perpignan.

C'est les vacances! A picnic spread, a cyclist, and a young man writing home, with the Mediterranean resort of Collioure as a backdrop, form an inviting summer vacation collage.

chapitre 11
Aventures au Maroc

One of Morocco's most popular attractions is the walled city of Marrakech. Marrakech is famous for its **Médina,** the Moslem quarter where merchants gather every day to sell their products in small stores called **souks.** Visitors come to shop and to enjoy the colorful activities in the early evening on the main square by the Médina. Close by is the Hôtel du Parc, where Josette Mustapha, the daughter of the owner of the hotel, works as a receptionist during the summer.

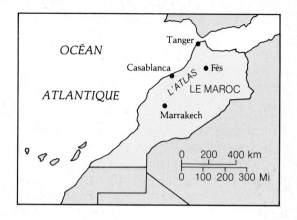

Arrivée à l'hôtel

Toute l'année, à l'Hôtel du Parc à Marrakech, il y a beaucoup de touristes marocains et européens. Josette Mustapha, la fille du propriétaire° de l'hôtel, travaille là pendant l'été comme réceptionniste. Cette année, non seulement elle s'occupe° des réservations et de la réception des clients,
5 mais elle aide aussi deux nouveaux employés à apprendre leur métier:° Ali, un porteur, et Mlle Farouk, qui va remplacer° Josette à l'automne.

owner

is in charge
job
replace

Aujourd'hui, c'est le premier août, et beaucoup de Français viennent au Maroc pour les vacances. Vers cinq heures et demie, un couple d'un certain âge° arrive à l'hôtel, et Josette se met gentiment à leur service.

middle-aged

10 — Bonsoir, monsieur, madame, dit-elle. Puis-je vous aider?

— Nous avons une réservation. Le nom est Marchand, dit l'homme.

— Oui, monsieur, répond Josette. Une chambre à deux lits avec salle de bains? Bon, donnez-moi vos passeports, s'il vous plaît... Et voulez-vous bien remplir cette fiche?

15 M. Marchand donne les deux passeports à la jeune fille, et un moment plus tard, la fiche. Puis, Josette appelle Ali et lui donne la clé de la chambre des clients.

— Tiens! Ali, dit-elle, prends les bagages de ces messieurs-dames. Ils ont la chambre quinze.

20 — Est-ce que nous sommes loin de la Médina? demande alors Mme Marchand.

— Non, madame, dit Josette, c'est tout près. Et les activités sur la place viennent de commencer.

M. Marchand n'a pas l'air enthousiaste.

25 — Ça vaut vraiment le coup? demande-t-il d'un air sceptique.°

— Oh oui, c'est très intéressant, dit Josette. Il y a des charmeurs de serpents,° des danseurs, des musiciens...

skeptical

snake charmers

La muraille de la ville de Marrakech

Mme Marchand, elle, a très envie d'aller voir ce spectacle.

— Nous avons peut-être le temps ce soir, Louis... Le dîner est à quelle
30 heure, mademoiselle?

— À vingt heures, madame. Mais un bon conseil! ajoute° Josette. Si   adds
vous avez des bijoux, ne les mettez pas pour aller à la Médina. Vous
pouvez les laisser dans le coffre-fort de l'hôtel, si vous voulez. Voilà une
enveloppe pour les mettre dedans.

35 — Oui, d'accord. Vous avez raison, mademoiselle. On peut laisser aussi
ton argent, Louis, suggère Mme Marchand à son mari.

— Tu sais bien, Marie-Madeleine, que je n'aime pas me séparer de mon
argent! proteste-t-il.

— Malheureusement, il y a toujours des pickpockets dans la foule à la
40 Médina! insiste Mlle Farouk. D'ailleurs,° l'hôtel a une assurance contre le   In any case
vol.

— Tu as pris beaucoup trop d'argent liquide,° mon ami, dit Mme Mar-   cash
chand à son mari. Il vaut mieux le laisser ici, ajoute-t-elle avec autorité.

M. Marchand n'a pas l'air content, mais il suit docilement° sa femme   follows obediently
45 vers l'ascenseur. Vingt minutes plus tard, ils descendent de leur chambre
et donnent l'enveloppe avec leurs bijoux et leur argent à Josette, qui
demande à Mlle Farouk de la mettre dans le coffre-fort.

Après le départ des Marchand pour la Médina, Josette range les fiches
des clients. Elle va les donner ce soir à la police, comme d'habitude.
50 Machinalement,° elle regarde la fiche des Marchand.   Routinely

— Tiens! dit-elle à Mlle Farouk. Ces gens arrivent de Marseille, mais
leur voiture est immatriculée à Paris. C'est bizarre!

Hôtel du Parc, Marrakech
Fiche de voyageur

PERSONNES: 2	CHAMBRE NO.: 15
NOM: Marchand	PRENOMS: Louis Michel Armand
NOM DE JEUNE FILLE: Leduc	Marie-Madeleine Marthe
DOMICILE: 92 avenue Mac Mahon Marseille	
NATIONALITE: français	
NO. DE PASSEPORT: 77AE 52230	NO. DE CARTE D'IDENTITE:
DELIVRE A: Marseille	LE: 6 juin 1983
VENANT DE: Casablanca	ALLANT A: Algers
NO. D'IMMATRICULATION DE LA VOITURE: 477 RV 75	
ARRIVEE: 1er août	DEPART: 5 août

There are ninety-six **départements** in France, and each one has both a name and a two-digit number. The last two digits of a car's license plate correspond to the department in which the car is registered. For example, Strasbourg is in department 67, **Bas-Rhin;** Rennes is in department 35, **Ille-et-Vilaine;** and Marseille is in department 13, **Bouches-du-Rhône.**

Department 75, **Paris,** is the only **département** that is a single city. The license plate number 477 RV 75 indicates that the car is registered in Paris.

questions

1. Où habitent les Marchand? Où sont-ils maintenant? D'où viennent-ils? Où vont-ils aller le 5 août?
2. Qui prend la fiche des Marchand? Qui prend leurs bagages? Qui leur parle des pickpockets à la Médina?
3. Qu'est-ce que Josette va donner à la police? Qu'est-ce que les Marchand donnent à Josette?

parlons du texte

The following drawing illustrates the beginning of the story in Marrakech. Interpret the drawing in as much detail as possible: identify the characters, explain what they are doing and what the circumstances are.

à vous, maintenant

1. Act out a scene at a hotel reception desk in a French-speaking country. The roles of guests, receptionist, porter, and other hotel employees can be played by different students. Think of ways to enliven the situation: for example, the family might be exceptionally large, or might include a pet; the receptionist might have no record of the reservation; there may be a great deal of luggage, or none at all.
2. Fill out a *fiche de voyageur* for yourself and your family. Choose any places and dates. You may need to make up a passport number.

Une affaire mystérieuse

Deux heures plus tard, les Marchand reviennent à l'hôtel.

— Ouf! je suis fatigué! se lamente M. Marchand. Je vais me reposer.

— Mais non, Louis, tu n'as pas le temps. C'est l'heure de nous habiller pour dîner, répond Mme Marchand. Tiens! Je vais mettre mon collier de perles et mon bracelet en or. Va donc° demander notre enveloppe à la jeune fille.

— Je vais aller la chercher, leur dit Mlle Farouk qui a écouté leur conversation. Elle va vers le coffre-fort dans le bureau et pousse un cri° d'horreur: Oh... non! ce n'est pas possible! Le coffre-fort est ouvert! Et il n'y a plus rien dedans!

Josette, affolée, appelle son père qui lui dit de téléphoner immédiatement à la police. M. Marchand est pâle comme la mort, et M. Mustapha s'empresse de° lui présenter ses excuses.

— Je regrette beaucoup, monsieur, madame. C'est la première fois que ça arrive à mon hôtel. Mais rassurez-vous, mon assurance va vous dédommager° de votre perte.

Pendant ce temps, Josette a téléphoné à la police. L'inspecteur Mahmud arrive très vite et questionne M. Mustapha et Josette. La jeune fille explique que, comme d'habitude, elle a mis° les objets de valeur des clients dans le coffre-fort. Mais quand Mme Marchand a demandé son enveloppe, continue-t-elle, Mlle Farouk a trouvé le coffre-fort vide.

therefore

utters a cry

hastens to

compensate

placed

Pendant toute cette conversation, Ali semble très nerveux et regarde les autres d'un air inquiet. Mais il ne dit rien à personne. Mlle Farouk essaie de° calmer Mme Marchand qui se lamente sur la perte de ses bijoux. M. Marchand est affalé° dans un fauteuil, complètement épuisé.

tries to
slumped

Ensuite, M. Mahmud interroge, en privé, chaque personne présente. Il leur pose des questions sur les petits et les grands événements de la journée, et leur demande s'ils suspectent quelqu'un. Quand il a terminé, il demande à Josette toutes les fiches de voyageurs et les examine attentivement. Puis, il décide de rentrer à son bureau pour téléphoner à la Sûreté° de Paris. Il relève d'abord les empreintes digitales° sur le coffre-fort, et s'en va, fort perplexe.

police department
takes fingerprints

À minuit, l'inspecteur revient à l'Hôtel du Parc pour arrêter deux suspects.

qui est-ce?

Vous êtes l'inspecteur Mahmud. Dites pourquoi vous suspectez ou vous ne suspectez pas les personnes suivantes: Ali, Mlle Farouk, Josette, M. Mustapha, M. Marchand, Mme Marchand. (La clé du mystère est dans la *lecture*, page 266.)

à vous, maintenant

1. Explain what circumstances cause you to experience different moods and feelings. Use the following adjectives.

   Je suis ravi(e) quand...

ravi(e)	sceptique	enthousiaste
inquiet, inquiète	content(e)	nerveux, nerveuse
timide	fatigué(e)	perplexe
épuisé(e)	affolé(e)	furieux, furieuse

2. Describe the way you think your classmates are feeling, based on how they look to you.

   [Jacqueline] a l'air nerveuse et perplexe.

petite scène

Act out a scene like the following, in which you and a classmate discuss whether or not a proposed outing — to the movies, for example — seems worthwhile.

VOUS	On fait quelque chose ce soir? Tu es libre?
ELLE/LUI	Oui, je suis libre à 19 h. On peut aller au cinéma, si tu veux.
VOUS	Bon, d'accord. On joue «Le mystère de minuit» au cinéma du coin.
ELLE/LUI	Ah oui? Tu penses que ça vaut le coup?
VOUS	Oui, c'est une histoire de vol de bijoux à Nice.
ELLE/LUI	Ça a l'air intéressant! Allons-y!

La Place Djema-el-Fna, à Marrakech

La Médina de Marrakech

Most cities in Morocco have a Moslem district called **la Médina.** The Médina in Marrakech is one of the most colorful. The narrow streets of the Médina form a labyrinth swarming with people in search of silver and gold jewelry, copper and brass utensils, leather goods, wool, as well as meat and produce. Bargaining is in order for most merchandise, especially jewelry, antiques, and rugs. Many people come just to admire the skill of the artisans, such as the wool merchants who dye wool and then hang it over the street to dry, providing a multicolored shelter from the sun. One can meander through the Médina for hours; without a guide, it is easy to get lost.

Each evening from about five o'clock to dusk, a colorful spectacle takes place on the Place Djema-el-Fna, the open square in front of the Médina. There are things to buy, but above all there are things to see: snake charmers, musicians, dancers, storytellers, and trained animal acts. Foreigners and Moroccans alike crowd around the performers to watch in wonder and amusement.

Étude de mots

Jouons avec les mots

A large group of masculine singular nouns ending in **-eur** identify performers of an action or members of a profession. Most of the nouns are formed by adding **-eur** to a verb stem. In the feminine, some of these nouns end in **-euse** and some end in **-rice**. A few of the nouns have no feminine form, even though they may refer to women.

Study the following list of nouns. You have seen many of them before.

le chanteur, la chanteuse   singer
le charmeur, la charmeuse   charmer
le coureur, la coureuse   runner, racer
le danseur, la danseuse   dancer
le flatteur, la flatteuse   flatterer
le joueur, la joueuse   player
le porteur, la porteuse   porter
le vendeur, la vendeuse   salesperson
le visiteur, la visiteuse   visitor
le voleur, la voleuse   thief
le voyageur, la voyageuse   traveler

l'acteur, l'actrice   actor
l'auditeur, l'auditrice   listener
le commentateur, la commentatrice   commentator
l'inspecteur, l'inspectrice   inspector

The following nouns have no feminine forms:

le chauffeur   driver   **l'ingénieur**   engineer
le docteur   doctor   **le professeur**   teacher

A   Complete each of the following sentences with the correct noun referring to a performer of an action or a member of a profession.

1. Mme Blanchard est un bon _____ de maths.
2. La femme de Léon est _____ de taxi.
3. Elle fait beaucoup de compliments à tout le monde. C'est une _____.
4. Cette femme est _____ à la Sûreté de Paris.
5. Le ballet de Paris a besoin de _____ professionnels.
6. Les _____ descendent fatigués de l'avion.
7. _____! Prenez les bagages de ces messieurs.
8. On a arrêté le _____ de bijoux à Nice. C'est un Américain.
9. Simone est une excellente _____ de tennis, n'est-ce pas?
10. L'_____ qui joue le rôle de Lady Macbeth est vraiment bonne.

Les moyens de transport

on voyage en bateau   on voyage en caravane   on voyage en motocyclette

on voyage en train   on voyage en avion   on voyage en autocar

B   Decide what means of transportation you would like to use to travel between the following cities, if you had plenty of time and an unlimited expense account.

▪▥   Paris–Rennes   *J'aimerais voyager en train de Paris à Rennes.*

1. Rennes–Douarnenez
2. Paris–Strasbourg
3. Paris–Dakar
4. Alger–Marrakech
5. Alger–Marseille
6. Marseille–Montréal

à vous, maintenant

Discuss with your classmates what means of transportation you usually take to go to various places in town. Use *en vélo, en métro, en autobus, à pied,* as appropriate.

▪▥   — *Comment est-ce que tu vas*   — *J'y vais en métro.*
        aux grands magasins?

au supermarché	à l'école	à la gare
au cinéma	en ville	à l'hôtel
au stade	à l'aéroport	chez des amis

Prononciation et orthographe

❚ /s/ le dessert
❚ /z/ le désert

/s/

RÉPÉTEZ

le dessert	décider	six
l'assurance	le cinéma	la prononciation
suspecter	le garçon	la réceptionniste
le soir	la scène	impatiemment

The sound /s/ is spelled **ss, s, c, ç, sc, x,** or **t** (when followed by the letters **-ion** or **-iemment**).

LISEZ

1. Ce soir, Sylvie va au cinéma avec un garçon français.
2. *Tongue-twister:* Si six cents scies scient six cents cyprès, six cent six scies scient six cent six cyprès.

/z/

RÉPÉTEZ

le désert	présenter	onze
la réservation	Josette	douze
poser	vous avez	dix hôtels
le magasin	nous allons	six enfants

The sound /z/ is spelled **s** (between two vowels), **z,** or **x** (when *liaison* occurs).

LISEZ

1. Je vous présente deux amies, Josette et Elisabeth.
2. Nous avons des réservations dans deux hôtels.

Cœur qui soupire n'a pas ce qu'il désire.

Vowel review

Repeat after your teacher or the tape:

/e/	/ɛ/	/ə/	/ø/	/œ/
la clé	bête	dedans	mieux	l'inspecteur
l'employé	prête	ce	mystérieux	la valeur
le collier	ouvert	contre	nerveux	le porteur
ces	cette	quelquefois	la flatteuse	le flatteur
le bracelet	frais	la première	la danseuse	le danseur

À la française

French-speaking people refer to 24-hour clock time mostly when they are traveling, going to a show, or making an appointment. One of the reasons is that time schedules for trains, planes, entertainment, and radio or TV announcements are given on a 24-hour basis. The hours 1 to 12 correspond to A.M. and the hours 12 to 24 correspond to P.M. Any fraction of the hour is given in minutes past the hour.

L'avion arrive à **quatorze heures.**   (2 P.M.)
Le train arrive à **seize heures quarante-cinq.**   (4:45 P.M.)

Here is a partial schedule for trains from Marseille to Paris:

MARSEILLE	21 42	19 22	23 53	08 00
AVIGNON	22 52	20 47		07 05
LYON	01 10	00 08	03 31	09 26
PARIS	06 12	07 27	08 30	13 30

Le Maroc et la ville de Marrakech

The North African kingdom of Morocco offers a variety of geographical features: a long seacoast on the Mediterranean and the Atlantic; the Atlas mountains, over four thousand meters high, with their winter ski resorts; and desert regions where summer temperatures reach 40°C. There are modern cities like Tangiers, Casablanca, and the capital, Rabat, and ancient walled cities like Fès, Meknès, and Marrakech.

Marrakech is situated on a plain at the foot of the Atlas mountains. With its striking ochre-colored walls and many palm trees rising like an oasis out of the desert sands, the city is an alluring sight for approaching travelers. Inside the adobe walls, temperatures remain relatively cool. People flock to Marrakech during every season of the year to visit the Médina and many other fascinating attractions. The Sultan's Palace, formerly a residence for Moslem rulers, is now a museum with beautiful gardens. Perhaps the most celebrated building in the city is the Koutoubyia mosque, which dates from the twelfth century A.D. At the top of the tall spire of the mosque, a crier called a **muezzin** chants five times each day, calling Moslem worshipers to prayer.

La mosquée Koutoubyia et un charmeur de serpents

Grammaire

The demonstrative adjectives **ce(t), cette, ces**

Masculine singular	ce (before consonant sound) cet (before vowel sound)	ce monsieur cet homme
Feminine singular	cette	cette dame
Plural (masculine or feminine)	ces	ces garçons ces filles

Ce, cet, cette (*this* or *that*), and **ces** (*these* or *those*) are demonstrative adjectives. They agree in number and gender with the nouns they modify.

A Call a friend's attention to various items at a department store.

■III une robe *Regarde cette robe!*

1. une chemise
2. des bijoux
3. un collier
4. une ceinture
5. des chaussures
6. des foulards
7. un bracelet
8. une jupe
9. un imperméable

B You are taking a tour of an old French city. Ask your tour guide during what period various structures were built.

■III un pont *Ce pont est de quelle époque?*

1. un hôtel
2. un château
3. une cathédrale
4. un lycée
5. une église
6. des monuments
7. un hôpital
8. des musées
9. des maisons

C After your first day in a resort hotel, you are very dissatisfied with the accommodations, the service, and the food. Complain to the manager about the following problems. Use demonstrative adjectives.

■III Le restaurant est vraiment mauvais. *Madame/Monsieur, ce restaurant est vraiment mauvais!*

1. La réceptionniste est insupportable.
2. Le porteur est un idiot.
3. L'ascenseur est dangereux.
4. La chambre est moche.
5. Le lit est trop dur.
6. Les fauteuils sont trop petits.
7. Les légumes ne sont pas frais.

Indirect-object pronouns **lui** and **leur**

In the third person only, the indirect-object pronouns are different from the direct-object pronouns. (In the first and second persons, **me, te, nous,** and **vous** are used as both direct and indirect objects.)

THIRD PERSON	INDIRECT OBJECT	DIRECT OBJECT
Singular	Tu **lui** parles?	Tu **la/le** regardes?
Plural	Tu **leur** téléphones?	Tu **les** invites?

1. The indirect-object pronouns **lui** and **leur** replace **à** plus a noun phrase designating a person or group of people.

> Je parle **à Josette.**   Je **lui** parle.
> Je vais demander **à mes amis.**   Je vais **leur** demander.

Note some common verbs that often take indirect objects:

demander (à)	**parler (à)**
donner (à)	**raconter (à)**
montrer (à)	**téléphoner (à)**

2. **Lui** and **leur** follow the same word-order patterns as other object pronouns. They precede the verb, except in affirmative commands.

> Tu **leur** donnes ce cadeau?   Donne-**leur** ce cadeau.
> Tu vas **leur** donner ce cadeau?
> Ne **leur** donne pas ce cadeau!

D Replace the italicized noun phrases with *lui* or *leur,* as appropriate.

> ▬▮▮ Il répond *à l'inspectrice.*   *Il lui répond.*

1. Il parle *à son père.*
2. Nous téléphonons *à Raymond.*
3. Tu vas demander *aux enfants?*
4. Téléphonez *au docteur.*
5. Elle dit bonjour *à ses parents.*
6. Ne parlez pas *aux joueurs.*

E Respond to the following questions either affirmatively or negatively. Use an appropriate object pronoun in each response.

> ▬▮▮ Tu écoutes le guide?   *Oui, je l'écoute./Non, je ne l'écoute pas.*
> ▬▮▮ Elle téléphone à Paul?   *Oui, elle lui téléphone./Non, elle...*

1. Tu téléphones à tes copains?
2. Elle regarde le passeport du client?
3. Elle parle à son amie?
4. Il répond à l'inspecteur?
5. Il va écouter les musiciens?
6. Mlle Mustapha parle aux employés?

F   During the first few hours in Marrakech, Mme Marchand has plenty of instructions for her husband. However, M. Marchand is feeling sulky and doesn't want to be bothered. Take the role of M. Marchand and reply that you don't want to do as you're told.

■III   Donne ton argent à la   *Non, je ne veux pas lui donner*
        jeune fille.   *mon argent.*

1. Donne cinq francs au porteur.
2. Montre la photo des enfants à ces employés.
3. Donne-moi les passeports.
4. Téléphone à mes cousins marocains.
5. Demande le chemin à la jeune fille.
6. Parle à ces danseurs là-bas.
7. Donne-moi la clé de la chambre.
8. Demande notre enveloppe à la jeune fille.

The **passé composé** with **avoir**

The **passé composé** is a verb tense used to refer to actions or events that occurred in the past. A verb in the **passé composé** has two parts: the past participle of the verb, preceded by a present-tense form of an auxiliary verb (usually **avoir**).

AUXILIARY VERB	PAST PARTICIPLE	ENGLISH EQUIVALENTS
j'ai		I worked (have worked, did work)
tu as		you worked (have worked, did work)
il/elle a		he/she worked (has worked, did work)
on a	travaillé	we/they worked (have worked, did work)
nous avons		we worked (have worked, did work)
vous avez		you worked (have worked, did work)
ils/elles ont		they worked (have worked, did work)

1. The past participle of an **-er** verb is the infinitive stem plus **-é.**

Infinitive	Past participle
jouer	joué
manger	mangé
expliquer	expliqué

2. In the negative, **ne** precedes the auxiliary verb; **pas** follows the auxiliary.

   La police **n'a pas** trouvé les bijoux.

G A group of tourists have just returned from Marrakech. Tell some of the things they did there, according to the cues.

▪▥ nous: trouver un bracelet en or

Nous avons trouvé un bracelet en or.

1. elles: regarder les danseurs
2. moi: acheter un collier
3. vous: manger du couscous
4. on: visiter la Médina
5. toi: parler aux vendeurs
6. nous: écouter les musiciens

H Deny that the following actions took place.

▪▥ Tu as mangé tous les gâteaux.

Mais non, je n'ai pas mangé tous les gâteaux!

1. Paul a travaillé tout l'après-midi.
2. Geneviève a écouté la radio.
3. Les enfants ont joué toute la journée.
4. Tu as trouvé tes bijoux.
5. Ils ont aidé leurs parents.
6. Vous avez laissé votre argent à la maison.
7. On a visité le premier étage du château.

I You are chief of police. Each morning, with your assistant, you make a list of responsibilities for the day. In the evening, the two of you go over the day's activities and enter them in the police journal. Based on the A.M. checklist below, what do you say to your assistant during your evening conference?

▪▥ Moi, je téléphone à la Sûreté de Paris.

Moi, j'ai téléphoné à la Sûreté de Paris.

1. Ledoux regarde toutes les fiches de voyageurs de l'hôtel.
2. Creuset et Duhamel étudient les empreintes digitales.
3. Toi, tu arrêtes les deux suspects.
4. Toi et Hoffmann, vous interrogez les suspects.
5. Toi et moi, nous expliquons la situation aux journalistes.
6. Moi, je déjeune avec le maire (*mayor*).

à vous,
maintenant

Tell your classmates five things that you have done in the past week. Then mention at least three things that you intended to do, but did not get around to doing.

Cette semaine, j'ai...
Malheureusement, je n'ai pas...

The verb **prendre:** present tense

SINGULAR	PLURAL
je prends	nous prenons
tu prends	vous prenez
on/il/elle prend	ils/elles prennent

The basic meaning of **prendre** is *to take*. It also means *to have, to eat*, and *to drink* when used in connection with meals or food.

Je prends le métro pour aller en ville.	I take the subway to go downtown.
Il prend de la salade.	He's having salad.

Apprendre (to learn) and **comprendre** (to understand) are conjugated like **prendre**.

J'apprends l'anglais.	I'm learning English.
Tu comprends la leçon?	Do you understand the lesson?

J Everyone is hungry or thirsty today. Say what foods people are having.

■||| nous: du pâté   *Nous prenons du pâté.*

1. moi: du chocolat chaud
2. vous: du fromage
3. lui: de l'eau minérale
4. eux: des pommes
5. nous: du saucisson
6. toi: des légumes
7. elles: du jambon
8. elle: du civet de lapin

K The following people are leaving on vacation today. Say how they are traveling and when they are departing.

■||| Pierre: l'avion à 15 h   *Pierre prend l'avion à quinze heures.*

1. Raymond: le bateau à 17 h
2. nous: le train à 20 h 30
3. toi: l'autocar à 14 h 45
4. moi: l'avion à 21 h 05
5. vous: le train à 18 h 52
6. elles: l'avion à 13 h 20

L State that the following people are learning the languages indicated, but that they don't understand them very well.

■||| Richard: le latin   *Richard apprend le latin, mais il ne le comprend pas très bien.*

1. toi: l'allemand
2. eux: l'anglais
3. elle: l'espagnol
4. nous: le français
5. vous: le latin
6. moi: l'espagnol

L'histoire du Maroc

Morocco, like the rest of North Africa, was part of the Roman Empire for several centuries. Following the decline of Rome, the Arab conquest brought the Moslem religion to the region in the 7th century A.D. From that time on, a succession of dynasties ruled in Morocco, as there were ongoing power struggles between the Arabs and the Berbers. The Berber dynasty of the **Almoravides** (Moors), which ruled Morocco and Spain during the 11th and 12th centuries, was one of the most influential in shaping the civilization.

Beginning in the 15th century, the Portuguese, Spanish, and French attempted to establish colonial holdings in the country, which had always had enormous strategic significance because of its location at the entrance to the Mediterranean. By 1850, French and Spanish forces had gained strongholds throughout much of the country. The French had become the dominant power in Morocco by 1912, and the country — except for an area on the Atlantic that was controlled by Spain — was in effect a protectorate of France.

Morocco gained its independence from European powers in 1956 and became a constitutional monarchy with a king who is both head of state and religious leader. The country maintains close economic and cultural ties with France, and French is widely spoken along with Arabic and Berber.

Lecture

Aux dernières nouvelles

«LE MATIN» de Marrakech   le 2 août

Coup° double pour un inspecteur de la police locale   triumph

L'inspecteur Joseph Mahmud de la police de Marrakech vient de réussir°   succeed
une double arrestation à l'Hôtel du Parc. Appelé à l'hôtel hier soir par
Mlle Mustapha, la fille du propriétaire, pour une affaire de vol de bijoux et
de monnaies étrangères,° Mahmud a mis la main non seulement sur la   foreign currency
5 voleuse, mais aussi sur un faux-monnayeur.°   counterfeiter

Interrogé, l'inspecteur Mahmud a déclaré: «L'affaire est très simple!
Lorsque° je suis arrivé à l'hôtel vers vingt heures, j'ai trouvé le coffre-fort   When
où on met les bijoux et l'argent des clients, ouvert et vide. Quand j'ai
demandé à la réceptionniste, Mlle Mustapha, de reconstituer les
10 événements de la journée, j'ai remarqué plusieurs choses:

«Premièrement, Mlle Mustapha et Mlle Farouk sont les seules per-
sonnes à connaître° la combinaison du coffre-fort. J'ai effectivement°   to know/indeed
trouvé les empreintes digitales des deux femmes sur le coffre-fort, mais pas
d'autres.

15 «Deuxièmement, d'après° Mlle Mustapha, c'est sa remplaçante, Mlle Farouk, qui a ouvert le coffre la dernière. En effet, c'est elle qui a pris l'enveloppe des clients de la chambre 15, à dix-sept heures trente pour les mettre en sûreté. Aucun° client n'a déposé d'objets de valeur à la réception entre ce moment-là et vingt heures. *(according to)* *(No)*

20 «Troisièmement, c'est Mlle Farouk qui est présente, comme par hasard,° quand les clients reviennent de la Médina, et qui leur offre d'aller chercher leur enveloppe. Donc, c'est elle qui découvre le coffre-fort vide. J'ai même appris qu'elle avait° encouragé les Marchand à laisser leurs objets de valeur à l'hôtel. Ce sont là des coïncidences assez étranges, vous ne

25 trouvez pas? *(as if by chance)* *(learned that she had)*

«Avant de retourner à l'hôtel pour interroger à nouveau° Mlle Farouk, j'ai téléphoné à la Sûreté de Paris. La fiche des occupants de la chambre 15, les Marchand, contenait un renseignement° qui m'a mis en alerte. J'ai pensé: Pourquoi leur voiture est-elle immatriculée à Paris, alors qu'ils°

30 habitent à Marseille? La Sûreté m'a renseigné tout de suite:° les propriétaires de la voiture sont recherchés° pour fabrication de fausse monnaie. Il fallait donc° que je retrouve l'argent des Marchand de toute urgence. Toujours d'après Mlle Mustapha, le mari ne voulait pas° laisser son argent à l'hôtel. C'est sa femme qui a insisté. *(again)* *(contained a piece of information)* *(since they)* *(informed immediately)* *(wanted)* *(It was necessary, therefore)* *(did not want)*

35 «À l'hôtel, j'ai trouvé Mlle Farouk prête à partir,° et n'ai eu aucune° difficulté à lui faire avouer° son crime. Elle m'a donné les enveloppes des clients presque sans protester. Et lorsque j'ai examiné celle° des Marchand, j'ai pu constater° immédiatement que leurs quarante billets de 500 francs étaient° faux. Vous connaissez la suite!° J'ai arrêté Mlle Farouk et

40 M. Marchand. Ils sont en ce moment à la prison de Marrakech.» *(ready to leave/had no)* *(admit)* *(the one)* *(I was able to see)* *(were/You know the rest)*

Les autres clients ont retrouvé leurs bijoux et leur argent. Nous leur souhaitons° une excellente fin de séjour° dans notre ville. Et nous faisons tous nos compliments à Monsieur l'Inspecteur Mahmud pour son coup double. *(wish/end of stay)*

une situation embrouillée

Unscramble the story below, so that it follows the facts as they happened.

1. Les Marchand vont regarder le spectacle à la Médina.
2. L'inspecteur relève les empreintes digitales sur le coffre-fort.
3. Mme Marchand a envie d'aller à la Médina.
4. Mlle Farouk insiste que l'argent des Marchand est en sûreté dans le coffre-fort.
5. Ali est nerveux quand il parle à l'inspecteur.
6. M. Mahmud téléphone à la Sûreté de Paris.
7. L'inspecteur Mahmud arrête M. Marchand.
8. M. Marchand donne sa fiche à Josette.
9. L'inspecteur interroge Mlle Farouk qui avoue son crime.
10. Josette aide deux nouveaux employés.

à vous, maintenant	1. Quel est votre moyen de transport préféré? 2. Est-ce que vous préférez voyager seul(e)? avec un tour? avec un groupe d'amis? avec un guide? 3. Quel pays voulez-vous visiter? Quel état? Quelle province? Quelle ville? Quel village? 4. Prenez-vous le temps de vous promener à pied? en vélo? de parler avec les gens de la région?
résumés oraux	Explain the role of each of the characters in the story as they participated in the events of the day: Josette, Ali, Mlle Farouk, M. Mustapha, M. Marchand, Mme Marchand, l'inspecteur Mahmud.
résumé écrit	The newspaper *Le Monde* in Paris wants to run a short article about the Marrakech incident. Find out the many "who's?", "what's", "where's", "when's", and "why's" that are contained in the *Le Matin* article. Use this information and the following questions as guides to write your own article. 1. Où l'action s'est-elle passée? 2. Qui a participé à l'action? 3. Qu'est-ce qui est arrivé? 4. Quand l'action s'est-elle passée? 5. Pourquoi?

Résumé grammatical

Demonstrative adjectives (A-C)

The demonstrative adjectives **ce, cet, cette** (this/that) and **ces** (these/those) agree with the nouns they modify. With masculine singular nouns, **ce** is used before a consonant, **cet** is used before a vowel. Feminine singular nouns take **cette.** All plural nouns take **ces.**

ce garçon   **cet** homme   **cette** femme   **ces** gens

Indirect-object pronouns **lui, leur** (D-F)

The third-person indirect-object pronouns **lui** and **leur** replace **à** plus one or more nouns; these pronouns refer to a person or to a group of people. They precede the verb except in affirmative commands. Note that **lui** means either (*to*) *him* or (*to*) *her*.

— Tu parles **à Anne?**   — Oui, je **lui** parle.

— Il va téléphoner **à Luc?**   — Oui, il va **lui** téléphoner.

— Je demande **aux voyageurs?**   — Oui, demande-**leur.**

The **passé composé** with **avoir** (G-I)

The *passé composé* is a tense used to relate actions or events that have already occurred. It is made up of two verbs: an auxiliary verb (usually **avoir**) in the present tense, and the past participle of the main verb. For **-er** verbs, the past participle is the infinitive stem plus **-é.** Below are examples of the verbs **jouer, manger,** and **trouver** in the *passé composé:*

J'ai joué au tennis avec elles.

On a mangé beaucoup de pain.

Vous avez trouvé votre parapluie?

The negative of the *passé composé* is formed by placing **ne** before the auxiliary verb **(avoir)** and **pas** after the auxiliary.

Je n'ai pas téléphoné à mon copain.

The *passé composé* corresponds to three English tenses: the simple past, the compound past, and the emphatic past.

elle a parlé = she spoke, she has spoken, she did speak

The verb **prendre:** present tense (J-L)

SINGULAR	PLURAL
je prends	nous prenons
tu prends	vous prenez
on/il/elle prend	ils/elles prennent

1. The basic meaning of **prendre** is *to take.* **Prendre** also means *to have* or *to eat* when used with foods.

Prenons le train.	Let's take the train.
Prends du fromage!	Have some cheese!

2. Other verbs with forms that follow the pattern of **prendre** are **apprendre** (to learn) and **comprendre** (to understand).

Il apprend à danser.	He's learning to dance.
Je comprends tout!	I understand everything!

Révision

A   State whether the following people travel sometimes, often, or never by the means of transportation indicated.

▪ⅲ   moi: l'avion   *Je ne prends jamais l'avion.*

1. nous: le train
2. toi: ton vélo
3. elles: l'autocar
4. on: le métro
5. vous: la voiture
6. lui: sa motocyclette

B   Ask if Inspector Mahmud has interrogated any of the following people.

▪ⅲ   le jeune homme   *Est-ce qu'il a interrogé ce jeune homme?*

1. la dame
2. les messieurs
3. la cliente
4. l'employée
5. les touristes
6. la jeune fille
7. le couple français
8. l'employé
9. le garçon

C   Report that the people have not yet performed the indicated actions.

▪ⅲ   Gilles: étudier sa leçon   *Gilles n'a pas encore étudié sa leçon.*

1. vous: rencontrer les touristes
2. on: préparer la salade
3. toi: acheter les légumes
4. elle: écouter les musiciens
5. nous: téléphoner à la police
6. l'inspecteur: arrêter le suspect

D   Find out if Inspector Mahmud is asking questions of the following people. Your classmates should reply in the affirmative or negative and use *lui* or *leur*, as appropriate.

▪ⅲ   l'employé   — *Il pose des questions à l'employé?*
— *Oui, il lui pose des questions. / — Non, il ne lui pose pas de questions.*

1. les touristes
2. les Marchand
3. la cliente
4. le porteur
5. la réceptionniste
6. le propriétaire

E   Which of the following people did you suspect had stolen the jewels at the Hôtel du Parc? Use at least two adjectives in your responses.

▪ⅲ   M. Marchand   *Je n'ai pas suspecté M. Marchand. Il est trop timide et pas très intelligent.*

1. Mlle Farouk
2. Josette
3. l'inspecteur Mahmud
4. Ali, le porteur
5. Mme Marchand
6. M. Marchand

F   Prepare a travel folder for Morocco. Use information from the culture sections of the chapter and other information you can find.

Vocabulaire

NOMS

l'acteur, l'actrice   actor
l'argent (*m.*)   money
l'assurance (*f.*)   insurance
l'auditeur, l'auditrice   listener
l'autocar (*m.*)   intercity bus
les bagages (*m.pl.*)   bags, suitcases
le bijou (*pl.* **bijoux**)   piece of jewelry
le bracelet (en or)   (gold) bracelet
le bureau   office
la caravane   trailer
le chanteur, la chanteuse   singer
le charmeur, la charmeuse   charmer
le chauffeur   driver
la clé   key
le client, la cliente   customer, hotel guest
le coffre-fort   safe
le collier (de perles)   (pearl) necklace
le commentateur, la commentatrice   commentator
le conseil   advice; piece of advice
le coureur, la coureuse   runner, racer
le danseur, la danseuse   dancer
le docteur   doctor
l'événement (*m.*)   event
le fauteuil   armchair
la femme   wife
la fiche   registration form
la foule   crowd

NOMS

les gens (*m.pl.*)   people
l'hôtel (*m.*)   hotel
l'ingénieur (*m.*)   engineer
l'inspecteur, l'inspectrice   inspector
le joueur, la joueuse   player
le lit   bed
le mari   husband
la mort   death
les objets (*m.pl.*) **de valeur**   valuables
la perte   loss
le temps   time
le train   train
les vacances (*f.pl.*)   vacation
le vendeur, la vendeuse   salesperson
le visiteur, la visiteuse   visitor
le vol   theft
le voleur, la voleuse   thief

ADJECTIFS

affolé(e)   frantic
ce (cet), cette   this, that; **ces** these, those
enthousiaste   enthusiastic
épuisé(e)   exhausted
fatigué(e)   tired
immatriculé(e)   registered
inquiet, inquiète   disturbed
nerveux, nerveuse   nervous
ouvert(e)   open
perplexe   perplexed
vide   empty

PRÉPOSITIONS

dedans   inside
contre   against

ADVERBES

attentivement   carefully
fort   very
immédiatement   immediately

VERBES

apprendre   to learn
arrêter   to arrest
comprendre   to understand
décider   to decide
dire   to say; **il/elle dit**   he/she says
donner   to give
expliquer   to explain
interroger   to question, interrogate
prendre   to take; to eat, drink, have (a meal)
remplir   to fill out
répondre   to answer; **il/elle répond**   he/she answers
se reposer   to rest
suspecter   to suspect
terminer   to finish
travailler   to work

AUTRES MOTS ET EXPRESSIONS

quelqu'un   someone

avoir l'air   to seem; to look
ça vaut le coup   it's worth it
c'est bizarre   that's rather odd
il s'en va   he goes away
plus tard   later
poser des questions   to ask some questions
la première fois   the first time
rassurez-vous   don't worry

chapitre 12
Une tragédie
dans les Alpes

Bruxelles (Brussels), the capital of **la Belgique,** is an important commercial, industrial, and cultural center. The city bustles with life and international business. Bruno Martin lives with his parents and his two sisters in the heart of the capital. It is Easter time, and the Martins have gone to the French Alps for a ski vacation — all except M. Martin, who is kept at home by his work at the Common Market.

Un communiqué de dernière minute

Ce soir, M. Martin est seul chez lui à Bruxelles. Ce sont les vacances de Pâques,° et sa femme et leurs trois enfants sont allés à Chamonix dans les Alpes françaises, pour y faire du ski. M. Martin n'a pas pu partir avec eux à cause de ses affaires. À huit heures, il décide d'écouter le journal sportif
5 à la radio. Comme il est passionné pour le football, il veut savoir les résultats du match entre l'Allemagne° et l'Angleterre.° Il s'installe confortablement dans un fauteuil et met la radio:

«Et maintenant, chers auditeurs, les nouvelles sportives. Tout d'abord, les résultats du match de football Allemagne – Angleterre qui° a eu lieu à
10 Cologne. Après un match très disputé, l'équipe allemande a gagné d'un but. Le score est de trois à deux. Les Allemands vont rencontrer l'équipe de France à Saint-Étienne le mois prochain.

Notre meilleur coureur cycliste depuis Merckx, Michel Parmentier, a annoncé aujourd'hui son intention de courir à nouveau cet été dans le Tour
15 de France. Son docteur déclare qu'il est complètement remis° de son accident en Espagne° l'hiver dernier.

...Nous interrompons notre journal pour vous apporter un communiqué de dernière minute: Aujourd'hui, une avalanche dans les Alpes, près de Chamonix, a causé la mort de plusieurs skieurs. L'un d'entre eux est un
20 jeune Belge âgé de seize ans. On ne nous a pas encore communiqué l'identité de ce malheureux jeune homme.»

À ces mots, M. Martin devient terriblement inquiet pour son fils. Pris° de panique, il se précipite au téléphone pour appeler l'hôtel où sa famille est descendue.° Mais il lui faut° d'abord appeler les renseignements° à
25 Chamonix, pour avoir le numéro de l'hôtel. Malheureusement, le standardiste n'arrive pas à obtenir la communication.°

— Je regrette, monsieur. Toutes les lignes sont occupées. Rappelez plus tard.

Après une autre tentative° au téléphone, M. Martin perd patience et
30 décide d'envoyer un télégramme à Chamonix.

Easter

Germany/England

which

recovered
Spain

Seized

is staying/he must/
    information

get the connection

attempt

```
┌─────────────────────────────────────────────┐
│  ╭──────────────────────────────────────────╮ │
│  │                                          │ │
│  │   TELEGRAMME                             │ │
│  │                                          │ │
│  ╰──────────────────────────────────────────╯ │
│                                               │
│   MME  RENE  MARTIN    HOTEL  DU  MONT-BLANC   │
│                                               │
│   74025   CHAMONIX   FRANCE                    │
│                                               │
│                                               │
│   INQUIET  A  CAUSE  AVALANCHE    ATTENDS      │
│                                               │
│   NOUVELLES  DE  VOUS    PRIERE  TELEPHONER    │
│                                               │
│   D'URGENCE   AFFECTUEUSEMENT    PAPA          │
│                                               │
└─────────────────────────────────────────────┘
```

télégrammes

Notice that in a telegram, no accents or punctuation marks are used.

If M. Martin had written out his message completely, this is what he would have said:

> Je suis inquiet à cause de l'avalanche. J'attends des nouvelles de vous. Prière de (*please*) me téléphoner d'urgence. Affectueusement, Papa.

Write out in full the messages contained in the following telegrams.

1. GAGNE CHAMPIONNAT TENNIS WIMBLEDON   SUZANNE
2. IMPOSSIBLE RENTRER   PERDU ARGENT ET BIJOUX   PRIERE TELEPHONER D'URGENCE   HOTEL DU PARC   LOUISE
3. ARRIVE DEMAIN PARIS TRAIN   ESPERE TE VOIR GARE ST-LAZARE 17H 45 RAYMOND

à vous, maintenant

1. Où êtes-vous allé(e) pour les vacances de Pâques?
2. Êtes-vous passionné(e) pour le ski? le football? le tennis? le base-ball?
3. Est-ce que vous gagnez souvent quand vous faites du sport?
4. Est-ce que vous avez déjà vu une avalanche? au cinéma? en réalité? Où?
5. Est-ce que vous avez déjà eu un accident? Quelle sorte d'accident?
6. Avez-vous déjà envoyé un télégramme? Quand?

petite scène

Pretend to be a radio sports commentator. Give the results of a recent game, and tell where and when the game took place. Model your comments on the information given in the sports report that M. Martin heard.

Chamonix

Chamonix, an important center for mountain climbing and winter sports, attracts visitors from all over the world. The town is situated in a valley at the foot of **le Mont Blanc,** the highest mountain in Europe. Mont Blanc forms part of the border between France and Italy. The scenery in the valley is breathtaking, with majestic peaks towering on all sides.

Looking up at Mont Blanc from the town of Chamonix, one sees a large glacier called **la mer de Glace** (sea of ice). Visitors can take a cog railroad up the mountain to a point close to the glacier for a truly magnificent view. From the glacier, experienced alpinists begin their climb toward some of the higher peaks, and skiers begin the ascent to Mont Blanc, where skiing goes on throughout the year.

One of the world's longest highway tunnels, **le tunnel du Mont Blanc,** cuts through the Alps and links France and Italy near Chamonix. The tunnel is 11.6 kilometers long. It took more than six years to build and was opened in 1965.

La mer de glace

Sain et sauf?

Toute la soirée, M. Martin, dévoré d'inquiétude,° attend des nouvelles de   consumed with worry
sa famille. Finalement, à dix heures, le téléphone sonne. Il décroche
l'appareil° aussitôt.   picks up the receiver

—Allô? Qui est à l'appareil? demande-t-il d'une voix° anxieuse.   voice
5 —Allô, Papa! C'est moi, Bruno! répond la voix de son fils.
—Bruno! Eh bien, tu sais, j'ai eu peur! Vous avez reçu° mon télégramme,   received
n'est-ce pas?
—Oui, Papa...
—Alors, tu vas bien? demande M. Martin. Et ta mère? Et tes sœurs?
10 —Toute la famille va bien, sauf Anne-Marie...
—Allons bon! Qu'est-ce qui lui est arrivé? s'exclame le père, inquiet à
nouveau.
—Elle est tombée en ski et elle s'est cassé la jambe°...   has broken her leg
—Oh, mon Dieu! Mais c'est épouvantable! se lamente M. Martin.
15 —Rassure-toi, Papa, dit Bruno. On a emmené Anne-Marie à l'hôpital, et
Maman est avec elle. Mais Papa... Soudain, Bruno sanglote° d'émo-   sobs
tion.
—Qu'est-ce que tu as? C'est plus grave? Tu ne me dis pas tout?
—Mais si,° Papa, je t'assure, elle va très bien se remettre°... Mais tu sais   si = oui (in response to
20 qu'il y a un Belge qui est mort sous l'avalanche?   non)/recover
—Oui, j'ai entendu ça à la radio, répond son père, et c'est pour ça que j'ai
envoyé le télégramme...
—Eh bien, continue Bruno, c'est Benoît Garnier. Tu le connais, n'est-ce
pas? Lui et son père sont arrivés ici hier, pour faire du ski.
25 —Oh, mon pauvre Bruno! C'est affreux! Je suis désolé pour toi... et c'est
bien triste pour la famille. Et son père, comment va-t-il? Est-ce qu'il a
été accidenté, lui aussi?
—Non, mais il est effondré,° bien sûr.   devastated
—Et sa mère, est-ce qu'elle le sait?
30 —Oui, M. Garnier lui a téléphoné. Elle arrive demain matin.
—Oh, la pauvre. C'est vraiment tragique, la mort d'un enfant... Je peux
peut-être l'appeler et lui demander si je peux faire quelque chose pour
elle? suggère-t-il.
—Oui, ce serait° gentil. Merci, Papa, répond Bruno. Dis à Mme Garnier   that would be
35 que j'ai beaucoup de peine.° Il va bien me manquer.°   I'm very sorry/I'll miss
—Bon. Je vais faire ça. Et je vais aussi téléphoner à l'hôpital pour prendre   him
des nouvelles d'Anne-Marie. À quel hôpital est-elle?
—Au Centre Hospitalier de Chamonix.
—Alors, au revoir, mon grand. Bon courage! Embrasse tes sœurs et ta
40 mère pour moi, et rappelle-moi demain pour me donner des nouvelles.
—D'accord, Papa. À demain!

Practice the following ways of inquiring about situations.

1. You meet a friend who is heavily bandaged. Ask what happened.

Qu'est-ce qui t'est arrivé?	Tu as eu un accident?
Comment ça se fait?	Tu es tombé(e)?

2. You arrive at a scene of confusion and excitement. Ask what all the fuss is about.

Qu'est-ce qui se passe?
Qu'est-ce qui s'est passé?

petite scène

Here is how you might start and end a French telephone conversation. Act out the exchanges with a classmate, supplying a topic of conversation.

VOUS	Allô? C'est toi, [Paul]?
ELLE/LUI	Allô? Non, c'est [Serge].
VOUS	Je voudrais parler à [Paul].
ELLE/LUI	C'est de la part de qui?
VOUS	C'est [Nicole] à l'appareil.
ELLE/LUI	Bon. Attendez un moment.

(Votre copain/copine vient au téléphone. De quoi parlez-vous?)

VOUS	Alors, au revoir. À bientôt.
ELLE/LUI	Je vais te rappeler demain pour te donner des nouvelles.

Étude de mots

Les sports

On joue...
au base-ball
au basket-ball (au basket)
aux boules (f. pl.)
au football (au foot)
au golf
au hockey
au ping-pong
au tennis
au volley-ball (au volley)

On fait...
de l'athlétisme (m.)   *track and field*
du cheval
de l'escrime (f.)   *fencing*
du judo
de la lutte   *wrestling*
de la natation   *swimming*
du ski
du vélo
de la voile

A   Identify the sports depicted in the following drawings.

On joue au tennis.

B   What sport(s) do you associate with each of the following things?

■ⅲ   une piscine   *On fait de la natation.*

1. une équipe de cinq joueurs
2. une table
3. la neige
4. un bateau et du vent
5. une équipe de neuf joueurs
6. l'expression «en garde!»

à vous, maintenant

Discuss with your classmates what sports you are interested in. Give the names of your favorite teams and players.

J'aime [le base-ball]. Mon équipe favorite est les [Red Sox].

Une partie de boules

Les sports en France

The French enjoy a wide variety of sports, both as spectators and as participants. One sport that is popular all over the country among people of all ages is **les boules.** The game can be played practically anywhere, between two teams of one to four players each. A wooden ball about the size of a golf ball **(le cochonnet)** is thrown a variable distance from the spot where the players stand. The **cochonnet,** wherever it lands, becomes the target. Each player then throws two **boules** — heavy metal balls about the size of a softball — toward the **cochonnet.** When all of the boules have been thrown, a point is scored for the one that lies nearest the **cochonnet.** Games of boules often lead to heated discussions and attract crowds of onlookers.

Bicycling is important as a form of recreation and as a practical means of transportation. Competitive cycling is also one of France's leading professional sports. The premier event is the annual **Tour de France,** a three-week race around the country that grips the attention of the nation.

France, with its numerous mountain ranges, has always produced excellent skiers and alpinists. French skiers have won many Olympic medals. A team of French climbers was the first to conquer the Himalayan peak Anapurna, one of the world's highest mountains. The country's long coastlines make sailing a favorite activity. Other sports in which the French have had considerable international success are tennis, fencing, and gliding, a sport that is subsidized by the government in order to encourage young people to join the air force.

The French, like people throughout the world, have a passion for **le foot** (soccer). Professional teams from various cities draw the support of millions of spectators each year. During competition for the World Cup, the international tournament that is held every four years, nationalistic fervor runs high in France.

Les parties du corps

1	la tête	8	la figure
2	les cheveux (*m. pl.*)	9	le cou
3	l'œil (*m.*), *pl.* les yeux	10	le bras
4	le nez	11	la main
5	la bouche	12	le doigt
6	les dents (*f. pl.*)	13	la jambe
7	l'oreille (*f.*)	14	le pied

1. The definite article (**le, la, les**) is generally used with parts of the body when the context makes clear whose body it is. (In English, possessive adjectives are usually used.)

Ferme les yeux.	Close your eyes.
Il a un livre à la main.	He has a book in his hand.

2. The expression **avoir mal à** is used with parts of the body to describe specific aches and pains.

J'ai mal au pied!	My foot hurts!
Tu as mal à la tête?	Do you have a headache?

C   **L'examen physique:** This is a pantomime game. The teacher is an army doctor and the students are recruits. All of the recruits hope to get medical excuses to get out of going on a week-long survival test. The doctor reads the list of parts of the body that are to be examined in determining the fitness of the recruits for the assignment. Each student complains of a pain in each area mentioned, and uses pantomime to show her or his discomfort. Recruits who convincingly act out all of the appropriate ailments are excused from duty; those who make mistakes are given KP duty (or other suitable punishment).

■⫶   les oreilles   *Aïe! J'ai mal aux oreilles!*

D   What parts of the body are involved in the following sports?

■ⅲ   Avec quelles parties du corps   *On joue au ping-pong*
       joue-t-on au ping-pong?   *avec les mains et les bras.*

1. Avec quelles parties du corps fait-on du ski?
2. Avec quelles parties du corps joue-t-on au basket?
3. Avec quelles parties du corps fait-on du vélo?
4. Avec quelles parties du corps joue-t-on au football français?

Jouons avec les mots

The verb prefix **re- (r-** before a vowel) means that the action expressed by the verb occurs *again*. Compare the following pairs of verbs.

appeler	to call	**rappeler**	to call again
commencer	to begin	**recommencer**	to begin again
entrer	to go in	**rentrer**	to go in again (to return home)
partir	to leave	**repartir**	to leave again
tomber	to fall	**retomber**	to fall again
venir	to come	**revenir**	to come again

E   Complete each sentence with a verb from the lists above.

1. ____! Vous êtes les bienvenus!
2. Papa va me ____ au téléphone demain.
3. Elle est ____ sur la piste et s'est cassé la jambe pour la deuxième fois.
4. Je ____ mes devoirs pour la troisième fois.
5. Notre bébé ____ à marcher. Il ____ souvent.
6. Ils sont partis à une heure. Ils vont bientôt ____.
7. Nous venons d'arriver à Nice. Nous allons ____ en train.

À la française

Every language provides ways of complaining about poor health or discomfort. In French, the expression **j'ai mal** is the usual way. The expression may be used in referring to any part of the body, but the most popular complaint is **J'ai mal au foie. Le foie** is the liver, which is considered the source of trouble for a wide variety of complaints, real and imaginary. Rich food, butter, and eggs are often blamed for the "national disease," liver complaint. Many people believe that the cure lies in going to health spas, usually located near mineral springs. The natural mineral water and the strict diets imposed are thought to provide relief to the liver.

Another frequently heard complaint is **J'ai mal au cœur**, which means "I feel nauseous." And a French-speaker reacts to a sharp pain by exclaiming **aïe!** — the equivalent for "ouch!"

Prononciation et orthographe

 /j/ mieux

/j/			
RÉPÉTEZ	mieux	les yeux	le travail
	le pied	Yolande	l'œil
	s'inquiéter	l'employé	le conseil
	le ciel	j'ai sommeil	l'oreille
	la rivière	le soleil	meilleur

The sound /j/ is spelled **i**, **y**, **il**, or **ill**.

LISEZ
1. Mireille regarde de tous ses yeux et écoute de toutes ses oreilles.
2. Je vais à mon travail à pied le long de la rivière.

Review of vowel sounds

Repeat after your teacher or the tape.

/a/	/ã/	/i/	/ɛ̃/
Jeanne	Jean	la marine	le marin
sa	sans	l'identité	l'intention
la caravane	le vent	dire	inquiet
les bagages	le temps	la fiche	rien
l'argent	l'agent	le lit	la faim
les Alpes	les gens	Chamonix	le pain

Oeil pour oeil, dent pour dent.

Le siège du Marché commun, à Bruxelles

La Belgique

La Belgique was once part of ancient Gaul, the name applied to France before and during the Roman occupation. Belgium was conquered by the Franks, a Germanic tribe, in the third century A.D., and over the centuries came under the rule of the Dukes of Burgundy, the Austrians, the French, and the Dutch. In 1831 Belgium achieved its independence, and became a kingdom under Leopold I. Belgium was invaded by the Germans during both world wars and suffered greatly. Today it is a highly industrialized and prosperous nation. It is an important center for the production of steel, chemicals, and textiles, as well as for the mining of coal, iron, and zinc.

Brussels is the commercial, industrial, and cultural center of the country. It is the headquarters of the Common Market, an organization established after World War II to try to unify the economies of six European countries: France, Belgium, Italy, Luxemburg, the Netherlands, and West Germany. Denmark, England, and Ireland joined the Common Market in 1973; Greece joined in 1981.

Belgium has two official languages: French and Flemish (a Dutch dialect). There is also a French dialect called **le wallon,** which is spoken in parts of northern France as well as in Belgium.

Grammaire

Present tense of **savoir** and **connaître**

SINGULAR	PLURAL
je **sais**	nous **savons**
tu **sais**	vous **savez**
on/il/elle **sait**	ils/elles **savent**

SINGULAR	PLURAL
je **connais**	nous **connaissons**
tu **connais**	vous **connaissez**
on/il/elle **connaît**	ils/elles **connaissent**

1. **Savoir** means *to know* in the sense of knowledge of general facts and acquired information. It may be used alone or with a direct object, a clause, or an infinitive. **Savoir** followed by an infinitive means *to know how to do something.*

Je ne sais pas!	I don't know!
Tu sais la réponse?	Do you know the answer?
Ils savent que c'est vrai.	They know that it's true.
Elle sait faire du ski.	She knows how to ski.

2. **Connaître** means *to be familiar with* or *to be acquainted with* people, places, and certain bodies of information such as school subjects. **Connaître** is used with a direct object.

Il la connaît.	He is acquainted with her.
Nous connaissons bien la ville.	We know the city well.
Tu connais l'histoire de l'art?	Are you familiar with art history?

A The big game ended two hours ago, but no one seems to know the result. Ask several classmates how the game came out.

> ▪️▥ toi — *Tu sais les résultats du match?*
> — *Non, je ne les sais pas.*

1. elles
2. vous
3. on
4. ta sœur
5. les garçons
6. lui

B Say that the following people are very familiar with the indicated people, places, or subject areas.

> ▪️▥ vous / les Alpes françaises — *Vous connaissez bien les Alpes françaises.*

1. nous / ce château
2. toi / les sciences naturelles
3. elles / cette famille
4. moi / ce monsieur
5. on / tous les sports d'équipe
6. lui / ce restaurant

| à vous,
maintenant | Find out who among your classmates and their friends and families knows how to do the following things. |

| jouer aux boules | danser la polka | préparer le couscous |
| faire de l'escrime | jouer du piano | parler allemand |

— *Qui sait [jouer aux boules]?* — *Moi, je sais [jouer aux boules].*
*Mon père sait... J'ai un cousin
qui sait...*

C Complete the following sentences, using the correct forms of either *savoir* or *connaître* as appropriate.

▪ⅲ Tu _____ ma sœur, n'est-ce pas? *Tu connais ma sœur, n'est-ce
pas?*

1. Vous _____ si le restaurant est ouvert.
2. Alice _____ jouer de la guitare.
3. Nous _____ bien cette région.
4. Ils _____ que Papa se repose.
5. Je _____ cette vieille dame.
6. Nous ne _____ pas la date.
7. Elle _____ ce vieux château.
8. On ne _____ pas qui a gagné.
9. Il _____ bien la littérature française.

Regular **-re** verbs

répondre to answer	
je répond**s**	nous répond**ons**
tu répond**s**	vous répond**ez**
on/il/elle répond	ils/elles répond**ent**
past participle: répond**u**	

1. The stem of a regular **-re** verb is the infinitive minus **-re.** The present-tense endings are **-s, -s, –, -ons, -ez, -ent.** Other verbs of this type that you have seen are:

   attendre   to wait (for)
   descendre   to go/come down
   entendre   to hear
   perdre   to lose

2. The past participle of a regular **-re** verb is formed by adding **-u** to the infinitive stem.

   attendre: attend**u**   perdre: perd**u**

D   Say that the following people are waiting for the train from Brussels.

> ▬ⅲ   lui   *Il attend le train de Bruxelles.*

1. nous
2. vous
3. elles

4. moi
5. toi
6. elle

E   Here are some partial scores that tell you who is winning various games or matches. Report on which team or player is *losing* in each contest, and by what score.

> ▬ⅲ   Les Canadiens et les Bruins: *Les Canadiens perdent de*
>   Les Bruins gagnent de 3 à 1.   *3 à 1.*

1. Vous et nous: Vous gagnez de 7 à 5.
2. Lise et Hélène: Lise gagne de 5 à 3.
3. Toi et moi: Je gagne de 17 à 13.
4. Les Martin et vous: Les Martin gagnent de 2 à 0.
5. René et moi: René gagne de 10 à 8.
6. Les Expos et les Pirates: Les Expos gagnent de 4 à 2.

F   Say that the following people all heard the results of the game on the radio.

> ▬ⅲ   moi   *J'ai entendu les résultats du match à la radio.*

1. eux
2. vous
3. toi

4. on
5. nous
6. elle

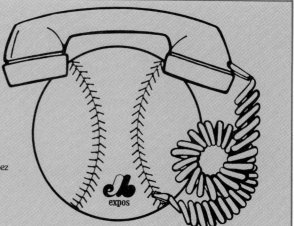

Irregular past participles

The following chart gives a partial list of verbs that have irregular past participles.

INFINITIVE	PAST PARTICIPLE	EXAMPLE
avoir	eu	J'ai eu peur.
connaître	connu	Nous avons connu cette dame.
être	été	Elle a été furieuse.
faire	fait	Tu as fait tes devoirs?
mettre	mis	Il a mis son manteau.
pouvoir	pu	Tu as pu faire du ski.
prendre	pris	J'ai pris du café au lait.
savoir	su	Il a su la réponse.
vouloir	voulu	Nous avons voulu sortir.

G   Restate each of the following sentences in the *passé composé*.

▬▬ Elles peuvent comprendre.   *Elles ont pu comprendre.*

1. Je suis heureux.
2. Vous avez de la chance.
3. Elles veulent nous voir.
4. Nous sommes en retard.
5. Elle peut partir.
6. Tu connais ce garçon?
7. Il met des lunettes de soleil?
8. Elles font du bateau.
9. Nous prenons le métro.

The **passé composé** with **être**

Several French verbs take the auxiliary verb **être** instead of **avoir** in the *passé composé*. The past participles of these verbs agree in gender and number with the subject. One such verb is **tomber** (to fall).

MASCULINE SUBJECT	FEMININE SUBJECT
je suis tombé	je suis tombée
tu es tombé	tu es tombée
il est tombé	elle est tombée
nous sommes tombés	nous sommes tombées
vous êtes tombé(s)	vous êtes tombée(s)
ils sont tombés	elles sont tombées

1. When the subject is feminine, **-e** is added to the past participle.
2. When the subject is plural, **-s** is added to the past participle.

The following verbs take **être** in the *passé composé*. Many describe motion.

INFINITIVE	PAST PARTICIPLE	ENGLISH EQUIVALENT
aller	allé	to go
arriver	arrivé	to arrive; to happen
descendre	descendu	to go/come down
entrer	entré	to enter, go in
monter	monté	to climb, go up
mourir	mort	to die
naître	né	to be born
partir	parti	to leave
passer	passé	to pass (by)
rentrer	rentré	to go back, go home
rester	resté	to stay, remain
retourner	retourné	to return
sortir	sorti	to go out
tomber	tombé	to fall
venir	venu	to come

H The tennis match began at two o'clock. Below are the times at which people arrived. Say whether they were *en retard*, *à l'heure*, or *en avance*.

▪ⅲ toi: 2 h 15   *Tu es arrivé(e) en retard.*

1. nous: 2 h 30
2. moi: 1 h 50
3. elle: 3 h
4. eux: 2 h 20
5. lui: 2 h
6. elles: 12 h
7. on: 2 h
8. vous: 2 h 10
9. Marie: 1 h 45

I The first person(s) went to Chamonix; the second stayed in Brussels.

▪ⅲ mon oncle / ma tante   *Mon oncle est allé à Chamonix, mais ma tante est restée à Bruxelles.*

1. toi / tes copains
2. vous / votre père
3. moi / ma cousine
4. mon frère / mes amies
5. nous / notre sœur
6. Maman / Papa

J Restate the following sentences in the *passé composé*.

▪ⅲ Elle descend rapidement.   *Elle est descendue rapidement.*

1. Elle vient en métro.
2. Nous descendons de la montagne.
3. Tu vas au match, Sylvie?
4. Ils entrent dans le stade.
5. Je tombe sur la piste.
6. Elles reviennent ensemble.
7. Vous retournez à Marrakech, madame?

Le Tour de France

Sous le soleil, la pluie ou le vent, dans les plaines et les montagnes, les coureurs pédalent, pédalent, pédalent chaque° année pendant trois semaines, au mois de juillet. Ils sont français, belges, italiens, espagnols. Ils sont déjà champions dans leurs pays, mais ils essaient° de gagner le
5 maillot° jaune, c'est-à-dire° la première place dans la plus fameuse course cycliste du monde, le Tour de France.

    Les noms des vainqueurs° restent dans la mémoire de millions d'enthousiastes qui suivent la course à la radio ou à la télévision, et plus spécialement dans la mémoire des habitants des villes et des villages par
10 où ils passent. Par exemple, Eddy Merckx, un Belge, et Jacques Anquetil, un Français, qui ont chacun° gagné cinq fois le Tour de France, un exploit formidable.

    each

    try
    jersey/that is

    winners

    each

Il y a environ° vingt-deux étapes° dans le Tour, et chacune couvre de °around/leg of a journey
cent cinquante à deux cent quarante kilomètres par jour. Le gagnant d'une
15 étape ne° porte le maillot jaune, ce prix tant convoité°, que si sa moyenne° °ne . . . que: only/this
est la meilleure de tous les coureurs depuis le départ. Ainsi,° le gagnant du much-coveted prize/
Tour est celui° qui a obtenu° la meilleure moyenne de tous sur la distance average time
totale. Certains coureurs ont peut-être porté le maillot une ou deux fois, Thus
mais ils ne se classent à l'arrivée qu'en deuxième ou troisième place, ou the one/obtained
20 même plus loin.

L'itinéraire du Tour change chaque année. Il peut partir de Brest, en
Bretagne, ou de Fleurance, en Gascogne, mais il fait toujours le tour des
côtes, il grimpe° toujours des cols° à plus de quinze cents mètres d'altitude, climbs/mountain passes
dans les Alpes et dans les Pyrénées. Le Tour fait quelquefois aussi un
25 détour en Belgique, en Allemagne, ou dans un autre pays° qui a des country
frontières° avec la France. Enfin, il se termine toujours à Paris, où, quel- borders
quefois, le Président de la République vient accueillir° le vainqueur sur les welcome
Champs-Élysées.

| avez-vous la question? | Make up questions on the *lecture* that would prompt the following responses. |

1. Ils sont français, belges, italiens et espagnols.
2. Le coureur qui a la meilleure moyenne de temps.
3. Sur les Champs-Élysées à Paris.
4. Il y en a vingt-deux en tout.

| situations | Life is full of happy and unhappy events and situations. Specify some of the circumstances that make you happy or sad. |

Je suis heureux/heureuse parce que...
Je suis malheureux/malheureuse parce que...
Je suis content(e) quand...
Je suis triste quand...

| résumés oraux | |

1. Describe briefly an accident (real or imaginary) you had last year.
   Where did the accident take place? Did you go to the hospital? How
   long did you stay in the hospital?
2. Describe briefly a sports event (real or imaginary) you went to last
   week. Where did the event take place? What teams played? Which
   team won? By how many points? Were you happy or unhappy at the
   final score?

| résumé écrit | **Bonne ou mauvaise nouvelle?** Write a short paragraph about a piece of good or bad news you received last month. What happened and where? To whom did it happen? Why did it happen? What were your reactions when you received the news? |

poème

Extrait de
«Chanson des escargots
qui vont à l'enterrement»

À l'enterrement° d'une feuille° morte   funeral/leaf
Deux escargots s'en vont
Ils ont la coquille° noire   shell
Du crêpe autour des cornes°   with crepe around the horns
Ils s'en vont dans le noir
Un très beau soir d'automne
Hélas° quand ils arrivent   Alas
C'est déjà le printemps
Les feuilles qui étaient° mortes   were
Sont toutes ressuscitées
Et les deux escargots
Sont très désappointés.

Jacques Prévert
Paroles, © *Editions Gallimard*

_____ Résumé grammatical _____

Present tense of **savoir** and **connaître** (A-B)

savoir	connaître
je sais	je connais
tu sais	tu connais
on/il/elle sait	on/il/elle connaît
nous savons	nous connaissons
vous savez	vous connaissez
ils/elles savent	ils/elles connaissent

Savoir means *to know* a fact or (when followed by an infinitive) *to know how* to do something. **Connaître** means *to be familiar* with a person, place, or subject area.

C'est difficile, tu sais.   Je connais sa sœur.
Il sait la réponse.   Elle connaît la ville.
Vous savez qu'il a raison.   Tu connais bien le latin?
Ils savent faire du ski.

Regular **-re** verbs   (D-F)

The verb **descendre** may be considered a model for the forms of regular **-re** verbs.

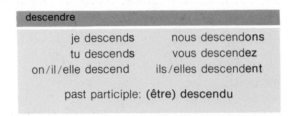

descendre

je descends	nous descend**ons**
tu descends	vous descend**ez**
on/il/elle descend	ils/elles descend**ent**

past participle: **(être) descendu**

Other regular **-re** verbs that you have seen are: **attendre, entendre, perdre,** and **répondre.**

Irregular past participles   (G)

infinitive	past participle	infinitive	past participle
avoir to have	eu	**pouvoir** to be able	pu
connaître to know	connu	**prendre** to take	pris
être to be	été	**savoir** to know	su
faire to do, to make	fait	**vouloir** to want	voulu
mettre to put (on)	mis		

The **passé composé** with **être**   (H-J)

infinitive	past participle	infinitive	past participle
aller to go	allé	**partir** to leave	parti
arriver to arrive	arrivé	**rentrer** to go home	rentré
descendre to go down	descendu	**rester** to stay	resté
devenir to become	devenu	**retourner** to return	retourné
entrer to enter	entré	**revenir** to come back	revenu
monter to go up	monté	**sortir** to go out	sorti
mourir to die	mort	**tomber** to fall	tombé
naître to be born	né	**venir** to come	venu

The past participle of a verb conjugated with **être** agrees with the subject, adding regular feminine and plural adjective endings.

Elle y est all**ée.**
Ils sont parti**s.**
Elles sont venu**es.**

Révision

A   Say which sports are played during the various seasons in the part of the country where you live.

> ▪ꓲꓲ   en hiver   *En hiver, on joue/on fait...*

1. en hiver
2. en été
3. en automne
4. au printemps

B   While shopping yesterday, Odette met her friend Hélène. Complete their conversation by using the appropriate forms of *savoir* and *connaître.*

ODETTE	Tu _____ bien ce magasin, n'est-ce pas?
HÉLÈNE	Oui, pourquoi?
ODETTE	Est-ce que tu _____ où est le rayon des chaussures?
HÉLÈNE	Là, à droite. Mais tu _____, ça coûte très cher ici.
ODETTE	Ça ne fait rien. Je _____ la vendeuse. Elle va me montrer quelque chose de bon marché.

C   Describe an outing with friends. Use the *passé composé* with *être* or *avoir.*

> ▪ꓲꓲ   Tout le monde vient chez moi.   *Tout le monde est venu chez moi.*

1. Luc et Suzanne arrivent en retard.
2. Nous partons ensemble.
3. Nous prenons la voiture.
4. Nous allons à la montagne.
5. On fait de la voile.
6. Je tombe à l'eau et tout le monde a peur.
7. On mange après.
8. Il commence à faire froid.
9. Nous mettons nos pull-overs.
10. Nous redescendons de la montagne très tard.

D   Say that the following people lose their way in the mountains. A classmate will reply that this has never been the case.

> ▪ꓲꓲ   toi   — *Tu perds souvent ton chemin en montagne.*
>   — *Mais non, je n'ai jamais perdu mon chemin.*

1. vous
2. elle
3. eux
4. nous
5. moi
6. on

E   Learn the name of the most recent winner of the *Tour de France.* Try to find a magazine article about the race. If possible, learn the route that was followed and trace it on a map. Then report on the event to the class.

Vocabulaire

NOMS

les affaires (*f.pl.*)   business
l'athlétisme (*m.*)   track
    and field
l'auditeur, l'auditrice
    (*m./f.*)   listener
la bouche   mouth
les boules (*f.pl.*)   a popular
    outdoor game
le bras   arm
le but   goal
les cheveux (*m.pl.*)   hair
le communiqué   bulletin
le cou   neck
le coureur cycliste   bicycle
    racer
les dents (*f.pl.*)   teeth
le doigt   finger
l'équipe (*f.*)   team
l'escrime (*f.*)   fencing
la figure   face
le football   soccer
l'identité (*f.*)   identity
la jambe   leg
le journal sportif   sports-
    cast
la lutte   wrestling
la main   hand
le mot   word
la natation   swimming
le nez   nose
l'oeil (*m.*) *pl.* **les yeux**   *eye*
l'oreille (*f.*)   ear
le pied   foot
le résultat   result
le skieur   skier
le/la standardiste   telephone
    operator
le télégramme   telegram
la tête   head

ADVERBES

affectueusement   affection-
    ately
aussitôt   immediately
complètement   completely
confortablement   comfortably
finalement   finally
soudain   suddenly
terriblement   terribly

VERBES

arriver (à)   to succeed (in)
attendre   to wait (for)
se casser   to break (a bone)
communiquer   to communi-
    cate
connaître   to know, to be
    acquainted with
courir   to run
déclarer   to state
décrocher (l'appareil)   to pick
    up (the phone)
devenir   to become
embrasser   to kiss
entendre   to hear
envoyer   to send
gagner   to win
s'installer   to settle down, to
    move in
interrompre   to interrupt
partir   to leave, to depart
se passer   to happen
perdre   to lose
se précipiter   to rush
rappeler   to call back
rencontrer   to meet
savoir   to know
sonner   to ring
suggérer   to suggest
tomber   to fall

ADJECTIFS

affreux, affreuse   awful
anxieux, anxieuse   anxious
dernier, dernière   last
disputé(e)   contested
épouvantable   terrible
grave   serious
inquiet, inquiète   worried
malheureux, malheureuse
    unfortunate
meilleur(e)   best
passionné(e)   keen on, enthu-
    siastic about
plusieurs   several
prochain(e)   next
sportif, sportive   athletic
triste   sad

PRÉPOSITIONS

depuis   since
entre   between
sauf   except for

AUTRES MOTS ET EXPRESSIONS

à nouveau   again
avoir lieu   to take place
bon courage!   have courage!
    don't despair!
c'est pour ça   that's why
descendre à l'hôtel   to stay at
    a hotel
faire du ski   to ski
l'un d'entre eux   one of them
mettre la radio   to turn on
    the radio
mon Dieu!   good heavens!
sain et sauf   safe and sound
qui est à l'appareil?   who is
    calling?

chapitre 13

C'est la fête du Carnaval!

295

In Nice, on the **Côte d'Azur** (French Riviera), **le Carnaval** lasts from Epiphany (January 6) to Ash Wednesday, but the big parade and main festivities take place on **Mardi gras** (Shrove Tuesday). On that day, beautiful floats covered with flowers parade through the streets of Nice. Masked balls are organized in various hotels and private homes, and fireworks on the beach light up the sky until late at night. Fanny Latour, who lives in Nice, is looking forward to the occasion. However, she has a romantic problem and is seeking some advice.

Le courrier du coeur

Nice, le 2 février

Chère Magali,

Mardi gras arrive dans deux semaines et *il* ne m'a pas encore invitée au bal. *Lui,* c'est un beau garçon intelligent et sportif que je connais depuis
5 quatre ans. Je suis amoureuse de lui et je crois qu'il m'aime aussi.

    Malheureusement, il est timide, et je suis sûre qu'il n'ose° pas me de-   dare
mander de l'accompagner. Nous sortons beaucoup ensemble, mais toujours avec un groupe de copains. On se voit à la plage ou au café, on joue souvent aux boules le soir après le travail. On fait aussi quelquefois des
10 balades° en vélo. Mais on n'est jamais sortis seuls ensemble.   outings
    J'ai déjà des invitations pour le bal — j'en ai même beaucoup — mais je voudrais y aller avec *lui* et personne d'autre.°   nobody else
    Que faire? Une de mes amies m'a dit d'aller me promener, comme par hasard,° sur le quai où il travaille sur le bateau de son père. Mais je ne suis   as if by chance
15 pas flirteuse et je ne saurais pas° quoi dire. Je ne peux pas non plus° jouer   I wouldn't know / either
à la femme libérée et lui demander de m'inviter! Je suis du reste° plus   in fact
timide que lui.
    Pouvez-vous me donner un conseil? Je ne sais vraiment pas quoi faire.

Fanny, la Grande Timide

Nice, le 7 février

20 Chère Grande Timide,

Ton problème n'est pas aussi insoluble° que tu le crois. D'après ta lettre,   difficult to resolve
j'imagine que tu as bon caractère et que tu es plus franche° que beaucoup   honest, frank
d'autres jeunes filles que je connais. La prochaine fois que vous sortez en
25 bande, pourquoi ne pas mentionner le bal et lui en parler franchement?
Sans te jeter à son cou, bien sûr! Vous êtes bons amis, et il ne va pas penser
que tu es flirteuse. Demande-lui simplement quels sont ses projets pour le
Mardi gras. S'il a l'intention de t'inviter, tu vas ainsi° lui donner l'occa-   thereby
sion° de le faire. Sinon,° tu vas pouvoir enfin savoir ce qu'il en pense.   chance / If not
30   Ne t'inquiète pas et bonne chance!

Magali

VILLE de NICE
CARNAVAL

FETES DU MARDI GRAS

le 19 février

Défilé sur la Promenade des Anglais, 11 heures
Feux d'artifices sur la plage, 20 heures
Bal masqué au Casino, 21 heures

Billets pour le bal: s'adresser au Casino

à vous,
maintenant

A friend calls and asks you for information about the Mardi gras ball in Nice. Pretend that you are going to go, and answer her/his questions as best you can.

1. Tu vas au bal du Mardi gras?
2. Tu y vas avec qui?
3. Où le bal va-t-il se passer?
4. C'est un bal masqué?
5. Qu'est-ce que tu vas mettre comme costume?
6. Tu vas aller voir le défilé? Où?
7. Où est-ce qu'il va y avoir des feux d'artifice?

Rubrique personnelle

The **courrier du cœur** appears in magazines such as *Elle, Marie-Claire,* and *Marie-France,* which are directed primarily toward young adults. It also appears in *Salut les copains!* and *Quinze ans,* magazines that are aimed at teenagers. The person in charge of the **courrier du cœur** column not only deals with letters from lovesick or heartbroken correspondents, but tries to give practical advice about many kinds of personal problems.

Un amoureux indécis

Chère Magali,

Nous nous connaissons depuis longtemps, et pourtant, je suis plus timide que jamais avec elle. C'est une fille charmante et très sympathique. Mes
5 copains la trouvent assez jolie, mais pour moi, c'est la plus belle de toutes les filles que je connais. Et puis, elle est toujours de bonne humeur, et elle s'entend bien avec tout le monde. On se rencontre souvent avec une bande d'anciens copains du lycée, mais je ne lui ai jamais demandé de sortir seule avec moi.
10   Je voudrais l'inviter au bal, la semaine prochaine, pour la fête du Mardi gras. Mais j'hésite à lui en parler. J'ai peur qu'elle refuse. Les copains me disent qu'on l'a déjà invitée, mais je ne sais pas si elle a accepté. Elle a toujours tellement de succès avec les garçons que j'en suis jaloux. Est-ce que vous croyez que je devrais° demander à un ami de l'inviter pour moi?   should
15 Ou bien est-ce qu'il vaut mieux lui envoyer une lettre?
       Quelle est la meilleure solution? Merci d'avance pour vos bons conseils.

Guy, l'Amoureux Indécis

Nice, le 10 février

Cher Amoureux Indécis,

20 Prends ton courage à deux mains, et invite-la toi-même de vive voix!° Ne   in person
te laisse pas influencer par tes copains. D'après ce que tu me dis dans ta lettre, cette jeune fille est gentille et sociable. Elle ne va pas être choquée°   shocked
par ton invitation. Et qui sait? Peut-être a-t-elle très envie d'aller au bal avec toi.
25   Amusez-vous bien!

Magali

opinions

Describe Fanny and Guy, based on information gathered from their letters to Magali and her answers to them.

Fanny est une jeune fille... Guy est un jeune homme...

**à vous,
maintenant**

1. À qui demandez-vous conseil quelquefois? Quels bons conseils vous a-t-on donnés?
2. Est-ce que vous lisez quelquefois le «courrier du cœur»? Quels problèmes avez-vous trouvés intéressants?
3. Est-ce que vous avez bon ou mauvais caractère?
4. Est-ce que vous êtes timide ou sociable?
5. Est-ce que vous aimez aller au bal? danser? aller à la plage? jouer aux boules? faire des balades en vélo? Avec qui?

courrier du cœur   You are Magali. How would you answer the following letters?

Chère Magali,

Je le connais depuis un an et je l'admire beaucoup. C'est un beau garçon intelligent et il a beaucoup de succès avec les filles. J'aimerais sortir avec lui, mais il est très flirteur. Je suis de nature jalouse et j'ai peur d'être malheureuse.

J'ai besoin de vos conseils.

Une victime passionnée

Chère Magali,

Mon père ne veut pas me laisser prendre la voiture le soir. Il dit que je suis trop jeune, et il me demande de rentrer le soir à dix heures. Mais j'ai dix-huit ans! Dix heures! Je trouve que c'est exagéré. Et quand je m'amuse avec les copains au café, je ne peux pas rentrer seul sans voiture.

Aidez-moi à le persuader de me traiter en adulte.

Victor le Désolé

La majorité

In France, young people are said to be **majeur(e)** (of age) when they reach the age of eighteen. This means legal freedom, including the right to vote and to drive a car. Many still feel obligated to ask their parents' permission to marry, however. Physically fit eighteen-year-old boys must serve for one year in the army or in **la coopération,** an alternative form of service similar to the Peace Corps, for one and a half to two years.

Paysages

la mer

1 le ciel
2 le soleil
3 la vague
4 la plage
5 le sable

la montagne

1 la lune
2 le nuage
3 l'arbre (*m.*)
4 le lac
5 le rocher

la campagne

1 la colline
2 le fleuve
3 la plaine
4 le champ
5 l'herbe (*f.*)
6 la fleur

à vous,
maintenant

1. Où est-ce que vous faites du bateau? du ski? du surf?
2. Où est-ce que vous habitez? Décrivez le paysage de votre région.
3. Est-ce qu'il fait souvent du soleil chez vous? En quelle saison? Y a-t-il souvent des nuages ou est-ce que le ciel est souvent bleu?
4. Regardez le paysage sur les photos pages 111, 272 et 302, et dites dans quelle région ces photos ont été prises.

Jouons avec les mots

As you have learned French words, you have probably noticed many word families — groups of words that have a common root. Being aware of word families is a good way to increase your vocabulary.

Study the following chart of related words.

VERBES	NOMS	ADJECTIFS	ADVERBES
	l'intelligence (f.)	intelligent(e)	intelligemment
rentrer	la rentrée		
	la jalousie	jaloux	jalousement
amuser	l'amusement (m.)	amusant(e)	
inviter	l'invitation (f.), l'invité(e)		
(se) promener	la promenade		
travailler	le travail	travailleur, travailleuse	
décider	la décision, l'indécision	indécis(e)	décidément
	la timidité	timide	timidement

A   For each word family in the chart, make up a sentence using at least one word from that group.

La Côte d'Azur et la Provence

La Côte d'Azur (The Azure Coast, or French Riviera), in the province **la Provence,** is one of the most famous coastlines in the world. It extends along the Mediterranean from Toulon to the Italian border. It includes the tiny principality of Monaco, an enclave on the coast that is smaller than Central Park in New York. St.-Tropez, Cannes, Antibes, Menton, and many other charming towns attract visitors the year round. The Mediterranean vegetation of the region includes lavender and other wildflowers, and cultivated flowers such as roses, mimosas, carnations, and violets. The petals of these flowers are used to make perfume in Grasse, the center of France's world-famous perfume industry, which lies in the hills above Cannes. With the Alps rising just beyond the coastal hills, Provence and the Côte d'Azur offer a rich scenic beauty that has enchanted some of the world's great painters, including Cézanne, Van Gogh, and Picasso.

Picturesque towns like St.-Tropez (top), fields of lavender, and miles of beaches (right, near Antibes) contribute to the charm of **la Provence.**

Prononciation et orthographe

	/g/	la **g**are
	/ʒ/	la **j**ambe

/g/

RÉPÉTEZ

la **g**are	la fi**g**ure	fati**gu**é
le **g**olf	**g**rand	le **gu**ide
ai**gu**	la ba**gu**ette	**G**uy

The sound /g/ is spelled **g** or **gu** (before **e, i,** or **y**).

LISEZ

1. Les bagages de Guillaume sont à la gare.
2. Ce garçon est un grand gourmand.

/ʒ/

RÉPÉTEZ

la **j**ambe	la **j**upe	l'ora**g**e
le **j**ardin	**j**ouer	les **g**ens
le **j**ournal	**J**eanne	**G**illes

The sound /ʒ/ is spelled **j** or **g** (followed by **e** or **i**).

LISEZ

1. Gilles et Gisèle jouent dans le jardin.
2. Je trouve ces gens gentils et généreux.

Vowel review

RÉPÉTEZ

/o/	/ɔ/	/õ/
le dos	bonne	bon
le mot	la porte	mon
beau	le tonnerre	le conseil
le manteau	encore	tomber
jaune	le collier	compter

Faute de grives, on mange des merles.

Collioure, un port méditerranéen près de la frontière espagnole

La géographie de la France

France offers a great diversity of climate and terrain, especially for a country that is not quite as big as Texas. The northern part of the country has mild summers and chilly, but not frigid, winters with much rain and occasional snow. The weather south of the Loire River is sunnier and warmer. With long coastlines on the north, west, and south, France's climate is largely influenced by the sea. Even though every point in France lies at a more northerly latitude than New York City, extreme cold and heavy snowfall occur only in the high mountains. In **le Midi,** the region in the southeastern part of the country that includes Provence and the Côte d'Azur, winter temperatures very rarely approach the freezing point.

France has large, modern cities in all of its regions, and particularly since World War II the nation has become quite highly industrialized. Nevertheless, the countryside remains predominantly rural in character and appearance. From the green, rolling **campagne** of Normandy to the spectacular peaks of the Alps and the Pyrenees, a wealth of natural beauty unfolds. Other mountain ranges are the Jura and the Vosges, north of the Alps in the east, and the Massif Central in the southern central part of the country. There are lakes, plains, forests, and canals. There is even a small desert in the **Camargue** region of the Rhone River delta. Wherever the land is not too rugged or forested, there are cultivated fields.

Four major rivers located mainly or entirely within France are the Seine, the Loire, the Rhone, and the Garonne. The Rhine River forms the border with Germany. Most of France's borders, like the Rhine, are natural boundaries: the Pyrenees, with Spain; the Alps, with Italy; Lake Geneva and the Jura, with Switzerland. Only the borders with Luxembourg and Belgium are relatively flat.

Throughout the country, countless towns and villages with picturesque gray slate or red tile roofs nestle in valleys or perch atop hills. Travelers in France are likely to be surprised and charmed by the truly remarkable variety of landscapes.

Grammaire

The pronoun en

The pronoun **en** may be used in place of a phrase beginning with **de, du, de la,** or **des.** Except in affirmative commands, **en** precedes the verb.

—Tu prends de la soupe? — Oui, j'**en** prends.
— Yes, I'm having some.

—Il parle du bal? — Non, il n'**en** parle pas.
— No, he's not talking about it.

—Je peux prendre des fleurs? — Oui, prends-**en.**
— Yes, take some.

The pronoun **en** is always used with numbers, expressions of quantity, or **un(e)** if the noun is not expressed.

—Tu as combien de frères? — J'**en** ai **deux.**
—Tu aimes le poisson? — Oui. J'**en** mange **beaucoup.**
—Qui a une voiture? — Moi, j'**en** ai **une.**

When used with the expression **il y a, en** is placed after **y.**

—Il y a du pain? — Bien sûr, il y **en** a!

A   Answer the following questions either affirmatively or negatively, using *en.*

▪▥   Tu as des copains français?   *Oui, j'en ai./Non, je n'en ai pas.*

1. Ils vont acheter des gâteaux?
2. Est-ce qu'il y a du lait?
3. Est-ce que vous avez de l'argent?
4. Jacques parle de l'accident?
5. Marie fait de l'athlétisme?
6. Vous revenez du bal?

B   Correct the person who makes the following statements. Each number is one too low.

▪▥   Elle a trois colliers.   *Non, elle en a quatre.*

1. Vous avez une voiture.
2. Nicole achète quatre baguettes.
3. On visite trois châteaux.
4. Il y a dix joueurs dans une équipe de football.
5. Les Latour ont deux enfants.
6. Il y a 95 départements en France.

Use *en* in answering the following questions.

1. Est-ce que vous allez faire du camping cet été?
2. Parlez-vous souvent des nouvelles sportives?
3. Est-ce que vous mangez beaucoup de viande? de légumes? de gâteaux?
4. Est-ce que vous avez un vélo? un bateau? des skis?
5. Est-ce qu'il y a quelquefois des feux d'artifice dans votre ville? À quelle occasion?

Object pronouns with the **passé composé**

In the *passé composé*, object pronouns immediately precede the auxiliary verb.

<table>
<tr><td>Il l'a acheté à Paris.</td><td>He bought it in Paris.</td></tr>
<tr><td>Je ne **leur** ai pas parlé.</td><td>I didn't speak to them.</td></tr>
</table>

When a direct-object pronoun is used with a verb in the *passé composé*, the past participle agrees with the direct-object pronoun. Agreement is shown by the ending of the past participle.

Marie? Bien sûr, je l'ai invit**ée**.   (**invitée** = f. sg.)
Voilà les billets. Je **les** ai achet**és** ce matin.   (**achetés** = m. pl.)
Où sont les clés? Tu **les** a mis**es** sur la table?   (**mises** = f. pl.)

No agreement occurs with indirect-object pronouns or with **en.**

Je **leur** ai téléphoné.
Des robes? Non, je n'**en** ai pas acheté.

C   Your teacher gave you the following commands. Report that you have done what was asked. Use object pronouns or *en*, as appropriate.

▬ᴵᴵᴵ   Commencez la lecture.   *Je l'ai commencée, madame/mademoiselle/ monsieur.*

1. Faites vos devoirs.
2. Étudiez le vocabulaire.
3. Répondez à Luc et à Marie.
4. Rangez ces livres.
5. Téléphonez à M. Duval.
6. Regardez cette carte.
7. Mettez des pommes sur mon bureau.
8. Apprenez la leçon.
9. Apportez du papier.
10. Écoutez cette cassette.

Answer the following questions about things you did yesterday. Use direct- or indirect-object pronouns or **en**.

1. Vous avez aidé vos parents?
2. Vous avez écouté la radio?
3. Vous avez pris l'autobus?
4. Vous avez fait du sport?
5. Vous avez compris les leçons?
6. Vous avez parlé à votre grand-mère?
7. Vous avez fait la cuisine?
8. Vous avez téléphoné à vos copains?

The verb **dire**

The irregular verb **dire** means *to say* or *tell*.

SINGULAR	PLURAL
je **dis**	nous **disons**
tu **dis**	vous **dites**
on/il/elle **dit**	ils/elles **disent**
past participle: **dit**	

D Report the comments made by the following people on an article they have just read.

▪▯ Pierre: (c'est vrai)   *Pierre dit que c'est vrai.*

1. Daniel: (c'est bien)
2. vos cousins: (c'est formidable)
3. nous: (c'est barbant)
4. toi: (c'est bête)
5. les vieux messieurs: (c'est bizarre)
6. vous: (c'est intéressant)

E Tell what each of the following people said upon hearing about a recent wedding.

▪▯ Mireille: «Zut, alors!»   *Elle a dit: «Zut, alors!»*

1. moi: «Ce n'est pas vrai!»
2. eux: «C'est formidable!»
3. nous: «C'est triste!»
4. mes amis: «Oh, mon dieu!»
5. vous: «Comment ça se fait?»
6. toi: «Oh là là!»
7. elles: «Chic, alors!»
8. lui: «C'est vraiment tragique!»

The verbs **voir** and **croire**

The verbs **voir** (to see) and **croire** (to believe, to think) have very similar forms.

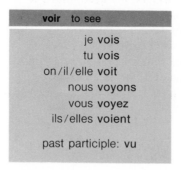

voir to see
je **vois**
tu **vois**
on/il/elle **voit**
nous **voyons**
vous **voyez**
ils/elles **voient**
past participle: **vu**

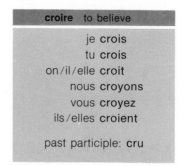

croire to believe
je **crois**
tu **crois**
on/il/elle **croit**
nous **croyons**
vous **croyez**
ils/elles **croient**
past participle: **cru**

F Describe what the following people think they see in an abstract painting at the modern art museum.

▪▥ Jacques: un cheval   *Jacques croit qu'il voit un cheval.*

1. moi: des nuages
2. vous: un fleuve
3. Hélène: des fleurs

4. toi: le soleil
5. nous: une ville
6. les enfants: un petit chien

G Say that the following people never believe what they are told.

▪▥ toi   *Tu ne crois jamais ce qu'on te dit.*

1. elle
2. vous

3. eux
4. son frère

5. ces messieurs
6. nous

7. moi
8. lui

H Report that the witnesses of the UFO last night couldn't believe their eyes.

▪▥ Mlle Leclair   *Elle n'a pas cru ce qu'elle a vu.*

1. nous
2. lui

3. moi
4. vous

5. les garçons
6. elles

7. on
8. toi

Comparative and superlative forms of adjectives

In a comparative statement, two or more elements (people, things, etc.) are judged to be either *unequal* or *equal* with respect to a particular characteristic. In a superlative statement, one element is judged to possess a characteristic to the *greatest* or *least* degree. The characteristics are often expressed with adjectives.

Comparisons expressing *inequality* follow the patterns:

plus + adjective + **que**	adjective + *-er* + *than;* or *more* + adjective + *than*
moins + adjective + **que**	*less* + adjective + *than*
Robert est **plus intelligent que** Marc.	Robert is *smarter (more intelligent) than* Marc.
Michèle est **moins sérieuse que** Jeanne.	Michèle is *less serious than* Jeanne.

Comparisons expressing *equality* follow the pattern:

aussi + adjective + **que**	*as* + adjective + *as*
M. Dubarry est **aussi inquiet qu'**elle.	Mr. Dubarry is *as worried as* she is.

1. The adjective agrees with the *first* element in the comparison.
2. Emphatic pronouns are used after **que.**

Superlative statements follow the patterns:

(noun) + definite article + **plus** + adjective + **de**	*the most* + adjective, or adjective + *-est,* (+ noun) + *of* or *in*
(noun) + definite article + **moins** + adjective + **de**	*the least* + adjective (+ noun) + *of* or *in*

Note that a noun is either expressed or implied at the beginning of the superlative phrase. The definite article and the adjective agree with this noun, expressed or implied.

Hélène est **la fille la plus gentille** de la famille.	Hélène is *the nicest girl in* the family.
Jacques est **(le garçon) le plus beau** de la famille.	Jacques is *the handsomest (boy) in* the family.

I   Make superlative statements using the following cues. You may use either *plus* or *moins.*

■III   le foot / dur / tous les sports   *Le foot est le plus/moins dur de tous les sports.*

1. l'amour / difficile / tous les problèmes
2. le français / intéressant / les cours
3. la mort d'un enfant / tragique / toutes les choses
4. le mariage / heureux / tous les événements
5. l'été / beau / toutes les saisons
6. Paris / grand / toutes les villes françaises

J Have a three-way argument about the following comparisons. Two of you express completely opposite views, while the third declares that there is no difference on the point in question.

▪▦ le football et le basket-ball
(passionnant)

— *Le football est plus passionnant que le basket-ball.*
— *Mais non! Le football est moins passionnant que le basket-ball!*
— *Ne vous disputez pas! Le football est aussi passionnant que le basket-ball.*

1. les sports et la musique (intéressant)
2. la mer et la montagne (beau)
3. les femmes et les hommes (intelligent)
4. les Français et les Américains (sympathique)
5. la ville et la campagne (agréable)

K Make as many comparative and superlative statements as you can based on the following pictures. Assign names to the characters as necessary to help you talk about them.

à vous,
maintenant

1. Use *plus...que, moins...que,* or *aussi...que* and the adjectives of your own choice to compare various friends, relatives, and acquaintances.
2. Prepare some items for your own book of records, using appropriate superlatives.

Le français est le cours le plus intéressant de l'école!

Lecture

Projets de mariage

Voilà la lettre que Fanny a envoyée à son amie, Nanette, après le bal.

Nice, le 5 mars

Ma chère Nanette,

Il y a bien longtemps que je n'ai pas reçu° de tes nouvelles. Comment vas-tu? Est-ce que tu es tellement occupée que tu n'a pas le temps
5 d'écrire?° N'oublie° pas ta vieille amie, je t'en prie!

Pour moi, j'ai été très occupée récemment. Imagine-toi que je viens de me fiancer avec Guy Carnot. Tu es surprise? Pas autant° que moi! Je suis très heureuse, très amoureuse... Nous allons nous marier le trente janvier de l'année prochaine, d'abord à la mairie de Nice et après, à l'église en
10 plein air° que tu connais. Et, bien sûr, j'aimerais t'avoir comme demoiselle d'honneur.° Tu acceptes, n'est-ce pas?

J'ai aussi l'intention de demander à mon amie Christiane et à Catherine, la sœur de Guy. J'envisage° des longues robes vertes pour les demoiselles d'honneur. Le vert vous ira° très bien à toutes les trois. Pour les garçons
15 d'honneur, un smoking avec un nœud papillon° blanc et un œillet° blanc. Moi, je vais mettre du blanc, naturellement, et ma mère va me donner le voile de dentelle° qu'elle a porté le jour de son mariage.

Ma bague° de fiançailles est très jolie: un saphir entouré° de petits diamants. C'est la bague de la grand-mère de Guy.
20 Naturellement (tu me connais!), je fais déjà des projets pour notre voyage de noces° et j'imagine aussi le mas° que nous allons habiter dans la montagne. Je vais te dire tout ça dans ma prochaine lettre.

À bientôt!

Gros baisers,°
Fanny

I haven't received for a long time	
to write / forget	
as much	
outdoor	
maid of honor	
picture	
will go	
bowtie / carnation	
lace	
ring / surrounded	
honeymoon / **mas** = **maison** (en Provence)	
kisses	

parlons du texte	Tell how the following things are connected with people mentioned in the *lecture*.

1. une fleur blanche
2. une lettre
3. une longue robe verte
4. un voile de dentelle
5. une bague
6. un mas

à vous, maintenant	1. Est-ce que vous avez déjà été à un mariage? Qui s'est marié?
	2. Est-ce que vous avez été garçon ou demoiselle d'honneur? Quels vêtements avez-vous portés ce jour-là?
	3. Aimez-vous les mariages?

résumé oral ou écrit	Give an account of what happened from the time that Fanny and Guy wrote letters to Magali in the *courrier du cœur*, to the day that Fanny wrote a letter to Nanette announcing her engagement to Guy.

À la française

The parents of the bride and groom usually send out an announcement **(un faire-part de mariage)** about the church ceremony to relatives and friends. The names of the grandparents and parents may be followed by the names of brothers and sisters and their spouses. Close friends and relatives usually receive another card inviting them to the wedding reception.

madame charles Forey
monsieur et madame henri Forey
jean et dominique
marc et françoise
catherine et claude

sont heureux de vous faire part du mariage
de jacqueline avec christophe Lecarme.

monsieur et madame jacques Lecarme
vincent et danielle
jérôme et claude
anne et jean-pierre
catherine
sylvie et françois

sont heureux de vous faire part du mariage
de christophe avec jacqueline Forey.

la bénédiction nuptiale leur sera donnée, en l'église
saint-germain-des-prés, le samedi 30 juin 1973,
à 13 heures.

Les fiançailles et
le mariage en France

 In France, most young people think of marriage as a step far too serious to be taken lightly. Very few marry before the age of twenty-one.

Although the need to secure parental approval has become far less common since the second World War, many young people still ask their parents for permission to marry. The engagement of couples is often celebrated at a party, during which the fiancé places an engagement ring on the finger of his bride-to-be. The period of the engagement may last up to a year.

Weddings often involve two ceremonies. A civil ceremony, which is required by law, is performed by the mayor at the town hall. On the same day or on the following day a religious ceremony, if it is desired, is held in a church.

_____ Résumé grammatical _____

The pronoun **en** (A-B)

The pronoun **en** may take the place of a phrase beginning with **de, du, de l',** or **des.** Except in affirmative commands, **en** precedes the verb.

Elle achète des bijoux?	Non, elle n'**en** achète pas.
	No, she's not buying any.
Il parle de l'accident?	Oui, il **en** parle.
	Yes, he's talking about it.
Tu veux acheter du pain?	Oui, je voudrais **en** acheter.
	Yes, I'd like to buy some.
Nous pouvons prendre des fleurs?	Oui, prenez-**en.**
	Yes, take some.

En is always used with numbers, expressions of quantity, or **un(e)** if the noun is not expressed.

Il a un frère?	Oui, il **en** a un.
	Non, il **en** a quatre.

When used with the expression **il y a, en** precedes **a.**

Il y a de la glace?	Oui, **il y en a** beaucoup!

Object pronouns in the **passé composé** (C)

In the *passé composé*, object pronouns and **en** immediately precede the auxiliary verb.

> Elle **l'**a apporté ce matin.
> Nous **lui** avons téléphoné hier.
> Il **en** a parlé.

The past participle agrees with direct-object pronouns, but not with indirect-object pronouns or with **en**.

> Cette robe? Je l'ai achet**ée** (*f.sg.*) à Rome.
> Ses devoirs? Il les a faits (*m.pl.*) ce matin.
> Tu les as vu**es** (*f.pl.*) au bal, mes sœurs?

But:

> Je ne lui ai pas parlé hier.
> Des stylos? J'en ai vu dans le tiroir.

The verbs **dire, voir,** and **croire** (D-H)

croire to believe
je **crois**
tu **crois**
on/il/elle **croit**
nous **croyons**
vous **croyez**
ils/elles **croient**
past participle: **cru**

dire to say, to tell
je **dis**
tu **dis**
on/il/elle **dit**
nous **disons**
vous **dites**
ils/elles **disent**
past participle: **dit**

voir to see
je **vois**
tu **vois**
on/il/elle **voit**
nous **voyons**
vous **voyez**
ils/elles **voient**
past participle: **vu**

Comparative and superlative forms of adjectives (I-K)

COMPARATIVE

plus + adjective + **que**   Paul est **plus égoïste que** Luc.
Paul is more selfish than Luc.

moins + adjective + **que**   Julie est **moins nerveuse que** Chantal.
Julie is less nervous than Chantal.

aussi + adjective + **que**   Je suis **aussi sérieux que** toi.
I'm as serious as you.

1. The adjective agrees with the first element in the comparison.
2. Emphatic pronouns are used after **que**.

SUPERLATIVE	le/la/les + **plus** + adjective	Jean est **le plus gentil** de tous les garçons.
		John is the nicest of all the boys.
	le/la/les + **moins** + adjective	Gisèle est **la moins sérieuse** de la classe.
		Gisèle is the least serious in the class.

1. The article and the adjective agree with the noun, expressed or implied, at the beginning of the superlative phrase.
2. After a superlative, *of* or *in* is expressed with **de.**

Quelques fêtes

Mardi gras (Shrove Tuesday) is the last day before Ash Wednesday, which begins the forty-day period of Lent that ends with Easter. **Mardi gras** concludes the period of **Carnaval,** a time of celebration before the solemn Lenten season.

Pâques (Easter) is celebrated at masses in churches and cathedrals. Certain traditions are similar to those in the United States. Children may roll colored eggs downhill and run to find them at the bottom, or they may hunt for chocolate eggs and rabbits. The day after Easter is a holiday.

Le premier mai is Labor Day in France. It is also a celebration of the coming of spring. On this occasion, it is traditional to offer a small sprig of lily-of-the-valley to good friends and members of one's family.

Le 14 juillet is the French national holiday. It is usually referred to in English as Bastille Day. July 14 commemorates one of the important events that began the French Revolution in 1789: the seizing of the Bastille prison by Parisians as part of the revolt against the monarchy.

Noël (Christmas) is an important religious holiday. Traditionally, Christmas trees are decorated, and children leave their shoes in front of the fireplace for **le Père Noël** to fill.

Un défilé de Mardi gras

Révision

A   Report where the following people say they are going.

     ▪III   Hélène: à la plage   *Hélène dit qu'elle va à la plage.*

1. Jean et Geneviève: à la montagne
2. Pierre et toi: près d'un lac
3. Mme Brunot: dans les magasins
4. vous et vos frères: à la campagne
5. les enfants: aux champs
6. toi: sur le quai

B   The hotel affords everyone a nice view. Tell what the following people see from their terraces.

     ▪III   on: le sable sur la plage   *On voit le sable sur la plage.*

1. nous: le ciel bleu avec des nuages
2. moi: une colline avec des arbres
3. vous: les montagnes
4. lui: des rochers
5. toi: des fleurs dans les champs
6. elles: des bateaux sur la mer

C   Confirm the fact that the people indicated saw the notice posted on the school bulletin board, but didn't believe it.

     ▪III   le professeur de français   *— Il a vu le communiqué, n'est-ce pas?*
                                              — Oui, il l'a vu, mais il ne l'a pas cru.

1. vous
2. lui
3. le directeur

4. votre sœur
5. eux
6. les élèves de seconde

D   An interviewer wants to know more about you. Respond either negatively or affirmatively, using *en*.

     ▪III   de l'ambition   *— Vous avez de l'ambition?*
                                  — Oui, j'en ai. (Non, je n'en ai pas.)

1. de la patience
2. de l'imagination
3. des idées
4. du courage
5. de l'enthousiasme
6. de l'expérience

E Compare the following people or things. Use either *plus...que, moins...que,* or *aussi...que.*

■ Bernadette est sympathique. (Chantal) — *Bernadette est plus/moins/aussi sympathique que Chantal.*

1. Henriette est timide. (Guillaume)
2. Le livre de sciences est intéressant. (le livre d'histoire)
3. La robe de Claudine est belle. (la robe de Martine)
4. Pascal est sérieux. (Yvette)
5. Marianne est grande. (Bernard)
6. Les problèmes de maths sont difficiles. (les problèmes de chimie)
7. Le Tour de France est passionnant. (la World Series)
8. Le poisson est cher. (la viande)

F Respond affirmatively or negatively to the following questions, using object pronouns or *en.*

■ Tu as vu les feux d'artifice? — *Oui, je les ai vus.* (*Non, je ne les ai pas vus.*)

1. Tu as mis ton chemisier bleu?
2. Tu as visité une ville célèbre?
3. Tu as invité des amis chez toi?
4. Tu as téléphoné à tes parents?
5. Tu as rencontré des copains en ville?
6. Tu as vu ce livre?
7. Tu as fait tes devoirs?
8. Tu as demandé à Magali?

G You are planning a trip to a new area and want to get the most for your money. Ask your travel agent appropriate questions about the following attractions, using superlatives.

■ une route pittoresque — *Quelle est la route la plus pittoresque?*

1. des monuments anciens
2. un spectacle intéressant
3. un joli jardin
4. un grand château
5. une belle église
6. des musées près d'ici

H

1. Gather information about Mardi gras celebrations in other French-speaking parts of the world, such as Quebec, Haiti, and Louisiana. Report your findings to the class.
2. Find out as much as you can about the French perfume industry and prepare a bulletin board display.

Vocabulaire

NOMS

l'arbre (*m.*)   tree
le bal   ball; dance
le café   café
la campagne   country, countryside
le champ   field
le ciel   sky
la colline   hill
le conseil   advice
la fleur   flower
le fleuve   large river
la fois   time
le groupe   group
l'herbe (*f.*)   grass
l'invitation (*f.*)   invitation
le lac   lake
la lettre   letter
la lune   moon
la montagne   mountain
le nuage   cloud
la plaine   plain
le projet   project
le rocher   rock, boulder
le sable   sand
le soleil   sun
le travail   work
la vague   wave

ADJECTIFS

amoureux, amoureuse   in love
ancien(ne)   old
charmant(e)   charming
flirteur, flirteuse   flirt
franc(he)   frank
indécis(e)   indecisive
jaloux, jalouse   jealous
libéré(e)   liberated
sûr(e)   sure

ADVERBES

enfin   finally
ensemble   together
franchement   frankly
simplement   simply; just
tellement   so much

VERBES

accompagner   to accompany
se connaître   to know each other
croire   to believe
s'entendre   to get along
hésiter   to hesitate
imaginer   to imagine
s'inquiéter   to worry
influencer   to influence
refuser   to refuse
se rencontrer   to meet
voir   to see
se voir   to meet

AUTRES MOTS ET EXPRESSIONS

déjà   already
en   of (it, them); about (it, them); from (there)
pourtant   even so

aussi...que (*comparative*)   as...as
avoir l'intention (de)   to intend (to)
bien sûr   of course
bonne chance!   good luck!
ce que   what
courrier du cœur   lonely hearts column
d'après   according to
depuis longtemps   for a long time
en bande   as a group
être de bonne humeur   to be in good humor
il vaut mieux   it's better
le/la moins... (*superlative*)   the least...
le/la plus... (*superlative*)   the most...
se jeter au cou de quelqu'un   to throw oneself at someone
moins...que (*comparative*)   less...than
plus...que (*comparative*)   more...than
plus...que jamais   more...than ever
que faire?   what to do?

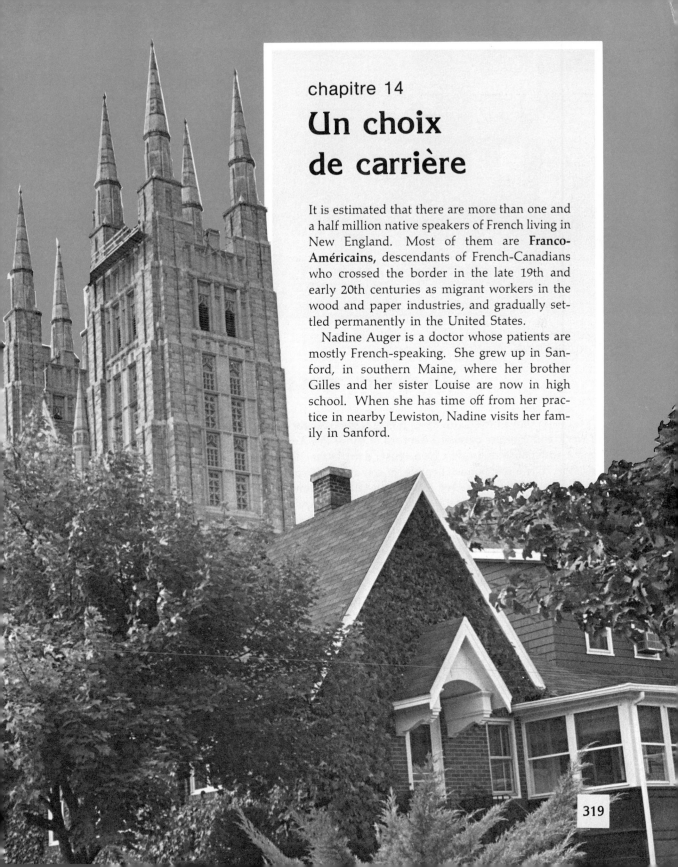

chapitre 14

Un choix de carrière

It is estimated that there are more than one and a half million native speakers of French living in New England. Most of them are **Franco-Américains,** descendants of French-Canadians who crossed the border in the late 19th and early 20th centuries as migrant workers in the wood and paper industries, and gradually settled permanently in the United States.

Nadine Auger is a doctor whose patients are mostly French-speaking. She grew up in Sanford, in southern Maine, where her brother Gilles and her sister Louise are now in high school. When she has time off from her practice in nearby Lewiston, Nadine visits her family in Sanford.

Un métier passionnant

À l'occasion de l'anniversaire de sa mère, Nadine Auger est venue passer un week-end chez ses parents à Sanford. L'aînée des Auger est une jeune femme ambitieuse qui a déjà bien réussi dans la vie. Elle est médecin à Lewiston. Elle a une bonne clientèle, et son avis médical est très respecté.

5 Pourtant, elle a toujours rêvé d'aller s'installer à Montréal, même pour quelques années seulement. Et voilà justement qu'une chance s'est présentée° pour elle de réaliser son rêve. Elle explique pourquoi à son frère Gilles, qui va finir ses études au lycée de Sanford au mois de juin. La plus jeune des Auger, Louise, écoute de toutes ses oreilles.

just such an opportunity has come up

10 — C'est un laboratoire pharmaceutique en France qui cherche un médecin bilingue pour un poste à Montréal. La recherche m'a toujours intéressée, et comme c'est un poste à mi-temps, je vais aussi pouvoir travailler dans un hôpital.

— Ça, c'est vraiment un coup de chance, tout à fait ce qu'il te faut!°
15 commente Gilles.

just what you need

— Oui, c'est vrai. Et par-dessus le marché,° il faut aller à Paris pour un stage de formation de quatre mois!

on top of that

— Quoi? Quelle veinarde! Tu vas passer un été formidable! s'exclame Louise, un peu jalouse.

20 — Mais ne te plains° pas, toi! Tu vas aller à Old Orchard Beach, n'est-ce pas? demande sa grande sœur.

don't complain

— Oui, j'ai été voir la propriétaire du motel et elle m'a embauchée. Je vais travailler de deux heures à huit heures, surtout pour servir d'°interprète aux clients qui viennent du Québec.

serve as

25 — Eh bien, tu t'es bien débrouillée! Ça ne va pas être un job trop difficile pour toi, dit Nadine. Tu vas avoir le temps d'aller à la plage le matin et de sortir le soir.

— Comment est-ce que tu as trouvé ce poste? demande Gilles à Nadine.

— J'ai vu une offre d'emploi dans *L'Express* international.

La filiale° canadienne d'un important laboratoire pharmaceutique français connu pour les résultats de sa recherche cherche

MEDECIN

Jeune, dynamique, bilingue anglais/français, avec si possible une expérience de l'industrie pharmaceutique pour un poste à MI-TEMPS:

D'ASSISTANT DU DIRECTEUR MEDICAL ET SCIENTIFIQUE

Pour:
–faire les expérimentations cliniques
–assurer la publication des recherches et les relations avec les médecins
–s'occuper de la correspondance médicale.

Après une formation° de 4 mois à Paris-Ouest le titulaire° sera° basé à MONTREAL Canada et pourra° éventuellement pendant la mi-temps libre travailler dans un hôpital pour maintenir le contact.

Adresser lettre avec curriculum vitae à: **SPMN-AP**
    125 Avenue Charles de Gaulle
    92522 Neuilly

branch

training period
jobholder / will be
will be able

questions

1. Quels sont les avantages de ce poste pour Nadine?
2. Pourquoi Louise est-elle jalouse?
3. Pourquoi est-ce que Louise a de la chance, elle aussi?

petite scène

Act out the following scene, which takes place at an employment agency. Then vary the situation according to your own interests or experience.

L'EMPLOYÉ(E)	Bonjour, mademoiselle. Puis-je vous aider?
MICHÈLE	Je cherche du travail à mi-temps pour l'été.
L'EMPLOYÉ(E)	Est-ce que vous parlez anglais? Nous avons une place dans un hôtel qui a beaucoup de clients américains.
MICHÈLE	Oui, je parle anglais. Ça a l'air intéressant! Le travail est de quelle heure à quelle heure?
L'EMPLOYÉ(E)	De cinq à dix heures du soir à la réception. Je peux arranger une interview, si vous voulez.
MICHÈLE	Oui, d'accord, j'aimerais bien. Merci beaucoup.

à vous, maintenant

1. Avez-vous déjà eu un emploi? Où?
2. Préférez-vous travailler à mi-temps et avoir du temps libre, ou travailler toute la journée et gagner plus d'argent?

Une offre d'emploi

— Et toi, Gilles, qu'est-ce que tu vas faire cet été? demande Nadine.

— Moi, je cherche du travail à plein temps. Je n'ai pas envie d'aller à l'université l'année prochaine. Je voudrais travailler au moins pendant un an.

5 — Ah, bon? Tu en as parlé à Papa et Maman? Qu'est-ce qu'ils en pensent?

— Oh, tu sais, répond Gilles, au début ils n'ont pas été très chauds pour cette idée. Mais je crois que maintenant, ils ne sont pas contre. Je voudrais trouver un job où j'utilise mon français, comme toi et comme Louise.

10 — Est-ce que tu as regardé les offres d'emploi dans le journal?

— Oui, bien sûr, mais je n'ai rien trouvé jusqu'à maintenant. Enfin,° je   Well, actually
n'ai pas encore vu le journal d'aujourd'hui. Passe-le-moi, s'il te plaît.

Pendant que Gilles étudie les offres d'emploi, les deux sœurs finissent de préparer les cadeaux d'anniversaire de leur mère.

15 — Tiens! s'exclame tout à coup° Gilles. Voilà quelque chose d'inté-   suddenly
ressant. Il lit° l'annonce à haute voix:°   reads/aloud

— Eh bien, si tu réussis à obtenir° cet emploi-   getting
là, ça sera° un beau cadeau d'anniversaire pour   will be
Maman. Tu sais qu'elle a toujours voulu faire
un voyage en France. Si chacun de nous a du
travail, les parents vont pouvoir mettre de
l'argent de côté pour le voyage.

— Bon, dit Gilles, je vais aller téléphoner à
cette entreprise. J'espère que la place n'est pas
déjà prise.

à vous, maintenant

1. Quel journal lisez-vous? Lisez-vous quelquefois les offres d'emploi?
2. Espérez-vous aller à l'université? Ou préférez-vous avoir un emploi?
3. Est-ce que vos parents sont souvent contre vos idées? Quelles idées?

demande d'emploi

Offer your services for a job that you think will suit your interests, abilities, and schedules. Prepare an ad in French with appropriate details about the kind of work you are looking for and your qualifications for it.

Les Français en Amérique

The history of the United States has been much affected by the French and people of French descent. In 1682, the explorer Robert de La Salle descended the Mississippi and claimed a vast territory west of the river for France. The territory, named **la Louisiane** for the French king, Louis XIV, was sold to the United States in the famous Louisiana Purchase during the presidency of Thomas Jefferson. The early French settlers and their children founded towns like **Saint-Louis, la Nouvelle-Orléans, Baton Rouge,** and **Mobile.**

During the second half of the 17th century, many French settlers were exiled by the British from the province of Acadia (in eastern Canada) to the east coast of the United States. From there, many went to Louisiana. The **bayous** of southern Louisiana, home to many descendants of the early Acadian immigrants, are often referred to as Cajun country. ("Cajun" is a mispronunciation of **Acadien.**) The suffering of the exiled Acadian families is described in Henry Wadsworth Longfellow's epic poem *Evangeline.*

The Cajuns and the **Franco-Américains** of New England today comprise the majority of French-speaking Americans. The language of members of these groups differs from so-called "standard" French, and most of the people are bilingual. They take pride in their French heritage, however, and a number of organizations have been formed to promote recognition of this heritage and the continued use of the French language.

Étude de mots

Les métiers

Most nouns referring to members of professions have both masculine and feminine forms, but some have only a masculine form. You are already familiar with many of the following nouns.

l'acteur (*m.*), **l'actrice** (*f.*)   actor
l'agent (*m.*) **de police**   police officer
l'architecte (*m./f.*)   architect
l'artiste (*m./f.*)   artist, painter
l'athlète (*m./f.*)   athlete
l'avocat (*m.*), **l'avocate** (*f.*)   lawyer
le chanteur, la chanteuse   singer
la/le comptable   accountant
l'écrivain (*m.*)   writer
le fermier, la fermière   farmer

l'infirmier (*m.*), **l'infirmière** (*f.*)   nurse
l'ingénieur (*m.*)   engineer
la/le journaliste   journalist
le mécanicien, la mécanicienne   mechanic
le médecin   doctor
l'ouvrier (*m.*), **l'ouvrière** (*f.*)   worker
la/le photographe   photographer
le pilote   pilot
la/le secrétaire   secretary
le soldat, la femme soldat   soldier

Note: Nouns that identify professions or occupations normally drop the indefinite article after the verb **être**, except in the phrase **c'est/ce sont**.

Elle est ingénieur.   *but:* C'est **un** ingénieur.

A   Say who uses the items pictured below in her or his work.

C'est un artiste ou une artiste.

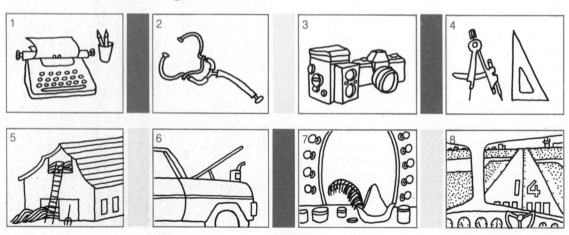

B   Match the following characters in this book with their occupations.

■▮▮   M. Le Hur   *M. Le Hur est pêcheur de langoustes.*

1. M. Le Hur   a. pêcheur de langoustes
2. Mme Cordier   b. réceptionniste
3. Mlle Auger   c. guide de musée
4. M. Farid   d. marchand de vêtements
5. Mlle du Pavillon   e. médecin
6. M. Mustapha   f. contrôleur aérien
7. Mlle Mustapha   g. propriétaire d'hôtel
8. M. Diop   h. fermière

à vous,
maintenant

Tell your classmates what kind of work you think you would like to do and why. If you do not know the French word for the occupation of your choice, ask your teacher to provide it.

Les hautes études en France

Studies for the **baccalauréat** degree in France are difficult and require a great deal of work. For many people, however, this work is worthwhile, because **le bac** opens the door to all universities in France. There are sixty-one universities in the country, thirteen of them in Paris. The most famous is **la Sorbonne,** in the section of Paris known as the Latin Quarter (so called because Latin was spoken at the University in the Middle Ages).

University studies are free and open to anyone who has **le bac.** Each university is divided into **facultés** that offer studies in a particular field: chemistry, literature, medicine, etc. A student might say, for example, «**Je vais à la fac de droit** (law school) **de Lyon.**»

There are several university degrees. **Le D.E.U.G. (diplôme d'études universitaires générales),** which requires two years of study, corresponds roughly to a bachelor's degree. Advanced degrees include **la licence** (three years' study), **la maîtrise** (four years), and the highest degrees of French education, **le doctorat** and **l'agrégation.**

Une sélection de journaux de Montréal

Prononciation et orthographe

▌ /ɥ/   lui

The sound /ɥ/ is a glide sound that has no equivalent in English. It is always followed by a vowel, usually /i/. It may help you in practicing /ɥ/ to pronounce the vowels /y/ (as in **tu**) and /i/ (as in **y**) in succession, more and more quickly until the two sounds are linked. The combination /y/ plus /i/ naturally leads to /ɥi/.

RÉPÉTEZ

lui	la cuillère	aujourd'hui
depuis	la cuisine	juillet
je suis	ensuite	la pluie
la nuit	huit	minuit

The sound /ɥ/ is always spelled **u** + vowel.

LISEZ
1. Minuit sonne dans la nuit chaude de juillet.
2. Aujourd'hui, il fait la cuisine depuis huit heures.

Consonants

Many French consonant sounds are very similar to English consonants. There is a noticeable difference, however, between French and English with respect to the consonants /p/, /b/, /t/, and /d/. At the beginning of a French syllable, these consonants are very soft, with little or no air passing between the lips. At the beginning of an English syllable, the consonants /p/, /b/, /t/, and /d/ are much stronger, and a puff of air is produced when they are pronounced. To become more aware of this difference between French and English consonant sounds, contrast the following pairs of words.

RÉPÉTEZ	**pas**	**tout**	**beau**	**des**
	Pa	two	bow	day

Vowel review

RÉPÉTEZ	/u/	/y/	/œ̃/
	où	j'ai **eu**	**un**
	v**ou**s	j'ai **su**	chac**un**
	s**ou**s	**su**r	quelqu'**un**
	le c**ou**p	r**éu**ssir	br**un**
	jal**ou**se	la l**u**ne	auc**un**
	surt**ou**t	**u**tiliser	le parf**um**

Le soleil luit pour tout le monde.

Grammaire

The **passé composé** of reflexive verbs

The *passé composé* of a reflexive verb is formed with the present tense of **être** plus the past participle. The reflexive pronoun immediately precedes the form of **être**.

> je me suis préparé
> il s'est promené
> vous vous êtes habillé

The past participle agrees in number and gender when the reflexive pronoun is the direct object, which is usually the case.

MASCULINE SUBJECT
je me suis levé
tu t'es levé
il s'est levé
nous nous sommes levés
vous vous êtes levé(s)
ils se sont levés

FEMININE SUBJECT
je me suis levée
tu t'es levée
elle s'est levée
nous nous sommes levées
vous vous êtes levée(s)
elles se sont levées

When the reflexive pronoun is not the direct object, no agreement occurs. There is no change in the past participle ending.

Ils se sont acheté des bottes. (The direct object is **des bottes.**)

Elle s'est cassé la jambe. (The direct object is **la jambe.**)

A It was a glorious day yesterday and all the following people took walks to the places indicated. Specify where they went.

◼▮ Bernadette: en ville   *Bernadette s'est promenée en ville.*

1. Christophe: sur la colline
2. Nicole et Micheline: dans les champs
3. Béatrice et Georges: près du fleuve
4. Alain et Yves: dans le jardin
5. Gisèle: à la campagne
6. Antoine et toi: dans le parc
7. nous: dans la montagne
8. moi: sur la plage
9. toi: dans la vallée

B   The following people went on a shopping spree. Verify what items they bought. Use the reflexive form of *acheter* in your responses.

> ■Ⅲ   Denis a acheté un bracelet?   *Oui, il s'est acheté un bracelet.*

1. Ta mère a acheté un foulard?
2. Tu as acheté des jeans?
3. Tes cousins ont acheté des sandales?
4. Ton frère et toi, vous avez acheté des ceintures?
5. Henriette a acheté une jupe?
6. Tes sœurs ont acheté des bas?

à vous, maintenant   Are you hard to get along with? Tell when, with whom, and why you last had an argument.

> *Vendredi je me suis disputé(e) avec ma petite sœur à cause de...*

The verbs **partir** and **sortir**

partir to leave	
je **pars**	nous **partons**
tu **pars**	vous **partez**
on/il/elle **part**	ils/elles **partent**
past participle: (être) parti	

sortir to go out	
je **sors**	nous **sortons**
tu **sors**	vous **sortez**
on/il/elle **sort**	ils/elles **sortent**
past participle: (être) sorti	

1. Note that both **partir** and **sortir** take the auxiliary verb **être** in the *passé composé,* and their past participles end in **-i.**
2. **Partir** and **sortir** are followed by **de** when the point of departure is indicated.

> Ils **partent de Paris** ce soir.   They are leaving Paris this evening.
>
> Ils **sortent de l'école** à une heure.   They get out of school at one o'clock.

C   Inquire when the following people are leaving. A classmate replies that they have already left.

> ■Ⅲ   Béatrice: en vacances   — *Quand est-ce que Béatrice part en vacances?*
> — *Elle est déjà partie.*

1. Luc: à la campagne
2. Les Auger: en vacances
3. votre famille et vous: en voyage
4. toi: des États-Unis
5. Nadine et Dominique: d'ici
6. les employés: du bureau

D   Ask if the first person indicated is still going out with the second. A classmate responds that this has never been the case.

> ▪ⅲ   toi: Jacques   — *Tu sors toujours avec Jacques?*
> — *Non, je ne suis jamais sortie avec lui.*

1. Juliette: ton cousin
2. Luc: Danièle
3. ton frère: la chanteuse canadienne
4. votre frère et vous: ces deux actrices
5. les Bertol: vous deux
6. toi: Chantal

Regular -ir verbs

réussir to succeed	
je **réussis**	nous **réussissons**
tu **réussis**	vous **réussissez**
on/il/elle **réussit**	ils/elles **réussissent**
past participle: **réussi**	

The present tense of regular **-ir** verbs is formed by adding the endings **-is, -is, -it, -issons, -issez,** and **-issent** to the infinitive stem. The past participle is formed by adding **-i** to the infinitive stem.

Other regular **-ir** verbs you have seen are:

> **atterrir**   to land
> **finir**   to finish
> **remplir**   to fill, fill out

E   It's the end of the school year. Say that all of the following people are finishing their studies in the indicated fields.

> ▪ⅲ   elle: médecine   *Elle finit ses études de médecine.*

1. toi: physique
2. lui: sciences naturelles
3. vous: chimie
4. moi: littérature française
5. nous: maths
6. eux: latin

F   Say that the following people have succeeded in their fields.

> ▪ⅲ   Louisette: avocate   *Elle est avocate et elle a bien réussi.*

1. eux: architecte
2. vous: fermier
3. moi: comptable
4. toi: photographe
5. lui: journaliste
6. nous: pilote

The relative pronoun **qui**

The relative pronoun **qui** (who, that, which) may be used as the subject of a *relative clause*. A relative clause describes or identifies a noun. (Note: a clause is any phrase that includes a subject and a verb.)

Nadine est une femme **qui a bien réussi.**	Nadine is a woman *who has had much success.*
Voilà une offre d'emploi **qui m'intéresse beaucoup.**	Here's a want ad *that interests me very much.*

1. The relative pronoun **qui** may refer to animate nouns (people, animals) or to inanimate nouns (things, places, concepts).
2. A relative clause introduced by **qui** immediately follows the noun(s) that it describes or identifies.
3. The verb form that follows **qui** agrees with the noun(s) modified by the clause.

> J'ai parlé à **Paul, qui est** de Lewiston, et à **Louise et Gilles, qui sont** de Sanford.

G   Combine each pair of sentences into a single sentence. Use *qui* to change the second sentence in each pair to a relative clause.

▪ⅲ Nadine sort avec Jean-Michel. Nadine est médecin à Montréal.	*Nadine, qui est médecin à Montréal, sort avec Jean-Michel.*

1. Sylvie a un emploi à Dakar. Sylvie est canadienne.
2. Dominique connaît une femme. Cette femme a 102 ans.
3. Cette église est la plus belle de la région. Cette église dâte du dix-huitième siècle.
4. J'ai vu des montagnes. Les montagnes sont plus hautes que les Alpes.
5. Martin va en France cet été. Martin adore voyager.
6. Nous avons parlé à Mlle Couret. Mlle Couret a été très gentille.

H   Several people tell you about some of their friends and relatives. Pass along the information to a friend.

▪ⅲ Guillaume dit: «Mon cousin habite à Rennes.»	*Guillaume a un cousin qui habite à Rennes.*

1. Maryse dit: «Ma cousine veut être avocate.»
2. Philippe dit: «Mes frères ont voyagé en Afrique.»
3. Marcel dit: «Ma tante travaille dans un hôpital à Chicago.»
4. Véronique et Anne disent: «Notre ami est journaliste à Washington.»
5. André dit: «Ma copine espère aller aux États-Unis cet été.»
6. Paul et Serge disent: «Nos cousins vont souvent au Maroc.»
7. Jacqueline dit: «Mon copain habite à San Francisco.»

Lecture

Votre horoscope

Do you sometimes have difficulty planning your future? If all else fails, consult your horoscope.

Bélier (21 mars–20 avril)
Vous êtes énergique et impulsif/impulsive. Vous aimez les sports.
Carrières: les sciences expérimentales, l'exploration, la publicité

Taureau (21 avril–20 mai)
Vous êtes déterminé(e), endurant(e). Vous aimez les maths. *Carrières:* la construction; ingénieur, fermier/fermière

Gémeaux (21 mai–21 juin)
Vous êtes adaptable, intelligent(e), versatile. Vous parlez beaucoup.
Carrières: les métiers manuels, le journalisme, le droit (*law*)

Cancer (22 juin–23 juillet)
Vous êtes romantique, imaginatif/imaginative, économe et un peu instable. *Carrières:* les affaires, l'art, l'histoire, les antiquités

Lion (23 juillet–22 août)

Vous êtes généreux/généreuse, magnanime, créatif/créative. Vous aimez lire. *Carrières:* la médecine, les sciences politiques; ouvrier/ouvrière

Vierge (23 août–22 septembre)

Vous êtes intelligent(e), analytique, modeste et un peu matérialiste. *Carrières:* la banque, la comptabilité, l'enseignement (*teaching*); écrivain

Balance (23 septembre–22 octobre)

Vous êtes charmant(e), intuitif/intuitive, idéaliste, indécis(e). *Carrières:* la diplomatie, l'assistance sociale, la politique

Scorpion (23 octobre–21 novembre)

Vous êtes discret/discrète, prudent(e), imaginatif/imaginative. Vous aimez écrire. *Carrières:* la psychiatrie, la recherche psychique, la détection, le journalisme

Sagittaire (22 novembre–20 décembre)

Vous êtes versatile, franc(he), philosophe, optimiste. Vous rêvez beaucoup. *Carrières:* la musique, l'enseignement, le clergé, l'entraînement (*training*) des chevaux

Capricorne (21 décembre–19 janvier)

Vous êtes ambitieux/ambitieuse, idéaliste, discipliné(e), persévérant(e). *Carrières:* l'architecture, la politique, l'administration, le service public

Verseau (20 janvier–18 février)

Vous êtes indépendant(e), non-conformiste, inventif/inventive, un peu mystérieux/mystérieuse. *Carrières:* la musique, l'astrologie, la sociologie, l'invention

Poissons (19 février–20 mars)

Vous êtes réceptif/réceptive, impressionnable, mais peu sociable. Vous êtes créatif/créative. *Carrières:* professeur, infirmière, metteur en scène, décorateur d'intérieurs

à vous,
maintenant

1. Est-ce que vous croyez à l'astrologie?
2. Quand êtes-vous né(e)?
3. Quel est votre signe du Zodiaque? Quels sont les signes de vos amis?
4. Quel est votre caractère?
5. Quelles sont les carrières qui vous sont ouvertes?

À la française

Some French people, like people in most parts of the world, have certain preconceptions of Americans and the United States. Some of the ideas have some limited basis in fact, while others are laughable to people who have actually visited **les U.S.A.** In any case, most people realize that stereotypes and generalizations should always be taken with a grain of salt, and very few take them as fact.

Many people still associate Americans with cowboys, Indians, and gangsters, even though they realize that the popular Hollywood images are well out of date. There is also a notion that nearly all Americans are wealthy, drive enormous cars, and spend a lot of money freely. They are thought to eat hot dogs, hamburgers, ice cream, and soft drinks — and little else — at all times of day. In general, Americans do dress and act in a more casual manner than most French people. For these reasons, they are sometimes considered **des grands enfants.**

On the other hand, American technology and business expertise are respected in France. People who take an interest in politics and international relations recognize the importance of American influence on the affairs of Europe. Many French people remember the important role of American troops in helping to liberate their country from enemy occupation during both World Wars.

As more French people visit the United States, fewer are willing to believe the popular stereotypes. Most people who take such a trip find it a rewarding experience, and while they surely perceive faults in American society, they generally recognize many qualities as well. Above all, most people, whether or not they have traveled abroad, realize that Americans, like themselves, are not all alike.

Were you aware of certain stereotypes of French people before you began to study French? Take a few minutes to discuss some of these stereotypes in class. You will probably conclude that they are no more valid than the ones that are sometimes applied to Americans.

The **passé composé** of reflexive verbs (A-B)

Reflexive verbs take **être** in the *passé composé*. The reflexive pronoun is usually the direct object, in which case the past participle agrees with the subject.

masculine subject	feminine subject
je me suis habillé	je me suis habillé**e**
tu t'es habillé	tu t'es habillé**e**
il s'est habillé	elle s'est habillé**e**
nous nous sommes habillé**s**	nous nous sommes habillé**es**
vous vous êtes habillé**(s)**	vous vous êtes habillé**e(s)**
ils se sont habillé**s**	elles se sont habillé**es**

If the direct object is different from the reflexive pronoun, no agreement occurs.

> Elle s'est cassé le bras.
> Nous nous sommes acheté une voiture.

The negative is formed by placing **ne** before the reflexive pronoun and **pas** after the verb **être.**

> Il **ne** s'est **pas** levé tôt.

The verbs **partir** and **sortir** (C-D)

The verbs **partir** (*to leave*) and **sortir** (*to go out*) are irregular verbs, and do not follow the pattern of **-ir** verbs like **finir.**

partir	
je **pars**	nous **partons**
tu **pars**	vous **partez**
on/il/elle **part**	ils/elles **partent**
past participle: (être) **parti**	

sortir	
je **sors**	nous **sortons**
tu **sors**	vous **sortez**
on/il/elle **sort**	ils/elles **sortent**
past participle: (être) **sorti**	

De is required after **partir** and **sortir** when the place being left is named.

> Je **sors de mon bureau** à cinq heures.

Regular -ir verbs (E-F)

The present tense of regular -ir verbs is formed by adding the endings -is, -is, -it, -issons, -issez, and -issent to the infinitive stem. The past participle is formed by adding -i to the infinitive stem. (The stem is the infinitive minus -ir.)

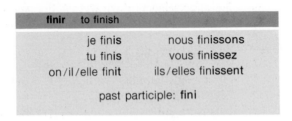

finir	to finish
je finis	nous finissons
tu finis	vous finissez
on/il/elle finit	ils/elles finissent

past participle: fini

Other regular -ir verbs you have seen are:

atterrir to land
remplir to fill, fill out
réussir to succeed

The relative pronoun qui (G-H)

A common way of describing or identifying a noun is to give additional information about it in a relative clause. (A clause is a phrase that includes a subject and a verb.) A relative clause may have as its subject the pronoun **qui** (who, which, that). **Qui**, as a relative pronoun, may refer to one or more persons, places, things, or concepts.

Voilà Isabelle, **qui a gagné la course cycliste.**	There's Isabelle, *who won the bicycle race.*
Les légumes, **qui sont moins chers que la viande,** sont aussi bons.	Vegetables, *which are less expensive than meat,* are just as good.
Il travaille dans une entreprise **qui a six cents employés.**	He works in a business *that has six hundred employees.*

A relative clause immediately follows the noun(s) that it describes or identifies. The verb form that follows **qui** agrees with the noun(s) modified by the relative clause.

Le garçon **qui se promène** là-bas s'appelle Claude.
Tu connais ces filles **qui viennent** d'arriver?

A From the descriptions of activities or places of employment below, say what kind of work the following people do. More than one answer may be possible.

> ▪ⅲ Mlle Sinclair travaille dans un hôpital.   *Elle est médecin (infirmière, secrétaire).*

1. M. Dupont arrête les voleurs.
2. Mme Moreau travaille pour *l'Express*.
3. Mlle Duclos navigue en avion.
4. M. Billetdoux fait des portraits.
5. Mme Voltaire participe aux jeux Olympiques.
6. Mlle Dubarry fait des plans de buildings.
7. M. Fourchet joue bien le rôle de *Hamlet*.
8. Mme Jolliet travaille dans un garage.
9. M. Louvet aime travailler dans ses champs.

B You have lost track of time. Say that the following people are leaving at the times indicated. A classmate contradicts you and says that they left at some previous time.

> ▪ⅲ Paul: demain   — *Paul part demain.*
>   — *Mais non, il est parti hier!*

1. Marie: en avril
2. Jeanne et Louise: à midi
3. Les Dupont: tard
4. Paul et Hélène: après le dîner
5. Roger: aujourd'hui
6. on: à huit heures

C Say that in April the following people never go out without their umbrella.

> ▪ⅲ on   *En avril, on ne sort jamais sans son parapluie.*

1. lui
2. toi
3. moi
4. nous
5. vous
6. elles

D It was a hot, lazy summer afternoon. Say where the following people were settled.

> ▪ⅲ Jacques: dans un fauteuil   *Jacques s'est installé dans un fauteuil.*

1. moi: sur la plage
2. on: sur une colline
3. lui: au stade
4. Paul et vous: sous un arbre
5. Yvette: dans son lit
6. nous: dans un cinéma climatisé
7. toi: dans le jardin
8. mes cousins: sous un parasol

E Today's newspaper contained a number of interesting articles under the following headlines. Ask your friends whether they saw the stories that attracted your attention.

▪▥ Médecins de 30 pays
se rencontrent à Bruxelles

Vous avez vu l'article sur les médecins qui se sont rencontrés à Bruxelles?

1. Jeune fille part pour l'Amérique en bateau à voiles
2. Famille de pigeons s'installe à l'hôtel de ville de Lyon
3. Équipe canadienne gagne à Chamonix
4. Pilotes refusent d'atterrir à Madrid
5. Gorille africain arrive au zoo de Montpellier
6. Trois Anglaises montent au Mont Blanc
7. Groupe de lycéens français revient de Tokyo
8. Actrice américaine achète entreprise à Bordeaux

F Prepare a list of possible careers where knowledge of French or another foreign language would be essential or helpful.

G See how many place names of French origin you can identify in your region and in your country. (Hint: The names of three states and five state capitals can be traced to French.)

Vocabulaire

NOMS

l'agent de police (*m.*) police officer

l'architecte (*m./f.*) architect

l'artiste (*m./f.*) artist

l'athlète (*m./f.*) athlete

l'avis (*m.*) opinion

l'avocat (*m.*), l'avocate (*f.*) lawyer

le chanteur, la chanteuse singer

la clientèle clientele

la/le comptable accountant

l'écrivain (*m.*) writer

l'emploi (*m.*) employment, job

l'entreprise (*f.*) firm, business

le fermier, la fermière farmer

l'idée (*f.*) idea

l'infirmier (*m.*), l'infirmière (*f.*) nurse

l'interprète (*m./f.*) interpreter

le journal newspaper

la/le journaliste journalist

le laboratoire laboratory

le mécanicien, la mécanicienne mechanic

le médecin doctor

le métier trade; profession

l'occasion (*f.*) occasion

l'offre (*f.*) offer

l'ouvrier, l'ouvrière worker

le photographe photographer

le pilote pilot

le poste job

la recherche research

le rêve dream

la/le secrétaire secretary

le soldat (la femme soldat) soldier

le stage de formation training period

la vie life

VERBES

se débrouiller   to work things
  out, to manage
embaucher   to hire
finir   to finish
intéresser   to interest
partir   to leave
passer (le temps)   to spend
  (time)
réussir (à)   to succeed (in)
rêver   to dream
servir de   to serve as
terminer   to finish
utiliser   to use

ADJECTIFS

ambitieux, ambitieuse
  ambitious
bilingue   bilingual
quelque(s)   some
respecté(e)   respected
veinard(e)   lucky

ADVERBES

au moins   at least
surtout   especially

AUTRES MOTS ET EXPRESSIONS

chacun(e)   each one
à mi-temps   part-time
à plein temps   full-time
ce qu'il te faut   what you
  need
il faut   one must; it is necessary
mettre de côté   to set aside
un coup de chance   a stroke
  of luck

troisième étape (a)

A   **Votre correspondance.** It's time to write another letter to your pen pal. Tell your friend about some of the interesting things you have done recently, and ask about her or his activities. You may also want to mention some of your plans and hopes for the summer, next year, and the more distant future.

B   **Un beau voyage.** Plan a trip, whether it is to be real or imaginary, to one of the places you have read about in this book. Tell the class why you chose that location, when you are going to go, how you will get there, and what you plan to do. If there are reasons that caused you to rule out some of the other places, explain what those reasons are. You might even wish to talk to a travel agent, who can give you some free information about fares, schedules, accommodations, attractions, and so forth.

C   **Qu'est-ce qu'ils sont devenus?** Choose one of the young people you met in chapters 1–14 and imagine some of the things that might happen to that person during the next fifteen years. Taking the role of that man or woman fifteen years from now, bring the class up to date on what has become of you. Give such information as where you now live, how old you are, what your current job status is, what kinds of work or study you have pursued, and how your friends and family are doing.

D   **Votre avenir.** Give some thought to the kind of work you would like to do when you finish school, and talk briefly about it to the class. Include some of the reasons for your choice and some of the things you will need to do in order to achieve your goal. Many people are not sure about this question until they are a good deal older, so you may want to mention several possible choices. See if you can think of ways in which knowing French could help you.

E **Le jeu des portraits.** Play another round of the game that was suggested in the **première étape** section, page 103, in which students try to guess the identity of a well-known person by asking **oui-non** questions. This time, however, individual students should choose the character and answer the questions. The person who correctly guesses the secret identity takes the next turn as "mystery guest."

F **Le journal.** Prepare a French-language version of a school newspaper. Give student reporters such news and feature assignments as: a student government meeting; a dance or other school social event; athletic contests; interesting projects in French class or other classes; and profiles of selected students or teachers. You might have editorials, **courrier du cœur,** a movie review, or a restaurant critic's column on the offerings in the cafeteria. Either compile the stories in a binder or simulate an authentic newspaper by pasting up the copy in columns on a large sheet of paper or cardboard. You could even add some advertisements from a French newspaper or magazine.

G **Critiques et réactions.** Conduct a class discussion of a current popular movie or television show, or of a book that many students have read recently (perhaps a novel assigned in English class.) Talk about the characters, the plot, the setting, and your reactions. A written review could be included in your newspaper, if you do Activity F.

H **Le journal sportif.** Present a brief sports report on your favorite team or individual athlete. Comment on the results of recent games or matches, the current standings (or the prospects for the coming season), key players, and injuries. If you are a devoted sports fan, you may wish to report on more than one of the teams you follow. If you aren't a sports fan, you can take this opportunity to declare your indifference.

I **Une interview.** Simulate a job-interview situation in which one student acts as the prospective employer and one or more students represent applicants. Each applicant might prepare a résumé, a written summary of a person's experience and qualifications. With a little imagination, this activity can take the form of a humorous sketch. For example, the job may have been advertised simply as "high-paying," "exciting," or "exotic," with no details given about the nature of the work. During the course of the interview, it could be discovered that the job is bizarre, dangerous, or deadly dull.

J **Des proverbes.** Working with one or more classmates, choose one of the proverbs included in the **Prononciation et orthographe** sections of Chapters 1–14. Then work out a very short skit to illustrate the meaning of the proverb. The proverb itself will probably be the last line of the skit. As a variation, act out a scene in pantomime, and let the rest of the class try to guess the proverb that is being dramatized.

K **Le français près de chez vous.** Do more research on a place in your area that has some French background, and give a report to the class in English. For example, it may be a historic site, a shop run by a French person, a community where many native speakers of French live, or just a town with a French name for which you can learn the origin. There is almost certainly "something French" not far from you. It might be fun to investigate.

L **Les grandes vacances.** Do any of the color pictures on pages 241–248 depict activities that you plan to participate in this summer? Are there scenes that make you think of where you will be? Maybe you like the photographs but feel that they don't represent what your vacation will be like. If so, which of the pictures would you most like to step into if you could? Talk about your plans and wishes for the coming summer vacation. Illustrate your talk with any of the photographs from this book that you find inviting.

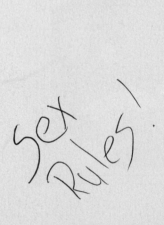

Reference
section

French first names

The following list includes some of the most popular French names. It is not a complete list of first names.

boys

Alain	Jean-Luc		
Albert	Jean-Paul		
André	Jean-Philippe		
Antoine	Jean-Pierre		
Arnaud	Jérôme		
Benoît	Joël		
Bernard	Joseph		
Bertrand	Jules		
Bruno	Julien		
Charles	Laurent		
Christian	Léon		
Christophe	Louis		
Claude	Luc		
Daniel	Marc		
David	Marcel		
Denis	Mathieu		
Dominique	Maurice		
Émile	Max		
Éric	Michel		
Étienne	Nicolas		
Eugène	Olivier		
Francis	Pascal		
François	Patrick		
Frédéric	Paul		
Gabriel	Philippe		
Gauthier	Pierre		
Georges	Raoul		
Gérard	Raymond		
Gilbert	René		
Gilles	Richard		
Guillaume	Robert		
Guy	Roger		
Henri	Rolland		
Hubert	Serge		
Jacques	Simon		
Jean	Thierry		
Jean-Claude	Thomas		
Jean-François	Victor		
Jean-Jacques	Vincent		
Jean-Louis	Yves		

girls

Alice	Laure		
Andrée	Laurence		
Anne	Lise		
Annick	Élise		
Annie	Louise		
Antoinette	Lucie		
Barbara	Madeleine		
Béatrice	Marguerite		
Bernadette	Marianne		
Brigitte	Marie		
Caroline	Marie-Claire		
Catherine	Marie-Christine		
Cécile	Marie-Françoise		
Chantal	Marie-Hélène		
Charlotte	Marie-Thérèse		
Christine	Martine		
Claire	Michèle		
Claude	Mireille		
Colette	Monique		
Danièle	Nathalie		
Denise	Nicole		
Diane	Noëlle		
Dominique	Pascale		
Élisabeth	Patricia		
Ève	Pauline		
Évelyne	Rachel		
Fanny	Renée		
Florence	Rose		
Françoise	Sara		
Gabrielle	Simone		
Geneviève	Solange		
Germaine	Sophie		
Gisèle	Suzanne		
Hélène	Sylvie		
Irène	Thérèse		
Isabelle	Valérie		
Jacqueline	Véronique		
Janine	Viviane		
Jeanne	Yvette		
Josette	Yvonne		

Supplementary word sets

The following word lists will help you to increase the number of things you can say and write during your study of each chapter. Some of the words may be introduced as active vocabulary in chapters later than the chapters for which they are listed here.

chapter 1

ADJECTIVES OF NATIONALITY

allemand(e)   German
anglais(e)   English
chinois(e)   Chinese
coréen(ne)   Korean
cubain(e)   Cuban
hollandais(e)   Dutch
irlandais(e)   Irish
israélien(ne)   Israeli
italien(ne)   Italian
japonais(e)   Japanese
mexicain(e)   Mexican
polonais(e)   Polish
russe   Russian
suisse   Swiss
vietnamien(ne)   Vietnamese

chapter 2

CLASSROOM OBJECTS

la bande   tape
le cartable   bookbag
la cloche   bell
la corbeille   wastebasket
la craie   chalk
le dictionnaire   dictionary
le drapeau   flag
l'écran (*m.*)   screen
l'étagère (*f.*)   bookcase; shelf
le feutre   felt-tip marker
la gomme   eraser
le magnétophone   tape recorder
la règle   ruler
le tableau d'affiches   bulletin board
l'horloqe (f.) clock

TRANSPORTATION

en mobylette   by moped
en moto   by motorcycle
en vélomoteur   by motorbike
en taxi   by taxicab

chapter 3

HOUSING AND FURNITURE

l'armoire (*f.*)   wardrobe (closet)
la cave   cellar
la commode   bureau, dresser
le congélateur   freezer
la cuisinière   stove
le divan   sofa
l'évier (*m.*)   sink
le fauteuil   armchair
le four   oven
le grenier   attic
l'immeuble (*m.*)   apartment building
la lampe   lamp
le lit   bed
la penderie   closet
le placard   cupboard
le réfrigérateur   refrigerator

chapter 4

TIME EXPRESSIONS

actuellement   currently
à présent   at present
de temps en temps   from time to time
en ce moment   at the moment
rarement   rarely
toujours   always

SCHOOL SUBJECTS

la comptabilité   accounting
la dactylographie   typing
la sténographie   stenography, shorthand

chapter 5

FAMILY

l'arrière-grand-mère (*f.*)   great-grandmother
l'arrière-grand-père (*m.*)   great-grandfather
le cadet, la cadette   youngest child
la marraine   godmother
le parrain   godfather
la petite-fille   granddaughter
le petit-fils   grandson

DESCRIPTIVE ADJECTIVES

faible   weak
fort(e)   strong
gros(se)   fat
insouciant(e)   carefree
jeune   young
maigre   thin
maladroit(e)   clumsy, awkward
marrant(e)   funny
têtu(e)   stubborn
triste   sad
vaniteux, vaniteuse   vain
vieux (vieil), vieille   old

chapter 6

CITY LOCATIONS

la bibliothèque   library
le gratte-ciel or **la tour**   skyscraper
le grand magasin   department store
le monument   monument
la papeterie   stationery
la pharmacie   drugstore
la quincaillerie   hardware store
le supermarché   supermarket
l'université (*f.*)   university
l'usine (*f.*)   factory

PREPOSITIONS

à côté de   next to, beside
autour de   around
entre   between
le long de   along
parmi   among

FAMILY

le beau-frère   brother-in-law
le beau-père   father-in-law; stepfather
la belle-mère   mother-in-law; stepmother
le demi-frère   stepbrother
la demi-sœur   stepsister

chapter 7

CLOTHING AND JEWELRY

l'anneau (*m.*) or **la bague**   ring
les boucles d'oreille (*f. pl.*)   earrings
le bracelet   bracelet
le cardigan   cardigan sweater
le chandail   heavy sweater
le collier   necklace
le costume or **le complet**   man's suit
la cravate   necktie
les gants (*m. pl.*)   gloves
la montre   watch
les pantoufles (*f. pl.*)   slippers
le papillon   bow tie
le tailleur   woman's suit
la veste   jacket

COLORS

(bleu) clair   light (blue)
(bleu) foncé   dark (blue)
blond(e)   blond
multicolore   multicolored
roux, rousse   red-haired

chapter 8

HOUSE AND GROUNDS

le balcon   balcony
le garage   garage
la pelouse   lawn
la sonnette   doorbell
la terrasse   patio, terrace
la véranda   porch
les volets (*m. pl.*)   shutters

REFLEXIVE VERBS

se baigner   to bathe
se brosser (les dents)   to brush (one's teeth)
se coucher   to go to bed
se déshabiller   to get undressed
se laver (les mains)   to wash (one's hands)
se maquiller   to put on make-up
se peigner   to comb one's hair
se raser   to shave
se reposer   to rest
se réveiller   to wake up

chapter 9

WEATHER

le brouillard or **la brume**   fog
le ciel est couvert or **il fait gris/nuageux**   it's cloudy
il grêle   it's hailing
il tombe de la neige fondue   it's sleeting

chapter 10

FOOD

l'ail (*m.*)   garlic
le bifteck or **le steak**   steak
le boeuf hâché   ground beef
la cerise   cherry
le citron   lemon
la confiture   jam
la côtelette   chop
les épinards (*m. pl.*)   spinach
le foie   liver
les frites or **les pommes frites** (*f. pl.*)   French fries
le hamburger   hamburger
les hors-d'oeuvre (*m. pl.*)   appetizers
le hot-dog   hot dog
l'omelette (*f.*)   omelet
le pain grillé   toast
le pamplemousse   grapefruit
la pêche   peach
la pizza   pizza
la poire   pear
le raisin   grapes
le rosbif   roast beef
le thon   tuna
le yaourt   yogurt

chapter 11

HOTEL TERMS

le chasseur or **le groom**   bellhop
la femme de chambre   chambermaid
le portier   doorman
le standard (téléphonique)   switchboard
le vestibule   lobby

chapter 12

GAMES

le backgammon   backgammon
le bridge   bridge
le canasta   canasta
les cartes (*f. pl.*)   cards
les dames (*f. pl.*)   checkers
les dominos (*m. pl.*)   dominoes
les échecs (*m. pl.*)   chess
le whist   whist

CARDS

le carreau   diamonds
le coeur   hearts
le pic   spades
le trèfle   clubs

l'as (*m.*)   ace; **l'as de (coeur)**   ace of (hearts)
la dame   queen
le roi   king
le valet   jack

CHESS

le cheval   knight
la dame   queen
échec   check
le fou   bishop
mat   mate
pat   stalemate
le pion   pawn
le roi   king
roquer   to castle
la tour   castle, rook

SPORTS

l'alpinisme (*m.*)   mountain climbing
l'aviron (*m.*)   rowing
le badminton   badminton
la boxe   boxing
le canoë   canoeing
le cyclisme   bicycle racing
le golf   golf
la gymnastique   gymnastics
le hand-ball   handball
le hockey sur gazon   field hockey
le judo   judo
le karaté   karate
le patin à glace   ice skating
le patin à roulettes   roller skating
la plongée   scuba diving

PARTS OF THE BODY

la barbe   beard
la cheville   ankle
le cœur   heart
le cou   neck
le coude   elbow
le dos   back
l'épaule (*f.*)   shoulder
le front   forehead
le genou   knee
la gorge   throat
la joue   cheek
la langue   tongue
les lèvres (*f. pl.*)   lips
le menton   chin
la moustache   moustache
l'orteil (*m.*)   toe
l'os (*m.*)   bone
la peau   skin
le poignet   wrist
la poitrine   chest
le sang   blood
le ventre   belly

chapter 13

NATURAL FEATURES

le bois   woods
l'étoile (*f.*)   star
la falaise   cliff
la forêt   forest

la planète   planet
le sommet   summit, peak
le volcan   volcano

chapter 14

JOBS AND PROFESSIONS

l'agent de change (*m.*)   stockbroker
l'agent immobilier (*m.*)   real estate agent
l'astronaute   astronaut
le/la biologiste   biologist
le cadre commercial   business executive
le chef de ventes   sales manager
le/la chimiste   chemist
le chirurgien   surgeon
la femme/l'homme d'affaires   business person
le maçon   stonemason
le mathématicien, la mathématicienne   mathematician
le musicien, la musicienne   musician
le peintre   painter, artist
le physicien, la physicienne   physicist
le plombier   plumber
le/la psychiatre   psychiatrist
le/la psychologue   psychologist

Phonetic symbols

vowels and semi-vowels

/a/	la, papa, femme
/ɛ/	mère, bête, français
/e/	et, préférer, mes
/œ/	peur, soeur, jeune
/ø/	peu, deux, heureux
/ə/	je, petit, devoirs
/i/	ami, ici, italien
/ɔ/	porter, joli, bonne
/o/	mot, beau, au
/u/	tout, sous, où
/y/	tu, autobus, d'habitude
/ɑ̃/	dans, en, temps
/ɛ̃/	pain, intéressant, canadien
/ɔ̃/	bon, montagne, montrer
/œ̃/	brun, lundi, quelqu'un
/w/	oui, jouer, joueur
/wa/	moi, trois, croire
/ɥ/	huit, depuis, aujourd'hui
/j/	envoyer, famille, sommeil

consonants

/b/	bébé, bien, s'habiller
/d/	des, aider, bavarde
/f/	faire, difficile, photographe
/g/	gare, degré, guide
/ʒ/	jeune, gentil, tragique
/ʀ/	kilomètre, cave, d'accord
/l/	les, belle, joli
/m/	manteau, mais, dame
/n/	nous, américaine, donner
/ɲ/	oignon, bourguignon, Bretagne
/p/	pour, après, étape
/ʀ/	rien, arrêter, finir
/s/	sous, réservation, français
/ʃ/	chien, acheter, moche
/t/	tu, attendre, toute
/v/	vers, avion, grave
/z/	zéro, saison, chaise

pronunciation of letters of the alphabet

A /a/	B /be/	C /se/	D /de/	E /ø/	F /ɛf/	G /ʒe/
H /aʃ/	I /i/	J /ʒi/	K /ʀa/	L /ɛl/	M /ɛm/	N /ɛn/
O /o/	P /pe/	Q /ky/	R /ɛʀ/	S /ɛs/	T /te/	U /y/
V /ve/	W /dublave/	X /iks/	Y /igʀɛk/	Z /zɛd/		

Grammatical summaries

Words that introduce nouns

articles

	SINGULAR Masculine	Feminine	PLURAL Masculine/Feminine
Definite	le l' (before a vowel)	la l' (before a vowel)	les
Indefinite	un	une	des
Partitive	du de l' (before a vowel)	de la de l' (before a vowel)	

demonstrative adjectives

ce cet (before a vowel)	cette	ces

possessive adjectives

mon	ma mon (before a vowel)	mes
ton	ta ton (before a vowel)	tes
son	sa son (before a vowel)	ses
notre	notre	nos
votre	votre	vos
leur	leur	leurs

Pronouns

		SUBJECT	EMPHATIC	DIRECT-OBJECT	INDIRECT-OBJECT	REFLEXIVE
Singular		je (j')	moi	me (m')	me (m')	me (m')
		tu	toi	te (t')	te (t')	te (t')
		il	lui	le	lui	se (s')
		elle	elle	la	lui	se (s')
Plural		nous	nous	nous	nous	nous
		vous	vous	vous	vous	vous
		ils	eux	les	leur	se (s')
		elles	elles	les	leur	se (s')

| y, en | The word **y** replaces **à** (or another preposition indicating location) plus a noun phrase. |

Il va **au lycée.** Il **y** va.

The word **en** replaces **de, du, de la, de l'**, or **des** plus a noun phrase.

Il achète **de la viande.** Il **en** achète.

When both words are used in the same phrase, **y** precedes **en.**

Il y a des hôtels ici? Oui, il **y en** a deux.

Adjectives

singular forms

MASCULINE	FEMININE
grand	grande
français	française

Feminine is masculine plus **-e.**

MASCULINE	FEMININE
timide	timide
sympathique	sympathique

Masculine and feminine forms are identical.

MASCULINE	FEMININE
bon	bonne
canadien	canadienne
gentil	gentille
bas	basse

Feminine doubles final consonant and adds **-e.**

MASCULINE	FEMININE
furieux	furieuse
généreux	généreuse
heureux	heureuse
sérieux	sérieuse

Masculine ends in **-eux**, feminine ends in **-euse.**

MASCULINE	FEMININE
beau (bel)	belle
blanc	blanche
frais	fraîche
nouveau (nouvel)	nouvelle
vieux (vieil)	vieille

Irregular adjectives. (Forms given in parentheses are used before a masculine singular noun beginning with a vowel.)

plural forms

SINGULAR	PLURAL
un **petit** garçon	des **petits** garçons
une **petite** fille	des **petites** filles

Regular pattern: plural adds **-s.**

SINGULAR	PLURAL
un film **français**	des films **français**
un élève **sérieux**	des élèves **sérieux**

Adjectives ending in **-s** or **-x**: no change in masculine plural.

SINGULAR	PLURAL
le **beau** château	les **beaux** châteaux
le **nouveau** chapeau	les **nouveaux** chapeaux

Adjectives ending in **-eau**: plural adds **-x.**

Verbs

regular verbs in **-er, -re, ir**

		parler	descendre	finir
Present	je (j')	parle	descends	finis
	tu	parles	descends	finis
	on/il/elle	parle	descend	finit
	nous	parlons	descendons	finissons
	vous	parlez	descendez	finissez
	ils/elles	parlent	descendent	finissent
Passé composé	j'/je	ai parlé	suis descendu(e)	ai fini
	tu	as parlé	es decendu(e)	as fini
	on/il/elle	a parlé	est descenu(e)	a fini
	nous	avons parlé	sommes descendu(e)s	avons fini
	vous	avez parlé	êtes descendu(e)(s)	avez fini
	ils/elles	ont parlé	sont descendu(e)s	ont fini
Imperative		parle	descends	finis
		parlons	descendons	finissons
		parlez	descendez	finissez

reflexive verbs

		s'habiller	se coucher
Present	je	m'habille	me couche
	tu	t'habilles	te couches
	on/il/elle	s'habille	se couche
	nous	nous habillons	nous couchons
	vous	vous habillez	vous couchez
	ils/elles	s'habillent	se couchent
Passé composé	je	me suis habillé(e)	me suis couché(e)
	tu	t'es habillé(e)	t'es couché(e)
	on/il/elle	s'est habillé(e)	s'est couché(e)
	nous	nous sommes habillé(e)s	nous sommes couché(e)s
	vous	vous êtes habillé(e)(s)	vous êtes couché(e)(s)
	ils/elles	se sont habillé(e)s	se sont couché(e)s
Imperative		habille-**toi**	couche-**toi**
		habillons-**nous**	couchons-**nous**
		habillez-**vous**	couchez-**vous**

stem-changing verbs

		acheter	préférer	appeler
Present	je/j'	achète	préfère	appelle
	tu	achètes	préfères	appelles
	on/il/elle	achète	préfère	appelle
	nous	achetons	préférons	appelons
	vous	achetez	préférez	appelez
	ils/elles	achètent	préfèrent	appellent
Passé composé	j'ai (etc.)	acheté	préféré	appelé
Imperative		achète	préfère	appelle
		achetons	préférons	appelons
		achetez	préférez	appelez

verbs with spelling changes

		manger	commencer	envoyer
Present	je/j'	mange	commence	envoie
	tu	manges	commences	envoies
	on/il/elle	mange	commence	envoie
	nous	mangeons	commençons	envoyons
	vous	mangez	commencez	envoyez
	ils/elles	mangent	commencent	envoient
Passé composé	j' (etc.)	ai mangé	ai commencé	ai envoyé
Imperative		mange	commence	envoie
		mangeons	commençons	envoyons
		mangez	commencez	envoyez

irregular verbs

		aller	avoir	connaître	dire
Present	je/j'	vais	ai	connais	dis
	tu	vas	as	connais	dis
	on/il/elle	va	a	connaît	dit
	nous	allons	avons	connaissons	disons
	vous	allez	avez	connaissez	dites
	ils/elles	vont	ont	connaissent	disent
Past participle		(être) allé	eu	connu	dit
Imperative		va	aie	connais	dis
		allons	ayons	connaissons	disons
		allez	ayez	connaissez	dites

		écrire	être	faire	mettre
Present	je/j'	écris	suis	fais	mets
	tu	écris	es	fais	mets
	on/il/elle	écrit	est	fait	met
	nous	écrivons	sommes	faisons	mettons
	vous	écrivez	êtes	faites	mettez
	ils/elles	écrivent	sont	font	mettent
Past participle		écrit	été	fait	mis
Imperative		écris	sois	fais	mets
		écrivons	soyons	faisons	mettons
		écrivez	soyez	faites	mettez

		partir	pouvoir	prendre	savoir
Present	je/j'	pars	peux	prends	sais
	tu	pars	peux	prends	sais
	on/il/elle	part	peut	prend	sait
	nous	partons	pouvons	prenons	savons
	vous	partez	pouvez	prenez	savez
	ils/elles	partent	peuvent	prennent	savent
Past participle		(être) parti	pu	pris	su
Imperative		pars		prends	sache
		partons		prenons	sachons
		partez		prenez	sachez

		sortir	venir	voir	vouloir
Present	je/j'	sors	viens	vois	veux
	tu	sors	viens	vois	veux
	on/il/elle	sort	vient	voit	veut
	nous	sortons	venons	voyons	voulons
	vous	sortez	venez	voyez	voulez
	ils/elles	sortent	viennent	voient	veulent
Past participle		(être) sorti	(être) venu	vu	voulu
Imperative		sors	viens	vois	veuille
		sortons	venons	voyons	veuillons
		sortez	venez	voyez	veuillez

Core material equivalents
Chapters 1–10

chapter 1   The French language in the world

Who are you?

Hello! My name is Pierre Legrand.
I'm French.
I live in Paris. And you?

Hi! *My* name is Yvette Lebeau.
I'm Canadian.
I live in Quebec City. And you?

You're speaking English?

PIERRE	You're speaking English? Are you American?
YVETTE	No, Canadian. I speak French, too.
PIERRE	Really? Where do you live?
YVETTE	In Quebec City. And you, are you French?
PIERRE	Yes. I speak a little English, but not very well.

Nationalities

Pierre Legrand is French.
He lives in Paris.
He doesn't speak English very well.
Yvette Lebeau is Canadian.
She lives in Quebec City.
She speaks English and French.

Salutations

—Hi, Jacqueline!
—Hi!

—Good-by!
—Bye, Marie, see you soon!

—Hello, sir. Hello, ma'am.
—Hello!

—Good-by, miss.
—Good-by, Alain.

chapter 2   At school

Here's my school

Hi! It's me, Pierre Legrand.
I'm a high school student.
I go to the Lycée Pasteur, in Paris.
Here's my school.
It's a big school, isn't it?

On the way to school

PIERRE	Hey! Danièle, are you going to school by subway?
DANIÈLE	Yes. Usually I go by bicycle, but when it rains....
PIERRE	By bicycle? But you live a long way from school!
DANIÈLE	A long way? Not at all! Sometimes I even walk!
PIERRE	Really? But the subway is much more practical.

Two students

Pierre is a high school student in Paris.
Pierre's school is called the Lycée Pasteur.
He goes there by subway.
Danièle is a high school student.
Usually, she goes to school by bicycle.
But when it rains, she goes by subway.
The subway is very practical, isn't it?
But Danièle's bicycle is practical, too.

How's it going?

PIERRE	Hi, Jean. Hello, Cécile. How's it going?
JEAN	Okay, thanks.
CÉCILE	Not too bad. How about you, Pierre?
PIERRE	Not good today!
CÉCILE	Why?
PIERRE	It's raining. . . . And I have a test!
PIERRE	Hello, ma'am. How are you?
MME BROCHOT	Fine, thank you. And you, Pierre?
PIERRE	Oh! Not very well, ma'am.
MME BROCHOT	What's the matter? Are you sick?
PIERRE	No, it's because of the test!

chapter 3   At home

Welcome to

Hello! I'm Yvette Lebeau, from Quebec City.

Quebec City!

I'm almost fifteen years old.
I live in a pretty little house.
It's not far from the Château Frontenac.
You're invited to my home.

Happy birthday!

YVETTE	Hi, friends! Welcome!
JOËL	Happy birthday! Here! There's a little gift for you.
YVETTE	Thanks a lot, Joël. That's nice.
SYLVIE	I have something for you too.
YVETTE	Thanks. You're sweet, Sylvie. Well, come on into the living room. Everyone's there.

Yvette's birthday

Yvette's house is near the Château Frontenac.
Yvette invites Joël and Sylvie to her home.
Joël has a little present for Yvette.
Sylvie also has something for her.
Why? It's Yvette's birthday!
She's fifteen years old today.

| Hospitality | Welcome! | Sit down. Make yourself at home. |
| | Welcome, madam. | Sit down! Make yourself at home. |

chapter 4   Studying

Lessons and homework

Hello from Strasbourg!
I'm in the living room with a friend.
I often study with her after school.
We're both in *seconde* (tenth grade).
Right now, we're studying a history lesson.
We also have some math homework.

Bad news!

BERNADETTE	Hello?
GÉRARD	Hello, is that you, Bernadette? It's Gérard.
BERNADETTE	Hi. How are you, Gérard? Are you sick?
GÉRARD	No, I'm okay now. Tell me, what do we have for homework tomorrow?
BERNADETTE	We have some math problems, and they're not easy, you know.
GÉRARD	How about the history lesson?
BERNADETTE	It's boring.
GÉRARD	Darn it! Bad news!

Lots of homework

Bernadette often studies with a friend, Marianne.
Today, they have some math homework.
They also have a history assignment.
Gérard calls Bernadette on the phone.
He doesn't know what homework they have for tomorrow.
Bad news! The homework is difficult, and the assignment is boring.

Excuse me, sir!

BERNADETTE	Excuse me, sir. I'm late!
TEACHER	Yes, Ms. Muller. You're often late. Why?
BERNADETTE	I go home for lunch, and...
TEACHER	Do you have your English homework for today?
BERNADETTE	No, sir. I'm sorry.
TEACHER	Well, then, you have a zero in English.
BERNADETTE	Oh, no, please, sir...!

chapter 5   With the family

A large family

Hello from Port-au-Prince!
I live here with my family.
It's a large family!
There are five children, and I'm the oldest.
I have three sisters and a brother.
I like my little sister Suze. She's adorable.
As for my brother, he's unbearable.

A piece of good news!	RAYMOND	Berthe! What's up?
	BERTHE	There's a new baby at my house.... It's a boy.
	RAYMOND	That's great! Are you pleased?
	BERTHE	I'm delighted.... There are two of us now!
	RAYMOND	Yes there aren't too many of you, like at my house!
	BERTHE	No, you're lucky! You play with your sisters all the time. It's good to have a big family.

Brothers and sisters

Raymond Calixte is Haitian.
His is a large family: there are five children.
Raymond likes his little sister, but he doesn't like his brother at all.
His friend, Berthe Rigaud, has a little brother.
She is delighted, because there are two of them now.
She likes large families.

A visit to grandmother's	GRANDMOTHER	Ah, Raymond, it's you! How are you, my boy?
	RAYMOND	All right, grandmother. And you?
	GRANDMOTHER	Oh, you know, so-so. And your father? And your mother?
	RAYMOND	Everything's fine at home, grandmother. Here, here's something for you.
	GRANDMOTHER	Thank you, dear. Well, come in for a minute.
	RAYMOND	Yes, okay.
	RAYMOND	Good-by, grandmother. Take care.
	GRANDMOTHER	Good night, Raymond. See you soon.

chapter 6   Distant relatives

Which way do we go?	M. LE HUR	We're late. Aunt Soizic's going to be furious.
	MME LE HUR	No, don't worry! We're bringing lobsters! She's going to be delighted!
	M. LE HUR	All right. They live at 22 Rue de la Monnaie . . . across from the cathedral. . . It's around here, but where?
	ANNICK	Should I ask the way? (*to a passerby*) Sir, where is the cathedral, please?
	PASSERBY	It's not far from here, miss. You go straight ahead up to the Place Foch. First, you pass in front of the Cinéma Gaumont.
	ANNICK	Is that the Place Foch, the little square at the corner, over there?
	PASSERBY	Yes. When you get there, you turn right. Follow the street to the cathedral.
	ANNICK	Thanks very much, sir.
	PASSERBY	You're welcome.
	ANNICK	Now, let's hurry!

At the Kervendals'	MME KERVENDAL	You walked from the station! You poor things!
	M. LE HUR	Here, Soizic, here are the lobsters.
	MME KERVENDAL	Thank you very much, Jacques-Yves. How nice of you.
	M. LE HUR	Oh, it's nothing. . .
	PATRICK	Lobsters! Fantastic!
	MME LE HUR	Is everybody here?
	M. KERVENDAL	Yes, everyone is in the living room.
	M. KERVENDAL	Well, Annick, how do you like our city?
	ANNICK	Oh, it's not bad... but there's no ocean.
	PATRICK	You're really a sailor's daughter. Are you going to go boating during the summer?
	ANNICK	Maybe. I'd like to do some sailing.
	PATRICK	I'm going to my friend Jean-Marie's place in Concarneau. He has a sailboat, you know.
	ANNICK	Oh, great! You're lucky!

chapter 7   In an Algerian shop

We bargain here	M. FARID	Come in, madam. What would you like?
	CUSTOMER	I'm looking for a scarf to go with my green dress.
	M. FARID	This way, madam. Si, show this lady the scarves.
	SI	Here's a nice green and red scarf.
	CUSTOMER	No, I don't care for red.
	SI	Do you prefer blue? Here's a beautiful scarf in blue silk.
	CUSTOMER	Yes, it is superb. How much does it cost?
	SI	One hundred fifty dinars, madam.
	CUSTOMER	That's too expensive, young man!
	SI	No, madam, that's really a good price for silk. And it goes well with your blue eyes.
	CUSTOMER	What a flatterer! I'll buy it for 100 dinars.
	SI	One twenty-five!
	CUSTOMER	All right. I'll take it.

Veils and handkerchiefs	WAITER	Here are two teas, M. Farid. Shall I put them on the table?
	M. FARID	Yes, thanks, Ahmed. How much is it?
	WAITER	Five dinars.
	M. FARID	There! Good-by, Ahmed. Well, Si, to your health!
	SI	Thanks, Dad. Should I close the shop now?
	M. FARID	Yes, all right. But before going to lunch, I'd like to prepare the Ben Kim order.
	SI	Are the wedding dresses for them?
	M. FARID	Yes, six white dresses and matching veils and handkerchiefs.
	SI	Okay. I'm putting the six dresses in the box. Where are the veils?
	M. FARID	Right here. Now count out six handkerchiefs.
	SI	There are only five handkerchiefs.
	M. FARID	What! Look in the table drawer.
	SI	Yes, here's a white handkerchief like the others.
	M. FARID	Put it with the rest and let's go home. Are you hungry?
	SI	Yes, Dad, I'm always hungry for couscous.

A visit to a museum

Château de Beauregard — Cellettes (Loire-et-Cher)
Renaissance chateau built in the 16th and 17th centuries. Historical monument: privately owned; museum open daily from 9:30 to noon and from 2:00 to 5:00. Admission: 8 francs. Gray slate roof and high chimneys typical of the region; beautiful stone walls. In the portrait gallery, three centuries of history: kings and queens of France, princes and princesses, and famous men of every period.

IVANA — Ladies and gentlemen, it's nine-thirty. The tour is beginning. On the ground floor, we have two rooms, the entrance hall and the kitchen. But we're going to begin with the second floor. On the way, notice the beautiful Dutch clock. . . .

VISITOR — What period does the clock date from, miss?

IVANA — The eighteenth century, madam. This way. . . . Watch your step!

IVANA — We are now in the portrait gallery. There are 363 portraits here. Look also at the beautiful painted wood ceiling. The blue tile floor is unique in France. It depicts an army on the march.

VISITOR — Are there any portraits of your ancestors on the walls, miss?

IVANA — Yes, ma'am, but they are very distant ancestors. In our blue living room we have a portrait of the Chevalier du Pavillon. He died during the American Revolution. That's a little more recent!

Ivana has a guest

PHILIPPE — What do you do all day that's interesting?

IVANA — Well, in the morning I get up at seven o'clock. I go horseback riding until eight. Then I get dressed for the day. After breakfast, I give guided tours until noon.

PHILIPPE — And do you continue the tours in the afternoon?

IVANA — No, in the afternoon I study in the library.... Sometimes, I go for a walk in the park with my dogs.

PHILIPPE — What are you studying?

IVANA — I'm preparing for the entrance exam at Sciences-Po. It's a hard school!

PHILIPPE — Yes, that's for sure. So you're really very busy....

IVANA — Yes, but not all the time. I have fun, too. What about you, Philippe? When do you return to Paris?

PHILIPPE — In a week. But I'd like very much to see you again before I leave. Are you free Tuesday evening?

IVANA — I think so.

PHILIPPE — Then I'll take you to dinner in Amboise, okay?

IVANA — With pleasure!

chapter 9   The rainy season

At Dakar airport

M. DIOP	What's the weather like outside? Is it hot?
M. CAMARA	Yes, very hot. I hope it's going to storm. Here we are in July, and it hasn't rained yet!
M. DIOP	It's true, we really need rain. But if the Air Afrique plane can't land because of the storm....
M. CAMARA	Is that the flight from Casablanca?
M. DIOP	Yes, with a stop in Nouakchott. It's late.
M. CAMARA	What's the weather report?
M. DIOP	There's good weather in Casablanca. But they've got a sand-storm at Nouakchott. The wind is blowing from the desert at 75 kilometers per hour. And it's 35 degrees in the shade!
M. CAMARA	Wow! What heat!
M. DIOP	Well, so long, and have a good day! It'll be nice here, with the air conditioning. Not at my house, unfortunately! But I'm tired and I'll sleep well....

**Going to listen
to the griot**

KARIM	Mom, I'm hot! I want to go outside!
MME DIOP	But it's raining, Karim.
KARIM	No, Mom, it isn't raining any more.
MME DIOP	You're right. All right, you can go outside with your sister.
YACINE	No! I don't want to play outside! I'm afraid of the thunder.
KARIM	Thunder doesn't hurt you! And you have your gri-gri, don't you?
YACINE	Yes, but I'm afraid anyway.
KARIM	Well, I'm going to go by myself to listen to the griot. He's singing right now at the neighbors'.
YACINE	Oh? What's he doing there?
KARIM	It's for the birth of the Sambènes' son. The whole family is there. The griot is going to tell the story of their ancestors.
YACINE	Then I want to go too!
KARIM	Okay, let's go, little sister.... Hey! There's the Air Afrique plane. Dad's going to be glad.

chapter 10   A Burgundian meal

The big eater

MME CORDIER	Do you have the cold cuts, Jacques?
JACQUES	Yes, mother. Here's the pâté en croûte, ham, and sausage.
MME CORDIER	Hmm, a piece of the pâté is missing! How did that happen? My pork butcher is usually honest!
JACQUES	Uh... Well... You know I love pâté, mother.
MME CORDIER	Oh, what a glutton you are, Jacques! Oh, well, it doesn't matter. We're going to have a good dinner.
JACQUES	What are we having?
MME CORDIER	Well, after the *charcuterie,* we have snails and rabbit stew. The vegetables are potatoes and fresh peas.

M. CORDIER	Should I go get the wine from the cellar, Suzanne?
MME CORDIER	Yes, if you like.
M. CORDIER	When do we eat?
MME CORDIER	In an hour. I've just killed the rabbit. Please ask Alice to bring some lettuce from the garden.
M. CORDIER	Sure.
JACQUES	Is there cheese and dessert, mother?
MME CORDIER	Of course! White cheese with cream, and a strawberry pie especially for you.
JACQUES	Oh, boy! Thanks, mother.
MME CORDIER	Now, leave me to my cooking!

Jacques is starving

JACQUES	That smells good! This stew is going to be all right! Ohh, I'm starving!
MME CORDIER	Well, then, do something to help me. Go set the table in the dining room.
ALICE	Mother, when Jacques sets the table, something is always missing... the little dessert spoons... the napkins...
JACQUES	Oh, you drive me crazy! You can do it, if you want!
MME CORDIER	Be nice, you two! Don't squabble! And don't stay here while I'm cooking. Alice, go put the bread on the table.
ALICE	Oh, bother! There's no more bread.... I'll run over to the bakery on my bike.
MME CORDIER	Okay, here's five francs. Buy two loaves.
ALICE	All right, I'll be back in a minute. Jacques, don't eat all the pâté while I'm away!
JACQUES	Oh, don't bug me!

French-English vocabulary

The French-English vocabulary contains the basic words and expressions listed in the chapter vocabularies, plus words that occur in headings, captions, and reading material. The symbol ~ signifies the key word (minus the definite article, if any) for that entry. For example, ~ **cause de** under **à** means **à cause de;** la ~ **à manger** under **salle** means **la salle à manger.** The numbers in italics following the definitions refer to the chapters in which the words are introduced.

a: elle/il ~ she/he/it has, *2* (see **avoir**)

à at; in, *1*; to, *5*; ~ **bientôt** see you soon, *1*; ~ **cause de** because of, *2*; ~ **droite/gauche** to (on) the right/left, *6*; ~ **l'heure** on time, *4*; ~ **la (française)** in the (French) way; ~ **la maison** at home, *5*; ~ **mi-temps** part-time, *14*; ~ **nouveau** again, *12*; ~ **plein temps** full-time, *14*

aboyer to bark

accepter to accept, *3*

accidenté(e) injured in an accident

accompagner to accompany, *13*

acheter to buy, *7*

l'acteur, l'actrice actor, *11*

l'activité (*f.*) activity

admirer to admire, *8*

adorable adorable, *5*

adorer to adore, to love, *9*

aérien(ne) aerial; pertaining to air travel

l'aéroport (*m.*) airport, *9*

l'affaire (*f.*) affair; **les ~s** business, *12*

affectueusement affectionately, *12*

affolé(e) frantic, *11*

affreux, affreuse awful, *12*

l'agent de police (*m.*) police officer, *14*

ai: j'~ I have, *2* (see **avoir**)

aider to help, *10*

aimer to like, to love, *5*; **j'aimerais** I would like, *6*

aîné(e) oldest, *5*

l'air climatisé (*m.*) air conditioning, *9*

l'algèbre (*m.*) algebra, *4*

algérien(ne) Algerian, *1*

alimentaire pertaining to food

allemand(e) German; **l'allemand** (*m.*) German language, *4*

aller to go, *2*; ~ **bien/mal** to be well/unwell, *2* **allons bon!** oh no! *7*; **allons-y** let's go, *9*; **ça va?** how are things? *2* **s'en ~** to go away, *11*

allez: vous ~ you go, *4*; **comment ~-vous?** how are you? *2* (see **aller**)

allô hello (*on the telephone*), *4*

allons: nous ~ we go, *4* (see **aller**)

alors then, so, *6*

alsacien(ne) Alsatian

ambitieux, ambitieuse ambitious, *14*

américain(e) American, *1*

l'ami, l'amie friend, *4*

l'amitié (*f.*) friendship

amoureux, amoureuse (de) in love (with), *13*

amuser to amuse; **s'~** to enjoy oneself; to play, *8*

l'ancêtre (*m.*) ancestor, *8*

ancien(ne) old, *13*

anglais(e) English; **l'anglais** (*m.*) English language, *4*

l'anniversaire (*m.*) birthday, *3*; **bon ~** happy birthday, *3*

annoncer to announce, *9*

anxieux, anxieuse anxious, *12*

août (*m.*) August, *9*

l'appareil (*m.*) instrument; telephone; **qui est à l'~?** who is calling? *12*

l'appartement (*m.*) apartment, *3*

appeler to call, *12*; **s'~** to be named; **je m'appelle** my name is, *1*

l'appétit (*m.*) appetite; **bon ~!** enjoy the meal!

apporter to bring, *6*

apprendre to learn, *11*

après after, *4*; **d'~** according to, *13*

l'après-midi (*m. or f.*) afternoon, *8*

l'arbre (*m.*) tree, *13*

l'architecte (*m./f.*) architect, *14*

l'ardoise (*f.*) slate

l'argent (*m.*) money, *11*

l'aristocratie (*f.*) aristocracy

l'armée (*f.*) army, *8*

l'arrestation (*f.*) arrest

arrêter to arrest, *11*

l'arrivée (*f.*) arrival, *11*

arriver to arrive, *6*; ~ **à** to succeed (in), *12*

l'art (*m.*)   art, 4
l'artiste (*m./f.*)   artist, 14
as: tu ~   you have, 4 (see **avoir**)
l'ascenseur (*m.*)   elevator, 8
assez   rather, quite, 8; enough
assieds-toi (asseyez-vous)   sit down, 3
l'assiette (*f.*)   plate, 10
assorti(e)   matching, 7
l'assortiment (*m.*)   assortment
l'assurance (*f.*)   insurance, 11
l'athlète (*m./f.*)   athlete, 14
l'athlétisme (*m.*)   track and field, 12
l'atmosphère (*f.*)   atmosphere
attendre   to wait (for), 12
attentivement   carefully, attentively, 11
atterrir   to land, 9
au (contraction of **à** + **le**)   at/in/to the, 6; **~ moins** at least, 14; **~ revoir** good-by, 1
l'auditeur, l'auditrice   listener, 11
aujourd'hui   today, 2
aussi   also, 1; **~ ... que** as . . . as, 13
aussitôt   immediately, 12
l'autobus (*m.*)   bus, 2
l'autocar (*m.*)   intercity bus, 11
l'automne (*m.*)   autumn, fall, 9
autre   other, 7
autrefois   formerly, in the past
aux (contraction of **à** + **les**)   to the, in the, 6
avance: à l'~, d'~   in advance; **en ~** early, 4
avant de (+ *inf.*)   before (. . .ing), 7
avec   with, 4; **~ plaisir** with pleasure, 8
l'aventure (*f.*)   adventure, 11
l'avenue (*f.*)   avenue, 6
aveugle   blind

avez: vous ~   you have, 4 (see **avoir**)
l'avion (*m.*)   airplane, 9
l'avis (*m.*)   opinion, 14
l'avocat, l'avocate   lawyer, 14
avoir   to have; **j'ai** I have, 2; **~ (16) ans** to be (sixteen) years old, 3; **~ besoin (de)** to need, 9; **~ chaud** to be hot, 9; **~ de la chance** to be lucky, 5; **~ envie (de)** to want, 9; **~ faim** to be hungry, 7; **~ froid** to be cold, 9; **~ l'air** to seem; to look, 11; **~ l'intention (de)** to intend (to), 13; **~ lieu** to take place, 12; **~ peur (de)** to be afraid (of), 9; **~ raison** to be right, 9; **~ soif** to be thirsty, 9; **~ sommeil** to be sleepy, 9; **~ tort** to be wrong, 9
avons: nous ~   we have, 4 (see **avoir**)
avril (*m.*)   April, 9

le baccalauréat (le bac)   French secondary school exam and diploma
les bagages (*m. pl.*)   bags, suitcases, 11
la baguette   a kind of French bread, 10
le bal   ball, dance, 13
la banane   banana, 10
la bande: en ~   as a group, 13
la banque   bank, 6
barbant(e)   boring, 4
bas(se)   low, 8
le bateau   boat, 6; **faire du ~** to go boating, 6
bavard(e)   talkative, 5
beau, belle   beautiful, 5
beaucoup   very much, 6
le bébé   baby, 1
belge   Belgian, 1

le besoin   need; **avoir ~ (de)** to need, 9
bête   stupid, 5
le beurre   butter, 10
la bibliothèque   library, 8
la bicyclette   bicycle
bien   well, good, 5; **~ sûr** of course, 13
bientôt   soon; **à ~** see you soon, 1
la bienvenue   welcome; **être le/la/les ~(e)(s)** to be welcome
le bijou (*pl.* **bijoux**)   piece of jewelry, 11
bilingue   bilingual, 14
le billet   ticket
la biologie   biology, 4
bizarre   odd, strange, 11
blanc, blanche   white, 7
bleu(e)   blue, 7
le blouson   windbreaker, jacket, 7
le boeuf   beef, 10; ox
le bois   wood, 8 **en ~** made of wood, 8
bon(ne)   good, 5; **bon courage!** have courage! don't despair! 12; **bon marché** inexpensive, reasonably priced, 7; **bonne nuit** good night, 5
bonjour   hello, 1
bonsoir   good evening, good night
le borgne   one-eyed person
les bottes (*f. pl.*)   boots, 7
la bouche   mouth, 12
la boucherie   butcher shop, 10
la boulangerie   bakery, 10
les boules (*f. pl.*)   a popular outdoor game, 12
le boulevard   boulevard, 6
bourguignon(ne)   from Burgundy
le bracelet (en or)   (gold) bracelet, 11
le bras   arm, 12

brun(e) brown, 7
bureau teacher's desk, 2; office, 11
le but goal, 12

ça this; that; it; **~ ne fait rien** it doesn't matter, 10; **~ sent bon** it smells good, 10; **~ va** O.K., things are fine **~ va?** how are things? **~ va mal** things are bad, 2; **~ vaut le coup** it's worth it, 11; **comment ~ se fait?** how can that be? 10
le cadeau gift, 3
le café coffee, 10; café, 13
le cahier notebook, 2; workbook
calme calm
le/la camarade de classe classmate
la campagne country, countryside, 13
le camping camping, 6
canadien(ne) Canadian, 1
le caractère character
la caravane trailer, 11; caravan
le Carnaval Carnival
la carotte carrot, 10
le carreau tile, 8
la carrière career
la carte map, 2; card; **jouer aux ~s** to play cards
le carton cardboard box, 7
casser to break; **se ~ (la jambe)** to break one's (leg), 12
la cassette cassette, 2
la cathédrale cathedral, 6
cause: à ~ de because of, 2
la cave cellar, 10
ce (pronoun) it; **c'est/ce n'est pas** it is/it is not, 1
ce (cet before a vowel) this, that, 11; **ce que** what, 13
la cédille cedilla
la ceinture belt, 7

célèbre famous
cent one hundred, 5
ces these, those, 11
c'est it is, that is, 1; **~ formidable!** it's fantastic! 5; **~ pour ça** that's why, 12
cet this, that, 11 (see **ce**)
cette this, that, 11
chacun(e) each one, 14
la chaise chair, 2
la chaleur heat, 9
la chambre bedroom, 3
le champ field, 13
la chance luck; **avoir de la ~** to be lucky, 6; **bonne ~** good luck, 13
la chanson song
chanter to sing, 9
le chanteur, la chanteuse singer, 11
le chapeau hat, 7
le chapitre chapter
la charcuterie pork-butcher shop, delicatessen; products sold in such a store, 10
le charcutier delicatessen owner, 10
charmant(e) charming, 13
le charmeur, la charmeuse charmer
le château castle, 3
chaud(e) warm, hot; **avoir chaud** to be warm, hot, 9; **il fait chaud** it is warm, hot, 9
le chauffeur driver, 11
les chaussettes (*f. pl.*) socks, 7
les chaussures (*f. pl.*) shoes, 7
le chemin way, 6; **le ~ de fer** railroad
la cheminée chimney; fireplace, 8
la chemise shirt, 7
le chemisier woman's shirt, 7
cher, chère expensive, 7; dear, 13

chercher to look (for), 7
le cheval horse; **faire du ~** to go horseback riding, 8
le chevalier knight
les cheveux (*m. pl.*) hair, 12
chez at the home of; **~ moi** at my home, 3
chic, alors! great! 4
le chien dog, 8
la chimie chemistry, 4
le chocolat chocolate, hot chocolate, 10
le choix choice
le ciel sky, 13
le cinéma movie theater, 6; the movies, films in general
cinq five, 2
cinquante fifty, 4
le civet rabbit stew, 10
la classe class, 4
se classer to be ranked
la clé key, 11
le client, la cliente customer; hotel guest, 11
la clientèle clientele, 14
le climat climate
le coeur heart
le coffre-fort safe, 11
le coin corner, 6
le collant pantyhose, 7
le collège French school comparable to junior high school, 2
le/la collègue colleague
le collier (de perles) (pearl) necklace, 11
la colline hill, 13
combien how many, how much, 3
la combinaison combination
la commande order, 7
comme as, like, 5; **~ ci, ~ ça** so-so, 5
commencer to start, 8
comment how, 1; **~ ça se fait?** how can that be? 10; **~ ça va?** how are things? 2; **~ est (ta soeur)?** what is

(your sister) like? *5;* **~ vas-
tu? (~ allez-vous?)** how
are you? *2*
**le commentateur, la
commentatrice** commen-
tator, *11*
le communiqué bulletin, *12*
communiquer to communicate, *12*
complètement completely, *12*
composer to dial (telephone);
en composant by dialing
comprendre to understand,
11
le/la comptable accountant,
14
le compte account; **le bon
~** paid-up account
compter to count, *7*
le comte, la comtesse count,
countess
conclure to conclude
confortablement comfortably,
12
connaître to be acquainted
with, to know, *12;* **se ~** to
know each other, *13*
le conseil advice; piece of
advice, *11*
content(e) happy, *5*
continuer to continue, *8*
contre against, *11*
le contrôleur controller;
le ~ aérien air traffic
controller
le copain, la copine friend, *4*
le corridor hall, *3*
le corps body
la côte coast
le cou neck, *12*
la couleur color, *7*
le coup strike, blow; triumph; **ça vaut le ~** it's
worth it, *11;* **un ~ de
chance** stroke of luck, *14*
le coureur, la coureuse
runner, racer, *11;* **le/la ~
cycliste** bicycle racer, *12*
courir to run, to race, *12*

le courrier du cœur lonely
hearts column, advice to the
lovelorn, *13*
le cours school subject,
course, *4*
la course race
le couscous couscous (North
African dish)
le cousin, la cousine cousin,
6
le couteau knife, *10*
coûter to cost, *7*
le couvert table setting; **mettre le ~** to set the table, *10*
le crayon pencil, *2*
la crème cream, *10*
la crémerie dairy store, *10*
le cresson watercress
croire to believe, *13*
la cuillère spoon, *10*
la cuisine kitchen, *3*

d'abord (at) first, *6*
d'accord O.K., fine, *3*
d'après according to, *13*
d'habitude usually, *2*
la dame lady, woman, *1*
dans in, *3*
le danseur, la danseuse
dancer, *11*
de from, of, *1*
se débrouiller to work things
out, to manage, *14*
décembre (*m.*) December, *9*
décidément decidedly, certainly
décider to decide, *11*
la décision decision
déclarer to state, *12*
décrocher (l'appareil) to pick
up (the phone), *12*
dedans inside, *11*
le degré degree, *9*
dehors outside, *9*
déjà already, *13*
déjeuner to eat lunch; **le
~** lunch, *4;* **le petit ~**
breakfast, *10*

demain tomorrow, *4*
demander to ask, *6*
la demeure dwelling
les dents (*f. pl.*) teeth, *12*
le départ departure, *8*
se dépêcher to hurry;
dépêchons-nous let's
hurry, *6*
depuis since, *12;* **~ longtemps** for a long time, *13*
dernier, dernière last, *12*
derrière behind, *6*
des some, *4;* (contraction of
de + les) of the, from the,
6
descendre to go down, *8;* to
stay, to spend the night
(while traveling)
le désert desert, *9*
désirer to want, *7*
le dessert dessert, *10*
le dessin drawing, *4*
détester to dislike, to hate,
10
le détour detour
deux two, *2*
deuxième second, *8*
devant in front of, *6*
devenir to become, *12*
les devoirs (*m. pl.*) homework,
4
le dieu god; **mon Dieu!**
good heavens!
difficile difficult, *4*
dimanche Sunday, *4;* **le ~**
on Sundays
le dinar Algerian unit of
currency
dîner to have dinner, *8;* **le ~**
dinner
dire to say, *11;* **dis donc!**
say! *4*
disputé(e) contested, *12*
se disputer to have an argument, to quarrel, *10*
distrait(e) inattentive, absent-minded
dix ten, *2*
dix-huit eighteen, *3*

dix-neuf nineteen, 3
dix-sept seventeen, 3
le docteur doctor, 11
le doigt finger, 12
donner to give, 11
dormir to sleep, 9
doué(e) gifted
douze twelve, 3
droite: à ~ to/on the right, 6
du some; (contraction of **de + le**) of the, from the
dur(e) hard, 8
d'urgence urgently; immediately

l'eau (f.) water; **l'~ minérale** mineral water, 10
l'échange (m.) exchange; **les ~s de politesse** courtesy expressions
l'école (f.) school, 1; **les grandes écoles** specialized graduate schools in France
écouter to listen (to), 9
écrire to write
écrit(e) written
l'écrivain (m.) writer, 14
l'éducation physique (f.) **(la gym)** physical education, gym, 4
l'église (f.) church, 6
égoïste selfish, 5
l'élève (m./f.) pupil, 2
elle she, 1; her, 3; it, 3
elles they, 3; them, 7
éloigné(e) distant, 8
embaucher to hire, 14
embêter to annoy, 10
embrasser to kiss, 12
embrouillé(e) mixed up
emmener to take with, to lead away; to escort, 8
l'emploi (m.) employment, job, 14; **l'~ du temps** schedule
en in, 5; **~ marche** on the march, 8

en some; of, about (it, them); from (there), 13
encore again, 11
l'enfant (m./f.) child, 5
enfin finally, 13
ensemble together, 13
ensuite then, 8
entendre to hear, 12; **s'~ (avec)** to get along (with), 13
l'enterrement (m.) funeral
enthousiaste enthusiastic, 11
entre between, 12
l'entrée (f.) entrance, 8
l'entreprise (f.) firm, business, 14
entrer to enter, to go in, 3
envie: avoir ~ (de) to desire, to want, 9
envoyer to send, 12
l'épicerie (f.) grocery store, 10
l'époque (f.) period, epoch, 8
épouvantable terrible, 12
épuisé(e) exhausted, 11
l'équipe (f.) team, 12
es: tu ~ you are, 2 (see **être**)
l'escale (f.) flight stop, 9
l'escalier (m.) stairway, 8
l'escargot (m.) snail, 10
l'escrime (f.) fencing, 12
espagnol(e) Spanish; **l'espagnol** (m.) Spanish language, 4
espérer to hope, 9
est: elle/il ~ she/he/it is, 1 (see **être**)
et and, 1
l'étage (m.) floor of a building, 8
l'étape (f.) stopping place; leg of a race or journey
l'état (m.) state; **les États-Unis** the United States
l'été (m.) summer, 6
êtes: vous ~ you are, 3 (see **être**)

étrange strange
étranger, étrangère foreign; **l'~** foreigner
être to be, 1; **~ en train de + inf.** to be in the process of . . .-ing, 9
l'étude (f.) study; **~ de mots** word study; **les hautes ~s** higher education
étudier to study
eux them, 7
l'événement (m.) event, 11
exagérer to exaggerate
l'examen (m.) exam, 2
excuser to excuse; **excusez-moi** excuse me, 4
l'exercice (m.) exercise
expliquer to explain, 11
l'extrait (m.) excerpt, extract

face: en ~ de facing, opposite, 6
facile easy, 4
la faim hunger; **avoir ~** to be hungry, 9
faire to do; to make; **~ attention** to be careful, to pay attention, 8; **~ du bateau** to go boating, 6; **~ du camping** to go camping, 6; **~ du cheval** to go horseback riding, 8; **~ la cuisine** to cook, 10; **~ le guide** to act as a guide, 8; **~ mal (à)** to hurt, 9; **~ du ski** to ski, 12; **~ du sport** to play sports, 6; **~ de la voile** to go sailing, 6; **fais comme chez toi (faites comme chez vous)** make yourself at home, 3; **ne t'en fais pas!** don't worry! 6; **il fait beau** the weather is nice 9; **il fait frais** the weather is cool 9; **il fait froid** the weather is cold 9; **il fait mauvais** the weather is bad, 9; **il fait du vent** it's windy, 9

fais: je ~ I do; I make, 8; **tu ~** you do; you make, 8 (see **faire**)

faisons: nous ~ we do; we make, 8 (see **faire**)

fait: elle/il/~ she/he/it does *or* makes, 8 (see **faire**)

faites: vous ~ you do; you make, 8 (see **faire**)

la famille family, 5

fatigué(e) tired, 11

faut: il ~ it is necessary, one must; **ce qu'il (te) ~** what (you) need, 14

la faute fault, mistake; **~ de** for want of

le fauteuil armchair, 11

faux, fausse false

la femme woman, 1; wife, 8

la fenêtre window, 3

la ferme farm

fermement firmly

fermer to close, 7

le fermier, la fermière farmer, 14

la fête name day; festival; holiday; festivity

la feuille leaf; **la ~ de papier** sheet of paper, 2

février (*m.*) February, 9

les fiançailles (*f. pl.*) engagement

la fiche registration form, 11

la figure face, 12

la fille girl; daughter, 5 **la jeune ~** young woman, 1; **la ~ unique** only child (female), 5

le fils son, 5; **le ~ unique** only child (male), 5

la fin end

finalement finally, 12

finir to finish, 14

le flatteur, la flatteuse flatterer, 7

la fleur flower, 13

le fleuve large river, 13

flirteur, flirteuse flirt, 13

la fois time, 13

font: elles/ils ~ they do; they make, 8 (see **faire**)

le football soccer, 12

formidable terrific, 5

fort very, 11; strong

fou, folle crazy

le foulard scarf, 7

la foule crowd, 11

la fourchette fork, 10

frais, fraîche fresh, 9

la fraise strawberry, 10

franc, franche frank, 13

français(e) French, 1; **le français** French language, 1; **à la française** the French way

franchement frankly, 13

le frère brother, 5

les frites (*f. pl.*) French-fried potatoes

froid(e) cold; **le froid** cold weather, coldness; **avoir ~** to be cold, 9; **il fait ~** it's cold, 9

le fromage cheese, 10

la frontière border

le fruit fruit, 10; **les ~s de mer** assorted shellfish

furieusement furiously, 10

furieux, furieuse furious, 6

le/la gagnant(e) winner

gagner to win, 12

la galerie gallery, hall

le garçon boy, 1

la gare railroad station, 6

le gâteau cake, 10

gauche left; **à ~ (de)** to/on the left (of), 6

généreux, généreuse generous, 5

les gens (*m. pl.*) people, 11

gentil(le) nice, kind, 3

gentiment nicely, 10

la géographie geography, 4

la géométrie geometry, 4

la glace ice cream, 10; ice

gourmand(e) fond of eating, 10

la grammaire grammar

grand(e) big, large, 2

la grand-mère grandmother, 5

le grand-père grandfather, 5

les grands-parents (*m. pl.*) grandparents, 5

grave serious, 12

le grenier attic, 8

le gri-gri African charm or amulet

le griot African historian

gris(e) gray, 7

la grive thrush

le groupe group, 13

la guerre war, 8

habiller to dress; **s'~** to get dressed, 8

habiter to live, 1; **habité(e)** inhabited

l'habitude (*f.*) habit; **d'~** usually, ordinarily, 2

haïtien(ne) Haitian, 1

les haricots verts (*m. pl.*) string beans, 10

haut(e) high, 8

l'herbe (*f.*) grass, 13

hésiter to hesitate, 13

l'heure (*f.*) hour; **il est (une) ~** it is (one) o'clock, 8; **une ~ (dix)** (ten) minutes past one; **(deux) ~s et quart** quarter past (two); **(deux) ~s et demie** half past (two); **(trois) ~s moins le quart** quarter to (three); **trois ~s mois (dix)** (ten) minutes to three; **quelle ~ est-il?** what time is it?

l'histoire (*f.*) history, 4; story

historique historical

l'hiver (*m.*) winter, 9

hollandais(e) Dutch, 8

l'homme (*m.*) man, 1

honnête honest, 10

l'hôpital (*m.*)   hospital, *6*
l'horloge (*f.*)   clock, *8*
l'hospitalité (*f.*)   hospitality
l'hôtel (*m.*)   hotel, *11;* **l'~ de ville** (*m.*)   city hall, *6*
huit   eight, *2*
l'humeur (*f.*)   mood; **être de bonne ~**   to be in a good mood, *13*

ici   here, *4;* **par ~**   around here, *6;* this way, *7*
l'idée (*f.*)   idea, *14*
l'identité (*f.*)   identity, *12*
il y a   there is, there are, *3*
ils   they, *3*
s'imaginer   to imagine, *13*
immatriculé(e)   registered, *11*
immédiatement   immediately, *11*
l'imperméable (*m.*)   raincoat, *7*
important(e)   important
indécis(e)   indecisive, *13*
l'indépendance (*f.*)   independence, *8*
l'infirmier, l'infirmière   nurse, *14*
influencer   to influence, *13*
l'ingénieur (*m.*)   engineer, *11*
inquiet, inquiète   worried, disturbed, *11*
s'inquiéter   to worry
l'inspecteur, l'inspectrice   inspector, *11*
installer   to install; **s'~**   to settle down, to move in, *12*
insupportable   unbearable, insufferable, *5*
intelligemment   intelligently, *13*
intelligent(e)   intelligent, *5*
intéressant(e)   interesting, *4*
intéresser   to interest, *14;* **s'~ à**   to be interested in
l'interprète (*m./f.*)   interpreter, *14*

interroger   to question, to interrogate, *11*
interrompre   to interrupt, *12*
l'invitation (*f.*)   invitation, *13*
l'invité(e)   guest
inviter   to invite, *5*

jalousement   jealously
la jalousie   jealousy
jaloux, jalouse   jealous, *13*
jamais   never; ever; **ne...~**   never, *9*
la jambe   leg, *12*
le jambon   ham, *10*
janvier (*m.*)   January, *9*
le jardin   garden, *10*
jaune   yellow, *7*
je   I, *1*
le jean   jeans, *7*
jeter   to throw; **se ~ au cou de quelqu'un**   to throw oneself at someone, *12*
jeudi   Thursday, *4;* **le ~**   on Thursdays
jeune   young; **la ~ fille**   girl, *1*
la joie   joy
joli(e)   pretty, *3*
jouer   to play, *5*
le joueur, la joueuse   player, *11*
le jour   day, *8*
le journal   newspaper, *14;* **le ~ sportif**   sportscast, *12*
le/la journaliste   journalist, *14*
la journée   day, *8;* **bonne ~**   have a good day, *9*
juillet (*m.*)   July, *9*
juin (*m.*)   June, *9*
jusqu'à   up to, as far as, *6;* until
juste   just; right, correct, appropriate
justement   just; exactly; in fact
justifier   to justify

le kilo (le kilogramme)   kilogram
le kilomètre   kilometer, *9*

la   the, *1*
la   her, it, *7*
là   there, *3;* **~-bas**   over there, *6*
le   the, *1*
le   him, it, *7*
le laboratoire   laboratory, *14*
le lac   lake, *13*
laisser   to let; to leave, *10*
le lait   milk, *10*
se lamenter   to lament, to bemoan
le langage   language
la langouste   spiny lobster, *6*
le lapin   rabbit, *10*
le latin   Latin, *4*
la leçon   lesson, *4*
la lecture   reading
le légume   vegetable, *10*
les   the, *4*
les   them, *7*
la lettre   letter, *13*
leur   their, *6*
leur   (to) them, *11*
la liaison   liaison, linking
libéré(e)   liberated, *13*
libre   free, *8*
lire   to read
lisez   read
le lit   bed, *11*
la littérature   literature, *4*
le livre   book, *2*
loin   far, *2*
lui   him, *3;* (to) him, (to) her, *11*
luire   to shine
lundi   Monday, *4;* **le ~**   on Mondays
la lune   moon, *13*
les lunettes (*f. pl.*)   glasses; **les ~ de soleil**   sunglasses, *7*
la lutte   wrestling, *12*

le lycée   French high school, 2

le lycéen, la lycéenne   high school student, 2

ma   my, 5

madame   Mrs., madam, 1

mademoiselle   Miss, 1

le magasin   store, 6

mai (*m.*)   May, 9

le maillot de bain   swimming suit, 7

la main   hand, 12

maintenant   now, 4

la mairie   town hall, 6

mais   but, 1

la maison   house, 3

la majorité   majority

mal   badly; **ça va ~**   things are not going well, 2

malade   sick, 2

malheureusement   unfortunately, 9

malheureux, malheureuse   unfortunate, unhappy, 12

(la) maman   mom, mother, 3

manger   to eat, 10

manquer   to miss; **il manque (quelque chose)**   (something) is missing, 10

le manteau   coat, 7

le marchand, la marchande   merchant, 10

marchander   to bargain

la marche   step, 8

le marché   market; **le Marché commun**   Common Market; **bon ~**   inexpensive, reasonably priced, 7

marcher   to walk, 9

mardi   Tuesday, 4; **le ~**   on Tuesdays; **le Mardi gras**   Shrove Tuesday

le mari   husband, 11

le mariage   marriage, wedding, 7

le marin   sailor, 6

marocain(e)   Moroccan, 1

marron   reddish brown, 7

mars (*m.*)   March, 9

le masque   mask

les mathématiques (les maths) (*f. pl.*)   math, 4

la matière   subject

le matin   morning, 8

mauvais(e)   bad, 9

me   (to) me, myself, 8

le mécanicien, la mécanicienne   mechanic, 14

méchamment   nastily, naughtily, 10

méchant(e)   mean; naughty, 5

le médecin   doctor, 14

méditerranéen(ne)   Mediterranean

meilleur(e)   better; **le/la ~**   best, 12

même   even, 2

la mémoire   memory

la menthe   mint

la mer   sea, 6

merci   thank you, thanks, 2; **~ beaucoup/bien**   thanks a lot, 3

mercredi   Wednesday, 4; **le ~**   on Wednesdays

la mère   mother, 2

le merle   blackbird

mes   my, 5

la météo   weather report, 9

le métier   trade, profession, 14

le métro   subway, 2

mettre   to put; **~ de côté**   to set aside, 14; **~ le couvert**   to set the table, 10; **~ la radio**   to turn on the radio, 12; **~ en alerte**   to alert; **~ à cuire**   to start cooking, 12

meurs: je ~   I'm dying (see **mourir**)

mi-temps: à ~   part-time, 14

midi   noon, 8; **le Midi**   southeastern France

mieux   better; **il vaut ~** (+ *inf.*)   it's better (to), 11

mille   one thousand, 6; **(deux) ~**   (two) thousand

un million   one million, 6

minuit   midnight, 8

moche   ugly, 5

la mode   style, fashion; **à la ~**   in fashion

moi   me; as for me, 1

moins   less; minus; **~ ... que**   less . . . than, 13; **au ~**   at least, 14; **le/la/les ~ ...**   the least. . .

le mois   month, 9

le moment   moment, 5

mon   my, 5

le monde   world

monsieur   sir, 1; **Monsieur (Legrand)**   Mr. (Legrand), 1; **le ~**   man, 1

la montagne   mountain, 13

monter   to go up, 8

montrer   to show, 7

le morceau   piece, 10

mort(e)   dead, 5; **être ~**   to have died, 12 (see **mourir**); **la mort**   death

le mot   word, 1

mourir   to die; **je meurs de faim**   I'm starving, 10

la moyenne   average

le moyen   means, method

le mur   wall, 8

la muraille   thick wall, fortification

le musée   museum, 8

la musique   music, 4

mystérieux, mystérieuse   mysterious

n'est-ce pas?   isn't that so? right? 2

la naissance   birth, 9

la natation   swimming, 12

la nationalité   nationality

ne: ~ ...pas   not; **~ ...jamais**   never, not ever, 9; **~ ...personne**   no one, nobody, 9; **~ ...plus**   no longer, not any longer 9; **~ ...rien**   nothing, not anything, 9

neiger to snow; **il neige** it's snowing, 9

nerveux, nerveuse nervous, 11

neuf nine, 2

le neveu nephew, 6

le nez nose, 12

le nid nest; **faire son ~** to build one's nest

la nièce niece, 6

noir(e) black, 7

le nom name; **le ~ de jeune fille** maiden name

le nombre number, 2

nombreux, nombreuse numerous, 5

non no, 1

nos our, 8

la note grade; note

notre our, 6

la nourriture food

nous we, 3; (to) us, 8

nouveau (nouvel), nouvelle new, 5

la nouvelle piece of news, 4

novembre (m.) November, 9

le nuage cloud, 13

l'objet (m.) object; **les ~s de valeur** valuables, 11

l'occasion (f.) occasion, 14

occupé(e) busy, 3

octobre (m.) October, 9

l'oeil (m.; pl. **les yeux**) eye, 12

l'oeuf (m.) egg, 10

l'offre (f.) offer; **l'~ d'emploi** want ad, 14

offrir to offer

l'oignon (m.) onion, 10

l'oiseau (m.) bird

l'oisiveté (f.) idleness

l'ombre (f.) shade, 9

on we; one, they, people, you, 4

l'oncle (m.) uncle, 6

ondoyant(e) sinuous, wave-like

ont: elles/ils ~ they have, 4 (see **avoir**)

onze eleven, 3

l'orage (m.) thunderstorm, 9

l'orange (f.) orange, 10; (adj.) orange, 7

ordinal(e) (m. pl. **ordinaux**) ordinal

l'oreille (f.) ear, 12; **écouter de toutes ses ~s** to be all ears

l'orthographe (f.) spelling

ou or

où where, 1

ouf! exclamation indicating amazement or relief, 9

oui yes, 1

ouvert(e) open, 11

l'ouvrier, l'ouvrière worker, 14

le pain bread, 10

le palais palace

le pantalon pants, 7

(le) papa dad, father, 3

par by; **~ ici** around here, 6; this way, 7

le parapluie umbrella, 7

le parc park, 6

parce que because, 5

pardon pardon me, 4

les parents (m. pl.) parents, 5

parler to speak, 5; **le ~ régional** regional dialect

la partie part; game

pas not, 1; **~ du tout** not at all, 2; **~ (trop) mal** not (too) bad, 2

le passage: au ~ on the way, 8

le passant passerby, 6

passer to pass, 6; **~ le temps** to spend the time, 14; **se ~** to happen, 12

passionnant(e) thrilling, exciting

passionné(e) impassioned; **~ de** or **pour** enthusiastic about, 12

le pâté finely chopped meat, 10; **le ~ en croûte** a kind of pâté with a pastry crust; **le ~ de foie gras** goose liver pâté

la pâtisserie pastry shop, 10; pastry

pauvre poor, 6

le pays country

le paysage landscape

la pêche fishing; peach

pêcher to fish

la peine pain, sorrow

peint(e) painted, 8

pendant during, 6

penser to think, 8

perdre to lose, 12

le père father, 5

perplexe perplexed, 11

la personnalité personnality

la personne person; **ne... ~** nobody, 9

la perte loss, 11

petit(e) little, small, 2; **mon petit, ma petite** (my) dear, 5; **petit à petit** little by little

le petit déjeuner breakfast, 8

les petits pois (m. pl.) peas, 10

peu little; **un ~** a little bit, 1

la peur fear; **avoir ~ (de)** to be afraid (of), 9

peut: elle/il ~ she/he/it can or may, 9 (see **pouvoir**)

peut-être perhaps, 6

peuvent: elles/ils ~ they can, they may, 9 (see **pouvoir**)

peux: je ~ I can, I may, 9; **tu ~** you can, you may, 9 (see **pouvoir**)

le/la photographe photographer, 14

la physique physics, 4

la pièce room of a house, 3

le pied foot, 12; **à ~** on foot, 2

la pierre stone; **en ~** made of stone

le pilote   pilot, *14*
la piscine   swimming pool, *6*
la place   plaza square, *6*
le plafond   ceiling, *8*
la plaine   plain, *13*
le plaisir   pleasure; **avec ~** with pleasure, *8*
plaît: s'il vous/te ~   please, *4*
plein temps: à ~   full-time, *14*
pleut: il ~   it's raining, *9;* **il ~ à seaux**   it's pouring
pleuvoir   to rain, *9*
la pluie   rain, *9*
plus   more; plus; **bien ~**   much more, *2;* **ne... ~**   no longer, *9;* **~ ...que**   more...than *13;* **le/la/les ~** ...the most..., *13;* **~ tard**   later, *11*
plusieurs   several, *12*
le poème   poem
le poisson   fish, *10*
la poissonnerie   fish market, *10*
le poivre   pepper, *10*
la politesse   politeness, courtesy, **les échanges de ~**   courtesy expressions
politique   political; **la ~**   politics
la pomme   apple, *10*
la pomme de terre   potato, *10*
le pont   bridge, *6*
le porc   pork, *10*
la porte   door, *3*
porter   to wear, *7;* to carry; **se porter: porte-toi/portez-vous bien**   take care of yourself, *5*
le portrait   portrait, *8*
poser   to put, *7;* **~ des questions**   to ask questions, *11*
la poste   post office, *6*
le poste   job, *14*
le poulet   chicken, *10*
pour   for, *3;* in order to, *7*
pourquoi   why, *2*

pourtant   however, still *10*
pouvoir   to be able, can, may, *9*
pratique   practical, *2*
se précipiter   to rush, *12*
préférer   to prefer, *7*
premier, première   first, *8;* **en première**   in 11th grade (next-to-last year of **lycée**)
prendre   to take; to eat, to drink, to have (a meal), *11*
prends: je le ~   I'll take it, *7*
le prénom   first name
préparer   to prepare, *7*
près: ~ de   near, *2;* **tout ~**   nearby, *2*
presque   almost, *3*
prier   to pray; **je vous en prie/je t'en prie**   don't mention it, you're welcome, *6*
la prière   prayer; **~ de (téléphoner)**   please (call)
primaire   primary; **l'école ~**   elementary school
les primeurs (*m. pl.*)   fresh fruits and vegetables, *10*
le printemps   spring, *9*
privé(e)   private
le prix   price
le problème   problem, *4*
prochain(e)   next, *12*
le produit   product
le professeur   teacher, *2*
le projet   project, *13*
la promenade   walk; boulevard
la propriété   property
se promener   to take a walk, *8*
la prononciation   pronunciation
le pull-over   sweater, *7*
le pupitre   pupil's desk, *2*
pur(e)   pure

le quai   pier; street bordering a body of water, *6*
quand   when, *2;* **~ même**   just the same, *9*

quarante   forty, *4*
quatorze   fourteen, *3*
quatre   four, *2*
quatre-vingt-dix   ninety, *5*
quatre-vingts   eighty, *5*
que   that; than; whom; which; **~ ...?**   what...? *6;* **ce ~**   what, *13;* **qu'est-ce qu'il y a?**   what's the matter? *2*
quel(le)   what, which, *4;* **quel âge as-tu?**   how old are you? *3;* **quel temps fait-il?**   what's the weather like? *9;* **quelle heure est-il?**   what time is it? *8*
quelqu'un   someone, *11*
quelque chose   something, *3*
quelque(s)   some, *14*
quelquefois   sometimes, *2*
qui   who, *1;* which, that, *14*
quinze   fifteen, *3*
quoi   what; **il n'y a pas de ~**   don't mention it, you're welcome, *6*
quotidien(ne)   daily

raconter   to tell, *9*
la radio   radio, *12*
la raison   reason; **avoir ~**   to be right, *9*
ranger   to put away; to straighten, *7*
rappeler   to call back, *12*
se rassurer: rassurez-vous   don't worry, *11*
ravi(e)   delighted, *5*
le rayon   shelf, *7*
réaliser   to realize, to succeed in, to fulfill
récemment   recently
récent(e)   recent, *8*
le/la réceptionniste   receptionist
la recherche   research, *14*
recommencer   to begin again, *12*
reconstituer   to reconstruct
refuser   to refuse, *13*

regarder to look (at), 7
regretter to regret
la reine queen
le relais stopping place
remplir to fill; to fill out, 11
rencontrer to meet, 12; **se ~** to meet, 13
le rendez-vous appointment, date
la rentrée return; beginning of school year
rentrer to go back; to go home, 7
repartir to leave again, 12
le repas meal, 10
répéter to repeat
répondre to answer, 11
se reposer to rest, 11
représenter to represent, 8
respecté(e) respected, 14
ressembler (à) to resemble
la ressource resource
le restaurant restaurant, 6
le reste the rest, 7
rester to stay, 10
le résultat result, 12
le résumé résumé, summary
retard: en ~ late, 4
retomber to fall again, 12
le retour return
réussir (à) to succeed (in), 14
le rêve dream, 14
revenir to come back, 10
rêver to dream, 14
la révision review
revoir to see again; **au ~** good-by, 1
le rez-de-chaussée first (ground) floor, 8
rien nothing; **ça ne fait ~** it doesn't matter, 8; **de ~** you're welcome, 6; **ne... ~** nothing, 9
rire to laugh; **rira bien qui rira le dernier** he who laughs last, laughs best
la rivière river, 6
la robe dress, 7
le rocher rock, boulder, 13
le roi king

romain(e) Roman
rose pink, 7; **la ~** rose
rouge red
la route road; way; **en ~ (pour)** on the way (to)
la rue street, 6
la ruine ruin
le royaume kingdom

sa his, her, its, 5
le sable sand, 9
sain(e) healthy, 12; **sain et sauf** safe and sound
sais: je ~ I know, 12; **tu ~** you know, 4 (see **savoir**)
la saison season, 9
sait: elle/il ~ she/he/it knows, 4 (see **savoir**)
la salade salad, lettuce, 10
la salle room; **la ~ à manger** dining room, 3; **la ~ de bains** bathroom, 3; **~ de classe** classroom, 2
le salon living room, 3
salut hi, hello, 1
les salutations (f. pl.) greetings
samedi Saturday, 4; **le ~** on Saturdays
les sandales (f. pl.) sandals, 7
la santé health; **à ta/votre ~** to your health, 7
satisfaisant(e) satisfactory
le saucisson salami, 10
sauf, sauve safe 12; except for, 12
savoir to know, 12
les sciences naturelles (f. pl.) natural sciences, 4
seconde: en ~ in 10th grade (first year of **lycée**), 4
le/la secrétaire secretary, 14
seize sixteen, 3
le séjour stay; **la salle de ~** living-dining room, 4
le sel salt, 10
la semaine week, 8
sénégalais(e) Senegalese, 1

sentir to smell; **ça sent (bon)** that smells (good), 10
sept seven, 2
septembre (m.) September, 9
sérieusement seriously, 10
sérieux, sérieuse serious
le serpent snake
la serviette napkin, 10
servir (de) to serve (as), 14
ses his, her, its, 5
seul(e) alone; **tout(e) seul(e)** all alone, 9
seulement only, 7
si if, 9
s'il vous/te plaît please, 4
le siècle century, 8
le siège seat, headquarters
la sieste nap
simplement simply; just, 13
le site spot, site
six six, 2
le skieur, la skieuse skier, 12
le smoking tuxedo
snob snobbish, 5
sociable sociable, 5
la sœur sister, 5
la soie silk, 7
la soif thirst; **avoir ~** to be thirsty, 9
le soir evening, 8
soixante sixty, 4
soixante-dix seventy, 5
le sol floor, 8
le soldat (la femme ~) soldier, 14
le soleil sun, 13; **il fait du ~** it's sunny, 9
le sommeil sleep; **avoir ~** to be sleepy, 9
sommes: nous ~ we are, 3 (see **être**)
son his, her, its, 5
sonner to ring, 12
sont: elles/ils ~ they are, 3 (see **être**)
sortir to go out, to leave, 9
soudain suddenly, 12
souffler to blow, 9

la soupe soup, 10
soupirer to sigh
sous under, 8
le sous-sol basement, 8
souvent often, 4
soyez: ~ gentil be nice, 10
spécial(e) special
spécialement especially, 10
le sport sport(s), 6
sportif, sportive athletic, 12
le stade stadium, 6
le stage (de formation) training period, 14
le/la standardiste telephone operator, 12
le stylo pen, 2
le sucre sugar, 10
suggérer to suggest, 12
suis: je ~ I am, 1 (see **être**)
suivre to follow; **vous suivez** you follow, 4
superbe superb, 7
le supermarché supermarket, 10
sur on, 6
sûr(e) sure, certain; **bien sûr** of course, 13
surtout especially, 14
suspecter to suspect, 11
sympathique nice, likeable, 5

ta your, 5
la table table, 2; **à ~** the meal is served
le tableau chalkboard, 2
la tante aunt, 6
le tap-tap Haitian rural bus
la tarte pie, tart, 10
te you; to you, 8
le tee-shirt T-shirt, 7
le télégramme telegram, 12
téléphoner to telephone, 5
tellement so, so much, 13
le témoignage testimony
la tempête storm, 9
le temps weather, 8; time, 11
le tennis tennis; **les ~** sneakers, 7

terminale: en ~ in 12th grade (last year of **lycée**), 4
terminer to finish, 11
terriblement terribly, 12
tes your, 5
la tête head, 12
le texte text
le thé tea, 7
le théâtre theater, playhouse, 6
tiens! why! well! look! here! 2
timide shy, 5
timidement shyly, 10
la timidité shyness
le tiroir drawer, 7
toi you, 1
le toit roof, 8
la tomate tomato, 10
tomber to fall, 12
ton your, 5
le tonnerre thunder, 9
tort: avoir ~ to be wrong, 9
toujours always, 4; still, 9
le tour tour; turn; **à votre ~** your turn; **le Tour de France** French bicycle race
le/la touriste tourist
tourner to turn, 6
tout(e) (*pl.* **tous, toutes**) all, every; **tous/toutes les deux** both, 4; **tout droit** straight ahead, 5; **tout le monde** everybody, 3; **tout le temps** all the time, always, 4; **tout près** close by, 2
le train train, 11; **en ~ de** in the process of, 9
la tragédie tragedy
tragique tragic
traiter to treat, **~ en adulte** to treat as an adult
tranquille quiet, peaceful, 10
tranquillement quietly, 10
le travail work, 13
travailler to work, 11
travailleur, travailleuse hard-working; **le/la ~** worker

treize thirteen, 3
trente thirty, 4
très very; **~ bien** very well, fine, 2
triste sad, 12
trois three, 2
troisième third, 8; **en ~** in 9th grade (last year of **C.E.S.**), 4
trop too; too many, too much, 5
trouver to find; **comment trouvez-vous...?** what do you think of. . . ? 6; **tu trouves?/vous trouvez?** do you really think so? 7
tuer to kill, 10

un(e) a(n), one, 2; **l' ~ d'entre eux** one of them, 12
unique unique, 8 **la fille/le fils ~** only child, 5
l'urgence (*f.*) urgency; **d'~** urgently; **en cas d'~** in case of emergency
utiliser to use, 14

va: elle/il ~ she/he/it goes, 4 (see **aller**)
les vacances (*f. pl.*) vacation, 11
la vague wave, 13
le vainqueur victor
vais: je ~ I go, 2 (see **aller**)
la vallée valley
vas: tu ~ you go, 2; **comment ~-tu** how are you, 2 (see **aller**)
vaut: il ~ mieux it's better, 13
veinard(e) lucky, 14
le vélo bicycle, 2
les vendanges (*f. pl.*) grape-picking
le vendeur, la vendeuse salesperson, 11

vendredi Friday, 4

venir to come, 10; **je viens de (manger)** I have just (eaten), 10

le vent wind, 9; **il fait du ~** it's windy, 9

le verre glass, 7

vers toward, 8

vert(e) green, 7

les vêtements (*m. pl.*) clothes, 7

veulent: elles/ils ~ they want, 9 (see **vouloir**)

veux: je ~ I want, 9; **tu ~** you want, 9 (see **vouloir**)

veut: elle/il ~ she/he/it wants, 9 (see **vouloir**)

la viande meat, 10

vide empty, 11

la vie life, 14

viens: je ~ I come, 10; **tu ~** you come, 10 (see **venir**)

vient: elle/il ~ she/he/it comes, 10 (see **venir**)

le vignoble vineyard

la ville city, 6

le vin wine, 10

vingt twenty, 3

violet(te) purple, 7

le visiteur, la visiteuse visitor, 11

le vocabulaire vocabulary

voilà there is, there are, here is, here are 2; **(nous)~** here (we) are, 9

le voile veil, 7

la voilette veil that covers face, 7

voir to see, 13; **se ~** to meet, 13

le voisin, la voisine neighbor, 9

la voiture car, 2

le vol flight, 9; theft, 11

voler to rob

le voleur, la voleuse thief, 11

vont: elles/ils ~ they go, 4 (see **aller**)

vos your, 6

voter to vote

votre your, 4

voudrais: je ~ I would like, 7 (see **vouloir**)

vouloir to want, to wish, 9

vous you, 3; (to) you, 8

le voyageur, la voyageuse traveler

vrai(e) true, 8

vraiment really, 7

les yeux (*m. pl.*) eyes, 7

zéro zero, 2

zut, alors! darn it! 4

English-French vocabulary

The symbol ~ signifies the repetition of the key word in that entry.

able: to be ~ pouvoir
accept accepter
accompany accompagner
according to d'après
accountant comptable (m./f.)
actor acteur (m.), actrice (f.)
admire admirer
advice conseil (m.)
affectionately affectueuse-ment
afraid: to be ~ avoir peur
after après
afternoon après-midi (m./f.)
again à nouveau; encore
against contre
ahead: straight ~ tout droit
airplane avion (m.)
airport aéroport (m.)
algebra algèbre (m.)
Algerian algérien(ne)
all tout, toute, tous, toutes
alone seul(e)
already déjà
also aussi
always toujours; tout le temps
ambitious ambitieux, ambitieuse
American américain(e)
amuse amuser
ancestor ancêtre (m.)
and et
announce annoncer
annoy embêter (familiar)
answer réponse (f.); **to ~** répondre
anxious anxieux, anxieuse
apartment appartement (m.)
apple pomme (f.)
April avril
architect architecte (m./f.)
arm bras (m.)
armchair fauteuil (m.)
army armée (f.)

arrest arrêter
arrival arrivée (f.)
arrive arriver
art art (m.)
artist artiste (m./f.)
as aussi; comme; ~ **(good)** ~ aussi bon que
ask demander; ~ **questions** poser des questions
at à; ~ **my house** chez moi; ~ **least** au moins
athlete athlète (m./f.)
athletic sportif, sportive
attic grenier (m.)
August août
aunt tante (f.)
autumn automne (m.)
awful affreux, affreuse

baby bébé (m.)
bad mauvais(e); **it's ~ weather** il fait mauvais; **not (too) ~** pas (trop) mal
bakery boulangerie (f.)
ball bal (m.)
banana banane (f.)
bank banque (f.)
bargain marchander
basement sous-sol (m.)
bathroom salle de bains (f.)
be être; ~ **(16) years old** avoir (16) ans; ~ **careful** faire attention; ~ **(cold)** avoir (froid); ~ **(well)** aller (bien)
beautiful beau (bel), belle; **it's ~ weather** il fait beau
because parce que; ~ **of** à cause de
become devenir
bed lit (m.)
bedroom chambre (f.)
beef bœuf (m.)

before avant
behind derrière
Belgian belge
believe croire
belt ceinture (f.)
best meilleur(e)
better meilleur(e); mieux; **it's ~** il vaut mieux
between entre
bicycle vélo (m.)
big grand(e)
biology biologie (f.)
birth naissance (f.)
birthday anniversaire (m.); **happy ~** bon anniversaire
black noir(e)
blow coup (m.); **to ~** souffler
blue bleu(e)
boat bateau (m.)
body corps (m.)
book livre (m.)
boots bottes (f. pl.)
boring barbant(e)
both tous/toutes les deux
boulevard boulevard (m.)
box carton (m.)
boy garçon (m.)
bracelet bracelet (m.)
bread pain (m.)
break casser; **to ~ a (leg)** se casser (la jambe)
breakfast petit déjeuner (m.)
bridge pont (m.)
bring apporter
brother frère (m.)
brown brun(e); **reddish ~** marron
bus autobus (m.); **intercity ~** autocar (m.)
business affaires (f. pl.)
busy occupé(e)
but mais
butcher shop boucherie (f.)

butter beurre (*m.*)
buy acheter

cake gâteau (*m.*)
call appeler; **~ back** rappeler; **who's calling?** qui est à l'appareil?
camping camping (*m.*)
Canadian canadien(ne)
car voiture (*f.*)
careful: be ~ faire attention; **~ly** attentivement
carrot carotte (*f.*)
cassette cassette (*f.*)
castle château (*m.*)
ceiling plafond (*m.*)
cellar cave (*f.*)
century siècle (*m.*)
certain sûr(e); **~ly** bien sûr
chair chaise (*f.*)
chalkboard tableau (*m.*)
charming charmant(e)
cheap bon marché
cheese fromage (*m.*)
chemistry chimie (*f.*)
chicken poulet (*m.*)
child enfant (*m./f.*); **only ~** fille unique (*f.*), fils unique (*m.*)
chimney cheminée (*f.*)
chocolate chocolat (*m.*)
church église (*f.*)
city ville (*f.*); **~ hall** hôtel de ville (*m.*)
class classe (*f.*); **~room** salle de classe (*f.*)
clock horloge (*f.*)
close fermer
clothes vêtements (*m. pl.*)
cloud nuage (*m.*)
coat manteau (*m.*)
coffee café (*m.*)
cold froid(e); **to be ~** avoir froid; **it's ~ (weather)** il fait froid
color couleur (*f.*)
come venir; **~ back** revenir
comfortably confortablement
communicate communiquer
completely complètement

continue continuer
cook faire la cuisine
cool frais, fraîche; **it's ~ (weather)** il fait frais
corner coin (*m.*)
cost coûter
count compter
country pays (*m.*); **~side** campagne (*f.*)
courage courage (*m.*)
course: of ~ bien sûr
cousin cousin (*m.*), cousine (*f.*)
cream crème (*f.*)
crowd foule (*f.*)
customer client (*m.*), cliente (*f.*)

dance danse (*f.*); bal (*m.*); **to ~** danser
dancer danseur (*m.*), danseuse (*f.*)
darn it! zut, alors!
daughter fille (*f.*)
day jour (*m.*); journée (*f.*); **have a good ~** bonne journée
dead mort(e)
dear cher, chère
death death (*f.*)
December décembre
decide décider
degree degré (*m.*)
delighted ravi(e)
depart partir
departure départ (*m.*)
desert désert (*m.*)
desk bureau (*m.*), pupitre (*m.*)
dessert dessert (*m.*)
die mourir
difficult difficile
dining room salle à manger (*f.*)
dinner dîner (*m.*); **to have ~** dîner
do faire
doctor docteur (*m.*); médecin (*m.*)
dog chien (*m.*)
door porte (*f.*)

drawer tiroir (*m.*)
drawing dessin (*m.*)
dream rêve (*m.*); **to ~** rêver
dress robe (*f.*); **to get ~ed** s'habiller
during pendant
Dutch hollandais(e)

each chaque; **~ one** chacun(e)
ear oreille (*f.*)
early en avance
easy facile
eat manger; prendre
egg œuf (*m.*)
eight huit
eighteen dix-huit
eighty quatre-vingts
elevator ascenseur (*m.*)
eleven onze
employment emploi (*m.*)
empty vide
end fin (*f.*)
engineer ingénieur (*m.*)
English anglais(e)
enjoy: ~ oneself s'amuser (bien)
enter entrer
especially spécialement; surtout
even même
evening soir (*m.*)
ever jamais
every tout (toute, tous, toutes)
exam examen (*m.*)
except sauf
excuse excuser
exercise exercice (*m.*)
exhausted épuisé(e)
expensive cher, chère
explain expliquer
eye œil (*m.*) (*pl.* yeux)

face figure (*f.*)
facing en face de
fall tomber
false faux, fausse
family famille (*f.*)

farm ferme (f.)

farmer fermier (m.), fermière (f.)

father père (m.)

February février

field champ (m.)

fifteen quinze

fill remplir; ~ out remplir

finally enfin, finalement

fine d'accord, très bien

finger doigt (m.)

finish finir, terminer

first premier, première; at ~ d'abord

fish poisson (m.); ~ market poissonnerie

five cinq

flight vol (m.)

floor sol (m.); étage (m.); ground ~ rez-de-chaussée (m.)

flower fleur (f.)

follow suivre

foot pied (m.)

for pour

fork fourchette (f.)

forty quarante

four quatre

fourteen quatorze

frank franc, franche

free libre

French français(e)

fresh frais, fraîche

Friday vendredi

friend ami (m.), amie (f.); copain (m.), copine (f.)

from de

front: in ~ of devant

fruit fruit (m.)

furious furieux, furieuse

garden jardin (m.)

generous généreux, généreuse

geography géographie (f.)

geometry géométrie (f.)

German allemand(e)

get: ~ along (with) s'entendre (avec); ~ together se rencontrer

gift cadeau (m.)

girl fille, jeune fille

give donner

glass verre (m.)

glasses lunettes (f. pl.)

go aller; ~ down descendre; ~ home rentrer; ~ in entrer; ~ out sortir

gold or (m.)

good bon(ne), bien; ~-by au revoir; ~ night bonne nuit, bonsoir

grandfather grand-père (m.)

grandmother grand-mère (f.)

grandparents grands-parents (m. pl.)

grass herbe (f.)

gray gris(e)

great grand(e); ~! chic, alors! formidable!

green vert(e)

grocery store épicerie (f.)

group groupe (m.)

guest invité (m.), invitée (f.)

guide guide (m.)

gym éducation physique (f.), gym (f.)

hair cheveux (m. pl.)

Haitian haïtien(ne)

hall corridor (m.)

ham jambon (m.)

hand main (f.)

happy content(e)

hard dur(e)

hat chapeau (m.)

hate détester

have avoir

he il

head tête (f.)

healthy sain(e)

hear entendre

heart cœur (m.)

heat chaleur (f.)

hello bonjour, salut; (on telephone) allô

help aider

her elle; (possessive) son (sa, ses); (dir. obj.) la

here ici

hesitate hésiter

hi salut

high haut(e)

hill colline (f.)

him lui; le

hire embaucher

his son (sa, ses)

history histoire (f.)

home: at ~ à la maison; at the ~ of chez; go ~ rentrer; make yourself at ~ fais comme chez toi

homework devoirs (m. pl.)

honest honnête

hope espérer

horse cheval (m.)

hospital hôpital (m.)

hot chaud(e); to be ~ avoir chaud; it's ~ weather il fait chaud

hotel hôtel (m.)

hour heure (f.)

house maison (f.)

how comment; ~ are things? comment ça va? ~ are you? comment vas-tu? ~ many (much) combien; ~ old are you? quel âge as-tu?

however pourtant

hundred cent

hunger faim (f.)

hungry: to be ~ avoir faim

hurry se dépêcher

hurt faire mal (à)

husband mari (m.)

ice cream glace (f.)

idea idée (f.)

if si

imagine s'imaginer, imaginer

immediately aussitôt

in dans, en, à

indecisive indécis(e)

inexpensive bon marché

inside dedans; dans

instrument appareil (m.)

insufferable insupportable

insurance assurance (f.)

intelligent intelligent(e)

intend (to) avoir l'intention (de)
interest intéresser; **to be ~ed (in)** s'intéresser (à)
interesting intéressant(e)
interrupt interrompre
invite inviter
it ce; elle, il; ça; (*dir. obj.*) la, le

January janvier
jealous jaloux, jalouse
jeans jean (*m.*)
jewelry bijoux (*m. pl.*)
job emploi (*m.*); poste (*m.*)
journalist journaliste (*m.*)
July juillet
June juin
just simplement

key clé (*f.*)
kill tuer
kind gentil(le)
kiss embrasser
kitchen cuisine (*f.*)
knife couteau (*m.*)
know savoir; connaître

lady dame (*f.*)
lake lac (*m.*)
last dernier, dernière
late tard; **to be ~** être en retard
Latin latin (*m.*)
laugh rire
lawyer avocat (*m.*), avocate (*f.*)
learn apprendre
least le/la moins; **at ~** au moins
leave partir; laisser
left gauche (*f.*)
leg jambe (*f.*)
less moins
lesson leçon (*f.*)
let laisser
letter lettre (*f.*)
lettuce salade (*f.*)
library bibliothèque (*f.*)
life vie (*f.*)

like aimer; **I would ~** je voudrais, j'aimerais
listen (to) écouter
literature littérature (*f.*)
little petit(e); **a ~ bit** un peu
live habiter
living room salon (*m.*)
living-dining room salle de séjour (*f.*)
longer: no ~ ne...plus
look (at) regarder; **~ (for)** chercher
lose perdre
loss perte (*f.*)
love aimer, adorer; **in ~** amoureux, amoureuse
low bas(se)
luck: good ~ bonne chance; **to be ~y** avoir de la chance
luggage bagages (*m. pl.*)
lunch déjeuner (*m.*); **to eat ~** déjeuner

make faire
man homme (*m.*), monsieur (*m.*)
map carte (*f.*)
March mars
marriage mariage (*m.*)
matching assorti(e)
math mathématiques (les maths) (*f. pl.*)
matter: it doesn't ~ ça ne fait rien; **what's the ~?** qu'est-ce qu'il y a?
May mai
me me; moi
meal repas (*m.*)
mean méchant(e)
meat viande (*f.*)
mechanic mécanicien (*m.*), mécanicienne (*f.*)
meet rencontrer; se voir
merchant marchand (*m.*), marchande (*f.*)
midnight minuit
milk lait (*m.*)
Miss Mademoiselle

miss manquer; **something is ~ing** il manque quelque chose
Monday lundi
money argent (*m.*)
month mois (*m.*)
mood humeur (*f.*)
moon lune (*f.*)
more plus
morning matin (*m.*)
Moroccan marocain(e)
most le/la plus
mother mère (*f.*)
mountain montagne (*f.*)
mouth bouche (*f.*)
movies cinéma (*m.*)
Mr. Monsieur
Mrs. Madame
much: so ~ tellement
music musique (*f.*)
must: one ~ il faut
my mon (ma, mes)

name nom (*m.*); **my ~ is** je m'appelle
napkin serviette (*f.*)
naughtily méchamment
naughty méchant(e)
near près de; **~by** tout près
necessary nécessaire; **it is ~** il faut
neck cou (*m.*)
necklace collier (*m.*)
need avoir besoin de
neighbor voisin (*m.*), voisine (*f.*)
nephew neveu (*m.*)
nervous nerveux, nerveuse
never (ne...) jamais
new nouveau (nouvel), nouvelle
news nouvelles (*f. pl.*)
newspaper journal
next prochain(e)
nice gentil(le), sympathique; **~ly** gentiment; **it's ~ weather** il fait beau
niece nièce (*f.*)

nine   neuf
nineteen   dix-neuf
ninety   quatre-vingt-dix
no   non
nobody   (ne...) personne
noon   midi
nose   nez (*m.*)
not   (ne...) pas
notebook   cahier (*m.*)
nothing   (ne...) rien
November   novembre
now   maintenant
nurse   infirmier (*m.*), in-firmière (*f.*)

o'clock: it's (one) ~   il est (une) heure
O.K.   d'accord; ça va
October   octobre
odd   bizarre
of   de
offer   offre (*f.*)
often   souvent
old   ancien(ne), vieux (vieil), vielle; **how ~ are you?** quel âge as-tu?
on   sur
one   un(e)
onion   oignon (*m.*)
only   seulement
open   ouvert(e)
opinion   avis (*m.*)
or   ou
orange   orange (*f.*)
other   autre
outside   dehors

pants   pantalon (*m.*)
pantyhose   collant (*m.*)
paper   papier (*m.*); **sheet of ~** feuille de papier (*f.*)
pardon me   pardon
parents   parents (*m. pl.*)
park   parc (*m.*)
part-time   à mi-temps
pass   passer
pastry shop   pâtisserie (*f.*)
peas   petits pois (*m. pl.*)
pen   stylo (*m.*)
pencil   crayon (*m.*)

people   gens (*m. pl.*)
pepper   poivre (*m.*)
perhaps   peut-être
photographer   photographe (*m./f.*)
physics   physique (*f.*)
pie   tarte (*f.*)
piece   morceau (*m.*)
pier   quai (*m.*)
pilot   pilote (*m.*)
pink   rose
plain   plaine (*f.*)
plate   assiette (*f.*)
play   jouer, s'amuser
please   s'il te (vous) plaît
police   police (*f.*); **~ officer** agent de police (*m.*)
poor   pauvre
pork   porc (*m.*)
post office   poste (*f.*)
potato   pomme de terre (*f.*)
practical   pratique
prefer   préférer
prepare   préparer
pretty   joli(e)
problem   problème (*m.*)
pupil   élève (*m./f.*)
purple   violet(te)
put   poser; **~ away** ranger

quarrel   se disputer
question   question (*f.*); **to ~** interroger
quiet   tranquille
quite   assez

rabbit   lapin (*m.*)
radio   radio (*f.*)
railroad station   gare (*f.*)
rain   pluie (*f.*); pleuvoir; **it's ~ing** il pleut
raincoat   imperméable (*m.*)
read   lire
really   vraiment
red   rouge
refuse   refuser
research   recherche (*f.*)
rest   se reposer
restaurant   restaurant (*m.*)
result   résultat (*m.*)

return   retour (*m.*)
right   droit(e); **on/to the ~** à droite; **to be ~** avoir raison
ring   sonner
river   rivière (*f.*); fleuve (*m.*)
rock   rocher (*m.*)
roof   toit (*m.*)
room   pièce (*f.*); salle (*f.*)
run   courir

√sad   triste
sailor   marin (*m.*)
salad   salade (*f.*)
salesperson   vendeur (*m.*), vendeuse (*f.*)
salt   sel (*m.*)
same   même; **just the ~** quand même
sand   sable (*m.*)
sandals   sandales (*f. pl.*)
Saturday   samedi
say   dire; **say!** dis donc!
scarf   foulard (*m.*)
school   école (*f.*); **high ~** lycée (*m.*); **junior high ~** collège (*m.*)
science: natural ~   sciences naturelles (*f. pl.*)
sea   mer (*f.*)
season   saison (*f.*)
second   deuxième
secretary   secrétaire (*m./f.*)
see   voir
seem   avoir l'air
selfish   égoïste
send   envoyer
Senegalese   sénégalais(e)
September   septembre
serious   sérieux, sérieuse; grave
serve (as)   servir (de)
set: ~ aside   mettre de côté; **~ the table** mettre le couvert
seven   sept
seventeen   dix-sept
seventy   soixante-dix
several   plusieurs
shade   ombre (*f.*)

she elle
shelf rayon (*m.*)
shirt chemise (*f.*); **woman's ~** chemisier (*m.*)
show montrer
shy timide
sick malade
sigh soupirer
silk soie (*f.*)
simply simplement
since depuis
sing chanter
sir monsieur
sister sœur (*f.*)
sit: ~ down assieds-toi (asseyez-vous)
six six
sixteen seize
sixty soixante
sky ciel (*m.*)
sleep dormir
sleepy: to be ~ avoir sommeil
small petit(e)
smell: it ~s (good) ça sent (bon)
sneakers tennis (*m. pl.*)
snobbish snob
snow neiger; **it's ~ing** il neige
soccer football (*m.*)
sociable sociable
socks chaussettes (*f. pl.*)
soldier soldat (*m.*), femme soldat (*f.*)
some quelque(s); **~one** quelqu'un; **~thing** quelque chose; **~times** quelquefois
son fils (*m.*)
soon bientôt; **see you ~** à bientôt
soup soupe (*f.*)
Spanish espagnol(e)
speak parler
special spécial(e)
spoon cuillère (*f.*)
sport sport (*m.*)
spring printemps (*m.*)
stadium stade (*m.*)
stairway escalier (*m.*)

start commencer
state déclarer
station gare (*f.*)
stay rester
steal voler
stew civet (*m.*)
still toujours
store magasin (*m.*)
storm tempête (*f.*); **thunder~** orage (*m.*)
strange bizarre
strawberry fraise (*f.*)
street rue (*f.*)
string beans haricots verts (*m. pl.*)
student élève (*m./f.*); **high school ~** lycéen (*m.*), lycéene (*f.*)
study étudier
stupid bête
subway métro (*m.*)
succeed (in) réussir (à); arriver (à)
suddenly soudain
sugar sucre (*m.*)
suggest suggérer
summer été (*m.*)
sun soleil (*m.*); **it's ~ny** il fait du soleil
Sunday dimanche
sunglasses lunettes de soleil (*f. pl*)
superb superbe
supermarket supermarché (*m.*)
sure sûr(e)
suspect suspect (*m.*); **to ~** suspecter
sweater pull-over (*m.*)
swimming natation (*f.*); **~ pool** piscine (*f.*); **~ suit** maillot de bain (*m.*)

T-shirt tee-shirt (*m.*)
table table (*f.*); **to set the ~** mettre le couvert
take prendre; **~ out** emmener; **~ place** avoir lieu
talkative bavard(e)

tea thé (*m.*)
teacher professeur (*m.*)
team équipe (*f.*)
telephone téléphone (*m.*), appareil (*m.*); **to ~** téléphoner (à)
tell raconter, dire
ten dix
terrible épouvantable
terrific formidable
thank you merci
theater théâtre (*m.*)
theft vol (*m.*)
them eux (*m. pl.*), elles (*f. pl.*); les (*dir. obj.*); leur (*indir. obj.*)
then alors; ensuite
there la; **~ is (are)** il y a; voilà
they ils (*m. pl.*); elles (*f. pl.*); on
think penser, croire; **what do you ~ of?** comment trouvez-vous (trouves-tu)...?
thirst soif (*f.*)
thirsty: to be ~ avoir soif
thirteen treize
thirty trente
this (that, these, those) ce (cet, cette, ces)
thousand mille
three trois
thunder tonnerre (*m.*); **~ storm** orage (*m.*)
Thursday jeudi
time fois (*f.*); temps (*m.*); **all the ~** tout le temps; **for a long ~** depuis longtemps; **on ~** à l'heure; **what ~ is it?** quelle heure est-il?
tired fatigué(e)
to à, en
today aujourd'hui
together ensemble
tomato tomate (*f.*)
tomorrow demain
too trop; **~ much** trop
tooth dent (*f.*)
toward vers
town hall mairie (*f.*)

track and field athlétisme (*m.*)

trailer caravane (*f.*)

train train (*m.*)

traveler voyageur (*m.*), voyageuse (*f.*)

tree arbre (*m.*)

true vrai(e)

Tuesday mardi

twelve douze

twenty vingt

two deux

ugly moche

umbrella parapluie (*m.*)

unbearable insupportable

uncle oncle (*m.*)

under sous

understand comprendre

unfortunate malheureux, malheureuse

up: ~ to jusqu'à

us nous

use utiliser

usually d'habitude

vacation vacances (*f. pl.*)

vegetable légume (*m.*)

very très, fort; **~ much** beaucoup

visitor visiteur (*m.*), visiteuse (*f.*)

wait (for) attendre

walk marcher; (y) aller à pied; **to take a ~** se promener

wall mur (*m.*)

want vouloir, désirer, avoir envie (de)

war guerre (*f.*)

warm chaud(e); **to be ~** avoir chaud; **it's ~** il fait chaud

water eau (*f.*)

we nous, on

wear porter

weather temps (*m.*); **~ report** météo (*f.*); **what's the ~ like?** quel temps fait-il?

Wednesday mercredi

week semaine (*f.*)

welcome bienvenue (*f.*); **you're ~** de rien, je vous en prie, il n'y a pas de quoi

well bien; **~!** tiens!

what quel(le); ce que; que

when quand

where où

which quel(le); qui

white blanc, blanche

who qui; **~ is it?** qui est-ce?

why pourquoi

wife femme (*f.*)

win gagner

wind vent (*m.*); **it's ~y** il fait du vent

windbreaker blouson (*m.*)

window fenêtre (*f.*)

wine vin (*m.*)

winter hiver (*m.*)

with avec

woman femme (*f.*); **young ~** jeune fille (*f.*)

wood bois (*m.*)

word mot (*m.*)

work travail (*m.*); **to ~** travailler; **to ~ things out** se débrouiller

world monde (*m.*)

worried inquiet, inquiète

worry s'inquiéter; **don't ~** ne t'en fais pas; ne t'inquiète pas; rassurez-vous

wrestling lutte (*f.*)

writer écrivain (*m.*)

wrong: to be ~ avoir tort

yellow jaune

yes oui

you vous, tu; on; te

your ton (ta, tes); votre (vos)

zero zéro

Index

à
  + definite article 123
accent marks 31, 52
acheter 150
adjectives
  agreement 76
  forms 76, 201, 208
  comparison 308
  demonstrative 260
  descriptive 89, 201
  interrogative **quel** 178
  of nationality 14
  possessive **mon, ton, son**
    95; **notre, votre, leur** 125
  position 145
  superlative 308
adverbs in **-ment** 219
age 55
aller 36, 75
  + infinitive for future 124
  passé composé 288
alphabet 352
articles
  definite and indefinite 34,
    74
  contractions with **à, de** 123
  partitive 224
avoir 54
  as auxiliary in **passé**
    composé 262
  to express age 55
  with meaning *to be* 192

body, parts of 280
buildings, types of 116

cedilla 52
c'est, ce n'est pas 13
circumflex accent 52
classroom objects 29
clock time 168
clothing 139
cognates 72

colors 140
commands 146
  with object pronouns 177
comparisons 308
connaître 284
consonants, final 16
contractions
  à + definite article 123
  de + definite article 123
courtesy titles, **monsieur,**
    madame, mademoiselle
    11
croire 308

dates 190
days of week 69
de
  + definite article 126
  to express possession 35
  + noun 77
definite articles 34, 74
  contractions with **à** and **de**
    123
  with dates 190
  with parts of body 280
demonstrative adjectives 260
dire 307
direct-object pronouns
  le, la, les 151
  me, te, nous, vous 173
  in commands 151, 177

élision 31
emphatic pronouns
  singular 55
  plural 149
en, pronoun 305
-er verbs
  present tense 94
  passé composé 262, 287
être 16, 54
  as auxiliary in **passé**
    composé 287
exclamations with **quel** 202

faire 179
  in idioms 191
family vocabulary 88
food 217
future expressed with
  aller + infinitive 124

geographical terms 300
gender 34, 53
greetings and farewells 11

holidays 315

indefinite articles 34, 74
indirect-object pronouns
  lui, leur 261
  me, te, nous, vous 173
  position 173, 177, 261, 306
interrogative expressions 126
-ir verbs 330

je voudrais 203

liaison 16
locatives 115

mettre 227
months 190

nationality 14
negation
  ne...pas 17
  ne...plus 200
  ne...jamais 200
  ne...rien 200
  ne...personne 200
  pas de 96
  in **passé composé** 262

nouns
  gender 34
  plural 74
numbers
  0–10 27
  11–20 47
  21–69 67
  70–100 87
  100-1,000,000 117
  pronunciation of 51
  ordinal numbers 167

occupations and professions
  255, 324
on, subject pronoun 75
ordinal numbers 167

partir 329
partitive article 224
  replaced by **en** 305
pas de 96
passé composé
  formed with **avoir** 262
  formed with **être** 287
  irregular verbs 287
  negative 262
  position of object pronouns
    306
  reflexive verbs 328
possession with **de** 35
possessive adjectives 95, 125
pour + infinitive 152
pouvoir 203
préférer 150
prendre 264
prepositions 115, 166
present tense
  -er verbs 94
  -ir verbs 330
  -re verbs 285
professions and occupations
  255, 324

pronouns
  direct-object 151, 173, 306
  emphatic 55, 149
  en 305
  indirect-object 173, 177,
    261, 306
  reflexive 174
  relative **qui** 331
  subject 16, 53, 75
  tu vs. **vous** 27
pronunciation: phonetic
    symbols
  /i/ 15
  /e/ /ɛ/ 30
  /a/ /wa/ 50
  /u/ /y/ 71
  /ʀ/ 91
  /ã/ 91
  /ə/ 119
  /o/ /ɔ/ /ɔ̃/ 142
  /ʃ/ /ʒ/ /ɛ̃/ 170
  /ø/ /oe/ /œ̃/ 195
  /g/ /ɲ/ 221
  /s/ /z/ 257
  /j/ 282
  /g/ /ʒ/ 303
  /ɥ/ 326
  /p/ /b/ /t/ /d/ 327
  review 258, 282, 303, 327

quel 202
questions
  inversion 229
  oui/non questions 92
  information questions 126
  with interrogative words
    126

-re verbs 285
reflexive verbs 174
  passé composé 328
rhythm and pitch 92
relative pronoun **qui** 331
rooms of house 48

salutations 11
savoir 284
school subjects 68
seasons 190
sortir 329
sports 277
stem-changing verbs 150
stores 216
stress 72
subject pronouns
  je, tu, il, elle 16
  nous, vous, ils, elles 53
  tu vs. **vous** 27
  on 75
  ils for mixed groups 53
superlative adjectives 308

telling time 168
transportation 256
tréma 92
tu vs. **vous** 27

venir 226
venir de + inf. 226
verbs
  regular **-er** 94
  regular **-ir** 330
  regular **-re** 285
  reflexive 174, 328
  stem-changing 150
  irregular *see individual verb
    headings*
voir 308
vouloir 203
  je voudrais 203

weather expressions 191
word families 281, 301

y 36

Art credits

ILLUSTRATIONS

Chris Demarest: pp. 15, 31, 50, 71, 91, 120, 142, 170, 193, 195, 221, 222, 257, 282, 291, 303, 327, 334.

Devera Ehrenberg: pp. i, viii–xi, 11, 13, 19, 25, 29, 40, 46, 48, 49, 65, 77, 85, 88, 89, 114, 116, 122, 138, 139, 158, 166, 167, 168, 169, 172, 189, 191, 204, 214, 216–217, 251, 256, 278, 280, 300, 310, 324.

James Loates: pp. xii-xiii, xiv, xv, 113, 159, 210, 249.

Susan Spellman Mohn: pp. 62, 136, 188, 295.

COLOR PHOTOGRAPHS

Cover: Walter S. Clark, Jr.

Stage 1: La vie quotidienne
P. 1, Owen Franken/Stock, Boston; p. 2, (top left) Bryn Campbell/Magnum, (top right) Carol Palmer/ Andrew Brilliant, (bottom) Gordon Gahan/Photo Researchers; p. 3, (top) Carl Purcell, (bottom) Joe Flowers/Black Star; p. 4, (top) Guy Le Querrec/Magnum, (bottom) © Peter Menzel 1978–80; p. 5, Dana Hyde/Photo Researchers, (inset, top) © Peter Menzel 1978–80, (inset, bottom) Owen Franken/Stock, Boston; p. 6, Owen Franken/Stock, Boston, (inset) Carol Palmer/Andrew Brilliant; p. 7, (top) Christiana Dittman/Rainbow, (bottom) Owen Franken/Stock, Boston; p. 8, Nicholas Devore III/Bruce Coleman.

Stage 2: Les petits événements
P. 105, © Peter Menzel 1978–80; p. 106, (top) Carol Palmer/Andrew Brilliant, (bottom and inset) Owen Franken/Stock, Boston; p. 107, Owen Franken/Stock, Boston; pp. 108–109, Owen Franken/Stock, Boston; p. 108, (bottom) Carol Palmer/Andrew Brilliant; p. 109, (top) David Burnett/Stock, Boston, (bottom left) Carol Palmer/Andrew Brilliant, (bottom right) Owen Franken/Stock, Boston; p. 110, (top) Christian Delbert/The Picture Cube, (bottom left) Carol Palmer/Andrew Brilliant, (bottom right) Owen Franken/ Stock, Boston; p. 111, Erich Lessing/Magnum, (inset) Carol Palmer/Andrew Brilliant; p. 112, John Launois/Black Star.

Stage 3: Les joies et les peines
P. 241, Carol Palmer/Andrew Brilliant; p. 242, (top) Carl Purcell, (bottom left) Nicholas Devore III/Bruce Coleman, (bottom right) Lou Jones; p. 243, Serraillier/Photo Researchers; pp. 242–243, William Carter/ Photo Researchers; p. 244, (top and bottom) Presse-Sports; p. 245, (top) Presse-Sports, (bottom) Hervé Donnezan/Photo Researchers; pp. 246–247, Carol Palmer/Andrew Brilliant; p. 247, (inset, top) J. M. Charles/Photo Researchers, (inset, bottom left and right) Carol Palmer/Andrew Brilliant; p. 248, Owen Franken/Stock, Boston.

BLACK AND WHITE PHOTOGRAPHS

Title page: Mark Antman/Stock, Boston.
P. ix, Owen Franken/Stock, Boston; p. x, Maje Waldo/Stock, Boston; p. 12, Mark Antman; p. 18, French Government Tourist Office; p. 21, Mark Antman; p. 22, French Government Tourist Office; p. 24, Carol Palmer/Andrew Brilliant; p. 26, Image Photos/Clemens Kalischer; p. 28, Mark Antman/Stock, Boston; p. 32, Olivier Rebbot/Stock, Boston; p. 33, (top) Alain Keler/Editorial Photocolor Archives, (center) Mark Antman, (bottom) © Peter Menzel 1978–80; p. 37, Owen Franken/Stock, Boston; p. 42, Owen Franken/ Stock, Boston; p. 44, Jean Gaumy/Magnum; p. 52, The Bettmann Archive; p. 57, Carol Palmer/Andrew Brilliant; p. 61, Quebec Government Bureau; p. 62, Editorial Photocolor Archives; p. 66, (left) Mark Antman/Stock, Boston, (right) H. C. Chapman/ICON; p. 73, (top and bottom) Owen Franken/Stock, Boston, (center) Carol Palmer/Andrew Brilliant; p. 78, Niepce/Photo Researchers; p. 83, John Lopinot/ Black Star; p. 86, Lynn McLaren; p. 87 and p. 90, John Lopinot/Black Star; p. 93, Documentation Française; p. 97 and p. 98, Charles Hogg; p. 102, Lou Jones; p. 118, Elliot Erwitt/Magnum; p. 119, Carol Palmer/ Andrew Brilliant; p. 127, © Peter Menzel 1978–80; p. 128, Image Photos/Clemens Kalischer; p. 129, (top) Marc Riboud/Magnum, (background bottom) Alain Keler/Editorial Photocolor Archives, (bottom front) Image Photos/Clemens Kalischer; p. 130, Image Photos/Clemens Kalischer; p. 136, Editorial Photocolor Archives; p. 141, Carol Palmer/Andrew Brilliant; p. 144, Owen Franken/Stock, Boston; p. 148, Marc Riboud/Magnum; p. 153, Marc Riboud/Magnum, (inset) Philippe Morel, Sipa Press/Black Star; p. 154,